Shine on Me

D. Dexter Vizinau

iUniverse Star
New York   Bloomington

Shine on Me
The Story of Margaret Vizinau, A Determined African-American Woman and Her Faith in God

iUniverse Star
an iUniverse, Inc. imprint

iUniverse books may be ordered through booksellers or by contacting:

iUniverse
1663 Liberty Drive
Bloomington, IN 47403
www.iuniverse.com
1-800-Authors (1-800-288-4677)

ISBN: 978-1-58348-037-3 (pbk)
ISBN: 978-0-595-89696-7 (cloth)
ISBN: 978-0-595-89694-3 (ebk)

Printed in the United States of America

iUniverse rev. date: 01/07/09

Train up a child in the way he should go: and when he is old, he will not depart from it.

Proverbs 22:6

Honour thy father and thy mother: that thy days may be long.

Exodus 20:12

To my wife, Katrina,
And my children,
Michelle, Duane, Aleah,
Justin, and Miles

Acknowledgments

There are several individuals to whom I would like to express my appreciation. These people have helped me by providing encouragement, input, criticism, and editing. Without them, I could not have written this book: Greta and Phil Johnson, LaWanda Harris, Mary Bobo, Cheryl Patterson, Stephanie Anderson, Donna Dill, Sandra Small, Michelle Gandy, Mattie Bess, Mark Friedman, and Leona Lee.

Prologue

It's a rainy Saturday in the Fillmore district of San Francisco. The year is 1959, and it's just before Christmas. Eight-year-old Dexter is looking out of his front window, watching the raindrops fall and keeping an eye on the cars as they travel up and down the busy streets. He's nervous and has a sinking feeling in his stomach. There's a chill over him that's causing him to shake, even though it's warm inside the house. His younger brother, Hank, is in their bedroom, playing with toys on the floor.

Margaret is adding the final touches to her makeup, applying a little face powder to her cheeks and some lipstick to her full lips. Dexter approaches the dresser and watches his mother make herself up in the mirror. He's used to seeing her look at herself in the mirror even though she's blind and can't see.

It's not easy being a female like Margaret in the big city of San Francisco in the fifties. She has four strikes against her that make it especially difficult: one, she's a woman in a man's world; two, she's a Negro; three, she's a single parent with two small boys; and four, she's been blind since birth.

When Margaret appears to be finished with her makeup, Dexter asks, "Baba, why can't I go with you?"

She cuts him short with a stern, "No, you can't go, and stop asking me. You have to stay here. I know how to get around by myself, boy. I got around on my own long before you were born, and I can get around just fine now."

Tears begin to form in his eyes, and he begs, "Please, Baba, please, you need me to take you." He has thoughts of someone trying to steal her purse or attacking her or, even worse, her being hit by a car.

Margaret is getting angry now and becoming impatient with him. "Look, you can't come, and stop asking me."

Since Margaret's two children have grown into little boys, they've been her guides. Being the oldest, Dexter has stepped up to the main responsibility of guiding her since their father left when he was five years old. Because Hank is the youngest, to Margaret, he has always been the baby and has had less responsibility. When the children are not escorting her on outings, Margaret's mother and friends usually take them about. On this occasion, no one is available, and she is Christmas shopping for gifts for the boys. She won't take them along because she doesn't want them to know what she's buying.

Margaret turns from the dresser, pauses, and takes two steps forward. She turns a perfect right and then a left. She walks through the bedroom door and makes a right, then walks down the hallway to the closet on the left. "Dexter, I need my blue overcoat."

He takes her hand and puts it on the blue coat, trying not to let her hear him cry. She quickly slides her hand toward the top of the coat, reaches for the hanger, and pulls the coat from the rack.

She stands by the front door, turns toward Dexter, and says, "Bring me my purse off the dresser."

When Dexter goes to get the purse, Hank comes out of the boys' bedroom and runs over to his mother. "Baba, where you going?"

"I have to go out and do some shopping."

Dexter returns, and Margaret opens the purse and brings out her money pouch. She instructs Dexter to check her money. First he counts the ones, then the fives, the tens, and the twenties. He confirms the money and stands by, sobbing. "Yes Baba, it's okay."

Margaret tells her sons, "You boys behave while I'm away, and don't let anyone into the house. Hank, if you get hungry, you can have anything in the refrigerator. Just don't make a mess, and, Dexter, there's some soup on the stove. All you have to do is heat it up. The crackers are in the cupboard. I'll be back before dark, and I'll call you a little later."

Hank says, "Okay, bye, Baba," and pulls on her coat sleeve.

She leans over to give him a kiss, and he heads back to the bedroom to watch The Little Rascals on television. Margaret puts her money pouch back in her purse and feels inside for her collapsible white cane with the red tip. She grabs the black knob at the top of the cane and lets it drop. She pulls on the leather strap, and the cane snaps taut. Dexter hands her an umbrella. Margaret steps toward the front door and searches for the door handle; she quickly turns the knob.

Dexter, now frantic, stops her and cries, "Please, Baba, please, take me with you. It's raining outside, and I need to go with you; something could happen."

Angrily she shouts, "Boy, if you don't stop and let me loose, I'm going to whip you till you don't see tomorrow. Now let me go, and behave yourself until I get back."

Margaret heads out the door and uses the cane to find the top of the stairs. "Tap, tap, tap," on the ground goes the cane. Once the cane slips over the edge at the top of the stairs, she reaches for the banister and begins her descent.

Dexter stares at her through the glass front door and watches helplessly as she reaches the sidewalk. He quickly runs to the front window to watch her travel down the street. The rain is pouring down, and the wind is fiercely blowing. He is looking for her, but he can't see her because she's under the overhang of the window, trying to get her umbrella up, which is useless because it's so windy. It just blows inside out.

With a plastic scarf over her head, Margaret begins her journey down the sidewalk. "Tap, tap, tap," goes the cane.

Dexter is at the window, attentively watching his mother, and crying, "Baba, Babaaaaa." His face is so close to the window that it fogs the glass.

The intersection of Waller and Fillmore Streets is a busy one. It's a major throughway in San Francisco, running from south to north. The bus Margaret wants to take is the twenty-two bus line, and the bus stop is one block up Fillmore Street at the corner of Haight Street. Cars travel fast, heading up Fillmore, and there's no stop sign or signal.

Margaret reaches the corner and stops when the tip of the cane slips over the curb. She decides to cross Fillmore rather than turn at the corner and cross Waller where traffic has to stop.

Eight-year-old Dexter begins talking to himself. "No, not that way; go the other way!"

Margaret is standing at the curb with her head turned and tilted; she's listening for the traffic, trying to determine when she should step off the curb and go. A man walking up Fillmore doesn't pay attention to her and keeps on walking. The sound of the traffic is dying, so Margaret steps off the curb and pauses, then proceeds. "Tap, tap, tap," goes the cane.

Dexter's eyes are full of tears, and the rain is beating down on the window; he wipes away the fog to get a better look. He watches as his mother steps into the intersection, tapping her cane as she crosses the street.

Suddenly, it seems out of nowhere, Margaret hears a loud engine heading in her direction. It's a large delivery truck, the kind with a big cab on the back. The driver doesn't see her because he's fumbling with the radio. Baba hears the truck almost upon her and freezes. Finally the driver sees her and slams on the brakes. He stops just short of hitting her.

Dexter sees this and yells, "Baba!"

The driver rolls down his window and yells at Margaret, "You black bitch, you almost got yourself killed."

Margaret just says, "Thank you, Lord," and continues to walk in faith.

Dexter continues to watch from the window. The wind is blowing, and the rain is pouring down. He watches as his mother reaches the curb, turns, and taps to the next curb to cross Waller Street where there's a stop sign. She again listens, then steps off the curb, taps across the street, steps up, and continues until she's out of his sight. He leans on the window, which is foggy and wet from his breathing and wiping, and just weeps.

1

A Gift

To say that growing up with a mother who is single and blind must have its challenges is an understatement. Being the older of two sons brought about a lot of responsibility. Basically, I had to be my mother's eyes.

Don't get me wrong—my brother shared greatly in this responsibility, but it just seemed there was something about being older that passed the torch of responsibility on to me.

As we begin this journey into the life of my mother, Margaret Vizinau, you have to understand that she was a woman of great faith. It is by virtue of her faith that I feel I have survived to tell this story.

In order to understand what I mean when I say that my mother was a person of great faith, we have to go back to the beginning to a time just before she was born.

Sam was standing at the pulpit, waiting to bless the offering as the plates were being passed from one parishioner to another. The congregation was singing along with the small choir:

Lord, keep me day by day,
In a pure and perfect way.
I want to live. I want to live, Lord,
In a building not made by hand.

Sam began to pray. "Dear Lord, we come before you with heads bowed, asking you to receive these tithes and offerings as just a small token of our appreciation of the blessings you have bestowed upon us. We ask that you bless us, Lord, as we go about our travels so that we can see another day to serve you. Bless the sick and shut in, Lord, for they need you, and bless the mothers of the church, Father. Touch our pastor; touch his heart, dear Father, and give him the words of wisdom to give us your message that will fulfill our souls. Dear Father, we ask these blessings in your Holy Son, Jesus's, name. Amen."

Just before his prayer, Sam couldn't help but notice that his young wife, Mary, wasn't looking too well. She'd complained earlier of a headache, and she seemed a little flustered. She was sitting there in the pews, fanning to keep cool, only it was not very warm in the church. It was late autumn, and there was a chill outside; it had already rained a couple days before.

The pastor finished his sermon and dismissed the congregation. Everyone went outside to socialize or began making his or her way home.

In the truck, Sam turned to Mary and asked, "How are my lovely wife and baby?"

Mary looked down at her big belly, rubbed it, and replied, "We're a little tired, I guess; I still have this headache, and I'm feeling a little chill."

"Well, let's get the two of you home so you can lie down and get some rest," Sam replied.

"That sounds good; let's go." Mary tried to smile. Sam started up the truck and headed home.

That night, Mary was very restless. Her temperature was rising, and uneasiness came over her that she'd never felt before. She drifted off into a deep sleep and began to dream.

It was the middle of the night, and there was a white man in a canoe on a lake. The water was eerily still. While squatting on his feet in the little boat, the man reached for his reel and began to bait the hook. But the bait was not normal bait. He was putting a chicken's foot on the hook. He stood, placed the rod over his shoulder and cast the line. It flew out a good five yards and dropped down into the lake. As soon as it hit the water, he had a bite. It had to be the biggest catfish he ever saw.

Peacefully, the man sat and waited for his next catch. "Lord, I sure pray I catch another big one tonight." There he sat, looking up at the heavens. The night was clear, and the moon was bright. He noticed one star in particular, shining brighter than the rest; and it appeared to be getting brighter. He then noticed the light from the star was coming toward him. He became frightened and jumped up to bring in his line. Suddenly, the light surrounded him, and he stood up with his arms outstretched. "Father, I stretch my arms to thee," he said.

Mary shouted out in her sleep, "O Lord, O Lord, O Lord!"

Startled, Sam awakened and then woke Mary up.

Mary sat up straight and cried out, "Oh, my God. Oh, my God. Sam, I dreamed about a fish. Somebody's gonna die, somebody's gonna die. Oh, my baby, my baby, I'm worried about my baby."

"Calm down, honey, the baby's gonna be all right. It was just a dream," said Sam, trying to give some comfort. Suddenly he got a good look at her; she was covered with spots all over her face, and she was drenched in sweat. "My God," he said, putting his hand on her forehead. "You're burning up, honey. You're sick, and I gotta get you a doctor. Lay down, sweetheart; let me get you a cold rag for your forehead." He returned with a wet rag and laid it across her brow.

Mary didn't look too well. Her face was flushed and her eyes were red, and Sam was beginning to think that it might not be a good idea to take her out in the night. He decided not to take her and said, "I'm going into town and get the doctor. Just try to stay cool and calm. I'll be back before ya know it."

Storms in Arkansas could be pretty fierce, and this night was no exception. It was a nice little haul from the farm to the small town of Colt, but Sam was determined to get help for his wife. He was worried about her, and he was worried about the baby too. As he began his journey down the road, the winds picked up, and the rain was heavy. Lightning flashed, and thunder rocked his truck. Sam began to pray, but the conditions just seemed to get worse. Up ahead, there was a big dip in the road that Sam was familiar with. It had become too flooded to pass on rare occasions in the past. He prayed that the road would be clear.

As Sam drove, he continued to pray. He soon approached the dip. He could see that it was flooded, and he knew he couldn't cross. It was the middle of the night, and no one was out on the road in this storm. He had only gone just over two miles toward town and needed to turn around. "Lord, please Lord, help us through this, please Lord," he prayed.

Sam stopped the truck, backed it up, and tried to turn around. But he'd gone a little too fast, and the truck backed up into the mud. "Damn," he said, cussing, which he rarely did. "Excuse me, Lord," he said. Sam stepped on the gas, but the truck didn't move; it was stuck in the mud with the rear wheels spinning. He kept trying, but the truck wouldn't budge. "Damn," he said again, then "Excuse me, Lord." Frustrated, he helplessly wondered, "What can I do?" He had to leave the truck and walk back home in the cold rain.

When Sam arrived home, Mary was asleep in bed. She was still very warm but was also shivering from a chill. Sam covered her up lightly and got another cool rag to place on her forehead. Feeling hopeless, he knelt down and prayed, "Dear Lord, merciful Father, I come to you, Lord, to ask you for your touch, dear Lord. Touch my wife and this baby. Give them your grace so that we may see another day and be whole as a family, Father. Heal my wife, dear Lord, for this child is a child of God. We know that you are a merciful Father and an almighty God. You can save them, Lord; only you can get them through the night. I promise, dear Father, that if you help us, Lord, we'll dedicate this child to you, dear Lord. All these blessings we ask in your Holy Son, Jesus's name. Amen."

The next morning when Mary awoke, Sam was still on his knees, asleep, with his head lying on the bed, near her. She smiled and reached over to touch him and gently shook him awake. Her fever was gone, and she was feeling a little weak but much better. Sam awoke and saw her smile. It was a smile he loved to see, because he loved her so dearly; she was everything to him.

"How do you feel, honey?" he asked. Then he again noticed the spots. They were still all over her face. "Mary, you're still covered in spots," he said.

She jumped up and ran to the mirror. "Oh, my God!" she cried.

Sam, still concerned, suggested, "Let's get you to the doctor. Can you make it?"

"Yes, I think I can," she replied.

By this time, the weather had cleared up, and Sam got a neighbor to help with the truck. The ride into Colt was an easy one since the roads were clear and the weather was calm. Mary was weak and a little uneasy, but she was still much better.

The doctor was one of only a few white doctors who would treat colored folk. Mary only wanted a white doctor to treat her; she didn't trust any Negro doctor. She got that kind of thinking from her mother, Annie Jones. Annie felt that the schools black doctors went to provided incomplete educations and intentionally taught bad habits.

At the doctor's office, they waited just outside for the doctor to see Mary. They had to wait until there were no more white folks waiting. A couple of white people came after them but were seen before them. Finally, the nurse came outside and said they could come in.

The doctor took one look at Mary and said, "Mary, you have the German measles."

"I ain't been around no German folk; how I get this?" she asked.

The doctor laughed and said, "That's just what they call it, Mary. You don't have to be around Germans to get it. Besides, it's been going around these parts lately. You'll be all right. I'm going to give you a shot, and you'll be fine in a few days."

"What about my baby? Is my baby going to be fine?" she asked.

"Yes, Doctor, what about the baby?" Sam asked with a worried look on his face.

"The baby should be fine. Did you have a fever last night?" asked the doctor.

"Yes, Doctor, she had a fierce fever last night, bad dreams and everything. But she woke up this morning and the fever broke," said Sam.

"Well that's good. If you still had a fever, then it would give us something to worry about. But I'm sure the baby is just fine," added the doctor.

Sam and Mary headed back to the farm. Mary was still concerned about her dream. She dreamed about a fish, and to her that meant somebody was going to die. She needed to talk with her mama, so she asked Sam to turn and head back to Forest City. Sam objected and said she needed to get home and have some rest like the doctor said. But Mary told him she was okay and needed to see her mama. Not wanting to get her upset and sick again, he decided to go.

Annie Jones was a strong, well-known Negro woman. She was petite and very sharp and witty. She knew how to deal with white folks and could sometimes put them in their places in a polite way. Because her husband was a preacher, he and Annie both had the respect of many white preachers in the area. If it looked as if she were going to have a problem with someone, Annie could drop the name of a white preacher whom she knew received a great deal of respect from the person she was dealing with. She was not to be disrespected. Her English was pretty good, and she really didn't have much of a southern accent. She was the daughter of Martin Van Buren Savage and Mosetta Savage, who had been slaves in Lawrence County, Mississippi, where she was born.

The Savages moved to Forest City when Annie was very young. Soon thereafter, they joined the New Sardis Baptist Church, a very prominent church that had been founded by former slaves. Annie met her husband at New Sardis. He became the pastor, the Reverend W. A. Jones. Being the pastor's wife gave Annie a certain amount of prestige and respect in the community, and she enjoyed it.

It didn't take very long to get to Momma's (Annie's) house. Forest City was only six miles from Colt. Annie saw her daughter and son-in-law drive up and park in front of the house. Sam got out of the car and ran around to help Mary get out of the car. Momma couldn't tell if Mary was just tired of being pregnant, or if she was tired because she was sick.

Annie went outside to help and immediately saw something was not right with her daughter. "Baby, what's wrong with you?" she asked. "You all covered with spots!"

"Momma, I dreamed of a fish last night," said Mary.

"Come on in the house now; we have to get you off your feet," responded Annie. They got Mary into the house and sat her on the couch.

"Whew, I don't know how much longer I can take this," Mary cried.

Annie put her hand on Mary's forehead. It was a little warm, but not enough to give her real concern. "Tell Momma what happened," said Annie.

Mary began to tell Annie about church yesterday and how she'd become ill with a headache and a fever. She told her about how she'd gone to sleep and had a dream about the white man fishing, and then woke up with spots all over. She also told her about the doctor and what he said about the baby.

"Momma, is my baby going to be all right?" asked Mary. "I dreamed about a fish."

"Sam, what did the doctor say? Did he give her something?" asked Annie.

Sam answered, "Yeah, Momma, he said she had the German measles, and he gave her a shot. Said she should get some rest and that the baby should be okay."

"Well, he's a white doctor and one of the best around these parts. I'm sure he knows what he's talking about," said Annie.

"Momma, what about the fish?" asked Mary.

"Baby, I don't know about the fish," she answered. She squinted at Mary and said, "You say you saw a light shine down from the sky, shining on this white man. You ever see this white man before?"

"No, Momma, I never saw the man before," answered Mary.

"Well, no telling what the dream means. Because of the light, it's hard to tell what it means. The light usually means life or everlasting, and the fish means death, so by having them both in the same dream, I can't tell what it means," Annie responded.

Sam couldn't take it any more and had to say something. "I can't take all this devil talk. All that foolishness is nothing but Satan. You need to stop talking about that dream. It's a dream. That's all it is! Ain't nobody gonna die, and the light don't mean nothing. What we need to do is pray."

"Well, amen to that, young man. There ain't nothing better in times like these than God," Annie replied.

They knelt down by Mary, and Sam began to pray. He prayed for his wife to be healed and for the baby to be born whole and strong. He asked God to bless this family and their household. He asked God to not let anyone in the family die.

After the prayer, Annie stood erect with her small frame. She was wearing a long dress that hung on her, being a size too big. She looked up at the ceiling, brought her hands up in front of her, and began to clap.

"I've got a feeling that everything's gonna be all right." Mary and Sam looked at each other and smiled and joined Annie in singing and clapping. "I've got a feeling that everything's gonna be all right," they said, louder now. "I've got a feeling that everything's gonna be all right, be all right, be all right, be all right. My momma told me, everything's gonna be all right; my momma told me that everything's gonna be all right."

Mary was smiling at her momma, and Sam was beaming and having a good time. "My momma, she told me, everything's gonna be all right, be all right be all right be all right."

Annie kept the lead going. "And then Jesus, he told me, everything's gonna be all right. Ohhhh, Jesus, he told me, everything's gonna be all right. Yes he did. Jesus, he told me, everything's gonna be all right, be all right, be all right, be all right."

They now doubled up. "Be all right, be all right, be all right …" After singing and clapping, everyone felt good.

Mary's papa came through the front door and asked, "What's going on in here? What's all the commotion about?"

"Just praising the Lord, honey, praising the Lord," said Annie.

"Okay, Mary, let's go home." Sam reached to help Mary, when suddenly she felt a sharp pain in her stomach.

"Baby, what's wrong?" Annie asked.

"Just a little pain, Momma, nothing to worry about," said Mary.

"When is the baby due?" asked Papa.

"In a couple of weeks," Mary replied.

Annie being concerned about her daughter suggested, "Sam, you better let Mary stay here; we can keep an eye on her for you. You know you got to work and tend to your chores. You better let her stay here."

Sam knew she was right; he was already missing from work. Lucky for him, he had a good boss who liked him because he was a hard and honest worker. His boss also knew he had a wife who was expecting. "All right, Momma, you probably right. I'll go home and get her some clothes and bring them back. But if I ain't back here when it's time for the baby to come, you got to send someone for me right away," said Sam.

A couple of weeks went by, and Sam was over at his in-laws' house every day right after work. Sometimes he'd spend the night, and other times they'd send him home. He loved his wife, and he was at her beck and call, waiting on her hand and foot. Everyone was just waiting for the baby, and Mary recovered well from the measles. It was all planned out how the delivery would take place. Annie's first cousin Katie was a midwife and had delivered many kids around Forest City. She didn't live too far away and could come over any time the need arose.

On November 30, 1927, the baby was born. That early evening, Mary went into labor while Sam was there, and he went right on over and picked up Katie. Sam and Papa waited outside on the porch, and the women took care of things with the delivery. Sam and Papa Jones prayed together and talked about when Mary was born. Soon they heard the sound of a baby crying. Sam jumped up and almost fell down because he was so excited. They just kept looking at the door and waiting for the women to come with the news.

Annie came to the door and announced it was a girl. "Hallelujah, glory be to God, I got me a daughter," Sam yelled. "Can I go in?" He didn't wait for an answer. Mary was propped up with a pillow and was holding the baby.

She smiled at Sam and said, "It's a girl, Sam, our daughter."

Sam was so proud. Mary tried to hand the baby to him, but he blushed and said, "No, not right now."

Mary smiled and asked, "You scared?"

Sam just blushed deeper and replied, "No, I ain't scared."

That evening, they all sat around the bed talking. The baby had all her hands, legs, fingers, and feet. She looked fine and had a healthy set of lungs. Boy, she could cry out loud. It almost seemed strange how loud she could holler. Sam said, "Man, she sure got a set of lungs on her."

Annie said, "She sure do! I ain't ever heard a baby that loud before."

"That means she gonna be a singer," said Mary. "She's gonna sing for the Lord," she continued.

"Amen," everybody said.

"What we gonna name her?" asked Sam.

"Betty. I like Betty," said Rev. Jones.

"No, Papa," said Mary, "that's too common. Margaret. I like Margaret; it sounds like class. That's what my baby's got—she's got class," said Mary.

"How about Neelmah?" asked Annie. "I like Neelmah," she said.

"Neelmah?" asked Mary. "Spell it."

"N-a-o-m-i," Momma spelled.

"You mean Naomi," responded Mary.

"That's what I said, Neelmah," said Annie.

They all laughed, and Mary said, "Margaret Naomi Hinton—that's it!"

Everyone chimed in, "Margaret Naomi Hinton," and then it was time to pray.

After a couple of days, Mary was ready to take the baby to the doctor to have her checked out. The family wanted Mary to continue to rest, but she was a strong woman, and stubborn. She was already up and about, out of the bed and ready to go home. When Sam arrived she was dressed and packed and had the baby ready to go. Sam was really surprised and wanted her to rest some more, but he knew there was no arguing with her. He could tell by her attitude and posture not to mess around. So he just grabbed her things and took them out to the truck. "I'll take you to the doctor tomorrow," he said. She didn't answer him.

The next day, Mary was up before Sam. She had gotten dressed, and all the baby's things were ready for the trip to Colt to see the doctor. Bacon was frying in the pan, and the smell of it awakened Sam. He was a little weary and still tired. All the excitement of the baby, the going back and forth, and work had taken a little toll on him. But Sam was a big, strong Negro, standing over six feet tall and weighing over two hundred pounds. His bronze skin tone gave him a permanently tanned look. His arms were so nice, large, and firm, they looked like they were always swollen. This was from doing heavy work at the lumberyard he worked at across county.

In a couple of hours, they were outside the doctor's office, waiting. It just seemed like one white person after another kept coming and coming. Finally, after about two hours, the nurse came outside and told them they could go in. The doctor was always nice and friendly, especially to Mary. Sam thought he had a crush on **her** and was a little jealous but could never say anything; besides the **doctor** was always friendly to him as well. Still, he felt that Mary liked the attention the doctor gave her, and he was right. White men always took a liking to Mary, and really Mary did like them too.

"Well now, Mary, let me see this fine little baby. I hear it's a girl," said the doctor.

"Yes, Doctor, this is Margaret, Margaret Naomi Hinton," replied Mary.

"Margaret, now that's a fine name, that's a dignified name, you know," said the doctor, smiling at Mary as she nodded her head and looked at Sam. Sam was flustered with their gushy talk.

The doctor began to examine little Margaret, and she made a few sounds as if to complain about all the handling, but she didn't cry. He checked her hands and feet, looked at her behind, and at her privates. He felt under her armpits and her joints. Next he rubbed around her head—no lumps anywhere, and all motion was normal. He listened to her heart, and there was a strong heartbeat. He pulled out his light and looked in her ears; she complained a little but still didn't cry. He then went to check her eyes, "Ump," he sighed, pulled the light away, then looked again. "Ump," he said again.

"What's wrong?" Mary asked.

For a moment, the doctor had thought that maybe he saw something to be concerned about, but he quickly decided to dismiss it. He said, "Oh, nothing, I'm sure it's nothing. She appears to be okay, but I want you to bring her back to me in about six weeks for another checkup. By then we can make sure everything is in working order. She looks like a fine child, Mary. You should be very happy."

Mary replied, "Okay, Doctor, we'll be back in six weeks."

In the truck, Mary expressed her concern to Sam about the doctor's reaction to the exam. "There was something wrong with my baby, and he didn't tell me; I know it," said Mary.

"Oh no, honey, he'd have said something, and he said she was fine. You are always so suspicious. You need to quit that," replied Sam. Mary didn't respond, but deep inside she felt it and would keep a watchful eye on Margaret.

She loved her baby with all her heart and kept Margaret by her side all day and night. She sang to the baby, and she read the Bible to her. When she did her chores around the house, she constantly talked to Margaret. It was nice having company while Sam was at work, and it was good to have someone to talk to.

After about four weeks, things really became suspicious for Mary. She was sitting in the rocking chair with Margaret, and she just kept looking at her baby's eyes. Margaret hadn't looked at Mary yet; she hadn't fixed her eyes on her. Margaret would smile and respond to Mary's voice, but she wasn't responding to movement around her. Mary took her baby and tried to make her look at her by putting Margaret right in front of her face. Margaret's eyes just wandered and never fixed. They would even sometimes kind of flicker back and forth. Mary's heart beat harder, and fear began to set in. She jumped up from the rocking chair and quickly went outside with the baby. The sun was up high in the sky and shining bright. Mary wanted to see if the light would make Margaret close her eyes. She positioned the baby so the sun was right in her eyes. Margaret never closed her eyes; instead, she seemed to look into the direction of the sun.

Mary's lips quivered, and then she started to sob. She cried, "My baby, my baby, she can't see, my baby can't see. O Lord. Please, Lord. Help us, dear Lord. My baby ..."

That evening, when Sam came home from work, Mary was sitting in the rocker, asleep, with Margaret in her arms. Sam went to pick the baby up and woke Mary up. He smiled and cradled his little girl, then he looked down at Mary who frowned, and then began to cry. "Hey, honey, what's wrong?" he asked.

"She's blind, our baby is blind. She can't see," she cried.

Sam answered, "Now, that's foolish talk. Why you going to talk like that? This baby is way too young for you to know something like that. Stop saying those things."

"I want to take my baby to the doctor now. I know what I'm talking about. There's something wrong with my baby's eyes!" shouted Mary.

Sam knew he couldn't win the argument, and he needed to pacify his wife. Maybe there was something wrong. He looked at little Margaret's eyes and couldn't see anything wrong, but he knew the doctor would know for sure. Even though the doctor wasn't expecting them for another two weeks, Sam knew the doctor would still see them now.

In deep thought, they both drove to town. Sam was wondering, "What if she's right? Suppose Margaret is blind. What would they do? How would they take care of her? Only God knows why."

Mary couldn't help but think of Margaret, and in her mind, all she could say was, "My baby, my baby, my poor little child, my poor sweet child. Mommy's here, Mommy's here. I'll take care of you, don't you worry, Mommy's gonna take care of you." She just kept rocking and rocking back and forth. She already knew what the doctor was going to say.

They were lucky; when they reached the doctor's office, there was no one else waiting to see the doctor. The nurse let them in after having them wait just a short minute to let the doctor know they were there. The doctor wasn't surprised they were early.

Right away Mary said, "My baby can't see."

The doctor paused and replied, "I wasn't sure; we needed some time." He took Margaret in his arms and laid her on the table. He then took his light scope and examined her eyes. Finally he stood up, leaned back against a table, folded his arms, looked at the both of them, and said, "Sam, Mary, I'm sorry, but your daughter is blind. She can't see, and I don't know if she ever will. Actually, I don't think she ever will."

Sam wanted to know why, and Mary began to cry. The doctor brought up the fact that Mary had contracted the German measles about a month before the baby was born, and that she'd probably run a very high fever. There were other cases of mothers getting the measles and babies being born with defects. He told them that there were people that might be able to help them and show them how to raise a

13

blind child. He could let them know if they were interested. They just nodded their heads.

Mary already had it set in her mind, so it wasn't a surprise to her, but hearing it come from the doctor was still terrible and disturbing. Sam was in shock and disbelief. Mary looked solemnly over at Sam with tears rolling down her cheeks, then she reached over, pulled on Sam's hand, and said, "Come on, honey, let's go." They both stood. Sam collected their things, then put his hand on Mary's elbow, and they walked toward the door. "Good-bye, Doctor," said Mary as they departed.

When they got into the truck, Mary started crying and feeling hurt. She was starting to feel like it was her fault. She felt that if she hadn't gotten sick, the baby would be whole. "I want to go to my momma's." Sam already knew that; he was headed that way anyway.

Annie saw the truck pull up outside, so she walked out on the porch to greet them. Sam couldn't even get around to the other side in time because, as soon as they stopped, Mary jumped out and ran to Annie with the baby, yelling, "Momma, Momma, Margaret is blind. The doctor said she couldn't see. Oh, Momma, my baby, my poor baby. What are we going to do?"

"Come on in the house," Annie said as she motioned for them to enter. She looked around to see if anyone was near as she entered from behind. They all went into the house and sat in the parlor. Annie was a superstitious woman from Mississippi. She had been raised around folk from Louisiana and had learned and heard a lot of things. But she was also a God-fearing woman. She always said the Lord works in mysterious ways.

Annie started right in. She asked, "You remember that dream you had about the fish?" Mary nodded her head. Annie continued, "At first I didn't know what it meant, because there was that light. This baby is what it meant."

The Reverend Papa Jones walked in and wanted to know what was going on. Sam filled him in, and then Annie started in with the voodoo stuff. Quickly, the reverend cut her off with a motion of his hand, and Annie knew she had to shut up. He looked over at his daughter and grandchild, and then went over to embrace them.

The reverend was a wise and mature man; he was the leader of one of the most prominent and oldest Negro churches in Arkansas. He smiled at his daughter and said, "You young people have got to understand what God has done here. Margaret is special; she is a very special gift. She may not be able to see, but you can believe she has something nobody else has. God has given this girl a gift, though we don't know what it is yet. But we do know he also gave this gift to the two of you. He has plans for this child. You just have to listen and do what he says. It's time to rejoice and give praise to the glory and mighty power of God. Mary, you stand tall and proud. Let anyone who tries to say different of your child understand that your child is a special child sent from heaven above, and that God blessed you with this child."

Mary smiled. Her father always knew what to say and how to make things better, and she also knew he was always right. It was time to pray!

2

Let the Light Shine

"What a Friend we have in Jesus," sang the choir.

Mary's father, Rev. Jones, was standing in the pulpit, looking out over the congregation. "It's a good crowd for a second Sunday," he thought. Margaret caught his eye, but actually it was her singing that got his attention. She sat there next to her mother, and it was clear that she was having a good time. Most seven-year-olds seemed to be a little bored in church, but Margaret always enjoyed it. She was more attentive than most her age. She'd always sing along, and more than just the pastor noticed this. Mary was well aware of what was happening with her daughter. Margaret could sing. Margaret loved to sing. She had a very distinctive voice, and not only could she carry a note, but it was also evident she could lead.

On this particular Sunday, Rev. Jones decided to let his son-in-law, Sam, the Reverend Hinton, preach. This was a real honor for Sam, because New Sardis was a good-sized church, and many prominent Negroes went there. If he preached a good sermon, he would gain the respect of many. It could lead to something else for him, no telling.

After the choir stopped singing, the pastor began to speak to the congregation, "My fellow Christians, deacons, choir, members, and friends, today we have a special treat: a child of God, other than myself, will deliver our message today. I'm happy to have my son-in-law, the Reverend Samuel Hinton, deliver this morning's message, and I pray that you will give him a warm reception like that you have always given to me."

There were a few amens as Sam approached the podium. "First, giving honor to God, our pastor, members, and friends, I come before you, a humble man, and I pray that the words that I speak, which are given from God, touch someone and deliver them unto our Savior and Lord, Jesus Christ."

Mary sat in her seat straight and attentive. She was very proud of her husband. He was a model for the community, a good provider, and a man of God. Margaret sat next to her mother, holding her head up, slightly tilted, with an ear in the direction that her father was speaking. She wore a slight smile on her face, because she too was proud of Sam. She knew that she was his heart and that he loved her more than anything in this world.

Sam continued, "Let us open our Bibles and turn to the Old Testament, chapter 27 in the book of Psalms, verse 1. After you have found it, let the church say amen." After a moment, there were a few amens. Sam said, "Let us read together, 'The Lord is my light and my salvation; whom shall I fear? The Lord is the strength of my life; of whom shall I be afraid?'" Sam closed his Bible and looked out over the pews. "Our message today is entitled, Who Is Your Light?"

The words that Sam was speaking were especially important to Margaret. When she heard her father saying these words, she felt that he was speaking to her. She clung onto every word of her father's sermon. It gave her new meaning and understanding of herself and her disability.

Margaret never complained about not being able to see. Her mother and father did a great job of providing her with everything she could possibly need. She went to a school where there were other kids who were like her. She was never taught that there was something that she couldn't do. Her grandfather always told her that she was gifted with a special gift from God and that it made her special. She felt special indeed. Still, she was always curious as to what it would be like to see.

Sam's message talked about the light representing a guide to show you the way. "… And if you follow the light, the Lord will see you through. Just stay in the light, and you will have no reason to fear anything. Wherever you want to go, God will take you there. Whatever you want to do, God will show you the way. He is the light. He is your strength, and he can make a way out of no way."

Soon Sam got away from his teaching style and began preaching. He started like most preachers do and went with the old standards, but it got the people moving, and it gave them what they wanted. They wanted to be moved and touched by the Spirit.

Sam was preaching, "He'll make a way out of no way. He's my rock in a weary land, my doctor when I'm sick, my lawyer in a courtroom, my food when I'm hungry, my water when I'm thirsty." He repeated the verse "The Lord is my light." He was jumping up and down, going back and forth on the pulpit. The congregation was full of the Spirit.

Sam continued, "I wanna know, do you know the Lord? Do you know Jesus? He died for our sins. I don't know about you, but I know my God is a mighty God. How many of you know the Lord? Raise your hands if you know Jesus. Raise your hands in the name of the Lord. Praise his holy name."

The people were raising their hands, calling his name "Jesus, yes Lord, yes Lord." By now, they were jumping in the aisles and a couple of women fainted. The pianist was banging on the piano, timing her playing to Sam's rhythm. Mary was sitting in her seat, rocking back and forth. Tears were flowing from her eyes, and she just kept wiping and wiping. This was what it was all about; they were having a mighty good time in the name of the Lord.

Little Margaret was sitting there next to her mother and the sermon was touching her. It was touching her in a way she'd never felt before. A chill came over her body, and a sharp jolt shot up the center of her back. She couldn't contain herself anymore. Margaret jumped up, stretched out her arms, and lifted her head up in the air. She started shouting, "O Father, dear Lord, yes Lord. You are my strength and my light. Show me the way, Lord. I love the Lord, I love the Lord."

Mary stopped dead in her tracks. She looked over at Margaret and couldn't believe what she was seeing. Here was this small child, only seven years old, shouting out to the Lord with tears coming from her eyes. Mary reached over and grabbed her daughter and hugged her tightly with joy. Her little girl had come to know the Lord. They just stood there, holding each other, rocking back and forth, and both saying, "Thank you, Jesus. Thank you, Lord. Thank you, Jesus. Thank you, Lord."

At least ten people must have joined the church that day. After church, it seemed like everyone came over to Sam to tell him what a good sermon he had preached. His father-in-law, the reverend, came over and said, "Boy, you keep preaching like that, you going to have to get your own church."

On the way home, Margaret sat in the backseat of the car, humming "Jesus Loves the Little Children," and at that moment, they were a happy family. They seemed happier than they'd ever been before. Both Sam and Mary knew they had a lot to be thankful for. Mary was especially happy that the Holy Spirit had touched her baby.

Once home, it was time to focus on dinner. Mary had a chicken she was planning on frying. Margaret wanted to help with the cooking and voiced her desire to her mother. As usual, she was allowed to help.

Sam and Mary went to great lengths to make their home as simple as possible for their blind daughter. Everything had its place and was always put back where it belonged after it was used. Little Margaret learned where just about everything was. She knew just how many steps it would take and how many turns to get anywhere in the home. She knew where the furniture was and how to maneuver her way around pretty well.

Margaret was also very independent and very stubborn. No one could tell her that there was something she couldn't do because she was blind. She would never accept being blind as a reason why she couldn't do something. The problem was that sometimes it was true— but Margaret wouldn't accept it. This kind of thinking wasn't always good.

Mary took the greens out and set them on the counter next to the sink and asked Margaret to clean them. Margaret walked over to the sink and felt the counter, finding the greens and the sink stopper.

She started the water and carefully began adding greens and scrubbing them. Soon thereafter, there was a knock at the door, and Annie walked in without waiting for an answer. The reverend followed in behind her and they found Mary and Margaret in the kitchen.

"Girls, we're hungry and came right over to eat," Annie announced.

"Momma, I'm helping Mother cook dinner, and we're gonna have fried chicken," said Margaret.

"Good," replied Annie, "I'm gonna help too."

"Good! That way we can have dinner cooked right away," Margaret replied with joy.

"Neelmah, let me show you how to fry chicken when you get through with those greens."

Margaret finished cleaning and seasoning the greens and put them in a pot of water and set them on the stove. Mary said she'd take it from there so she could add the soulful touches, including some browned salt pork.

"Mother, where's the chicken?" Margaret asked.

"It's sitting on a plate on the table, baby," Mary answered.

Margaret walked over to the table and felt around. She found the plate and took it over to the counter. "Momma, we need to cut up the chicken to get it ready."

"All right, Neelmah, I'll teach you how to cut the chicken," said Annie. "You take the chicken and find the two back legs and spread them apart wide," Annie instructed. "Now take the left leg in one hand, and use your other hand to feel deep down where the joint is, where it attaches to the body."

Momma gave her the knife and Margaret put the edge to the chicken, in the joint next to her fingers, and sliced right down through the joint. Sam kept those knives razor sharp, so it went through without too much effort.

"Good, baby, good," said Annie.

They continued and finished cutting the chicken. "Now let's get the seasonings," instructed Annie.

Margaret went over to the cupboard and felt around, and Annie told her what she needed. Together they seasoned the chicken, and

Annie told her that normally she'd have the chicken sit for a while to let the seasonings take well to it, but they didn't have time to do that.

Mary was already putting the frying pan on the stove and had the lard in it, heating up. Annie instructed, "Get you some flour and put it in a sack and season it too." Margaret did as she was told.

Now came the difficult part; it was time to put the chicken in the hot pan. This made Mary and Annie nervous. "All right, Neelmah, you take a couple pieces of chicken, one at a time, and dip them in the egg, then put them in the sack and shake them up good, and then add them to the pan to fry," said Annie.

Mary always put pots on the stove, with the handles pointing inward, toward the center of the stove, so Margaret would never bump them or knock something over and get burned. Margaret knew that this was a practice. After getting three pieces ready, she went over to the stove and faced it. She was just tall enough to be able to reach the top of the stove, which was about at her neck.

Annie instructed her to wait, and got a stool for her to step on. Margaret stood there with the hot pan in front of her. She started to feel from the front surface over to the edge and back, over to the other edge, and then back to the center. Her hand moved up slowly from front center toward the back of the stove and found the panhandle. She asked for a long fork so she could feel the pan. Mary gave her the fork, and she and Annie watched as Margaret tapped and found the edges of the pan, then put the fork into the pan and measured how wide it was. Momma and Mary were on pins and needles, and now they really didn't want her to go any further, but they knew she'd have a fit if they tried to stop her.

Margaret handed Annie the fork, and then reached down into the sack and grabbed a piece of chicken. Carefully she pulled the piece out and moved it out in front of her, using good judgment, then slowly lowered it into the pan. When she heard the popping sound of it beginning to fry, she knew she had touched down, so she then gently let it fall into the pan. Mary and Annie both sighed in relief as Margaret continued with the rest of the chicken. It was a long and exhausting ordeal, and they both watched over Margaret every step of the way. They were glad when it was finally time to eat.

As time moved on, Margaret was developing into a fine young lady. She wanted to try to do lots of different things, as most children do. She even asked her father to teach her how to ride a horse. Mary was against this, but Sam felt that he could have her ride a pony while he guided it on another horse.

Against Mary's wishes, Sam decided to do it. From a neighbor, he borrowed a pony that was used by fairs for children to ride. He sat Margaret on the saddle and got onto his horse and told little Margaret to hold on. She was so giddy and excited that Sam almost couldn't hold himself together from all the joy and fun he was having too. "Hold on now, honey, here we go. Giddy-up, horsey," Sam said, giving his horse a little kick.

The horses took off with a little trot, and Margaret jerked back a little. She called out to the horse, "Whoa," and held on tight. The pony bounced up and down, and she bounced up and down in the saddle.

Sam's horse was getting a little ahead, so he kept looking back to see how she was doing. All of a sudden, down she went. Margaret fell off the pony. She took a very hard fall. She landed on her shoulder, and bumped her head on the ground. The fall knocked her out cold. Sam jumped off his horse and ran to Margaret, and the pony trotted off. He reached down, scooped her up, and began to run to the house.

Sam could see the bruise on the right side of his baby's forehead as she lay in his arms with her eyes closed. "Lord, O Lord, what have I done? My baby, please, Lord, help my baby." Sam ran up the steps of the porch and almost tripped going up. He ran into the house and yelled, "Mary, come quick!"

She came running out of the kitchen and yelled, "My God, what happened?" Sam had to tell her she'd fallen off the pony. Mary didn't have to say a thing; she knew Sam already knew she was upset. She ran to the kitchen to get a cold wet rag.

When Mary placed the cold rag on Margaret's forehead, she came to. "Ohhhh, ummmmm, owww. Mother, I fell off the horse," said Margaret.

Mary started in on her. "You just lie there and take it easy. If it wasn't for the Lord, you might be dead. I told you I didn't want you riding no horse. You can't see, and you don't have any business on a horse."

Margaret didn't like to hear this. She began to protest and started to speak, but was cut off quickly by her mother who said, "I don't wanna ever find you trying to get on a horse again, do you understand me?"

Margaret didn't respond. "Do you understand me, Naomi?" Mary asked sternly.

Margaret knew when her mother called her Naomi she meant business, so she answered, "Yes, ma'am."

"Sam, I'll get to you later!" Mary told him. He just held his head down and walked out.

3

My Savior

Margaret was a fast learner; she was very bright and intelligent. Her diction was good, and she spoke with a nice vocabulary, especially for a country girl in the South. She had good teachers who enjoyed her desire to learn and excel. They always took the extra time to give her the attention she needed.

Mary found Margaret a good tutor, and she started to read and write in Braille. One of the problems with her learning Braille was that it took someone who knew Braille to read it. Mary tried to learn but just couldn't pick it up. However, Sam was starting to get it, and this made Margaret very happy.

The main benefit of Margaret learning Braille was that she learned the letters of the alphabet, and then learned to spell and read. She'd sit in her chair with a sheet of paper, similar to cardstock; a stylus, which looked similar to a short ice pick; and the slate, which was made of metal and had a hinge on one end so it could open up and clamp down on a sheet of paper, holding it in place. There she'd sit, embossing the paper with dots, which made up the letters of the alphabet and became words. Her parents were very proud of her.

In church, Margaret loved to sing, and her voice was always audible as the choir sang. She'd sit in the front row next to her mother, and she knew all the words to all the songs. As soon as the choir started to sing, Margaret would start too. She never knew that she was drawing a lot of attention to herself and never felt the eyes of choir members peering over at her as they tried to focus on their songs. Actually, she was doing a lot better job than most of them.

One day after church, the reverend approached Sam about Margaret's singing. "You know, Sam, that little girl of yours has got some voice. She's starting to drown out my choir!"

Sam replied, "I know, Pastor, I can talk to her and get her to tone it down a little."

"No, no, I wouldn't do that. I think it's good; she's singing for the Lord. You can tell she's got the Spirit in her heart, and I think we should encourage it," said the reverend.

Sam nodded with agreement. "You ever think about getting her piano lessons?" asked the reverend.

"No," replied Sam, "but that's probably a good idea."

"Well, I know a good teacher, and I can talk to her if you like. She could probably come over to your house to give the lessons. We've even got an old piano in the back shed you can take. I'm sure the deacons won't mind. Shucks, she may wind up playing for the church, for all we know," the reverend suggested.

"That sounds like a great idea, Rev. I'll run it by Mary, and we'll talk to Margaret. I'll pick it up on my way home tomorrow evening," said Sam.

"You do that, son, you do that!" replied the reverend.

Sam talked with Mary, and she was elated. She felt it was a good idea and would keep Margaret busy. When they spoke with Margaret about it, she jumped with joy.

"Mother, I always wanted to play the piano. I always listen to the sister at church playing, and I can hear her tapping on the floor and hitting the keys. I can play it, I'm sure I can. I know I can play it, Mother!" said Margaret.

Sam got ready to pick up the piano on his own to get it into the house. He was a big, strong man, and he always enjoyed doing something to show off his strength to his wife. She offered to help, but he refused and said, "Nah, this is man's work. I got this!"

Sam struggled and fought with the piano and finally got it up the porch and into the house. It was an old upright, a Kohler & Campbell. The keys were stained, and the wood was dirty. It was a dark brown color, and it looked old, with some decorative carving here and there. Mary took a long look at it and kind of grumbled a little, but Sam stopped her short and said, "Ah, a little polish and some elbow grease, and it will be good as new. Clean it up, Mary," Sam said and smiled as he walked out the door. Mary just gave him a look like he was crazy, but she got to work.

Margaret was in her room studying, and Mary was surprised that she hadn't heard the commotion of the move. But once she started to clean the keys, Margaret heard them bang. She came running and almost ran into the door. "Mother, it's here, my piano, it's here!" She carefully traced every inch of the piano with her touch. She said, "It's beautiful, Mother. What color is it?"

"Dark brown," replied Mary, almost frowning. But it actually looked a lot better since she'd polished it up.

Sam came in from outside, holding the bench seat in his arms. He brought it over to the piano, and then said, "Here, honey, try it on for size."

Margaret felt her way to the bench and the piano, and Mary helped her position herself. Margaret took notice as to how the seat was in position to the piano so she could remember it. She smelled the scent of old wood and then felt the keys softly, feeling the height, length, the different sizes, and how many there were. She gently pressed down on the keys and listened to the sound. It needed tuning badly, but she said, "It sounds beautiful," and added, "When can I start the lessons, Mother? I want to start right away."

"Well, we have to contact the teacher. The reverend said he was going to talk to her. He'll let us know," Mary replied.

"Aw, Mother, I need to get started now. Come on, when? When?" Margaret pouted.

Mary replied, "Now don't start that pouting. I said it won't be long. You just hold your horses, little girl. You'll be making a bunch of noise soon enough."

The piano became a vehicle that Margaret could channel her energy into. She never wanted to miss a lesson, and she practiced aggressively. Soon she was all consumed by the piano, and Sam and Mary were very pleased that Margaret had found something that she really loved and worked hard to be good at it. Even though she couldn't see the keys, her hands would glide over them so naturally.

Soon Margaret began to focus her piano playing on gospel songs. As far as she was concerned, the teacher wasn't going fast enough. The teacher would come over and Margaret would be way ahead of her. She was experimenting on her own and learned the keyboard very well, better than most of the children who could see. The difference with Margaret was that she was really listening to the sound that the piano was making, in a different way than other children. She really appreciated the sound.

Margaret would take a song that she'd heard sung in church and sit and try to figure out how to play it, and the next thing you knew, she could play the song.

The teacher saw great promise in Margaret, who never ceased to amaze her. She finally had a conversation with Mary and Sam. She sat them down and told them that Margaret was a very gifted child. Of course, they already knew it. She told them that eventually they should try to get her into a school for artistic children so she could really excel. They thanked her and she left.

Sam was a hard worker; he did what he could to care for his family. Trying to work the small farm and work at the lumber mill was tough on him. He made decent money, for a Negro, and the extra money he could get from the farm served them well, so they never wanted for anything. But putting Margaret into a special school was not something they could afford. Sam and Mary talked about it and decided to let the Lord take care of it; he would provide!

4

Dedicated to the Lord

By the time Margaret was twelve years old, singing and playing the piano had become second nature to her. There was no mistaking that she was a musician and a singer. She was growing and beginning to fill out as a young woman. She became someone that you couldn't miss in a crowd. Her purse, where she kept her collapsible cane, was with her at all times. She used her cane to get around and always walked with her head held high, displaying a sense of pride. To Margaret, the fact that she was blind was never a disability to her or a hindrance that kept her from anything she wanted to do.

People all around the county began to recognize the young Negro blind girl who could sing and play the piano. Even some of the white folks around town began to hear about her and were kind of curious. One Sunday, there was a guest church coming to visit from another part of the county, and there was going to be a musical. The church music director asked Margaret if she'd sing a solo, which, of course, she was more than willing to do.

The Hintons were in church all day. They went to Sunday school, then to morning worship, and after morning worship, they stayed to eat at the church. They ate the works—fried chicken, greens, beans and rice, ham, dressing, and sweet potato pie. The family was full and, in about an hour, the program would start. Margaret went into the church and sat in a corner to take a snooze.

Margaret was awakened by the sound of the deacons beginning the service with an old hymn. One of the deacons shouted out the verse, "Father I stretch my hands to thee."

Then the congregation joined in, singing and dragging out every syllable. "Faaaatherrrr, I streeeetch myyyy haaaand to theeee."

Next the deacon shouted out, "No other help shall I know."

The church followed and sang, dragging out every word, "Noooo ooootherrrr heeeelp shaaaall I knoooow."

Margaret sat up quickly and joined in and tried to act like everything was normal, as if she hadn't been sleeping at all. Sam was watching her and began to chuckle.

The deacon read a scripture from the Bible, and then the pastor got up to say a few words. Sam was in his usual seat in the pulpit. "Today we have a special treat in store. We will have an evening of praising and rejoicing our Lord and Savior, Jesus Christ." The congregation's immediate amens followed. The pastor continued, "The way our program will proceed is that there will be a prayer by Minister Hinton, followed by a song from our choir, then a solo by our own young sister, Margaret, and then we will turn over the program to our musical guest."

Sam got up and said his prayer, keeping it short and simple. The church musical director got up, instructed the choir to stand, and instead of sitting down at the piano, he stood with a stick in his hand and began to direct them like a symphony conductor. He tapped his stick on the piano and then counted off—one, two, three, four:

> Calvary, Calvary
> Calvary, Calvary
> Calvary, Calvary
> Surely he died on
> Calvary

The choir was singing a cappella with no musical instruments accompanying them. They sounded great; all voices sounded as one. The lead singer sang the verse:

> Can you hear him,
> Calling to his Father?
> Can you hear him,
> Calling to his Father?
> Can you hear him,
> Calling to his Father?
> Surely he died on
> Calvary

Her voice was like a nightingale's. The whole congregation lit up; everyone was excited. The preachers all leaned forward and looked back at the choir with big smiles. The pastor just sat there, looking forward with a stare, not showing much emotion, but there was a sense of pride all over his face. He already knew what they were going to sing, and he knew what effect it would have over his church and the guest. Margaret, too, was visibly taken by what was taking place. It was almost overwhelming.

The choir started back with the chorus, but this time they doubled up and split up between two groups. It was very moving and deep with emotion. The song drew up images of the slaves who had come before and suffered but still had hope and looked to the Lord and Savior, Jesus Christ, to deliver them out of bondage.

When the song was over, church members were moved. There were shouts of, "Yes, Lord," and "Thank you, Lord! Thank you, Jesus! Thank you, Jesus!"

The pastor got up and addressed the congregation, "Oh, we're going to have a good shouting time tonight. How many of you know the Lord? Do you know that Jesus died for your sins?" There were shouts in response as he continued, "Ohhhhhh, we're gonna have a good time tonight."

Margaret sat thinking, "How am I going to follow that?" She had already picked a song to sing but now it wouldn't do. She had to think fast. What could it be? What should she sing?

The pastor stood in the pulpit and announced, "And now we're going to have a song from one of our own home-grown members. This young lady was born and raised right here in this church. She's become a fine young lady and serves as an example to others of good Christian living. This young lady lives to serve the Lord. Margaret, will you come up?"

An usher went over and touched Margaret on her shoulder; she stood up and let the usher guide her to the piano. It wasn't obvious from looking at her that she was trying to figure something out. She sat down and started to play on the piano keys; it was no particular song at that point. She began to speak. "Well, I had a song I was going to sing, but that selection by the choir had me calling on the Lord, seeking to play what he wants me to play and not what I want to play."

Margaret paused her playing and then began to play and sing:

> Precious Lord, take my hand.
> Lead me on.
> Let me stand.
> I am tired.
> I am weak.
> I am worn.
> Through the storm.

Her voice rose as she continued, "Through the night." Margaret's voice was that of a grown woman, not of a twelve-year-old child. She was singing from her heart, and she was singing to God. The audience was there, but that was not who she was singing to. Everyone could sense there was a connection taking place between her and a higher power.

It didn't matter if the people were there or not. As far as Margaret was concerned, she was singing a song and having a conversation with God. Her voice was strong and smooth. But what was even more impressive was that her voice was unique. She sang like no one else, and no one else sang like her. Her voice was not the voice of someone who could just sing and carry a note: she was an artist, with her own signature style.

The song was one that everyone had heard before. But no one had heard it sung like this. It took on a whole knew meaning with Margaret. She was a person who, in most people's opinion, needed to be led. But here she was, asking the Lord to lead her, in front of any- and everybody, and she didn't care who heard it or saw it. It was a strong visual presentation that, unless you were a log, you couldn't help but be touched by.

Margaret was winding down the song. She was in touch with her Lord, and she became very emotional. She continued to sing, "Take my hand, Precious Lord, lead me on."

Margaret began to shout. There were already several members shouting out to the Lord, "Thank you, Jesus, you know that I love you, Lord." She began to bang on the piano like they do when a preacher is wrapping up. Bang, bang, went the piano. "Oh, thank you, Jesus," she cried. Bang, bang, went the piano again. "I wouldn't be anything if it wasn't for you, Father." Bang, bang, went the piano. She stretched out her arms and stood up.

By now, the church was full of the Spirit. An usher moved over toward Margaret, and she stood up and knocked the bench over. But it didn't faze her as she continued, "O Lord, you brought me from so far, Father." Her arms were stretched out wide and her head lifted up toward the heavens.

The pastor got up and signaled to the usher, who began to fan Margaret. The church was on fire, and the musical director moved in and took over the piano. Margaret was still calling out to the Lord while she was being moved.

The pastor spoke to the congregation, "I want to know, do you know the Lord?" "Yes!" yelled out the crowd. "Do you know that Jesus died for your sins?" he asked. "Yes!" yelled the crowd. "Raise your hands if you know Jesus for yourself," he called. Everyone raised his or her hands. "Ahhhhhhh, my God is a mighty God. He's all things and everything," said the pastor. The church was in an uproar; even the guest choir had members shouting and fainting. The ushers had their hands full, and the deacons had to help carry people out.

"Now, folks, what we want to do is have our choir come down and let our guest move up into the choir stand," said the pastor, motioning to the ushers as he tried to bring calm to the congregation. The choirs worked to get themselves together to have some order while the ushers began to direct the change, and the program continued.

Later that night at home, Mary had set the tub for Margaret to take a bath. Sam and Mary were in their bedroom while Margaret was bathing. "Mary, our baby is no longer a little girl," said Sam.

"I know," answered Mary as her eyes began to tear.

Sam reached out to her and put her head on his shoulder, "Ah, honey, it's okay. She'll always be our little angel, and she's not ready to leave the nest yet!"

"It just seems like she's growing up so fast. I'm scared, Sam, I'm scared. I don't know what's in store for our baby. What's going to happen? How will she turn out? What will she do?" Mary just wept.

"Now, you know my answer for that question," he said.

She looked up in his eyes and nodded her head. She knew his answer would be, "The Lord will provide."

Mary went into the bathroom to wash Margaret's hair.

"Mother, can I wash my hair myself?" Margaret said.

Mary was a little shocked. She always washed her daughter's hair. It was almost a ritual. But she caught herself and simply replied, "Yes, dear. You know where the soap is, and the towels. Let me know if you need my help," she added and walked out of the bathroom.

Later that night, Margaret woke up from a deep sleep. She opened her eyes wide as if she'd been startled awake, and she was sweating. She tried to remember what she'd been dreaming about but couldn't. She began to think about the service that day and how she hadn't known what to sing. But as soon as she sat down to sing, the song came to her. She had never played that song before, nor had she ever sung it, at least not as a solo. Maybe she'd sung it along with the choir. She asked herself, "How did I know how to play that song? I never played that song before. How did I know it?" She lay there thinking and trying to figure it out. Finally, she just said, "Well, Lord, only you know."

Margaret lay there with her eyes open, in total darkness, and then something began to happen. Something was out there, something in the darkness. It was really small at first, and then it seemed to grow. It was really white. "It must be white," she thought, because she had only ever seen darkness. It was light! It had to be light because it was so bright.

At this point, Margaret began to be afraid. She was afraid because she had never seen anything before, and now she was seeing something. It grew more quickly now, and it was getting brighter and larger. She tried to move but couldn't. It was as if her body was no longer hers. "Lord, help me; help me, Jesus," she thought.

Now it felt as though she were floating in air, as though she had no body. The light had consumed her, and it was all around her. She felt a long way from home, as though she were no longer in her bed. Then she heard a voice. "Margaret, I have come unto you as I have come to others before you. I want you to know that I am with you wherever you go. Life will not always be easy for you, but I want you to know that one day we will be together. I want you to go and sing for me. Sing and praise me in song everywhere you go. You have been given a special gift, and this gift is also your gift to me."

Suddenly the light was gone, and Margaret fell limp and went into a deep sleep.

The next morning, Margaret told her mother and her father about her vision. Her mother said that maybe she'd had a dream. But her father said that the Lord had touched her and that it should not be questioned. "When the Lord calls on you, you must answer," he said. He also told her he believed her. Margaret felt she now had really come to know the Lord and that it was time for her to be baptized. Sam told her to come before the Lord at church on Sunday.

That Sunday when the doors of the church were opened, Margaret took out her cane, got up, and stepped into the aisle. An usher escorted her before the altar, and she was accepted into the Lord's flock. When asked if she knew the Lord and knew that his son had died for her sins, she responded, "I know the Lord. I know him for myself. He has spoken to me and told me that this is what I am to do. I will sing and praise his name all the days of my life."

"Praise God," said the pastor. "Let everybody say amen. I don't think there is one among you that would say that young Margaret isn't a child of God. Margaret, you have a gift that was given to you by the Lord, and we have all been touched by it. Deacons, let all of you who feel we should accept Margaret as a member of this church say 'Aye,'" requested the pastor. "Aye," they all said. "The ayes have it. Margaret, the next first Sunday, you will be baptized, and unless someone objects, your father, Minister Sam Hinton, shall conduct the baptism."

Sam was very happy, and the other ministers were all shaking his hand. Mary was standing right behind Margaret the whole time, and she just kept wiping the tears from her eyes, she was so filled with joy. From that day forward, God would be the single most important thing in Margaret's life.

The Hinton family was doing pretty well. Mary was doing some housework for some white folks in town, and Margaret was doing well in school. Sam tended to some of his chores early in the morning before going to work and tended to the rest when he got home. Margaret got up in the morning, washed up and got dressed, and helped with the breakfast. She was able to help in the house as well as with some of the outside chores. She did things like feed the chickens. Her main job was to become as independent as possible.

One Saturday morning, Annie and the reverend came over to visit. The reverend wasn't doing so well. He had come down with a terrible cold; he was coughing and hacking and was running a little fever. Annie fixed him some lemon and honey and told him to lie down and take it easy while she helped Mary cook supper.

That evening they went home and the Hintons decided to turn in early because they were going to visit the reverend's church in the morning. After breakfast the next morning, they headed out toward town to go to the church. When they got there, everyone was standing and milling around.

One of the deacons approached Sam and pulled him aside. Mary was puzzled. What was happening? Why was everyone looking at them? She noticed some of the members were crying. She looked over at Sam and saw him shaking his head and holding his head down. She knew it was bad news.

Before Sam made it over to Mary, Margaret reached over and grabbed her on her arm and said, "Mother, Papa Jones is dead."

Mary was overcome with grief. She knew that Margaret knew because she could hear like nobody else could. She had overheard someone whispering about it over twenty feet away. Mary and Margaret embraced each other and cried. "Where is my momma?" Mary asked.

She was at home, someone said. "Sam, let's go to Momma," she begged.

When they arrived at the Jones's home, Annie was sitting out on the porch in her rocker chair, rocking back and forth and staring ahead. There were church members, family, and neighbors milling about. It seemed like Annie was there, and then she wasn't there. Her sisters, Bee and Mine, were there, and they were tending to the visitors.

Bee came over to Mary to console her and Margaret, and they all began to cry. Next they walked up the steps toward Annie. Annie looked toward them as they approached and said, "He knew he was going to die; he told me last week. He said he wasn't going to be on this here earth much longer and that the Lord was going to be coming for him. He said the Lord told him in his sleep. Well, I guess he was right; he's with the Lord now." She began to cry out loud, "O Lord, dear God, what am I going to do without my Rev?" All the women huddled together and wept.

Rev. Jones's funeral was a grand affair. He was well known in the church community throughout Arkansas and Tennessee. People came from Little Rock, Mississippi, Forest City, Memphis, and all over the county. There were many flowers and cards, and there were preachers from all over. Sam didn't want a long, dragged-out funeral; he had always said that about when it came time for him to go. So they were going to honor that.

Annie wanted Margaret to sing a solo. Margaret didn't know if she'd be able to do it. Before Margaret was to sing, there was a selection by the choir. The lead singer was a member of the congregation who had a beautiful voice. The church was quiet when she began to sing because the last speaker had talked about the humorous moments he'd had with the reverend, and everyone had had a little chuckle.

The woman stepped over to the podium and the pianist began to play. Margaret sat thinking about her grandfather and the good times they'd had and how he'd always given her words of encouragement. The reverend had always told her that she was a child of God, that there were great things in store for her, and to always walk in faith.

The reverend had been a strong man who was very confident, even bordering on arrogant. He'd been a no-nonsense type of preacher, but he'd always been kind and sweet to Margaret. She would miss him.

The choir began to sing. Little did Margaret know that the song they were about to sing would have a profound impact on the rest of her life. They began to sing:

Chorus
>Shine on me, shine on me
>Let the light from the lighthouse
>Shine on me
>Shine on me, shine on me
>Let the light from the lighthouse
>Shine on me

Verse
>I heard a voice of Jesus say
>Come unto me and rest
>Let the weary and worn lay down
>Lay your head upon my breast
>I came to Jesus and I drank
>From thy chilling stream
>My thirst was quenched
>My soul was revived
>And right now I live in him

Chorus
>Shine on me, shine on me
>Let the light from the lighthouse
>Shine on me

The song touched Margaret in a way that no other song had. To her, Jesus was the light of her salvation. She had dreamed of a light and heard the voice of God telling her that he would lead her and to have no fear. For this song to be sung on this day at this time meant that this song was especially for her and that God had given it to her.

When it came time for Margaret to sing, she was sitting next to her mother, weeping and thanking and praising the Lord. The usher had come over to assist her to the piano but didn't know what to do because Margaret didn't seem to respond. "Naomi, Naomi, baby, are you all right?" asked Mary.

"Yes, Mother, I'm okay," Margaret answered.

Margaret sat at the piano and started to play an introduction. As she played, she began to speak. For a twelve-year-old to play so confidently and speak so eloquently was amazing to behold. Margaret said, "My grandfather was a man who dedicated his life to the Lord. He and my grandmother, Momma, paved the way for us to come to know the Lord and Jesus Christ, and I thank them for this. The song I'm about to sing is a favorite of my grandfather's, and he always used to ask me to sing it. So I'm going to sing it again today, and every time I sing it, I'll think of him. I ask that, when you hear this song as you go through your trials and tribulations, think of my grandfather, and know that the Lord will see you through."

She began to sing, "Amazing grace, how sweet the sound that saved a wretch like me. I once was lost but now am found, was blind but now I see." Margaret tried to sing as best she could, but the loss of her grandfather was difficult to bear. Several times throughout the song, she almost broke down. This affected everyone in the church, and many began to cry openly.

After the burial, everyone was invited over to the Jones's place to eat, which was customary. Mary told Margaret to go outside with the other children while she and Annie got everything ready. All the aunties, cousins, and relatives began to arrive and wouldn't let Mary or Annie do anything. Soon the afternoon began to take on a joyous atmosphere, with children playing, music playing in the house, and singing.

After everyone left and the house was cleaned, it came time for Mary, Margaret, and Sam to leave. Sam told Margaret to go and sit in the parlor. He and Mary went into the kitchen where Annie was doing some final cleaning. Sam approached Annie and said, "Momma, we think it's best if you come live with us."

But Annie shook her head. "Sam, I appreciate the offer, but I got to stay here and hold on to what me and Sam worked so hard for."

Sam wanted to keep on, but he knew by her tone and action that he wouldn't be able to change her mind.

"You all go on home. I'm goin' be all right," she said, motioning for them to leave.

It wasn't too long before what Sam had predicted began to take place. The church had given Annie some money, but it didn't last long. Annie tried to get work but could only get odd jobs here and there, which didn't pay much. The farm was paid for, but she couldn't keep up the taxes.

Before long, things began to come undone around the property, but Annie was stubborn and wouldn't take much help. She soon sold off all the animals, and since she didn't know how to drive, she sold the car too. Winter would be coming around soon, and something needed to happen.

Something did happen! There were white folks around who had been eyeing the property and wanted it. They put pressure on the county to do something. The next thing Annie knew, the sheriff was at her door, telling her she had two days to pay the money or three days to leave. Annie couldn't come up with the money to pay the back taxes, and so she moved in with Mary and Sam. Mary was not happy about the farm situation, but she was happy that Momma was at home with them.

It was good to have Annie around the Hinton household. Sam and Mary would go off to work, and Annie would help Margaret get to and from school. Dinner was always ready when they got home.

One morning, they were all gathered around the breakfast table getting ready to eat and Sam said grace, "Dear Lord, we thank you for this food we are about to eat. Bless this food so that it will nourish our bodies and souls. Watch over us, Lord, as we go about our daily travels. And bless us that we all make it home to see one another again. All these blessings we ask in your Holy Son, Jesus's name. Amen."

"Amen. Rise, Peter, slay and eat!" said Annie.

They all chuckled because Annie always said that after grace.

Sam went off to the lumber mill, ready for the day. He knew they were getting a new shipment of logs for cutting that day, and the trucks would be rolling in. As always, when the trucks came in, it was a real busy day. The logs would have to be unloaded and stacked in the yard nice and neat. Everything had to be done precisely and correctly. The boss was very meticulous, and he drove his men hard. He liked Sam because he was big, bright, and strong.

One of the trucks rolled around and lined up to be unloaded. One of the workers walked around to one side and began to loosen the straps holding the logs in place. There were four straps, spaced evenly from front to rear. First they'd loosen the front, then the rear, and then the two in the middle. Two workers would do the loosening with one on each side of the truck working in tandem with the other. Sam would be on one side with another worker on the other.

Everything seemed to go without a hitch. All the straps had been loosened, and Sam was standing on one side of the truck when one of the workers called out to him, "So, Sam, what did your wife fix you for lunch today? Are you sharing some of them vittles?" Sam just laughed and replied, "Nah, my honey only fix grubs for this man."

Suddenly, Sam heard a creak coming from the logs. He looked and saw the bottom one starting to slip out. He tried to get out of the way, but it was too late. The stack of logs hit him and knocked him down, pinning him facedown on the ground with a large log across his back.

"Sam!" the co-worker shouted, running over to where he was lying. "Get a truck to pull this log off Sam!" he shouted.

Sam was lying there with his eyes wide open and coughing up blood. "Ben, Ben," he said.

"Stay still, Sam, we'll get you out. Just hold on, Sam, we'll get you," Ben said.

Sam was drifting, "Tell Mary I love her, Ben."

Ben was getting tearful now. He knew Sam wasn't going to make it. "Get this log off! Get it off now!" Ben shouted. The workers were moving as fast as they could, but by the time they got the log off, Sam was dead.

The foreman had the grim task of traveling out to the Hinton farm to tell the family. Driving out there, he tried to think about what he should say, but no matter how hard he tried, the words did not come easily.

Annie was the first to see the trucks pull up; one was Sam's truck, only there was a white man driving it. "Mary, there's a couple of white men outside, and they driving Sam's truck," Annie shouted.

Mary dashed out of the kitchen and ran outside. Right away she recognized the foreman. "Where's Sam? What's wrong with Sam?" she shouted.

The foreman looked at Mary and held his head down, then looked back at the car toward the backseat. Sam was set up in the backseat, leaning against the door, head slumped over.

Mary looked at the car and saw the silhouette of Sam in the backseat. "Sam," she shouted, running to the car.

Annie walked over to the foreman, and he told her what happened.

Mary had opened the back door to the car, and she had Sam braced in her arms. She wept and cried and called out to the Lord, "God, dear God, why? Why take our Sam from us? Why, Lord?" She was overcome with grief.

Ben, who had driven the truck back, walked over to her and told her Sam's last words. Mary just cried out loud.

The foreman told Annie that the sheriff would be over any minute and asked if there was anything she needed them to do. Annie asked if he could take her over to the school to pick up Margaret.

Momma had never come early to take her out of school, so right away Margaret knew something was wrong. She was caught totally by surprise.

"Neelmah, come on, we got to go home," Annie said.

"Momma, what's wrong?" asked Margaret.

"Baby, it ain't no easy way to tell you …" Annie paused. Margaret got frightened and asked again.

"Neelmah, your daddy's done died." Margaret fainted right into Annie's arms.

On the drive back to the house, Margaret came to and began to weep. She started asking all kinds of questions. She was getting ahead of herself. "What happened to Father? Where is he? What are we going to do? What's going to happen now? First we lost Grandfather and now Father! What's going to happen to us, Momma?" she asked, sobbing and crying. "O dear God! Why? Why?" she yelled out.

"The Lord will provide," replied Annie.

Annie knew she had to be strong. Now it was only she and her daughter and her granddaughter, and they needed each other now more than ever. When she got to the farm, the sheriff was there. It was the same one who had evicted her, so there was some bad blood there. Annie didn't trust the sheriff; as far as she was concerned, he was the white folks' henchman.

"Afternoon, Annie," the sheriff nodded.

"How do, Sheriff?" she replied.

"Annie, I investigated the matter and determined that it was an accident. It wasn't anyone's fault. It's just one of those God-awful things. I'm sorry, Annie. Sam was a fine man, and everyone liked and respected him. He was a good Negro!" he said.

Annie just looked at him and could see that he was being sincere and was doing the best he could. "Thank you, Sheriff. Thank you for your kind words," she said.

"You let me know if there's anything you want me to do. The mortuary folks will be coming around soon to get Sam." He tipped his hat and walked off.

Annie knew she'd be seeing the sheriff again soon enough. With Sam gone and the three women trying to hold down the property, it was ripe for the local white folks to try and get a hold of it.

News spread fast around St. Francis County. By that evening, aunts, cousins, family, and friends were all coming by the farm to pay their respects. People were bringing food, flowers, and gift baskets, and some even brought money. All the women were gathered in the parlor around Annie, Mary, and Margaret. They were all speaking about what a fine man Sam was and how he had touched their lives. Margaret was sitting at the piano, playing quietly while everyone talked.

The men were all gathered outside on the porch. One of them spoke up. "It's not going to be easy for these women with no man around to care for them."

Another one chimed in, "This is a shame. It ain't been long since they buried the reverend and they took the farm from Annie."

Still another one came forward and offered some words of encouragement. "Let me tell you something. Mary's still a spring chicken, and she's a fine-looking woman with a nice figure on her. There's goin' be some man around going to want to come calling. You can believe that!" he said.

"Amen," the others agreed.

5

A Change Goin' Come

Just a closer walk with thee
Just a closer walk with thee
Just a closer walk with thee

The choir sang. It was a nice sunny day that Sunday in church. It was a good service; the pastor had preached a good sermon, and everyone was walking around paying his or her tithes and offerings.

It had been almost a year since Sam had died, and the ladies were doing fine. Annie found out that she really didn't have much to worry about. Sam and Mary had worked hard and always saved their money. They never spent money foolishly, and Mary was good at managing the money. She had enough to get by as long as she kept working. The farm had been paid for, and all they had to do was to pay for upkeep. Mary also had taken in a boarder who worked around the farm for food and shelter.

After church let out, they were outside mingling around with folks when a young man came over and approached Mary. Now, anyone that knew Mary knew that she was a nice lady, but she was also very strong, and you had to approach her correctly or she'd put you in your place.

Charlie was new to the church, but he had been coming around for about six weeks now, and it was rumored that he was looking for a wife. Mary noticed him coming to the church, and she also noticed how he looked at her. She thought he was kind of cute, but he was no Sam. Sam was tall, big, and strong, a redbone with large arms and huge hands. Charlie was shorter than she was and dark-skinned. Charlie also seemed a little timid. He seemed to tiptoe around, especially since he didn't know many people there. Mary remembered seeing him cry, teary-eyed, after a heartfelt sermon one day. That let her know he was a sensitive man.

"Hello, Miss Mary. My name is Charlie, ma'am," he said.

"Well hello, Charlie. You're new around here, aren't you?" she replied.

"Yes, ma'am. Work brought me up this way, and I'm looking to settle around these parts," he said.

"Mother, come on!" Margaret said, pulling on her mother's arm.

"Now, you mind your manners, Margaret," Mary responded. "This is my daughter, Margaret, and this is my mother. We all call her Momma," said Mary, motioning to her mother.

Annie didn't seem to take too kindly to Charlie, but she wasn't rude. "How do?" Annie offered her hand.

"Nice to meet you, ma'am," Charlie said.

Charlie just kind of stood there for a moment and seemed to not quite know what to do next. Mary decided to help him out. "Charles, is there something I can do for you? Is there something you want to say?" She had called him Charles. That was his name, but hardly anyone called him that.

"Ah yes, ma'am. I was wondering if I could have a word with you in private," he said.

Mary answered, "If you have something you want to say, you can say it in front of my mother and my daughter. I ain't got anything to hide from them." Margaret and Annie both snickered; it was funny to them because they knew how tough she could be.

"Oh, well, ah … yes, ma'am. Well, I was, ah, I was just kinda wondering if I could come calling on you one evening and take you into town for something to eat," he mumbled.

"And, why would you want to do that? Why do you want to take me out to dinner?" she shot at him.

Charlie was in over his head, out of his league; he could see that now. He actually already knew that before he approached her. But she was so beautiful to him, and she had a blind daughter who could sing like a bird and who had made him cry once. He just couldn't help himself. "I'm sorry, ma'am. I meant no harm," he said.

"Did I say no? Momma, did I say no?" Annie shook her head. "Margaret, did you hear me say no?"

Margaret responded "No, Mother."

This caught Charlie by surprise. He lit up, smiled, and before he could say anything else, Mary said, "You come around and pick me up at 6:30 Friday evening. Ask around; you can find out where I live. Come on, Momma, let's go." She grabbed Margaret by the arm and walked off.

Charlie just stood there, speechless, not knowing whether to say something or just walk off. He didn't have to think too long. He just walked off and shook his head, mumbling to himself. He thought out loud, "Boy, that woman's something else."

One of the deacons had seen what happened and walked over to Charlie and said, "I see you got your eye on one of the flowers in our garden." Charlie had almost walked into the man when he was cut short.

"Ah, yes, sir. I been looking at her for a few weeks now, and I noticed she ain't got nobody," Charlie said.

"Son, it's a plenty men in this county wouldn't mind getting next to that woman. There are a few that have tried, even some from this church. But she ain't an easy woman to get at. Plus it just seems like she just getting over her husband dying and all," said the deacon.

"Well I got a date with her Friday evening," Charlie said proudly to the deacon.

"Then you've done better than most," the deacon replied.

"But she didn't tell me where she lives. She told me to find out myself," he told the deacon.

The deacon laughed so much he was almost ready to fall over. "Son, that's funny. I knew she was a tough one," he responded, giving Sam the information on where the farm was. "Good luck, son," said the deacon as he walked away.

Mary was driving the truck home from church, and they were listening to some gospel music on the radio. Margaret was humming the song that was being played, and she had a little smile on her face. "What you so happy about, Naomi?" Mary asked.

Margaret replied, "You seem like you like that man at the church. Is he handsome, Mommy?"

"Not really, honey. But there is something about him that is cute," Mary said thoughtfully. She smiled and said, "He's shorter than me, about your height. He's darker than Sam was. I usually don't take to dark-skin men. But he seems nice—kind, and a little shy. I like that in a man. It means he's the caring type," Mary said as she smiled.

Annie spoke up with a little sass. "Don't seem like it's been that long since Sam died to me. Just don't seem like the time to be looking out your own barnyard just yet. Hell, the body ain't even cold."

"Momma, that's not a nice thing to say to Mother. You know she loved my father," Margaret responded.

"Well, I ain't ever going to marry no one else. Just don't seem like the way God intended it," said Annie.

"That's cause ain't nobody looking at you, Momma," said Mary.

"Girl, you don't know who looking or ain't looking at me," Momma replied.

Mary and Margaret laughed.

"Margaret, you know, you getting to be a grown woman pretty soon. You're fifteen now, and I see how some of these young men are starting to look at you," said Mary.

"Who's been looking at me, Mother? Who?" asked Margaret.

"Oh, just a few I noticed," said Mary. "You just need to stay close to your mommy and keep your mind on your schooling, young lady. You hear what I'm saying?" Mary said, almost in a snapping way.

"Yes, ma'am," replied Margaret. Margaret sat there, riding along and wondering who was looking at her. She was now more curious than ever.

Charlie was right on time; he pulled up in a nice, shiny, 1938 Pontiac and was dressed to kill. Annie was sitting on the porch and almost let it slip that she was impressed.

When Charlie approached the steps, he tipped his hat to her and said, "Howdy, Miss Jones. I come to call on your daughter. Is she ready?"

"She's inside; you can go on in and have a seat in the parlor. She'll be with you in a few," answered Annie.

Charlie opened the screen door and stepped inside.

Annie just mumbled a "Humph," as she rocked.

Once he was inside, standing just before him was Margaret with her hands folded. She had heard the car pull up and the conversation with Momma. She held out her hand, "Hello, Mr. Charlie," she said. It caught Charlie by surprise. He knew Mary's daughter was blind, and he had never interacted with her. She seemed so educated and poised, and she was dressed so neatly.

"Well, how do, young lady. I believe it's Margaret, right?" said Charlie.

"Yes, sir. You can have a seat. Mother will be right out," replied Margaret, as she motioned her hand toward the sofa seat.

Charlie sat down, and Margaret went over to the piano and sat on the stool, facing Charlie. He was wondering how she knew where to go to sit and how she knew where he was sitting, because she was facing directly in his direction.

"I've seen you in church playing the piano and singing. You're really good—almost made me cry one Sunday," said Charlie.

"Oh, thank you, sir," she responded.

"You can call me BD; that's what everyone calls me," he said.

"Yes, sir. Would you like me to play you something?" said Margaret.

Just then, Mary walked into the room. "Hello, Charles, sorry it took me so long. Margaret been keeping you good company?" she asked.

"Yes, she has; she was going to play me a song," he replied.

"Well, maybe some other time. Naomi, we've got to go now. Don't you stay up too late, you hear me?" asked Mary.

"Yes, ma'am," responded Margaret.

47

Margaret followed them to the door and stood in the doorway; Annie was still sitting on the porch rocking in her chair. "You come back at a decent hour. Where you heading?" asked Annie.

As Charlie opened his car door, he yelled back "The Top Hat in Blackfish."

"Top Hat? What's the Top Hat?" Annie wondered to herself.

Mary was all dressed up in a nice flower-print dress; it was white with pink roses on it. It fit snug up top and down to about the waist, and then swung out and full below the waist. She had made up her face and looked as good as Sunday morning.

"You look great," said Charlie.

"Thank you, Charles," replied Mary.

"Call me BD. That's what my friends call me."

"All right, BD," said Mary as she looked at the fine car. "Where are we going?"

"Blackfish. It's only about a half hour or so from here," said Charlie.

"I know where it is," Mary said bluntly. "I meant, where in Blackfish?"

"The Top Hat—it's a juke joint," responded Charlie.

"A juke joint. What are we going to do there?" asked Mary.

"See some blues," answered Charlie.

Mary had never been to a juke joint. Sam would never have taken her to one. He was strictly into the church. Mary didn't know much about the blues, but she knew what it was and had heard it as she traveled from one place to the other around the county. Sometimes she'd hear it on the radio as she scanned the stations, but it was supposedly the devil's music. Nonetheless, she always thought it sounded pretty good.

"Sonny Boy Williamson is playing there tonight. Do you know who that is?" asked Charlie.

Mary shook her head.

"Boy, let me tell you, you're in for a treat. He's only the best blues man around these parts. He's even got his own radio show, King Biscuit Time. You ever hear it?" asked Charlie.

Mary thought BD was trying to show off, trying to impress her. She just shrugged and said, "No." Actually, it was a little intimidating.

The blues was big in Arkansas. Colt wasn't very far from West Memphis, and Beale Street in Memphis was considered the blues capitol. Highway 61 was the main route for the Delta Blues, and all the great blues musicians traveled up and down the highway, playing in the juke joints along the way—greats, like Charley Patton, a man of Negro, white, and Indian blood who was a legend along the Delta. His blend of guitar playing, singing, writing, and arranging brought about a whole repertoire of blues, ballads, and spirituals. He mentored such legends as Willie Brown, Son House, and Howling Wolf.

The great Robert Johnson played up and down the Delta and amazed audiences with such classics as "Come on in My Kitchen" and "Cross Road Blues." It was said that Robert Johnson gained his guitar playing talent by striking a deal with the devil. Bukka White, who also was a boxer and baseball player, was fierce on a guitar. He made a name for himself while recording under the Victor label in Memphis before he was sent to prison for shooting a man.

Another great blues man on the Delta Circuit was Howling Wolf, formally known as Chester Arthur Burnett, who learned to play the harmonica from Sonny Boy Williamson. These men made the harp as much a part of the blues as any guitar.

Charlie was a big fan of the blues and got out every now and then to try and catch somebody performing at one of the local juke joints. Some weekends, Charlie traveled out to Osceola, Arkansas, and went to the Dipsy Doodle, a juke joint owned by Son House's father.

Charlie and Mary arrived at the Top Hat early enough to get something to eat before the show. Charlie got them a nice table, not too far from the front, but to the side of where the band was going to play. It was a cozy little table where he could sit next to her rather than across from her. He didn't want his back, or hers, to the band. Plus, he could court better sitting beside her. Mary thought it was a good place to sit as well.

It was early, about an hour before the show, but the joint was already getting busy. Black folks were coming in and getting set up to have a good time. The rules of the juke joint were that no matter what kind of problems you might have, they were left at the door. Just mind your business and have a good time, and you'd be fine. Sometimes it could get a little rough if someone had too much to drink. But they ran a good joint at the Top Hat, and the owners kept a sharp eye out for troublemakers.

A waitress approached to take their orders, and Charlie said, "Let me have a set up and we'll take two orders of fried chicken."

"Now, how you know I want fried chicken?" asked Mary.

"Well, everybody likes fried chicken," Sam responded.

"What else you have, sugar?" Mary asked the waitress.

"Fried catfish, smothered steak, fried pork chops, and chitterlings," answered the waitress.

"I'll have the pork chops with a little chitterlings on the side," Mary told her.

Charlie was a little flustered and almost felt uneasy.

"Let me tell you something, BD, if that's what you call yourself, Charles. I always order my own food, I take care of myself, and I don't need no man trying to tell me what to do or how to eat. Now if you think you going to be able to boss me around, you can take me home right now. If we stay, you're gonna have to respect me," Mary said, looking him straight in the eye and sitting tall.

BD sat up and looked like he just got caught stealing or something. "I didn't mean no harm, Missy. I'm sorry. I apologize. It won't happen again!"

Charlie thought back on what the deacon had told him. Mary was a strong woman, and she didn't take much from anyone. Actually, he liked that in a woman. He knew that she was the kind of woman he needed in his life, because he could get sidetracked real easy with women, wine, and gambling. He really wanted to do right and make something of his life, and he needed a good woman to help make that happen.

It was quiet between the two of them until the food came and they started to eat. The Top Hat had a brand new Wurlitzer juke box, and a song by Robert Johnson was playing. The guitar was picking and Robert began to sing, "I'll Dust My Broom."

Mary was listening to the music, and it was sounding good to her. She was tapping her feet and shaking back and forth. Charlie couldn't help but notice her breasts moving back and forth; he had to catch himself to keep from staring. "You know who's singing that song?" he asked. Mary shook her head no while chewing on some pork chop.

"That's Robert Johnson; he's the father of the blues. That's, I believe, 'I'll Dust My Broom,'" he offered.

"I heard him," said Mary.

They continued to eat and listen to the music. Bessie Smith was now playing on the juke box, "'Taint Nobody's Business If I Do." The waitress came with a set up for Charlie with two glasses. Out of his jacket pocket, Charlie pulled a small bottle. "What's that?" Mary asked.

"Whiskey," said Charlie.

"Oh no, I can't have no whiskey. I don't drink, and I sure can't have no whiskey," said Mary.

"Ah, you can take just a little nip; it won't hurt you. I'm with you, and I'll get you home okay," replied Charlie.

"I know you'll get me home okay. I'm gonna make sure of that. You don't need no drink no way," said Mary, sounding very stern.

"Come on, Mary, don't be so stuffy. Loosen up a little. How about something milder? How about some wine?" Charlie offered.

Mary looked at him, and then she looked around the room. Everyone was drinking, even the women. She didn't want to seem out of place, so she thought maybe she could take a little. Momma always kept a little gin in the house; she had taken a sip once and thought it was awful. She finally agreed and said, "Oh all right, I'll have some wine."

Charlie motioned for the waitress. "Please bring some of your best wine," Charlie instructed the waitress.

"We only got one kind of wine, sir," replied the waitress as she walked off.

The show was about to start. The owner of the Top Hat came out and was just about to introduce Sonny Boy, when two white couples walked in the door. Everyone stopped talking and looked at them as they went to try to find a seat. "Hold on one second, folks. Be right back," he told the crowd as he motioned for someone to start the juke box again.

It was rare that white folks came into a juke joint. There was a Negro man with them who was dressed very sharp. He looked important, and so did they. The club owner hurried and brought out a table and chairs from another room. Someone was mumbling that they were from a record company.

Once back on stage, the club owner said, "Okay, folks, sorry about the little delay." He gathered himself together and continued. "We have a real treat for you here at the Top Hat. Sonny Boy was born in Mississippi and now lives near here in Helena, Arkansas. He's played with all the great blues artists, including Robert Johnson. Hopefully, you've been listening to his show on the radio, King Biscuit Time. If you haven't, then you got to listen to it. Let's give a hand and bring him out—Sonny Boy Williamson!"

Sonny came out, dressed up from head to toe, looking like Dapper Dan. With him onstage, playing acoustic guitar, was Elmore James, who would one day make a name for himself with the electric guitar. Elmore was in the background, picking the guitar, while Sonny was talking to the audience. He started talking about the blues and how it was the Negroes' own music. He talked about his harmonica and how he got into playing it. In between sentences, he'd play a little. Everyone was smiling and excited. They were either tapping their feet or tapping their tables or tapping something.

Sonny now went into full swing. He started out playing "Your Funeral, My Trial." Mary was really excited; the wine was taking effect, the music was great, and so were the people. It was a whole new world to her. Sam was the farthest thing from her mind. Charlie was buzzing from the whiskey, and he was laid back, foot tapping, with his arm stretched out behind Mary.

Sonny continued on his blazing harmonica with more songs, including "Early One Morning," "Harmonica Blues," "Don't Start Me Talking," and "All My Love In Vain." When the show was over, he reminded everyone to listen to his radio show.

Charlie and Mary had a good time. He was a little buzzed but not drunk. She was a little more than tipsy but not drunk. Her speech was a little slurred. "So, Mr. BD, tell me about yourself. I see you at the church and all, but I didn't know you had a little devil in you."

"I just like to have a good time now and then. It's not like I do this all the time. I can't afford to waste my money. I work hard for it," replied Charlie.

"So what kind of work do you do that you can afford that fine car and all?" asked Mary.

Charlie answered, "I work at the county garbage dump. I also get a lot of junk that people throw away, and I sell it to make extra money, which is how I can afford this car."

Mary responded, "That's nice. You work hard and do whatever you can do. That's nice, BD, real nice!"

Charlie was driving Mary back home. They were about five miles from the farm, and he was going a little too fast on the two-lane road. Ahead of them was an old truck. BD overtook the truck and crossed out into the oncoming lane to pass. There were two white men inside, and BD looked over at them. It was something that you just didn't do with white folks.

"You see that Nigger look at me?" the driver said to his friend. It was late at night, and there were not many cars on the road. "I'm going teach that Nigger a lesson," he said as speeded up. The white man pulled up alongside Charlie's nice shiny Pontiac. "Will you look at that Nigger's car?" said the man to his rider.

Just as the white man rolled down the passenger window, they passed a crossing where the sheriff was parked on the side of the road. The white man driving saw the sheriff and slowed down and fell back behind Charlie. Charlie continued to speed because he didn't see the sheriff. After they passed him, the sheriff pulled out onto the highway and took off after them. The sheriff passed the truck and looked at the men inside, recognizing them. The driver waved at the sheriff as he passed. The sheriff nodded and took off after Charlie.

Soon the sheriff caught up to Charlie who didn't even realize that the sheriff was tailing him. By the time he realized it, it was too late. The sheriff pulled Charlie over and yelled for him to stay in the car. Charlie rolled down his window, and Mary said simply, "Oh, you in trouble now."

The sheriff approached the car and said, "Boy, you know you were speeding back there?"

"Sorry, sir, I didn't mean to. Just trying to get the lady home sir," said Charlie.

The sheriff bent down, looked over and saw Mary sitting in the car. "Well, how do, Mary?" said the sheriff.

"Good evening, Sheriff," she responded.

"Everything all right with you, Mary?" asked the sheriff.

"Yes, sir, Sheriff, everything is all right," responded Mary.

"Boy, I'm going to let you go this time. You slow this fancy car down and get Mary home to her momma. She's going to be looking for her. You think you can do that, boy?" the sheriff asked.

"Yes, sir, I can do that just fine, sir," replied Charlie.

"All right, you can go," said the sheriff.

The sheriff nodded his hat at Mary, returned to his patrol car, and drove off. Charlie started up the Pontiac and pulled onto the road.

"Boy, the sheriff must really like you. How do you know him?" Charlie asked Mary.

"My former husband was a well-respected man in this county. Both Negro and white folks respected him and my granddaddy. So they also have respect for me."

Charlie was impressed. Being with Mary probably saved him from a night in the poky.

Soon they arrived at the farm, and Charlie parked the car in front of the house. All the lights were out, which meant Annie and Margaret were asleep. "I hope you had a nice time, Mary," said Charlie.

"Yes, BD, I had a great time. I've never been to a juke joint before. I was told it was nothing but the devil in there, but I didn't see any devil. It's just a bunch of county folks having a good time. I could see how you can get into trouble if you don't have God in you. But I take God with me everywhere I go. What about you, BD, do you take God with you?" asked Mary.

"Yes, Mary, that's how I come to you. It was God brought me to that church. He brought me there," replied Charlie.

"We'll see, BD; we'll see," said Mary.

Charlie started coming around pretty often after that. He'd check on the ladies and see if there was anything that needed a man's touch, and of course, there always was, even though there was a boarder around. Annie began to get used to having him around, and Margaret was getting used to having Charlie around as well. He was a good-natured person who wouldn't harm a fly.

Anything they wanted him to do, he'd do, no questions asked, and Mary liked that. Mary needed to have a man around the farm, and it was good security. She didn't like being out in the middle of nowhere, just the three of them. She didn't feel secure. But BD wasn't no Sam. Sam had been big and strong and the head of the household. His presence and demeanor demanded respect, and whatever he said, you just did.

Charlie was totally different than Sam, but he had other qualities that Mary liked. One thing was for certain—it was Mary who would be in charge in this relationship; she was just too strong.

It wasn't long before Charlie and Mary got married. Charlie moved to the farm, and the family was whole again. Everything was at peace on the farm, but America was in the middle of war. Every day, the newspaper headlines and radio announcers talked of war. There was war in the Pacific, war in Europe, and problems in the Middle East.

Negroes were called up to fight, but they were still second-class citizens. Slavery was abolished over seventy years ago, but Negro people were reminded every day to keep in their place. Jim Crow was in effect, and everything was segregated—the restaurants, buses, bathrooms, swimming pools, schools, parks, and water fountains. "Colored only" and "White only" signs were everywhere in the South.

One Sunday after church, Annie's sisters came over to visit. Margaret loved it when her aunties and cousins came over. There was Aunt B and Aunt Mine and her cousin, Wilda. Margaret always liked to spend time with her cousin, Wilda, who was just a few years younger than she was.

The sisters were all gathered in the kitchen while Mary was cooking. Aunt Mine spoke about how depressing the war was, and Annie was complaining about how the white folks treated colored people. Aunt B spoke out, "I hear it ain't like this in California. They say colored folks is treated just like everybody else out there. They say colored people can live anywhere they want to live as long as you have the money."

"I heard that too!" said Mary.

"Shoot, I'm tired of all these white folks telling me where I can go and where I can't go. Always yes, sir, and yes, ma'am," said Annie.

Mary was at the sink washing some greens, then headed over toward the stove and suddenly stopped. She grabbed her stomach and ran to the toilet. Annie followed her and patted her on the back as Mary vomited. "Whew," said Mary when she'd finished.

"Girl, what's wrong with you?" asked Annie.

"Momma, I'm late, and I'm feeling sickly. I think I'm with child," said Mary.

When Mary and Annie came back into the kitchen, Annie announced that Mary was having a baby. All the sisters got up and came over to Mary, congratulating her, and they were all happy.

"Oh, baby, that's great news. It's always nice to have a new baby in the family. Keeps us all together and families happy," said Aunt Mine.

But Aunt B added, "Yes, that's true, but we don't need to keep bringing up babies around these parts, as messed up as it is around here for colored folks."

"Momma, why can't we move to California?" Mary asked Annie.

"Baby, maybe one day we will. But it takes some planning. We need to sit down with BD and try to figure things out. You can't just jump up and go. We've been around these parts a long time. It's got to be done right," responded Annie.

Soon Annie, Charlie, and Mary sat down and talked about moving. They all knew someone who had moved out West, and they decided to get in touch with some folks. They'd wait until the baby was born, then sell the farm and move to California. There were white people always coming around wanting to buy the farm, so they knew that would be no problem because they owned it outright. This would give them enough money to make the move. Plus, Charlie had done well with his hustle of selling off junk he got at the dump. They had some money saved and could hustle up more money before it came time to try and move.

Little Charles Dillard was born in January of 1944. Mary was thirty-five, Annie was fifty, and Margaret was now seventeen years of age. The family sold off the farm, packed up, and moved to Richmond, California. Charlie had no problem getting a job because of his experience in garbage. He got a job as a street sweeper with the Sanitation Department in San Francisco, and he'd catch the bus over the Bay Bridge every day and leave the car with Mary and the children.

The Dillards quickly found a church home in Richmond at the Seaport Baptist Church, and under the Reverend Richard Dotson, BD became a deacon. The church was always a good place to get help in transition. For Negroes, it served as more than just a place to get religion. It was also a place for networking, politics, and social services. If you needed a babysitter, you could find one there. If you needed a referral to a doctor, you could get one at the church. Whatever you needed, someone in the church knew where to get it. It wasn't long before the family made friends and got comfortable.

6

Color Blind

The Dillards were living in a small cottage in Richmond. California was a much different place than Arkansas. The Bay Area was beautiful—not that Arkansas wasn't beautiful, but it was a different kind of beautiful. The view of city of San Francisco across the bay was a sight to behold. There were so many people, and everybody seemed so busy. Everyone seemed to always be going somewhere.

One of the first things the Dillards noticed was that there were so many different kinds of people in California—Chinese, Japanese, Mexicans, Arabs, Jews, Negroes, and whites. Everyone seemed respectful of everyone else, and there was more of a mixing of the races, even though people still seemed to stick to their own kind.

It was 1945, and Margaret was eighteen. Mary was very busy with the baby, and she needed Margaret to become more independent than ever, and that was just what Margaret wanted. Margaret enrolled in the College for the Blind in Berkeley. She learned how to take the bus to and from school, and every day was an adventure for her. She used her cane to make her way down the sidewalks, and she'd listen for someone near to ask for assistance crossing streets. Usually someone came, but there were times when no one was near. It was then that it was stressful. She'd have to listen for the traffic to die down and then attempt to cross. This always seemed to be a challenge and was never an easy feeling for her. Some days, Mary drove Margaret to school and picked her up. Other days, Margaret had to make it on her own.

Soon, Aunt B and Aunt Mine moved out and found a place in Berkeley, so there was family that was local, and there was a support structure in place. Aunt B's daughter, Wilda, and Margaret were close in age and they were able to bond closer together.

There was so much for teenage girls to do in the Bay Area. Wilda and Margaret would catch the buses and go to the movies, go to the park, or, even better, go shopping. Margaret soon had a job playing piano at church and was making her own money. She and Wilda would catch the bus over to San Francisco and go to Union Square, where they'd buy clothes, makeup, and costume jewelry. After shopping, they'd go home, dress up, and make themselves up like they had someplace to go.

Wilda helped teach Margaret how to put her makeup on, and they'd stand in front of a mirror to practice. Margaret always had a hard time with the lipstick. Somehow she'd either put on too much, go over the lip line, or not put on enough. Wilda then showed her how to use a napkin, place it between her lips to get off the excess, and then wipe around the ridge of her lips.

Margaret would stand in front of the mirror and practice and practice. She'd hurry away from the mirror, go to her mother, and ask, "How do I look? Is it on right?" And Mary would just smile and say, "Yes, it looks as good as I told you last time."

Mary had started pressing Margaret's hair just before they left Arkansas. But now they were in California, and Margaret wanted to go to the beauty parlor and have it done professionally. Mary told her it was okay since it was her own money. So she found a hair salon in Richmond and started going every other week. Margaret's hair was dark and thin, and when it was pressed, it was silky and could hold curls well. Beauticians liked to work on her hair because it was so easy to work with. She usually kept it cut just above the shoulder.

Music was always Margaret's first love, next to the Lord. In college she stayed very active in the music department. She participated in musicals. She directed and coordinated numbers with groups and solos. The college had a small student body, so the kids were pretty close. Margaret was a favorite of both the faculty and the student body. She became very popular.

Margaret knew how to write using Braille before attending college. She could write with the slate and stylus almost as a fast as a sighted person could write with a pencil and paper. But the most significant thing she learned in college was how to use a typewriter. She took up typing so she could write things that sighted people could read if she needed to communicate.

To Margaret, her singing and playing ability was a gift given to her by God, and she used that gift every chance she could. Her voice had matured into a voice of inspiration, and when she sang, no one was immune to its effect on the human spirit. When she sang people listened, and when they listened they were moved.

Her soul and her heart flowed with every note until her music reached down inside the listener and made them chill. It made people happy, and some people cried, but whichever way it went, people couldn't help but be moved. It was because of this gift and her sincerity and charm that she became so popular.

Membership in the small church began to rise as a result of Margaret's singing and playing. She could take a small group of people, maybe four or five, teach them a song, and come Sunday morning, they'd have the church rocking.

At school, she got involved in opera music. The college had a collection of opera and symphony records, and Margaret would sit and listen to them on the phonograph. She'd learn the words then play the music. It wasn't long before Margaret came to the attention of people outside her immediate circle. Soon Berkeley city officials came to know that there was an extremely talented blind Negro girl at the local College for the Blind. She was constantly invited to attend Berkeley city functions to sing and play. Margaret loved to go to these events because she got to interact with a diverse group of people that were not in her immediate circle.

At the school, the student body was made up of a diverse range of people. The diversity represented the makeup of the community. Margaret made friends with everyone she met. This was exciting to her because in Arkansas, it was mostly black and white. She was glad they'd made the move to California, because she felt that none of the things that were happening to her would have happened back home. She loved Arkansas, but she was in love with California.

There was a young man attending the college with Margaret who was not totally blind. He could see well enough to walk around without a cane or any assistance but not well enough to drive. He needed very thick glasses to read but did not need to wear them to move about, see the streetlights, or converse with people. When speaking with him, one could almost not notice that he had poor vision.

Duane was a bright and intelligent young man. He had taken a liking to music in his early teens, and he liked all kinds of music. Duane could pick up an instrument and begin to learn how to play it. He sometimes took a lesson or two, but he'd only stay with the lessons long enough to learn the keys or notes, and then he'd drop out and figure out how to play it on his own.

Duane would learn one instrument then go on to another. Soon he could play the drums, harmonica, piano, and guitar. Duane really didn't attend the college like most students. It was more like he just hung out there. He'd pop in and out of classes. Sometimes he'd go, and sometimes he wouldn't. But whenever he was in class, he was always in tune with the subject matter. He kept his books with him at all times, and he was always reading in his spare time.

Margaret met Duane on campus, and she heard him speak up in classes. But she never really paid much attention to him. Unbeknownst to her, however, he was really paying attention to her.

One day after class, Duane approached Margaret. "Hi, Margaret," he said.

"Hello, Duane," she responded.

"May I walk you to your next class?" he asked.

This took her by surprise. The reason it took her by surprise was the way that he asked her. His tone was not that of a friend, but a tone of admiration that was more than friendly. Margaret almost blushed. She hadn't had a boyfriend and never really entertained the thought of one. Margaret paused, and then responded, "Sure, yes, you can walk with me."

"I really like the way you sing and play the piano," Duane said as he took her arm to guide her down the hallway.

"Thank you," she responded.

There was a pause, then Duane said, "I play a little piano too, but not as good as you do. I don't take it that serious, but I do like to play around with it."

"I notice that you play a few different instruments. It seems like you're always playing something different every time you come to class," said Margaret.

"Yeah, I like to try different things. I don't want to just know one kind of instrument. I want to know a little about them all," Duane said.

"That's interesting. I never met anybody like that. I guess that's pretty nice to know different things," said Margaret.

"Yeah it is, but you just don't get really good at any particular one. That's the drawback," he answered.

They soon reached the class. "We're here," Duane informed Margaret.

"Thank you, Duane, thank you for walking me to class." She began to turn toward the door of the class and bumped into another student. "Excuse me," she said.

Duane stopped her and said, "Hey, Margaret, I'd really like to see you again."

"Silly, you see me in school all the time," she said and kind of giggled. She knew what he meant, but she wanted him to say more. "I've got to get to class, Duane."

"Okay, but just a moment. Would you like to go to the city with me on Saturday?" Duane asked.

"I go to choir rehearsal on Saturdays," she responded.

"How about Sunday?" he asked.

"I go to church on Sundays. Duane, I have to go; I don't want to be late for class," she added.

"All right, how about if I call you?" he asked.

"Sure, you can call me at Underwood 5782," she said.

"Great, that's great, I'll call you," answered Duane.

"Good-bye, Duane." Margaret turned and entered the class. Duane stood there and watched her as she navigated to her seat. Margaret could feel him watching her.

Later that evening, Margaret was at home going over music for choir rehearsal, Mary was in the kitchen cooking, and Charlie was outside cleaning the car, when the phone rang. Mary answered the phone, "Hello."

There was a pause, then, "Hello, how are you?" the voice on the other end said.

"I'm fine. Who is this?" Mary asked.

"I'm Duane. I'm calling for Margaret. Is she in?" he asked.

"Margaret?" Mary held the receiver away from her ear and looked at it. "Yes, Margaret is here," she answered.

Just then Margaret came over to Mary. "Mother, it's for me; may I have the phone?"

Mary was stunned. She handed over the phone and stood there with her jaw dropped. As Margaret started her phone call, Mary snapped to and started to eavesdrop.

"Hello, Duane, is that you?" Margaret asked excitedly.

"Yeah, hi, Margaret. I told you I'd call," he said.

"Yes, you did, you did," said Margaret. "Where are you?" she said, then stopped and faced her mother. "Mother, I'm on the phone," implying that her mother should give her some privacy.

Mary didn't know what to do; she just shook her head and walked out of the hallway with her hand on her hip.

Annie walked in from going to the grocery store and saw Margaret in the hallway, seated by the phone table, talking on the phone. She noticed that Margaret was giddy. She'd never seen her like that before. Annie walked into the kitchen. "Mary, who's that Neelmah chatting to?" she asked.

"I don't know who he is—some boy named Duane," Mary responded.

"You don't know? How you don't know? You supposed to know whom your daughter's talking to. Especially if he going to come courting her. Boy's supposed to ask the young gal's folks before he comes a calling on her. I tell you, it's something else out here in California. People ain't got no respect for people. What's this world coming to?"

Annie was getting Mary all worked up. Now Mary had to find out what was going on; she'd get to the bottom of it as soon as Margaret got off the phone.

Mary heard Margaret say good-bye and hang up the receiver. "Naomi, come here to the kitchen," she yelled out to Margaret.

"Yes, Mother?" Margaret responded as she entered the kitchen and stood in the doorway.

"Who's this boy Duane? Why is he calling you?" asked Mary.

"Girl, don't you know a boy supposed to come calling on your folks before he calls on you?" interjected Annie.

"Momma, you let me handle this," Mary said "Naomi, who is this boy, and where did you meet him?"

Margaret answered, "Mother, he's just a friend. He goes to my school; he's in a couple of my classes."

"Is he a blind boy?" asked Mary.

"I don't know, Mother. Our school is for blind people, but he moves around like he can see. I haven't had a chance to talk with him about that. He wants to come and take me to the city on Saturday after choir practice," said Margaret.

"Well, good. I want to see who this boy is. You have him pick you up here at the house," ordered Mary.

"Yes, ma'am," Margaret humbly answered.

Saturday couldn't come around soon enough. Since that phone call from Duane, Mary had gone through all kinds of emotions. She would be angry, then happy, then scared. Her little gifted daughter had grown up overnight. Margaret had grown into a fine young lady. She was well groomed, shapely, educated, talented, and a Christian. Most important was that she was a Christian.

Margaret knew right from wrong. She studied her Braille Bibles regularly and always prayed and gave thanks to the Lord. Deep inside, Mary knew she didn't have to worry about Margaret in the world. California, and the Bay Area, was a great place full of wonderful things, but it was also a place of much sin. Mary would just pray on it.

It was about 2:30 in the afternoon on Saturday when they heard a knock on the door. The two ladies were all in the kitchen, waiting for Duane. Mary told Margaret to stay there until she called for her, then went to the door and opened it. She was shocked at what she saw.

It was a white boy! A very handsome white boy! Duane stood before Mary and said, "Hello, I'm Duane. You must be Margaret's mother," and he held out his hand.

Mary grinned with excitement and invited him in. "Come on in; have a seat here in the parlor." She motioned to the living room sofa. As she was closing the door, she noticed a car outside with a young white couple sitting in the front seat. They were watching and smiled; the driver waved. Mary waved back and closed the door.

Duane was a handsome young man. He was short and slender, just a little bit taller than Margaret. He had a handsome face with dark features, almost Italian looking. His hair was jet-black, and he had a slight mustache, jet-black eyebrows, and deep-set eyes. There was something about his eyes; they would sometimes twitch. Duane was dressed in a white shirt and slacks, with dress shoes. He had a great smile. Mary couldn't get over how handsome he was.

"So tell me about yourself, Duane. Margaret tells me you go to the same college?" asked Mary.

Duane felt the good attitude that Mary expressed toward him and began to put on the charm. "Well, my folks are from Michigan, and they now live in Los Gatos," he said.

"Los Gatos, where's that?" asked Mary.

"It's in the mountains, not far from San Jose which is just south of here, heading toward Santa Cruz," responded Duane.

Mary had heard of San Jose and Santa Cruz, but she really hadn't ventured too much outside of the immediate Bay Area. "What's it like there?" she asked.

"Oh, it's really nice. There's a small lake right near the back of the house. You can fish there and swim there, and it's really beautiful," said Duane.

"So where do you live, Duane?" asked Mary.

"I'm living with some friends of mine while I go to school," replied Duane.

"Oh, okay, I guess that's nice," said Mary.

"Naomi!" yelled Mary. "Duane is here for you, come now."

"You don't keep my daughter out too late. We have to go to church tomorrow. You understand me, young man?" she instructed Duane.

"Yes, ma'am, I do. I'll have her back okay," answered Duane.

Mary watched them leave as they entered the backseat of the coupe. Duane was very helpful in getting her in. He let her know to duck her head and step into the backseat and scoot over. Mary was glad to see that he was courteous and attentive. She had to sit down and think about what was happening. She liked the fact that Duane was white because, without admitting it, she was prejudiced about her own people. Since Mary was a redbone and most of her family were redbones or light skinned, she was color struck. She never really did care for dark-skinned men even though BD was dark. BD was a kind and simple man. Whatever she needed she could get BD to do it, no questions asked.

Mary never wanted a dark-skinned man for Margaret; she felt that, if you had a light or red-skinned man, you would have beautiful children. It was an ugly fact that many dark-skinned Negroes were prejudiced toward light-skinned Negroes and vice versa.

Annie was walking up the sidewalk toward the house, and she saw the car pulling out from in front of the house. When she entered the house, Mary was still sitting in the living room. Annie asked, "Mary, who was that coming from this house?"

"That was the young man come by to take Naomi out. He's a white boy," Mary said.

"A white boy?" shouted Annie.

"Yes, Momma, a white boy," Mary responded soundly.

"Do Neelmah know he's white?" asked Annie.

"I don't know. She probably does, but she doesn't care. She can't see him anyway. Don't make no difference to my baby. She's color blind," said Mary. "Must be nice to not care what color anyone is. Must be nice."

"What's the boy look like? What's he like?" asked Annie.

Mary was in a somber mood now. Her little girl was growing up, and she knew that one day she'd want to leave home. It saddened her but also made her happy.

"Mary! What's the boy look like?" yelled Annie.

"Oh, he's a handsome young man. He kind of looks like a ladies' man! But different, kind of like the freehearted type. He seems a little different than most white folks—an easy-going type," answered Mary.

"Well, you better talk with her about this. She may not know what she's getting herself into. I don't know about this white boy stuff and all. She could be getting in over her head," Annie said, shaking her head as she walked out of the room. Mary sat there and stared out the window and a tear came to her eye.

Even though Margaret was now almost twenty-four years of age, to Mary she was still her little girl. She had sheltered Margaret away from boys and had her focus on her music and the Lord. She knew this day would come and was able to accept it, but it was still difficult.

Margaret and Duane and the other young people were having a good time. They drove over to the city and went to Golden Gate Park. Duane knew where some folks were having a little jam session, playing some music. They sat on the blankets listening to music and drinking some soda pops and eating some cheese and crackers. The sun was out, and Margaret was enjoying the warm sunshine, listening to the music, and having light conversation with Duane.

Duane was really attentive to Margaret. He made sure everything was all right for her and that she was comfortable and having a good time. After the music stopped, they decided to go over to Stow Lake in the park and take a walk. It was about 5:00 and there were still a couple of hours of sunshine left, but the trees were blocking the sun in some areas around the lake, so it was a little cool there. Margaret had been carrying a sweater with her, and Duane offered to put it on her.

"I'll just put it over my shoulders," she said as Duane helped her. Margaret could hear the birds chirping, and she could smell the trees. She could also feel the tranquility of the park as they started to stroll. "I like it a little chilly out," she said.

"You do?" asked Duane.

"Yes, it's different from Arkansas. Arkansas is usually so hot and humid. It's not like here in California. It can be warm during the day here, then get real cool at night. I like that; it's refreshing," said Margaret.

"That's true; it is nice," Duane responded.

"Duane, describe what it looks like here for me," said Margaret.

Duane began to describe the setting. "Oh, it's beautiful. There's a small lake we're walking around, with a little island in the middle. There's a bridge where you can cross over to the island so you can stroll there. The trees are beautiful and full, and it's as though we're in a forest. It's hard to believe we're still in the City of San Francisco."

"It sounds like there are a lot of birds," said Margaret.

"Yes, there's ducks swimming in the lake and seagulls from the ocean and pigeons all around," said Duane.

"Seagulls from the ocean? Are we near the ocean?" asked Margaret.

"Yes, we're not far from the ocean beach," answered Duane.

"Ohhhh, I've never been to the ocean. Can we go sometime, Duane? Can we?" asked Margaret.

"Sure, we can go. We can go anytime," Duane answered.

Duane had been holding Margaret on her arm most of the time, near her elbow. He reached for her hand, and Margaret smiled. They were walking a little behind the other couple, who were holding hands as well.

"Duane, you know, there's so much about this place that I don't know and haven't experienced. My mother has sheltered my life, and she has really been very protective of me. My life has centered on the church and my music. I'd like to learn more about San Francisco, but I don't always have a lot of time. Perhaps you can show me around?" asked Margaret.

"I'd love to. I have a lot of friends here, and I've learned many things about this place. There are many things to do and many places to visit. It's an exciting place, and there's so much we can do together," answered Duane.

They continued to walk around the lake and hold hands. Margaret hadn't really had the attention of a man before, and she liked the feeling of being around Duane. He seemed so vibrant and full of life.

Margaret began to think about church and what she had to do the next day. "Oh, Duane, we'd better leave and head home. I've got to start preparing for church tomorrow. How would you like to come and visit my church? We have a real good time, and I'm sure you'd love it." There was a pause. Margaret spoke out to him, "Duane?"

"Umm, I don't believe in God. I'm sorry, but I won't come to your church," answered Duane.

This caught Margaret by surprise. She'd never really thought that he was someone who didn't believe. "Oh, I'm sorry to hear that," Margaret responded.

There was now silence between them. Margaret began to think about this situation, and the more she thought about it, the more she sensed that this was an opportunity to save a soul.

Margaret was a Christian, and Christians were to evangelize the sinners. Duane was now someone who needed to have his soul saved. He needed to find Jesus Christ. God had sent him to her so that she could help save his soul. Otherwise he would be doomed.

"Duane, have you ever heard of Jesus Christ?" asked Margaret.

Duane smiled and, with a little humor, answered, "Yes, I've heard a lot about Jesus Christ. I even studied the Bible. I've probably read all of it."

Margaret was puzzled now. "Well, if you know of the Lord and the studies of his Word, then why is it that you don't believe?" asked Margaret.

Duane explained to her that his parents were devout Jehovah's Witnesses and that his father was a leader at the Kingdom Hall. He told her how they had tried to raise him in the Kingdom and how he'd felt trapped, and when he became of age, he decided that he didn't believe. He also told her about how the situation had caused some friction between him and his father. Margaret was not deterred by this news. It now made her more determined. She'd leave it alone for now, but she'd come back to it soon enough.

When Margaret arrived home, her mother was waiting for her. She wanted to know how things went, and she wanted to know more about Duane. As soon as Margaret got into the house and Duane had left, the questions started. "Margaret, did you know Duane was a white boy?" her mother asked.

"No, Mother, I didn't," Margaret said sharply.

"You watch your tone with me, Naomi," Mary snapped.

"Oh, Mother, you're worrying about nothing. I didn't know what he was; I only knew he didn't sound colored. But that doesn't matter to me anyway; you should know that."

Mary thought for a moment, then said, "It doesn't bother me that he's white either, but what about his parents? How do you think they'll feel when they find out you're a colored girl?"

"I don't think they'll have a problem with me; they're Christians. Well, Jehovah's Witnesses, which is almost the same thing," said Margaret.

Mary had to think about that for a minute.

"They'll probably be happy that he likes me," said Margaret.

"And why is that?" asked Mary.

"Because he doesn't believe in God," said Margaret.

"He doesn't believe in God? Now what kind of foolishness is that? What does he believe in?" Mary asked.

"He was talking about some theory of evolution he's been researching," answered Margaret.

Mary was getting worried now. This white boy wasn't sounding so good anymore. "Margaret, baby, this Duane doesn't sound like he's the best boy for you to be going around with. I don't think you should see him anymore."

"Mother, what would happen if, every time we met a sinner, we just left them alone? How would they be saved?" Margaret asked her mother.

"Baby, I know what you're trying to say, and that's fine. Try and save his soul as a sinner and a friend, but I wouldn't think about him for anything beyond that," Mary said. "You can't take him serious as a boyfriend if he ain't saved. It just won't work, baby. It just won't," said Mary. "There's other boys out there, and I know you can find a good Christian one someday."

Margaret dismissed what her mother said and replied, "I'm tired, Mother. I'm going to get ready for bed."

That Sunday, after the preacher finished his sermon, the choir was singing.

> And I'm calling you, Savior, Savior
> Hear my humble cry
> While on others I am calling
> Do not pass me by

Four people had come before the congregation to join the church. The pastor was standing in front of the candidates, waiting for the choir to finish, then he signaled for the organist to wrap it up. Margaret followed the organist's cue. There were two young children and a mother joining. The mother had Christian experience, and the two children were candidates for baptism. After the pastor acknowledged the mother and children, the secretary of the church began to announce the fourth candidate. It was a man who'd been in trouble, someone who had never known the Lord.

The pastor asked the young man to stand before the church. He asked him if he had found Jesus Christ and if he was willing to accept him as his savior and make him a part of his life. The young man said, "Yes," and the church was full of praise and was thankful to the Lord.

"Is there something you'd like to say?" asked the pastor.

"Yes," said the young man.

The young man began to offer testimony. He talked about how he'd been living a life of sin, about how he'd never known the Lord, and that his momma had never talked about God. He spoke about meeting a young lady in the church who had helped him turn his life around. He felt there must be a God, because it must have been God who sent the young lady to him—a nobody who was headed for trouble.

The young man went on to say how he and the young lady had prayed together and that he had soon found a job, and they had fallen in love. He said God had touched his heart and had saved his soul. He wanted to do the right things, and he knew he had to have a church home. Everyone rejoiced, and the new member was accepted into the fold. To Margaret this was a sign from God. This was exactly the situation she was in with Duane, and it was encouragement for her to press on.

On the way back home, Margaret made mention to Mary that God had given her a sign of what she needed to do. Mary really didn't have anything to say. What could she say? She couldn't say anything. She knew just what her daughter was implying.

Margaret and Duane were now going steady. Mary became accustomed to him coming around the house and really appreciated him helping to get Margaret around here and there. They caught the buses together, and Duane taught Margaret how to get around on her own.

Duane had been visiting the music department at the UC Berkeley campus when he found out about a regional talent competition that was going to be held in San Francisco. He spoke with the music professor about Margaret. The professor had already heard about Margaret from the College for the Blind and said he'd see if he could help to get her into the competition.

Duane went over to Margaret's house to let her know about the competition. By now, they were used to him coming over unannounced. He went into the parlor and played with little Charles while he waited for Margaret and Mary, because he wanted to speak with both of them.

Duane had done some research on the competition and informed them that it was the Dale Carnegie competition, which was a prestigious event. He said that there would be recording industry people there who'd be looking for new talent to sign. Duane then informed them that the professor at the campus was going to get Margaret into the competition. He also informed them that the competition was going to be tough. He couldn't find out who was going to be in it. But he did find out that there was a young man in San Francisco named Johnny Mathis, who had made a name for himself as an athlete and was a favorite to win.

Johnny Mathis was well known around San Francisco. He was making a name for himself as an extraordinarily talented singer. His father had worked with him since he was very young and had given him all the resources he could in preparing him to sing. He had a fantastic voice and was also a good showman.

Mary was excited about the contest. She didn't know very much about Johnny Mathis, nor did she much care. Margaret had been in a number of talent shows over the years, and she'd always won. There was no reason to think that she wouldn't win this one. Even so, she made sure that Margaret had decided what she was going to sing and practiced it over and over again. She also purchased a nice two-piece suit for Margaret to wear.

On the day of the event, BD washed the car and helped to get little Charles dressed. Mary was fussing over Margaret, trying to get her hair just right and get her makeup in order. It was about time to leave, but Duane had not yet arrived. "Come on, Margaret, we have to get ready to go," Mary said, fussing at Margaret. Time was running short.

BD called up to them, "Come on, we're going to be late if we don't leave now."

"Be right there," Mary shouted back.

"Mother, we can't leave until Duane gets here," Margaret said, concerned that they'd leave.

"If he's not here when we're ready to leave, we have to go without him. Duane knows he needs to be on time. If he doesn't make it here, he knows how to get there on his own," responded Mary.

After another five minutes or so, it was time to leave. They had to cross the Bay Bridge and drive through the city to get to where they needed to be, and they had to be there with enough time for Margaret to check in.

On the way over to the city, Margaret was fussing about leaving Duane; little Charles kept asking questions about where they were going and why; BD was listening to the radio, trying to hear the ball game; Annie was trying to answer little Charles; and Mary was a nervous wreck. "Quiet! Quiet, all of you! I can't even hear myself think," Mary shouted.

Everybody got quiet, and Mary said, "Now this is an important day for Margaret. She's never been in a show like this one. We need to pray before we get there so that the Lord will bless her singing. BD, turn off that radio so we can pray." Mary said a prayer while everyone closed his or her eyes, except for BD who was driving.

When they arrived at the auditorium, there were so many people there, and it was so crowded, Margaret had to have a tight grip on Mary, and BD had to have a good hold on little Charles and Annie. It was an exciting place to be, and the air was full of anticipation. Margaret was still harping over leaving Duane and maintained her bad attitude.

After they checked in, only Mary was allowed to go backstage with Margaret. Annie, BD, and little Charles had to be seated in the audience. The competition was tough; the best amateur singers in the Bay Area were there, about thirty in all. The judges would pick ten for the finals, in which they'd each sing a second song, and then the judges would select the final three, ranking them first, second, and third.

It was soon time for Margaret to go out on stage to perform. When Mary and Margaret walked out onto the stage, you could hear the surprise of the audience. People were whispering and chatting. "Oh, she's blind," someone said.

Margaret and Johnny Mathis both made the final cut without a problem. Margaret was to go second to last, and Johnny was to go last. Margaret kept asking Mary if Duane had arrived, but Mary had not yet seen him. Suddenly, Duane arrived, about two singers before Margaret was to go on. Somehow he had managed to get backstage, and he walked up to Margaret and Mary.

"I'm sorry I'm late. I had to catch a ride," said Duane.

"Duane, you made it," Margaret said, beaming with joy. "Oh, goodie, I was afraid you weren't going to be here," she added, sounding giddy.

"So what happened; what did I miss?" asked Duane.

Margaret started to respond, but Mary cut in and told her to pay attention to the show so she could hear what was happening. Margaret didn't stop; she just lowered her voice and started to whisper to Duane. Next, they called for Margaret to come out onto the stage to perform.

Mary started to walk Margaret out onto the stage, but Duane intercepted and said, "I'll take her out." Before Mary could respond, they were on their way out onto the stage. Duane took her over to the piano to get her situated, and Margaret was blushing. Mary felt a little jealous, but she also felt Margaret wasn't concentrating on what she needed to do.

Margaret began to play the introduction for her song. Her hands were flowing over the piano keys as if they were married to each other. Her playing was beautiful, and she began to sing. "Somewhere over the rainbow, bluebirds fly ..." She had picked a song that was an American favorite. It was a song that everyone knew and loved, and she performed it as well as Judy Garland ever did. It was a great and commanding performance. The audience jumped to their feet with applause.

Up to this point, the competition had been stiff, but it was clear that Margaret was by far the best. It was time for Johnny to take the stage. Most people in the know knew he was the favorite. Johnny walked out onto the stage, and he looked magnificent. He was wearing a white dinner jacket with black tuxedo slacks and black patent leather shoes. His skin was smooth, a tanned bronze color, and his hair was jet black. When he walked out on stage, the women were awestruck. As far as they were concerned, all he had to do was stand there. The women were going crazy before he even started.

Johnny opened his mouth to speak, and someone screamed. He smiled and chuckled and continued. Johnny sat at the piano and began to play. The words just flowed out of his mouth. He sang an old standard, "My Blue Heaven." Johnny had received some formal voice training, and his voice was groomed to perfection. His showmanship was masterful, and he played to the crowd. He'd look out and smiled into the audience and at the judges, and they couldn't help but be touched. He commanded attention!

When the ballots were in and counted, the announcer began with third place. He announced another singer as the third-place winner. Mary and Margaret and Duane were on pins and needles backstage. The announcer walked out onto the stage and made the announcement, "And the winner in second place is Margaret Hinton." Margaret was elated, and so was Duane. She was jumping up and down and clapping, and Duane was celebrating with her. Duane walked her out on the stage to her place and returned backstage, smiling all the way. Duane looked at Mary, and he saw disappointment on her face.

There was much excitement in the air. People were now in anticipation of the inevitable, because it was obvious that, out of the group of ten, the only one who may have been some competition for Johnny was Margaret, and she had won second place. The announcer started, "And now for the moment we've all been waiting for. The winner of the Dale Carnegie Talent Competition is Johnny Mathis." The audience was on its feet giving Johnny a standing ovation. Johnny walked out onto the stage, walking ever so gracefully and elegantly. He accepted his trophy, shook the presenter's hand, turned to the audience, and bowed. The crowd loved it. He was a first-class act. At fifteen, he was already a professional.

After the show, strangers were walking over to Margaret, congratulating her and telling her how much they enjoyed her singing. One man came over and said he was from a recording company and was interested in talking with her. Mary gave him their information; however, the call never came.

Everyone piled into the car for the ride back home. BD and Annie talked about how good the show was and how good Margaret was and all the other singers too.

Annie said, "That boy who won was really good. He was something else, and all the girls were just fickle over him."

"Yeah, he was real good. You can tell he's a professional," added Duane.

Mary was disappointed; she knew that Johnny had won, but she also felt that Margaret could have won if she hadn't been so distracted and giddy over Duane. Inside she felt that, if Duane hadn't been there, Margaret would have won. Later, when Duane wasn't around, she'd make her feelings known. In the meantime, she didn't want to spoil the enjoyment everyone was having, so she kept quiet.

The fact of the matter was that Margaret had a great voice; it was a one-of-a-kind voice, and she sounded like no one else. But Johnny was polished. He was groomed to be a professional showman. Margaret was just a good singer with special talent, but she was not polished in the same manner as Johnny. His voice and his stage presence were exceptional. Margaret could not compete with him.

News of Margaret's success at the talent competition spread throughout the local community. She was beginning to make a name for herself, not only in the church community, but in the artistic musical community as well.

The renowned opera vocalist, Marian Anderson, was coming to perform a concerto at the Paramount Theater in Oakland, and the producers wanted to include someone local in the production. Someone recommended Margaret, and she was contacted to audition.

Margaret performed at the concert and was well received by the audience and critics. Doors were beginning to open for Margaret, and there were many options available to her. But fame and fortune were not a motivation for her. Duane and her mother both tried to persuade Margaret to take advantage of some of the offers she was presented with.

It was difficult for Margaret to turn down the many possibilities in front of her. But early on in her life, she had made a commitment that the gift that the Lord had bestowed upon her was going to be used to serve God. None of the offers were for gospel; therefore, they were not options she wished to pursue.

7

Heaven and Hell

Now that Duane and Margaret were a couple, Duane was getting tired of holding hands; he wanted more. For Margaret, the only way anything more was going to happen was if they were married. She was a good Christian and committed to God and his Word. Jesus Christ was her role model, and she tried to live her life like his.

Duane was getting frustrated with Margaret's refusals. He wanted her bad. Duane was infatuated with Margaret. He loved the way she looked, her brown complexion and silky hair. She was buxom and vivacious, and she had the voice of a nightingale. He knew she was special.

Margaret really liked the attention that Duane gave her. He was really the only man who had entered her life as a significant other. She couldn't see what he looked like, but she knew he was handsome because everyone had told her so. All of Margaret's friends and relatives loved Duane. He was pleasant, polite, and very knowledgeable in just about any subject, and he treated her very well.

Somehow, their religious beliefs, or nonbeliefs, were not a major factor in their relationship. Margaret felt that one day she'd be able to convert and save Duane, and Duane felt everyone had a right to believe or not believe. He had his own beliefs and wouldn't judge those who had theirs. It was a mutual respect for each other that had allowed this not to be an issue—yet.

Duane was not a man who really cared for working. Because of his disability, he was able to draw disability compensation from the county. It was enough money to live on, but not for much more than that. Day jobs were difficult for Duane because he was a night owl. He'd leave Margaret's house in the evenings after studying and go and visit friends of his who liked to party. They'd sit around and listen to jazz and blues, drink beer, smoke, and jam on their instruments. They'd be up until late into the middle of the night, and Duane wouldn't be able to get up in the morning.

Margaret was not aware of Duane's lifestyle after he left her; she never really thought to ask about it. She was aware that his attendance at the college was lackadaisical and that the college tolerated it. Therefore, if Duane couldn't make it to classes, it was not an apparent problem. Duane didn't go to school for grades anyway. He just went to learn. He wanted to know as much about everything on any subject that he could. It was his self-motivation for knowledge that drove him to go to school. A career in any given field was not of any interest to Duane.

Everywhere Duane went, he kept a few books with him. He read three or four books at a time. When he wasn't in class or with Margaret or with his buddies partying, he'd be reading. He had a pair of glasses that were very thick, and when he had them on and he looked at you, his eyes seemed so large that he looked like an alien or something. He looked really funny and it made people want to laugh. His buddies joked about it all the time, and Duane got a kick out of it as well. But as soon as he took them off, there was this handsome man standing in front of you. It was like Dr. Jekyll and Mr. Hyde. When Duane wasn't using his glasses to read, he used a magnifying glass.

Whenever Duane needed more money than what he was getting from the county, he'd just do odd jobs, anything for a buck. He'd wash cars, do garden work, manufacturing work, or whatever came along.

After thinking long and hard, Duane decided he wanted to marry Margaret. She was a good woman, and he knew that, for him, there was no one any better. She would be his, all his, and she had never been with anyone else. Margaret was saving herself for her husband, and he wanted her.

Duane went to work to raise the money to buy a ring. When he finally got enough money, he brought the ring and proposed to Margaret. Margaret was very happy that Duane had asked her to marry him. She was in love with Duane, and she knew that he loved her too. Upon hearing the news that Duane had proposed to her daughter, Mary was very happy. The whole family loved Duane, and he had already become a part of the family. Mary's only concern was Duane's commitment to work and his ability to support her daughter. Duane committed to get a job and do right by Margaret, and that was good enough for Mary.

Margaret and Duane decided to get married as soon as possible. Duane contacted his parents and informed them that he was engaged and would let them know the date of the wedding. His parents were surprised but were happy. They hadn't met Margaret or her parents, but Duane had talked a lot about them, and from what they knew about her, she sounded great for Duane.

Duane and Margaret were going to have a small church wedding with only a few friends and relatives. The date and the place were set, and everyone was informed of where and when. On the wedding day, Mary went over to the church a little early to decorate. Her cousin, Wilda, also came over to help. BD and Annie were in charge of getting Margaret to the church on time. Duane was with a few of his buddies, getting ready. He was a little hung over from the party they'd had for him the night before.

As Mary and Wilda were adding the final touches to the decorations, a couple came in. They were about an hour early for the wedding. Mary saw them and walked over to greet them. "Hello, I'm Mary, the bride's mother. Nice to see you."

"Oh, we're Duane's parents. I'm Muriel, and this is my husband, Henry," the lady responded.

"Oh, my dear, it's nice to meet you. Duane has said so much about you. I almost feel I already know you," said Mary.

Duane's parents were not at all what Mary thought they might look like. She expected two dark-haired, slender people that would be maybe Italian or French. But Muriel was short and pudgy with blond hair and blue eyes. She was Swedish. Duane's father was about average height with dark hair, and he was Native American.

Because Duane's last name was Vizinau, Mary had assumed that he was French or maybe Italian. After seeing his parents, she wondered where the name Vizinau had come from. Although she was curious, she'd never ask.

Duane's father was a descendent of the Chippewa Nation, Sault Ste. Marie Tribe, in the Michigan area. When the French had migrated to the United States, many of them had integrated with the Native Americans. Hence, the name of Vizinau had come into being in the tribe.

"Would you like to help me with a few last-minute decorations?" Mary asked Muriel.

"I'd love to," Muriel said, smiling, as they both walked off and left Henry standing alone. Henry just smiled and took a seat.

As the ladies were decorating, Henry was inspecting the church. He was expecting to have his own congregation some day because he was being groomed by his overseer to expand their faith. It wasn't a Kingdom Hall of the Jehovah's Witnesses that Duane was getting married in, but at least it was a Christian church. Henry was thankful for that. Actually, he was a little surprised when he heard Duane was going to marry a Christian woman.

Henry was disappointed that Duane had elected to leave the faith after he became an adult. They had raised Duane to be a devout Witness. But Duane felt stifled and had begun to doubt in his early teens.

Friends and family were beginning to arrive and, to Mary and Muriel's surprise, Duane was on time. All they needed now was the bride. Finally the bride arrived, and the wedding was ready to start. There were about thirty or so people there. Margaret was wearing a two-piece suit with a nice hat that had a net on it. Duane was wearing a nice gabardine double-breasted suit with a white shirt and tie.

It was a simple wedding with a pianist and a soloist. After a few words from the preacher and the saying of the vows, the minister then pronounced, "I present to you Mr. and Mrs. Duane Vizinau." They kissed and walked down the aisle.

After the wedding, everyone went to a small local hall for the reception. The reception grew with a few more of Duane's friends and a few of Margaret's church members. It was an interesting mix of people. Margaret's invitees consisted of mainly Negro people that were either family or friends from the church and a few from the school. Duane's invitees consisted of a mix of mainly whites plus a couple of Latinos and Asians who were family or buddies.

Everyone was having a pretty good time, chatting and eating. There was a pianist who played a few gospel songs while everyone ate. The food was prepared and served by Margaret's family. After everyone had eaten and they'd cut the cake, someone asked Margaret to play and sing a song. A small group of folks gathered around the piano while Margaret played. She sang a short gospel tune just to appease the guests, but she really didn't feel like performing. At least it gave Duane's parents a chance to hear her sing.

Duane had been going outside now and then with a few of his buddies, and Margaret noticed that he had alcohol on his breath. This annoyed her, but she decided it was not the place to say anything, and she knew he was really enjoying himself.

After Margaret finished playing the piano, a couple of Duane's friends sat down on the stool, and Duane walked over to them. "Hey, Duane, play a little something. Come on, let it rip," said one of Duane's friends.

"All right, move over," said Duane.

Duane sat down at the piano and jumped right in with the boogie-woogie. Duane's friends in the room walked over to the piano; one of them went outside and came back with a guitar; another came in with some drumsticks and started beating on the piano. Now they had a jam session, and Margaret was having a fit.

They were playing the devil's music at her wedding. She started heading toward the piano to complain, but Mary stopped her and told her to settle down. Annie took Margaret by the hand and led her away to sit down, all the while fussing along with Margaret. Mary could hear Annie say, "'Tain't nothing but the devil."

BD and Mary had made their way to the piano and stood by, tapping and clapping their hands. One of Duane's friends pulled out a flask with some liquor and took a swig. BD looked in his direction, and the friend held it up, offering him a swig. BD took the flask and put it

up to his mouth and leaned his head back to take a swig. "Ahhhhhh."
Then he tried to take another swig, but Mary grabbed it and gave it
back to Duane's friend.

A few of Margaret's church friends sat across the room near
Margaret and were a little uncomfortable with what was going on.
They could sense Margaret's uneasiness. Duane's parents went over to
Margaret and started chatting with her, trying to calm the situation.
They too were uncomfortable with the situation. But Duane and his
friends and a few of Margaret's friends, along with her parents, were
enjoying themselves and having a good time listening to the group
play the blues and the boogie-woogie.

After the reception was over and it was time to leave, Margaret
was ready to go home. Duane said his good-byes to the last few folks
still lingering and thanked them for coming. They all piled into the
car—Mary, Margaret, Annie, BD, Duane, and little Charles.

On the way to the house, Duane had an announcement to make.
He told everyone that he had gotten a place for Margaret and himself
to live in, and that it was in San Francisco. Margaret was happy to
hear the news. They hadn't talked about what they were going to do
after they got married, and she had assumed that Duane was going to
move in with them. Mary had assumed that too, and she was a little
disappointed that it wasn't what Duane intended to do.

Mary asked, "San Francisco? What about Margaret's schooling?"

"Margaret only has two weeks left until she gets her degree. We can
stay at our house on the weekends, and she can come and stay with
you during the week until she's done," said Duane.

"Yes, Mother, that will work out. Right?" said Margaret.

"I guess so," replied Mary.

Margaret and Duane moved into their own apartment in San
Francisco, and soon Margaret graduated from college. Duane found
a simple job working in a kitchen, cleaning up and washing dishes.
Money was tight, and Margaret was no longer working at the church.

It wasn't long after Duane and Margaret got married that she
became pregnant. Mary became concerned about Margaret being in
the city alone while Duane worked evenings, so she decided to move
to San Francisco as well. The move would be easy because BD was also
working in the city, and they'd saved enough money to buy a home.

The Dillards purchased a home in San Francisco in the Potrero Hill district at 560 Missouri Street. It was a nice three-level home, with the top two levels as their residence and a rental unit on the ground level. The Potrero Hill district of San Francisco was a very nice and diverse neighborhood, made up of people from all ethnic backgrounds. Like many parts of San Francisco, it was also very hilly. The hills stretched five and six blocks high, maybe even more. Most of the homes were two- and three-level homes that were built crammed next to each other. Their designs were a mix of old Victorian to Edwardian, with a few contemporary stucco and aluminum-siding homes.

Potrero Hill also had some of the best weather in San Francisco. During the summer months, the fog usually burned off during the day, giving rise to sunshine and warm weather.

The Dillards joined the Macedonia Baptist Church on Post Street in the Fillmore district, and BD became a deacon there. On Sundays, they would pick up Margaret on their way to church so that she could sing with the choir.

Margaret's pregnancy was going well, but she felt uncomfortable trying to play the piano; she couldn't play for very long. Her stomach was beginning to get very large and heavy, and it was getting close to her time to deliver.

On July 21, 1951, at San Francisco General Hospital, Margaret gave birth to an eleven-pound, four-ounce son. Duane wanted to name the boy after himself, and Margaret wanted to name him Dexter. They came to a compromise and decided to name the boy Duane Dexter Vizinau, and they'd call him Dexter so as to not confuse him, because then there would be two people named Duane in the household.

Margaret and Duane were very happy with the baby. Mary visited almost daily to help Margaret with the chores and to teach Margaret how to care for the baby. But Margaret was very stubborn and felt she could take care of the baby all by herself. Margaret did pretty well with preparing the bottles and changing the diapers. But every so often, Dexter would cry out when his mother was changing him because she'd accidentally stuck him with the safety pins.

When Dexter was just over three months old, Mary came over to visit and found Margaret not feeling well. She was very nauseous and sickly. She'd get a little dizzy and start vomiting. Mary took Margaret to the doctor, only to find out Margaret was pregnant again.

"Margaret, what are you and Duane doing? You've just had a baby, and now you're going to have another one? You can't afford to have another child, nor is it going to be easy for you to take care of two!" Mary said, expressing her disapproval.

"I can take care of my babies," said Margaret. "Duane wants several children, and so do I. We know what we're doing, and the Lord said to be fruitful and multiply," Margaret said in rebuttal.

"Oh, shut up," said Mary. "Don't be so stupid; I can't talk no sense to you. You wait until I see Duane. I'm going to tell him he better keep that thing in his pants, or he better use some rubbers or something," scolded Mary.

"You and BD had another child. Why can't I?" asked Margaret.

Mary answered, "Look, I waited many years before I had another child, and if Sam hadn't died, we might not have had another child. BD wanted a baby, and he is my husband, and we can afford one. There is a big difference between you and me. Good Lord, you ain't got one out of diapers and now you having another one."

Mary gave Duane a piece of her mind, and he knew not to argue with her. He just let her say what she had to say and simply gave a "Yes, ma'am."

Margaret's pregnancy was going as expected, only this time she was gaining even more weight than she did with Dexter. She was becoming very uncomfortable.

When Margaret was about seven months pregnant, Duane came home one day with an announcement. "Margaret, we're moving to Los Angeles."

"What do you mean we're moving?" asked Margaret.

"I've heard that there are some jobs down there. I know someone who can get me one, and they make good money," said Duane.

"But you have a job, and we're not doing so bad right here," replied Margaret.

Duane had actually lost his job, but he hadn't told Margaret. He'd leave the house as though he were going to work every day. But he was actually out looking for a job. He was having a tough time finding work. Whenever he got interviews, he'd get close to being hired, but when they saw that he couldn't see well, he wouldn't get the job.

The unfortunate thing about Duane was that his intelligence was actually above all the work he was trying to get. He was very knowledgeable in many areas, but he hadn't received a formal education in the areas he was interested in. What was fortunate was that he did get a steady check each month from the government, but it still wasn't enough.

Margaret never felt well enough to work because she now had Dexter, who was just ten months old and was getting ready to walk, and the new baby was due in two months. Leaving now to venture to a new place was not a wise option to Margaret. Nor was it a wise option to her mother.

When Margaret told her mother they were moving to Los Angeles, it prompted Duane and Mary's first argument. Mary strongly objected, saying that there would be no one who could help if they got into trouble. There would be no close family there. Still, in spite of Mary's objections, Duane was set on leaving. Mary wanted Margaret to leave the baby with her until they got settled, but Margaret wouldn't part with her baby. By the next week, they had packed up and left for Los Angeles.

Los Angeles was a busy place in 1952. Hollywood was turning out more movies than ever, and going to the motion picture theaters was one of America's favorite pastimes. The Vizinaus moved in with a friend of Duane's, who had a two-bedroom apartment near downtown Los Angeles.

Margaret, Duane, and Dexter stayed in one bedroom, while Duane's friend, Stan, lived in the other. Stan had helped Duane get a job working with him moving furniture and props around between sets at a movie studio. Margaret stayed home and did the chores and took care of Dexter while the two men were at work.

Mary worried about Margaret constantly. At least Stan had a telephone and Mary was able to call. Still, that wasn't enough for Mary. She and BD and little Charles would drive down to Los Angeles just about every other weekend, and it was taking a toll on BD and little Charles. It took almost eight hours of driving to get there, and little Charles always got restless and cranky during the long drive there and back. Sometimes they had to leave him with Annie.

Duane's sight was beginning to become a problem at work. As long as he worked with Stan, he could get the job done okay. When they had a job to do, Stan always coached Duane on what they were going to do and how they'd go about it. Duane could get around fine in familiar territory. If one didn't know any better, it would be hard to tell that he had trouble seeing. But when he got around unfamiliar terrain, he'd need to use his special glasses that he hated.

Stan and Duane tried to work together as much as possible. But there were those times when Duane would be called up to work with someone else, or even alone. It was these times that became a challenge for Duane, and on more than one occasion he had problems. It soon became apparent to the management that Duane might become a liability.

The Vizinaus moved into their new apartment. Margaret had been pregnant for nine months now, and she was expected to deliver any day. Dexter was going to be one year old, and Duane wanted to have a little birthday party for him. Margaret was tired and felt they couldn't have a party at that time. But Duane convinced her that she wouldn't have to do anything because he'd take care of everything. There would only be a few people since they didn't know many people.

Dexter's first birthday party was a very simple one. Duane invited a few of the children who lived in the same apartment building and a couple of his own friends. Margaret didn't do much; she just sat in a chair while Duane catered to her every need. She tried to be cheerful, but everyone could see that she was exhausted. Little Dexter kept climbing on her and calling for his baba (bottle).

At one year old, Dexter seemed pretty attentive to his mother. He was walking and waddling like most one-year-olds, but he was unusually obedient. Margaret could call his name, and he'd run over to her. It seemed as though he understood that his mother couldn't see.

Margaret was a good mother, and she was always very attentive to Dexter. Since they lived in a small, two-room apartment, which was only one room and a kitchen, it was easy to keep track of where Dexter was at all times. There wasn't much furniture in the apartment—a couch and a couple of chairs, a bed and a crib, a chest, and a table with a radio and lamp on it. Most of the time, Dexter slept with his mother and father.

After the party, Duane and Stan cleaned up while Margaret bathed Dexter so she could put him to sleep. After Stan left, Duane fixed something for the two of them to eat and fixed a few baby bottles for Dexter. Margaret ate all that Duane prepared; she had a strong appetite because of the baby. Dexter was now asleep, and Duane and Margaret were both tired as well. Margaret lay down on the bed, cradling Dexter near her. Duane then went over to the bed and lay down next to both of them.

"The party was very nice, Duane," said Margaret. "Dexter had a good time."

"Yeah," Duane laughed, "he didn't know what all the fuss was about. But I think he finally figured it was all over him. He was really tearing into that cake, and he got it all in his hair."

"Duane?" asked Margaret.

"Yes?" responded Duane.

"Tell me again what my child looks like. Everyone always says what a beautiful baby he is," she said.

Duane began to describe her son to her. "Well, he has dark hair that's real soft and curly. His skin color is a nice golden tan, and he has pretty brown eyes with long eyelashes. His smile is wonderful and loving, and he smiles all the time. You can tell he's a happy baby and well loved. He has these cheeks that make you want to pinch them or kiss them. He also looks really strong and sturdy." Margaret was smiling and stroking Dexter's hair while Duane described him to her.

Margaret continued the conversation. "Yes, he's a happy baby. He knows that he's loved. It's funny; I can never get him to call me Mama. He always calls me Baba. It's as though he associates me with the baby bottle, and that we are the same. I wonder if it's because he was breast fed for a while."

Duane just shrugged his shoulders and murmured, "Uh huh."

"Duane, can I tell you something and you promise not to tell anyone?" asked Margaret.

"Yes," replied Duane.

"Not even my mother!" she demanded.

"Yes, not even your mother," replied Duane.

"It's never really bothered me that I can't see. I think I've always accepted the fact that God made me this way because I'm his special

86

child. But the only thing I wish I could see is my child. I just wish that for one day, I could see him," she said with a crack in her voice as though she was about to cry, but she caught herself.

They lay on the bed; Duane was stroking Margaret's stomach, and Margaret was stroking Dexter's hair, and they fell asleep.

Three days later, Duane was at work in the middle of a moving job when a woman from the front office came out and called him. The woman told him that his wife had been taken to General Hospital and that she was about to deliver. Duane took off running and took a cab to the hospital. When he arrived, Margaret was still in labor, and a nurse was caring for Dexter. She gave Duane little Dexter, and the two of them stayed in the waiting room, waiting for Margaret to deliver.

Duane called Mary to let her know that Margaret was about to deliver; Mary asked how Margaret was doing and wanted to know if she needed to come down right away, or if she could wait another day and come on Friday after BD got off work and little Charles was out of school. Duane told her he thought she could wait and that he felt everything would be fine until they got there.

It was Thursday, July 24, 1952, and Margaret gave birth to another baby boy—Henry Ray Howard Vizinau. Duane insisted that Henry should be named after his Indian grandfather, Henry Vizinau. Margaret liked "Ray," and Mary liked "Howard," so he was named all three names. He weighed more than fourteen pounds, and he'd had to be delivered by Cesarean section.

After the baby was born and Margaret and the baby were all cleaned up, a nurse offered to hold Dexter while Duane went in to visit. Duane was beaming with joy that he had another baby boy. Margaret was exhausted and in pain; the operation had taken its toll on her. She was breastfeeding Henry, and he had taken to it right away, unlike Dexter who'd had to be taught to breastfeed. Dexter always preferred a bottle.

The first thing that Margaret wanted to know when Duane came into the room was, "What does he look like?" Duane told her that the new baby boy looked just like Dexter. He was the spitting image of his older brother, only he had a little more red in his color. Just like Dexter when he was born, Henry had a head full of hair. It went all down his back. He was a pretty baby boy. He almost looked like a girl.

"Hank—that's what I'm going to call him—Hank!" Duane said.

Margaret smiled through the pain.

"Hank and Dexter, my two sons," Duane said. He was a proud father, and he was glad he had boys. He was being a typical man. "Margaret, thank you for these two boys. I'm going to take them everywhere I go and teach them everything I know," he boasted.

Margaret just replied with an "Uh huh."

Duane went home that evening. He stayed home from work the next day to take care of Dexter and to go back to the hospital to visit Margaret. Mary, BD, and Charles would be driving down and arriving late Friday night.

When the Dillards arrived, it was late, and they needed to rest. Everyone crowded into the two-room apartment. Mary and Dexter slept in the bed, and the men and Charles slept on the floor.

Mary was up early the next morning and had breakfast done when the fellows woke up. "Get up! It's time to eat, and we have to get dressed and get out of here to go see Margaret," Mary told them. They all lazily got themselves together, ate, and dressed.

On the way to the hospital, Duane filled Mary in on how the delivery went and also on how the new baby was fine and looked just like Dexter.

When they arrived at the hospital, Margaret was sitting up and feeding the baby. She was still in some pain from the Cesarean operation, but other than that, she was fine.

"Naomi, you need to let me take Dexter back home with me until you get up and able," Mary told Margaret. Right away Duane objected, but Mary cut him off. "Duane, you need to get back to work. You can't afford to be off, and Margaret can't take care of both of these babies by herself." Margaret knew her mother was right and knew by the tone in her voice that there could be no argument.

Duane looked at BD but got no help from him. He then tried to get the work out, "Margaret."

But she responded with, "Duane, I think Mother is right. We better let her take Dexter home with her just for a little while until I can be up and about. It shouldn't be for long."

Duane started to sulk, but he knew they were right and agreed.

Right away Duane cheered up and shouted, "Well, how do you like Henry? Isn't he the biggest baby you ever saw?"

They all smiled and agreed, and BD said, "Boy, I don't know how you carried that big old boy around, Margaret. He's the biggest baby I've ever seen. How much did he weigh again, fourteen pounds?"

"Oh, Lord, yes, he felt like fourteen pounds to me. I was so glad to get this over. Lord knows I couldn't go another day!" Margaret exclaimed.

"Duane, what you been feeding Margaret that's making these big babies? Dexter was eleven pounds, and now Henry is fourteen pounds," BD added.

"Hank, that's what we'll call him, Hank," responded Duane.

BD chuckled and said, "That's a good name for a big old boy like that: Hank!" said BD.

"Well, I hope that's the last one," said Mary.

"Lord, yes," said Margaret. Duane didn't respond.

They stayed at the hospital all day, taking turns in the waiting room with little Charles and Dexter. Little Charles liked to help with Dexter. He felt as though Dexter was his little brother. Charles was now eight years old and was very helpful. But he got tired of staying in the hospital all day. Just before nightfall, they all left the hospital and went back to the apartment to rest and eat.

When they got back to the apartment, there was a note from Stan for Duane to contact him right away. Charles was the first one at the door and saw the note and gave it to Duane. Mary inquired as to what it was about, but Duane just said it was from a friend. He told them to go on in and he'd be back soon.

When Duane contacted Stan, he told Duane that he had been fired and was told not to come back. Duane had not contacted them to inform them that he wouldn't be there the next day, nor had he informed his boss that he was leaving when Margaret was about to deliver. Stan told Duane how he had tried to defend him, because they all knew that his wife was expecting any day. The boss said that Duane still had a responsibility to inform him before he left. The truth of the matter was they needed an excuse to let Duane go because they felt he was a liability.

Duane returned to the apartment, and Mary could sense that something was wrong. She didn't waste any time in inquiring with Duane what it was. He informed them that he'd been fired from his job.

Mary began to question Duane about what had happened. He didn't want to discuss it, but she continued, "What are you going to do?"

Duane was getting frustrated. "Mother, I'll take care of it. I'll get another job. In the meantime, we have a little money saved, and they're giving me a check for two weeks' work plus my current check. For right now, I can stay home for a little while and help Margaret with the babies, and you won't have to take Dexter right now." Mary decided not to argue and went into the kitchen to cook.

The next day they picked up Margaret and Hank from the hospital, brought them to the apartment, and helped get them situated. That evening, Mary, BD, and Charles headed for the long ride back to San Francisco. They needed to get back to work the next day, and Charles needed to get back in school.

Margaret was disappointed that Duane had lost his job, but she was glad he was able to stay home and help with the boys. Mary had left her some money to help them out for a while, and they felt good to be home as a family. Duane was very helpful with the boys and with Margaret. He helped cook and clean and run errands to the store.

As time went on, things got harder for the Vizinau family. Duane was not having much luck getting work, and money was getting very tight. Mary always needed to send money, and Duane's checks were barely enough to pay the rent and get a little food. Margaret couldn't work, and it was bothering her that she didn't get to go to church very often and that she didn't even have a church home. Learning to take care of two boys without being able to see and Duane gone all day looking for work was taking its toll on her. Duane was also getting frustrated with not being able to find work. He'd get little jobs here and there—washing dishes, cleaning floors, and sometimes a little hauling. The money was coming a little, day by day, but it was still not enough.

It was now four months since Hank had been born, and Duane was feeling as though he wasn't getting much attention. Just about all of Margaret's attention was going to the needs of Hank and Dexter. At night, Margaret would sleep in the bed with the babies. Dexter slept at the foot and Hank slept at the head with Margaret. Duane always slept on the couch. On this particular night, Duane was feeling depressed and needed some attention.

He asked Margaret if he could make a cot on the couch for the boys so that he could sleep with her that night. Margaret knew that this was coming, and she had mixed feelings about it. She was disappointed in Duane, but she also knew that he was trying very hard. At first she tried to say she was tired and maybe another night, but Duane pressed her. He started to beg and plead and appeal to her loving and caring nature.

Margaret had been anticipating this conversation, so she mentioned that she wanted him to begin using condoms. Duane did not have any condoms nor did he really want to use them. He began to explain how they could still make love without one and that he could control himself. Margaret was very apprehensive, but she finally agreed.

That night, the boys slept on the couch, and Duane made love to Margaret. Margaret was not very comfortable, but she felt she needed to accommodate her husband.

The next day, Duane was in better spirits and was up and out early looking for work. He came home that evening and had made $150. He brought home some food and supplies, and he also bought himself a little wine. It was the weekend, and he wanted to party. He invited Stan over for dinner, and the two of them sat around and drank the wine, talked, and played with the boys.

Margaret was getting tired, and Stan sensed it was time for him to go. When Stan announced he was ready to leave, Duane said, "No, no, you don't have to leave yet."

Margaret then said, "Duane, it's getting late, and the boys have got to go to bed."

Duane looked at her, then at Stan. He wanted to object, but he quickly thought of the night before and decided he wanted more. Duane then agreed and said, "Okay, all right, Stan. We'll catch you later. Thanks for coming by."

Stan left, and Duane put Dexter down on the floor and walked over to Margaret who was now going to breast feed Hank since Stan had left. She was tired and ready for sleep. "Honey?" Duane said to Margaret.

"Uh huh," Margaret replied. Anticipating what his next question might be, she said, "I took care of you last night. You let that hold you for a while."

"Ah, baby. Come on, just one more time. I'll tell you what, just let me sleep with you, and we don't have to do nothing. I just want to lie next to you. Let's let the boys sleep on the couch tonight."

Margaret gave in, and Duane fixed a cot for the boys on the couch. Margaret and Duane got in the bed, and Duane snuggled up to Margaret. Margaret turned her back to Duane to try to sleep. Duane moved over next to her and tried to go to sleep as well. But the urge was overcoming Duane, because he'd had a little too much to drink. He started poking at Margaret, but she was shaking off his advances. Duane begged and pleaded with Margaret until she finally gave in. Duane had sex with her and began to ejaculate. He tried to pull out, but a little had stayed in. Margaret had felt the seepage and was upset. She complained to Duane and told him that, from then on, he'd have to wear condoms. Duane didn't respond and turned over and went to sleep.

In a few weeks, Margaret was feeling sickly, and having felt that way before, she feared what was wrong with her. After a visit to the county hospital, it was confirmed that Margaret was again expecting a child. Having another baby was the last thing that Margaret and Duane needed. Things had become strained in their relationship, and they were broke. Duane could barely make enough money to care for his family. Trying to care for the essential necessities of shelter, food, clothing, and transportation seemed like an insurmountable task for Duane.

When Margaret informed her mother of her condition, Mary was at a loss for words. Her immediate response was to scold her, telling Margaret about all the problems this would cause and how they were already doing badly. But Mary caught herself and simply said, "I'll be down this weekend."

Mary was getting tired of having to continue to travel back and forth between San Francisco and Los Angeles. It was almost an eight-hour drive each way, and BD and Charles were getting tired as well. But there was nothing that could be done. Margaret was her daughter; Mary was always there for her, and she always would be.

After talking with her mother, Margaret informed Duane that her mother was coming down to visit.

"Why does she have to come down here? We can take care of this ourselves," Duane said.

"Because she cares for us, and she knows we can't do it all on our own," responded Margaret.

"Well, go call her back and tell her she can stay home and that we'll be fine," Duane demanded.

"I will not," Margaret responded sternly.

"Yes, you will," Duane shouted.

"No, I won't. I want to see my mother; I need her here. I need her here now," said Margaret, refusing to do as Duane wanted.

Duane was getting angry. He was feeling hopeless and not in control of the situation. He knew he had messed up, and he felt he needed to do something. The last thing he wanted was Mary coming down and getting in their business.

The shouting was now starting to affect the children. Hank, lying in the crib, was waking up. Dexter was toddling around the floor playing but was becoming anxious when the voices were raised.

Duane shouted back at Margaret, "Look, you're going to call your mother back right now, and you're going to tell her not to come down this weekend."

"Look, man, you better leave me alone. I'm not going to play this game with you," Margaret asserted.

Duane reached out and grabbed Margaret on the arm as if trying to make her walk over to the phone to call her mother. Margaret pulled back on her arm, and then pushed toward Duane, catching him off balance and sending him stumbling backward. Duane got angry, reached back, and backhanded Margaret across the face. The force made her fall back across the bed.

"How dare you hit me! How dare you! Man, I will kill you. I will get me a gun and blow your head off. My daddy didn't even hit me, and you ain't either," Margaret said, jumping up as if she were going to hit Duane.

Duane was not even in the vicinity of where she was standing, but she was ready to defend herself. He looked at her. He realized that he'd struck her across the mouth, and her lip was bleeding and getting puffy. He felt bad now and knew he'd done wrong. Right away he began to say he was sorry, but it was too late.

The baby woke up and began crying, and then Margaret began to cry. When Dexter saw his mother crying, he ran to her and he began to cry too. Duane now felt about as small as a fly. He went and got a wet towel and approached Margaret to try to aid her, but she pushed away his advance and asked him to leave. Duane left and went over to Stan's because he needed someone to talk to, and he needed a drink. Stan was always there when Duane needed him. He was a good listener and a good advice giver. But Stan wasn't home when Duane got there, so he just milled around outside Stan's apartment waiting for him to return.

After a couple of hours, Stan arrived and was surprised to see Duane just waiting around. "Hey, Duane, what's shaking?"

"Me and my woman had an argument," replied Duane.

"Oh?" asked Stan as he opened the door. "Come on in, have a seat. I'd offer you a drink, but I see you already have one." Stan eyed the whisky bottle in a paper bag Duane was carrying.

"Man, I couldn't wait. So I had to go and get me something," said Duane as he raised his bag in salute.

Stan had a phonograph and walked over to it to put on a record. He had a good collection of some blues and pulled out an album by John Lee Hooker. "Boogie Chillen" started playing through the small speaker.

"Ah yes, that's what I need. Play me some blues. 'Cause that's what I got, man. Man, I got the blues," said Duane.

"So tell me all about it, good buddy. What's bothering you?" asked Stan.

So Duane laid it all out for Stan. He talked about no money, no job, Margaret's having another baby, and his mother-in-law.

Stan tried to be encouraging, but he knew it was difficult for Duane. Every time it looked like he could get a decent job, the boss would find out that Duane couldn't see too well, and then he would either not get the job or get fired soon if he did get it. But Stan also knew that Duane was also lazy. He'd sleep all day if he could. He'd also party all night if he could.

Duane was starting to feel a little better. Stan told him he had a joint of some grass. So they smoked the joint, drank a little more, and listened to some more blues. Duane copped a seat on the floor and then started to doze off. He finally fell over and slept all night on the floor.

That Saturday, when Mary and BD arrived, Duane was still away. They had decided to leave little Charles with some relatives on this trip down. When they entered the apartment, it was in a mess. There were clothes everywhere, dishes in the sink, garbage in the trashcan, and toys all over the place. Not only was it a mess, but it was also a dangerous situation for Margaret, because she could easily stumble over something, fall, and hurt herself, or even hurt one of the children.

Mary told BD to pick up the trash, take the garbage out, and then take Dexter out for a trip to the park so he could play. After BD finished with the garbage, he went to pick up Dexter, but Dexter ran over to his mother and started calling for her to pick him up. "Baba, Baba, up, up," Dexter yelled, looking up at his mother and pulling on her dress.

"Now, you go with Granddaddy, and Baba will get you when you come back," Margaret told Dexter.

"Baba?" Dexter said begging.

"Go on now, go on," said Margaret.

Dexter stopped pouting and let BD pick him up. Mary went over to BD and Dexter and said, "Nana will play with you when you get back, okay?"

"Okay," answered Dexter.

Dexter was now eighteen months old, and he was learning to talk very quickly. His vocabulary seemed much broader than that of most eighteen-month-old children. He also seemed to have a good understanding about his mother's not being able to see. He seemed to look out for his mother, and he was also more obedient than most children his age.

In spite of the tough situation the Vizinaus had, the boys were very happy babies. Hank was just six months old, and he and Dexter were happy and cheerful all the time. Hank was too young to walk, but he'd lie down on the floor with a blanket and get a kick out of watching Dexter play around him.

After BD and Dexter left, Mary told Margaret to have a rest and take care of Hank while she cleaned up the house. First, she went into the kitchen and started washing up the dishes. She then decided to wash some diapers and clothes before beginning to straighten up the place. As she was separating the clothes, Mary noticed a towel with bloodstains, and then she noticed the dress.

Mary looked over at Margaret and asked, "What's this blood on your dress? What happened?"

This caught Margaret off guard; she hadn't thought that her mother might find out that Duane struck her. "Oh, ah, Mother, I tripped and fell," Margaret replied.

It hadn't dawned on Mary that Duane wasn't there until that moment. She also knew her daughter, and she could tell Margaret was lying, which was something she rarely did.

"Where's Duane?" asked Mary.

"He's not here right now," responded Margaret almost cynically.

"I can see that he's not here. Where is he?" Mary asked.

"I don't know," Margaret answered curtly.

Mary looked at Margaret and squinted, peering more closely at her daughter, and then she noticed the cut on Margaret's lip. She immediately walked over to Margaret and put her finger on Margaret's chin and inquired, "How did this happen?"

Margaret pulled her chin away and said, "It happened when I fell."

"Has Duane been beating on you?" Mary asked sternly.

"No, Mother, I fell," Margaret said, and a tear fell from her eye. She wanted to start crying, but she knew if she did, it would add to the situation, so she held back her tears. "He hasn't been beating on me, and I'm all right."

"Look, I'm not going to take him beating on you. I'll call the police on him. What's his problem where he thinks he can hit on you?"

"Mother, I said that I fell; now, just leave it be. I'm okay," Margaret replied.

Mary stopped, pondered, and decided to let it go, but she'd keep a watchful eye. She continued to clean and straighten up the apartment while Margaret saw to Hank. She went to the icebox and saw that there wasn't very much food in there. She also noticed that Margaret had lost a lot of weight. The situation wasn't good, and she didn't like what she was seeing.

"Naomi, why don't you come back home and stay with us for a little while, just until Duane is able to get things together?" Mary asked.

"Mother, I can't leave my husband, and I can't take his boys away from here. It would just kill him, and he wouldn't understand. Duane is trying; he's trying very hard, and I can't leave him here all alone," responded Margaret.

"Then let me take the boys back with me. We can take care of them just for a while, while you and Duane work things out," begged Mary.

"No, Mother, I can't do that either. It just wouldn't work. Duane wouldn't accept it, and I couldn't let my baby go. Hank needs his mother," answered Margaret.

"Well, just let me take Dexter. He is so busy and running around, and you have to take care of Hank, and now you're having another baby. You need to be able to take care of yourself. It's too much; it's just too much for you to do. You need to let me at least take Dexter for a little while," said Mary, sounding more demanding.

Margaret was thinking about it. She was always tired, and she wasn't feeling well. Dexter and Hank were just too much sometimes, and in a little while Hank would be crawling. It was already getting tough to keep track of what Dexter was always getting into. He was exploring everything in the apartment, even though there were only two rooms.

"Well, I guess it would help out a lot, but only for a little while. We have to ask Duane, and if he says it's all right, then it will be fine for Dexter to stay with you," said Margaret.

Duane didn't come home that night, and Mary and BD had to leave and head back to San Francisco. Margaret didn't want Dexter to leave without asking Duane first, but Mary insisted, and she was upset that Duane hadn't come home. Margaret told her that Duane was a little depressed and that she knew where he was. She stated that she'd deal with him when he got home and not to worry.

Mary and BD packed up and were soon on their way, driving back to San Francisco. Little Dexter was uncomfortable and wanted to play. He had never been in a car for such a long period of time. Mary put him in the backseat and let him play with his toys on the bench seat and on the floor. He was a typical toddler who tried to look for things to get into, but there wasn't much. Mary was enjoying watching him play and trying to figure out what he was trying to say.

Over the next few months, Mary and BD didn't get down to visit Duane and Margaret too often. Their visits were down to about once a month. It was just enough for Margaret and Duane to get to see Dexter and for Dexter to see his parents. He missed his parents and always cried when it was time to leave. Mary never liked what she saw when she visited because things didn't seem like they were getting better.

Margaret was not gaining the weight that she should have while being pregnant, Duane was struggling with trying to keep work, and they were not eating like they should. The one thing they did do was to make sure that Hank had everything he needed.

For Margaret and Duane, the time seemed to move very slowly, but for Mary, it seemed to move by quickly. In a short period of time, Margaret was eight months pregnant. Margaret was not doing well during her pregnancy. Her weight was not right, and she was always tired and sickly. Duane had put together enough money to stay home with Margaret during her last month of pregnancy and a couple of weeks after delivery. That way he could take most of the responsibility of taking care of Hank who was now almost one year old and had started walking.

Late one evening, Margaret was awakened by pain. It was unbearable pain, and she needed to get to a hospital right away. Duane called for an ambulance, which took about a half an hour to arrive. They wouldn't allow Hank to ride in the ambulance, so Duane had to ask a neighbor to mind him while he went to the hospital. Margaret cried out each time she felt the sharp pain, and Duane tried to comfort her. When they arrived at the county hospital, they quickly moved Margaret up to delivery. Duane had to wait in the waiting room, and he was getting nervous. Margaret had already delivered two babies, and neither one seemed to be as painful for Margaret as this. He sensed that something was wrong.

A doctor came out and told Duane that Margaret was not yet dilating but that she seemed to be in so much pain, they might have to operate and deliver with another Cesarean. The doctor also warned Duane that it was still a few weeks premature to deliver the baby and that it would be risky. Duane told the doctor he understood. After another fifteen or twenty minutes, the doctors decided they needed to take the baby, because there was some concern they couldn't hear a heartbeat from the child. They made preparations and began to operate.

In about an hour, the doctor came out to see Duane. The doctor informed him that the baby hadn't made it. It had been a baby boy, and it was stillborn, but he told Duane that Margaret was going to be fine, and they'd given her something to help her sleep. He said she'd sleep for several hours and encouraged Duane to go home and get some rest and come back a few hours later.

Duane was devastated and began to sob. The doctor called a nurse who tried to comfort Duane and gave him some aspirin. Duane asked if he could see Margaret. The nurse tried to discourage him, but Duane insisted. He was permitted to enter the room where Margaret was sleeping. He wanted to know if she knew about the baby, and the nurse said that she didn't. They thought they'd let him tell her. Duane thanked them and decided to stay at the hospital until she wakened.

As Duane sat beside Margaret, he had some time to reflect upon his life and the current situation. He thought about his parents who loved him dearly, and he thought about Margaret and his love for her. Duane was still very much in love with Margaret, but he was beginning to realize they were two different kinds of people. He began to wonder what the future would bring. Margaret was a devout Christian, and he was an atheist. Her devotion to him and their children had gotten her away from the church and her music. He realized that his selfishness had also gotten in the way of his appreciation for her.

Hank and Dexter meant the world to Duane. He loved his two boys more than he ever loved anything else in the world. They were two fine-looking, handsome kids, and Duane thought they looked just like him. The love that the boys had for him was more precious than gold. Hank was now one, and Dexter was two. He had to do right by them and his wife. He decided that he was going to do better regarding his family. He had made some mistakes, but it wasn't too late to make a change. The first thing they needed to do was leave Los Angeles and get back to the Bay Area. He had always been more able to find work there, and the transportation system was much easier for both Margaret and him to get around on. He decided, when Margaret awakened, he'd tell her they would be moving back.

Duane stood up and moved over next to Margaret. He was watching her and wondering how he was going to tell her they had lost their son. She was lying there so peacefully at rest. He stroked her forehead, and she started responding to his touch. He moved his hand because he wasn't trying to awaken her, but she started to wake up anyway.

Margaret woke up and sensed someone next to her. She could smell Duane's scent. "Duane?" she asked.

"Yes, Margaret, it's me," he replied.

"Oh, wow, how long have I been asleep?" she asked.

"I guess about ten hours. They gave you something to sleep," answered Duane.

"Where's the baby?" she asked.

"Margaret, you need to brace yourself. I don't have good news," said Duane.

"What's wrong, what's wrong with my baby?" Margaret asked nervously.

"Honey, the baby didn't make it," answered Duane. Before he could say anything else, Margaret began to cry.

Margaret wasn't able to contain herself; she was sobbing out loud. A nurse came into the room while Duane was trying to comfort her. "My baby, O Lord, why, Lord, why?" Margaret asked as she was sobbing. The nurse approached Margaret and mentioned to Duane that maybe he needed to leave the room. "No, Duane, don't leave me; stay here, stay near me, Duane," said Margaret.

Duane held on to Margaret and told her, "I'm here, honey, I'm here." He motioned for the nurse to leave the room, and she saw that she should go. Once the nurse left, Margaret and Duane held onto each other and wept.

Once the tears had ceased and both were composed, Duane dried his eyes and began to speak. "Margaret, I've been doing a lot of thinking. I know that I haven't always been the best husband and father that I should be. You've put up with a lot of my mistakes, and I want to make them up to you and the children. I think it's time for us to move back to San Francisco."

Margaret was surprised, but it was the news she wanted to hear. She'd been being as patient as she could because she was committed to her husband. But she missed her parents, and she felt trapped in Los Angeles.

"Oh, honey, I'm so happy to hear you say that. I've been praying so hard and so long for God to help you to see that going back to San Francisco would be the best thing for us," said Margaret.

Duane was in agreement, but he didn't think God had anything to do with it. He only answered with, "I think it's the best thing for us to do."

Margaret saw this as an opportunity to approach Duane about his soul. "Duane I have to tell you that I'm concerned about your soul."

This was something Duane did not want to hear, but Margaret continued, "This world is so full of sin, and the devil is busy. He's been trying from the start to tear us apart. Don't you see? I think losing our son is a sign from God that is meant to pull us closer together and closer to God."

Suddenly Duane became angry. "Hell, no!" he shouted. "What kind of God would take the life of a child? Our son didn't have a chance; he never did anything to anyone. He didn't deserve to die. If your God had anything to do with this, then I don't want any part of him," Duane said angrily.

Margaret knew that she had to be careful with Duane and that religion was a sensitive subject. But she continued, "Duane, I know you've heard this before, but it's true. Sometimes God works in mysterious ways. Can't you see, and don't you feel that this is bringing us closer together?"

Duane knew that Margaret was sincere in how she felt, so he calmed down, but he had to answer her. He said, "I feel we're going to come closer together because we love each other and it's the right thing to do. No god has anything to do with it. Now, I respect you for believing in whatever you want to believe in, but I don't believe in it, and I never will. Please let's not go over this now. Let's just hurry up and get you well enough to get out of here and go home to San Francisco."

8

Closer to You

The furthest back I can remember is when I was two years old. My mother and father and brother moved back to San Francisco, and we were together again as a whole family. The reason I can remember that far back is that there were a few events that took place that are prominent in my memory.

We had moved into an apartment building on Sutter Street near the corner of Baker Street. It was a three-story building, with the two top floors as living space and the ground floor a garage with storage. I don't remember exactly how many apartments there were in the building, but I believe there were three on the floor that we lived on, which was the top floor. There were two front doors at the top of a flight of stairs in the front of the building. When you went through the door on the left, you entered to a staircase that went to the top-floor apartments.

Our apartment was the door directly in front at the top of the stairs, and there was another door next to ours on the right that led to a second apartment. Opposite the door to the right across the short hallway, was another door leading to the third apartment. One thing about this building was that every tenant on our floor was blind. I don't know if it was some type of special program set up by a government agency or what. It probably was due to some program, because both my parents were resourceful people.

Anyway, I can remember the guy next door because he was an interesting character. I didn't see much of him, but when I did see him, I'd stare at him because he made me a little nervous. He was a tall, brown-skinned Negro man, and he had the type of eyes you see on some people who are blind that are sunken deep into the skull. He had a large protruding forehead as if he had an enormous brain. It was abnormal. His eyeballs would twitch back and forth and go up and down as if he were trying to scan. My mother and father would speak to him, but he never visited us. They always talked with him in the hallway. I didn't know his name, but my parents called him John. I didn't realize it at the time, but much later in life, I'd see him again and become shocked when I learned his name.

Across the hall was another blind Negro man, Wilber, who became a good friend of the family and was like a godfather to me.

My mother and father would argue quite frequently, and their relationship rapidly began to change. There was always a lot of action at my house.

Margaret was glad to be back in San Francisco. Her mother was near, and she had really missed Charles and Momma. She was able to go to church every Sunday with her family. She and the boys would walk to Macedonia Baptist Church, which was only four blocks down Sutter Street.

One Sunday, Margaret was up early, getting breakfast together in the kitchen. Duane got out of bed and walked into the kitchen to get some orange juice. "Good morning," said Duane.

"Good morning," answered Margaret.

"I want to keep the boys with me today. We're going to go out to Golden Gate Park on an adventure. We'll probably be gone all day," Duane said, matter-of-factly.

Margaret paused for a moment. She was about to consider it, but then she thought about the way in which Duane had said it, so she responded with, "I'm sorry, but the boys are going to church with me today. They go to church with me every Sunday."

Duane snapped back, "I know! They go to church with you every Sunday! I can't never take them anywhere with me, because you keep them with you everywhere you go."

Margaret just dismissed his reasoning. "I'm sorry, but you can live your life as a sinner if you want to. But these boys are going to know Jesus Christ. When they grow up, they are going to know who God is. I promised the Lord that I would raise these children in his name so they could be with me in heaven when we leave this place."

Duane threw up his hands in disgust. "Jesus Christ!"

"Don't you use the Lord's name in vain," Margaret blurted.

"My God, you are impossible, woman," Duane replied.

"There you go again. I wish you wouldn't do that, especially around the children. Next thing you know, they will say it," responded Margaret. Duane just walked out of the kitchen and went and sat on the bed.

Dexter ran into the bedroom and jumped on his dad's lap. He looked at his father and could see his father was upset. "Dada?" asked Dexter.

"Yeah?" Duane mumbled.

"Go bye-bye?" Dexter asked his father.

"No, you're going to go with Baba. You're going to church," Duane told his son.

"I go with you, Dada. Dada, I go with you," Dexter appealed to his father.

"No, no, son. You go with your mother; she needs you," Duane said with a tear in his eye. "Hey, son?"

Little Dexter looked up at his father with an alert look on his face. "What, Dada?"

"You always look after your mother when I'm not around. You take care of her. You're getting to be a big boy now," said Duane.

"I a big boy, huh, Dada?" Dexter responded feeling proud.

"Yeah, you're almost three years old now," Duane answered as he looked down at his son. He didn't have the best vision, but he could see faces when they were in front of him. He could see that Dexter was a handsome boy. He wasn't an infant anymore, and he was the cutest thing you ever wanted to see. Whenever Duane looked at his boys, his heart would just melt. They were both pretty boys, real handsome, something to be proud of.

Duane got up, hurried to put his clothes on, and left. He didn't know where he was going to go, but he wasn't going to sit around the house. It was a nice day in San Francisco, and he wanted to enjoy it.

Margaret had the boys all dressed up for church. She took one their hands in each of hers and headed down the street. After they'd walked a ways, Hank stopped and pulled on his mother's dress, then asked her to pick him up. She picked him up, and then said to Dexter, "Dexter, you know how to walk to the church, right?"

"Yes, Baba," Dexter answered.

"Good, now we're going to walk; we're not catching the bus today, okay?" she asked.

"Okay, Baba," Dexter answered.

Margaret and the boys started walking, with Dexter leading the way. They came to a corner and stopped, and Margaret told Dexter to look for cars. His father had taught him how to look both ways and also how to look at street lights. When the way was clear, Dexter said, "Come on, Baba," and they continued to walk.

Margaret counted the blocks; she always knew where to turn. She could actually make the trip on her own because she knew the route. But it was always good to test Dexter because he was in training. Hank couldn't do it yet because he wasn't quite two and couldn't yet be as attentive as Dexter. Whenever Margaret and the boys walked down the street, people looked at them. For most folks it was a sight to see.

They got to the church right as Sunday school let out; Mary, BD, Annie, and Charles were already there. Margaret was a little late and had missed Sunday school because of Duane. He'd gotten her off track. Once they were joined together, they all went into the church and sat together in one row, with the exception of Annie who was dressed in white and took a seat with the mothers of the church.

Margaret sat down and tried to have one boy sit on each side of her, but Hank didn't want to sit down on his own. He always wanted to sit in his mother's lap, so Margaret would have to hold him. He'd put his head on his mother's breast and start sucking his thumb. He was content in his mother's arms.

Dexter was always inquisitive; he would sit, look around, and inspect the church. He'd look at all the details of the building. He'd look up at the ceiling and at the floor, check the benches, and put his hands in the holders that held the communion glasses. Any pictures of Jesus or angels would really get Dexter's attention. The eyes on the pictures were especially of interest to him. Sometimes it looked like they were looking at him.

The deacons entered the sanctuary from a side door and walked over to a group of chairs that were sitting in front of the pulpit. They stood toward the front of the church facing the pews, each in front of a chair. All of them were carrying Bibles. Soon one stepped forward and began to sing, "I know the Lord; he heard my cry."

The congregation followed the deacons, singing, "I know the Lord; he heard my cry." They dragged every word out and let them hang in the air and dangle up and down with every syllable.

The deacon continued the lead and sang out quickly, "Long as I live, my soul shall rest."

Again the congregation chimed in, dragging out each word again, "Long as I live, my soul shall rest."

The program usually followed the same format. After the deacons sang, they'd have everyone stand and read a scripture, and then pray. The choir would come in and sing a couple of songs, and then the pastor would come out, say a few words, and have altar call.

On this particular Sunday, there was a guest preacher. He was visiting from a nearby church. His name was Reverend Reason, and he was the pastor of the First Union Baptist Church.

After altar call, the pastor made an announcement that, after the choir sang another selection, Rev. Reason would provide the day's sermon. He then said that he wanted to ask a favor of someone who was the daughter of one of the church members. The pastor said, "I'd like to ask Sister Dillard's daughter, Margaret, if she would come and give us a solo."

Margaret was surprised, and she blushed. Although she occasionally sang with the choir, she hadn't yet joined the church to become a member. So it wasn't very often the pastor requested her to sing. When she did sing, she seldom led. "Oh well, I guess so," she said under her breath. Mary motioned to the pastor, nodding her head that Margaret would sing. An usher came over to the end of the aisle to escort her to the pulpit. Mary took Hank and sat him up in her lap, and Margaret made her way to the end of the aisle. She asked the usher to take her to the piano.

Margaret sat at the piano and she had everyone's attention. She then began to play and sing:

> O Lord, my God,
> When I, in awesome wonder,
> Consider all
> The worlds thy hands have made.

When Margaret sang that song, it touched the heart of every Christian soul in the sanctuary. The people gave praise to God and thanked him for his grace. Tears came down in the choir stand, in the pews, and even on the cheeks of the ushers. Joy and worship filled the congregation. Everyone was thinking about God and "How Great Thou Are!"

Rev. Reason was overcome by what he had just witnessed. He had heard of Margaret a few years back when she was in the East Bay at Seaport Baptist Church in Richmond, but their paths had never crossed.

Rev. Reason had a growing congregation of his own, and he wanted more members. He needed another choir director and pianist to assist in his goal. To him, this was a blessing from God.

After Margaret sang, the pastor got up, and after acknowledging her solo, gathered himself together. When the congregation calmed down, he then introduced Rev. Reason and asked the congregation to accept his presence with a saying of ayes and a raising of hands. Everyone said, "Aye," and a few raised their hands.

Rev. Reason approached the podium. "I have to say that that young lady sang that song like I've never heard it sung before. It was as though I heard it for the first time. My soul is on fire, and I'm glad that I know the Lord. God has touched my soul, and he is in me now, right now!"

"Amen!" shouted several members.

"Margaret?" the reverend inquired, as he looked over to the pastor, wanting to make sure that was her name. The pastor nodded. "I tell you, if you're looking for a job, we got one for you over at First Union."

"Well, I say," Margaret mumbled to her mother. Mary was grinning from ear to ear as she nudged her daughter.

After church, Mary took Margaret over to meet Rev. Reason. He was a burly man with a round figure. He was wearing a three-piece suit with a watch hanging on a chain from the front pockets. He was standing, with his belly bulging out, as though it gave him authority. Rev. Reason was a no-nonsense preacher. He was an old-time kind of person. He spoke his mind, never biting his tongue. His voice was loud, strong, and commanded respect.

"Well, hello ladies," Rev. Reason said as Mary and Margaret approached him. "You be Sister Mary and you be Sister Margaret." He shook Mary's hand and then took hold of Margaret's.

"Hello, Reverend," said Margaret.

"Margaret, I'll get right to the point. I need someone new at my church that can work with me to get my choirs together. I have a vision about how many choirs I want, and I need somebody who can help us grow. From what I can see, I think you can do the job. That is, if you are interested," said the reverend, looking at Mary to see if she approved.

Margaret responded, "Yes, I'm interested. I'm not working right now, and we can use the work. I need to be about my Father's business."

"Well, that sounds great," said the reverend sounding delighted. "Why don't you come around Thursday evening about seven o'clock? I'll introduce you to the choir, and you can get started. Now, we don't pay a lot, but we're not cheap either," the reverend offered.

"That will be fine, Reverend; we'll be there," Margaret said as Hank and Dexter ran over to their mother. BD had been holding them back while their mother was talking with the reverend.

The reverend looked down and saw the two little boys. They were both looking up at him; Hank was holding onto his mother's dress, sucking his thumb, and Dexter was holding her hand. "Look at these handsome boys. Are these your boys, Margaret?" asked the reverend.

"Yes, sir, this is Hank and Dexter," replied Margaret, smiling.

"Well, these are two of the most handsome boys I've ever seen. Girl, the Lord is blessing you," stated the reverend.

Immediately, the reverend wondered who the boys' father might be. Whoever he was, he wasn't there. He also thought that the father must not be a Negro because those boys sure didn't look it; they looked mixed.

After church, Margaret and the boys went over to Mary's house. Annie was going to cook some fried chicken, and she had prepared some greens the night before, which she was dying to get to. Once they arrived at the house, Margaret changed the boys' clothes so they could play. Charles played with the boys while all three women prepared something in the kitchen. BD went into his room, turned on the radio, and listened to the ball game.

Dexter and Hank always had a good time playing with their Uncle Charles. To Dexter, it was just like having a big brother. Charles was ten years old now, and he was becoming a fine athlete. He loved baseball, basketball, and tennis, but baseball was his first love. His father, BD, was a faithful baseball fan and sometimes took him out to Seal Stadium to watch the Giants play.

Charles sometimes got a little rough with the boys. He liked to wrestle with them and toss them about. Sometimes one of the boys would get hurt. Dexter usually brushed it off and went back for more. But if Hank got the least bit hurt, he'd start crying and run to his Baba. Charles and Dexter would just keep on playing.

When dinner was ready, everyone sat around the table where the food was laid out. There was fried chicken, greens, rice, macaroni and cheese, and cornbread. Mary usually baked a pie, and Annie, a cake.

They'd gather around to say grace. "Hank, Dexter, fold your hands," Margaret would tell the boys. Dexter would fold his little hands, close his eyes, and bow his head. Hank would take his little hands and cover his eyes. Everyone would look at him and just smile because it was the cutest sight. He hadn't quite got it right.

BD would say grace. "Dear Lord, we're thankful for this food which is for the nourishment of our minds, bodies, and souls, and all that is within us. Praise thy holy name. Amen!"

"Amen!" everyone else would chime in.

"Rise, Peter, slay and eat," Annie always added.

This was what it was all about—family, and being together as a group, enjoying one another and loving one another. Everyone was happy, and everyone was getting full. After dinner, the women cleaned up the kitchen while the boys continued to play. BD generally snoozed by the radio.

Whenever it was time to leave, Dexter never wanted to go. He loved his grandmother as if she was his mother. Mary showered the boys with love, and they loved it. Dexter's relationship with his mother was becoming more like he was taking care of her, rather than she taking care of him, like most mothers and sons. Therefore, his grandmother seemed to play more of a providing role. He loved her love and affection. Since Hank was the baby, he was a momma's boy, and his relationship with Margaret seemed more like a mother and son relationship.

Mary had BD take Margaret and the boys home. It wasn't that far a ride from Potrero Hill to the far end of the Fillmore district, but Hank and Dexter usually fell asleep in the backseat of the car on the way home. BD walked Margaret up to the front door and went back to bring the boys up.

It was just after six o'clock in the evening when they arrived home. When Margaret opened the front door, she could hear music coming from the top of the stairs where they lived. She hiked up the stairs with BD and the boys in tow. The music was coming from her apartment. She banged on the door. The music stopped, and Duane opened the door. "Hey," he said. Smoke rushed out the door and hit Margaret in the face. Dexter ran by his mother and jumped into his daddy's arms. "Daddy!" he yelled, smiling and happy to see his father. Hank copied his brother.

"What are you doing?" Margaret asked Duane.

"Oh, me and a couple of the fellahs are sitting around playing some music," Duane answered. Before Margaret could get out another word, Duane shouted, "Hey, BD, how you doing? Want to come in and sit a spell?"

BD's eyes lit up, and he grinned. He saw they were drinking beer and smoking, and he wanted in on the party. He'd been holy all day, and Duane and his friends looked like they were having some fun.

"Ah, yeah. That sounds like a good idea. I can set a spell," answered BD, walking on in. One of Duane's friends handed him a beer.

Margaret was upset, but she contained herself. She and Duane had an understanding that she had her music and likes, and Duane had his. He respected hers, and she respected his. But she didn't like it; she thought it was devil's music, and she was worried about its influence on the children. So she just walked into the house and went into the bedroom.

"Okay, boys, let's hit it," Duane said. The music started, dah dah dah dah, and one of the men sang:

> Now when I was a young boy
> About the age of five,
> My mother said
> I was going to be the greatest man
>   alive.
>
> But now I'm a man
> Way past twenty-one,
> I want you to believe me, baby,
> I have lots of fun.
>
> I'm a man
> I spell it M—A—N,
> That represents Man.
>
> I'm a Man,
> A grown Man;
> I'm a Man,
> A natural born lover's man;
> I'm a Man,
> I'm a rolling stone,
> I'm a Man,
> I'm a hoochie coochie man.

They were jamming and having a ball. Duane was on the harmonica, Stan was on Margaret's piano, one man was on a small

111

set of drums, and another was singing and playing a guitar. Wilbur, from across the hall, was sitting on a chair with his shades on, sipping on his beer and tapping his foot. Hank and Dexter started dancing in the middle of the floor, and BD looked so excited, as if he were going to piss on himself. Margaret was in the bedroom, talking to herself, mumbling about how it ain't nothing but the devil. But she couldn't help acknowledging to herself that they sounded good. She sure didn't like the song though.

The guys kept playing and having a good time. Margaret finally got up and went into the kitchen. She felt around and determined that the kitchen was a mess. There were bottles, trash from take-out food, and dirty plates and utensils. So she started cleaning up the kitchen.

In the front room, the men finished playing a tune and were trying to decide what to play next. Stan said, "Wilbur, why don't you sing a song with us."

"Yeah, Wilbur, come on; sing a song," Duane added.

"Oh now, you know I can't sing, Duane. Shoot, if I started singing, you'd be ready to quit. I'm enjoying this; I ain't ready for it to stop," replied Wilbur.

"Yeah, I'll guess you're right," laughed Duane, and everyone else joined in the laughter.

"Who wants another beer?" asked Stan.

"That sounds really cool, man," responded Duane.

Stan headed for the kitchen to get the beers and saw Margaret standing at the sink washing dishes. "Hey, why don't we get Margaret to play a song with us. I bet she can really wail," Stan shouted.

"Ah, man, I know you're loaded now. That beer done gone to your head," Duane shouted back. "She don't know nothing about playing no blues," Duane said, laughing.

Wilbur jumped in, "Huh, I bet she can play. When you play like Margaret can play, you can play anything and sing anything."

Margaret stood there and said, "No, I can't play that music. I don't know nothing about that kind of music," she said, with a smirk on her face.

"Come on, Margaret, I bet you can, I bet you can play. Come on, it's not going to hurt you," Stan begged.

Margaret had been listening to the guys play, and it really was sounding good to her. Duane had challenged her. She was thinking,

"He doesn't know as much as he thinks he does." Stan was about to walk out of the room when Margaret said, "All right, I'll play one short song. That's all."

"All right, come on in; let Margaret through; let her have a seat," yelled Stan, as he guided her to the front room.

Duane was shocked; he couldn't believe what was happening. Now, this was something he had to see. BD was surprised too, and the grin on his face went from ear to ear. Wilbur sat straight up and acted as though he were proud, like he knew what he was talking about. He was mumbling under his breath "Uh huh, I told you. I told you. I knew it."

Margaret sat down at her piano, pulled the bench up, and got positioned as she felt the black and white keys. Then she counted off "One, two, three, four," and began pounding on the keys. She started playing the boogie-woogie. Duane leaned closer, looking at her and the piano. Then he turned his head and looked up at Stan with amazement in his eyes and his mouth wide open. Margaret was playing that piano and stomping her feet on the pedals like she'd been playing the boogie-woogie all her life.

The fellows started hooting and hollering and jumping up and down. BD was dancing with Hank and Dexter, and the boys were all giggles and full of laughter. Margaret finished her song and got up, turned toward Duane, and said, "Well, I guess you don't know as much as you think you know." Duane's eyes were open wide. He looked at the fellows, and they just burst out laughing.

That was enough for the evening; it was getting late, so it was time for the guys to go. Wilbur went home across the hall, and Stan went to stay with some relatives while he was in town. BD drove back across town, and the other gentlemen said goodnight and left. Margaret went into the kitchen, and Duane grabbed the boys up, one in each arm, and went to the bedroom to get them ready for bed. He played with them and tickled them while he got them ready. He rubbed his rough, stubbly chin on them, and the boys loved it.

After the boys were in bed asleep, Duane went and washed up and got in bed with his pajamas on and waited for Margaret. She took her time cleaning up the kitchen. After she finished, she felt her way into the bedroom and over to the closet. She opened it, pulled out her nightgown, and went into the bathroom. Duane lay there, watching her as she went back and forth. He was on full, and had something on his mind. Margaret's senses were sharp as a razor, and she knew what lay ahead. Duane thought he was being smart by washing up and brushing his teeth before he got in bed. He even put on a little Old Spice, just a little dab; he didn't want it to be too obvious.

Margaret changed into her nightgown and got into the bed. There was silence at first. Neither one said anything to the other. Duane let his foot touch her leg. Margaret didn't respond, but she didn't move her leg either. Duane then moved closer to her and leaned over on his side and said, "You know, I didn't know you knew how to play like that. You never played like that for me."

Margaret answered, "I don't play like that. It's not my kind of music. I just wanted you to know that I could play it if I wanted to."

"Well, didn't you enjoy it? Wasn't it a good time?" asked Duane.

She answered him "Yes, it was nice and it felt good. I never said it wouldn't be."

"Well then, why don't you like to do it? Why don't you like to party," asked Duane.

"I do like to party. I have a party when I go to church. I have fun praising the Lord. Duane, the feeling I get when I sing and play for Jesus Christ is a much greater feeling than anything else in the world. If I have a choice between the feeling I get when God is in me and the feeling I get with the devil in me, I'll chose God's feeling any day, because it feels so much better. We have a party at church. We party all the time."

Duane couldn't understand; there was no way he could. He also knew it wasn't debatable. He decided not to even try and approach Margaret for any love that night. So he turned over to go to sleep. Margaret got out of the bed and got on her knees to pray. Duane hadn't realized that Margaret had decided to service him that night, so long as he used protection.

Thursday night came fast. BD drove over to take Margaret to the church. One good thing about working at First Union Baptist Church was that it was very close to where Margaret lived on Sutter Street. It was only three blocks away, at the corner of Geary Boulevard and Baker Street. Once they got to the church, she inquired if someone would be willing to take her home so that BD wouldn't have to wait. The boys stayed home with Duane.

Rev. Reason greeted Margaret when they approached the front door to the church. He was sitting in a window to the right of the entrance looking out for her. There was an apartment that had a separate entrance in the front of the church, which the pastor and his wife used.

"Margaret, I'm glad you could make it. This is an exciting day for our church home. We're hoping you find it an exciting place for you and that maybe someday you'll make it your home too," said the reverend.

"Thank you, Reverend. I'm very glad to be here too. I've heard some good things about this church, and I'm looking forward to being a part of it," answered Margaret.

The reverend looked around to see if anyone was near, and then said, "Well, I hope so. I wanted to chat with you before we went in to meet the choir members." Just then a car pulled up with a woman driving, and she moved to take advantage of a space right near the front.

The reverend continued, "Margaret, I want you to know that this ain't going to be no easy job. It's a fairly decent-size choir, and there are some stubborn women in the group. Now, there are a couple of names you might want to make note of that can help you get along okay. They are some really nice ladies, and they'll cover your back."

As he continued, the woman from the car approached them. She was a tall, slender, fair-skinned woman who was very graceful. BD was standing there, about to leave, and couldn't help but notice how striking she was. She had the most pleasant smile, and when she walked, she moved liked a cat, and her hips swayed back and forth. He had to catch himself.

"Here's one of the ladies now. Hello, Molly, let me introduce you to someone. Margaret, this is Molly. She's our organist. She'll be accompanying you here at First Union. Molly, this here is Margaret; she's our new choir director. Molly, I told Margaret you'd look out for her," said the pastor.

"Sure, Pastor, you know I will," Molly said, smiling, as she took Margaret's hand to shake it. She looked over at BD who said, "Howdy, ma'am," nodding his head.

"Oh, I'm sorry; it's so rude of me. This is my father, Mr. Dillard. Daddy, this is the Reverend Reason, and this is Molly," Margaret said apologetically.

"How do?" said BD as the reverend remembered him from Sunday.

BD dismissed himself, and the reverend dismissed Molly, and then he gave Margaret a couple more names before they went inside to meet the choir.

They walked into the church, and Margaret could hear a lot of chatter coming from up ahead. Suddenly, the chatter stopped, and she could hear a few whispers. The choir members knew they were to meet a new choir director, but they didn't know that she was blind. One of the choir members recognized Margaret and began to gossip about how well she could sing and play. They had either seen or heard of her before. Another member was heard saying, "What?" as she stared.

Rev. Reason then shouted out, "All right, you chickens and roosters, listen up now. Pay attention, everybody. I got an announcement to make. This here's Margaret. She's your new choir director, and I want you to give her your undivided attention and make her feel comfortable and welcome. You know I ain't going to stand for no foolishness." A few of the members chuckled.

Margaret smiled and thought, "Well, I say."

Rev. Reason ran a tight ship and everyone was used to him treating his members like they were his children. It was a trait either you liked or hated.

"Now, Margaret, Brother Perry is our choir president. Perry, speak up," said the pastor, motioning to Brother Perry.

"Right here," yelled Perry.

"Gussy, you see that Margaret gets her way around the church okay," instructed the reverend.

"Yes, Pastor," responded Gussy.

"All right now, you got two weeks for some practicing with Margaret, and I want to hear some sho' nuff shouting good music come the first Sunday. Is everybody all right with that?" asked the pastor.

"Amen," responded the choir.

The pastor then patted Margaret on the shoulder and said, "Margaret, they're all yours."

Margaret jumped right in. She was experienced and it showed. She knew that she did not want to start out by trying to teach them any new songs. Instead, she asked about what songs they'd already been singing so that she could practice with them to determine who the lead singers were.

She decided on two songs they came up with. First, they would practice "It Took a Miracle," then they'd practice "It Is No Secret What God Can Do." Both of these songs would give her some sense of how tight the choir was and if each section knew their parts.

It didn't take long for Margaret to see that they needed some work on getting tighter. She took the time to go over everybody's parts. First, she went over the sopranos' parts, then the altos', and then the tenors' and basses'. She instructed the lead singers to stay an additional ten minutes after rehearsal.

After they rehearsed the two selections, she wanted to try one other song. The choir was tired and was ready to leave, but she kept them anyway. Since the first two selections were a little down tempo, she needed them to practice something that was easy but more of an up-tempo.

Margaret had them practice "Give Me That Old Time Religion." It was a song that everyone knew. They could have some fun with it, and it would also wake them up. The song accomplished just what she needed it to do. They had fun singing it, and it also woke them up.

After practice, Margaret told the choir that she'd see them next week and that she was glad to be there. She also told them that she was very impressed with their singing and that they all had beautiful voices. Brother Perry then had the choir stand for prayer and dismissal. Once the choir was dismissed, Margaret was flooded by the members all wanting to shake her hand and introduce themselves. It got to where Brother Perry had to tell them all to go home, since Deacon Wade was waiting to lock up the church. Everyone then started heading toward the door.

Molly locked up the organ and approached Margaret and told her that she'd done well. Gussy took Margaret by the hand and asked her if she needed anything. She showed Margaret to the ladies' room, and then turned her over to Brother Perry. He and his wife drove Margaret the three blocks to her home.

Brother Perry arrived at Margaret's home and walked her to the door. When Margaret opened the door, both the boys ran to the door to see their Baba. They immediately saw Brother Perry and froze, then huddled under their mother. Margaret said, "These are my two boys, Hank and Dexter. Say hello, boys."

Dexter said, "Hello," and Hank just looked at the man.

Duane came to the door and said, "Hello" while offering his hand.

Margaret introduced her husband. "Brother Perry, this is my husband, Duane."

"Hello, Duane. Brother Perry," answered Perry.

They shook hands and then Duane asked, "So how did it go?"

Before Margaret could answer, Brother Perry jumped in, "It went just fine. Margaret is going to do just fine at First Union."

"Thank you, Brother Perry. You really think it went well?" asked Margaret.

"Oh, I know it did," answered Perry.

"Great," said Duane as he grabbed the boys and pulled them back into the house. Margaret thanked Brother Perry for the ride and closed the door.

The next week, Margaret was back at First Union for her second choir rehearsal. They hadn't seen her or heard from her at the church since the last one. She'd gone back to Macedonia on the past Sunday. Rev. Reason had hoped to see her at his church but didn't make a big deal about it.

She practiced the same songs they'd sung the week before. Now she wanted to teach them a song that she would lead. The song she chose to sing as her first solo was "Shine on Me."

Margaret began by teaching them the choruses. Once they knew the choruses, she was ready for them to go through the entire song, with her singing the verses. She played the introduction, and then directed them to sing the first chorus. The choir sang out "Shine on me," and then again, "Shine on me." They continued, "Let the light from the lighthouse shine on me," and repeated the chorus.

It was now time for Margaret's part, "I heard the voice of Jesus say, come unto me and rest. Let the weary and worn lay down. Lay your head upon my breast."

She continued and sang the second part of the first verse, "I came to Jesus and I drank. From thy chilling stream, my thirst was quenched, my soul was revived, and right now I live in him."

It was time for the choir to join in with "Shine on me," but they fell apart. The choir was so in awe over Margaret's singing that they almost forgot to sing. They knew she could sing because they'd been practicing with her, and she'd sing when she'd teach them their parts. But until now, they hadn't really heard her sing.

In that moment, they realized they had someone special who was truly gifted by God. Her voice touched each and every one of them. There was going to be some soul-stirring going on in First Union. When she sang, they all felt like they'd been hit with a bolt of lightning, and they all looked at each other in amazement. It all made sense now, about how Rev. Reason had made such an abrupt change in the order of things to have Margaret take over the choir.

Margaret stopped playing the piano and asked the choir, "What's wrong? Did you all forget your parts?"

"No, Margaret, we're sorry. We just hadn't heard you sing like that before. We'll be ready now," said Gussy.

Margaret took it from the top, and this time the choir belted out their parts on cue and without error. They had a hard time keeping it together because it was only supposed to be rehearsal. But several members just couldn't help themselves and couldn't keep from being touched. There were more than a few wet eyes when they finished.

After rehearsal, everyone was excited and couldn't wait until the next day when they would sing. Many of the members gathered around Margaret to tell her how happy they were to have her. Margaret thought it was funny because she thought all the welcoming had been done the week before. But this time they showed her much more love. She felt the love and was touched by the sincerity.

The next morning, Margaret got up early to get the boys ready. She had told Brother Perry not to pick her up and that she'd make it to the church just fine without his help this time. She had decided that she and the boys were going to walk. Then Margaret did something that she rarely did: she asked Duane if he cared to attend. Of course he declined, and she had no problem with it.

Mary had decided that she and BD were going to visit First Union on Margaret's first day. She was very proud of her daughter and couldn't wait for the moment when the church secretary asked for visitors to rise and speak if they felt the need to. Mary would get up and announce to everyone that Margaret was her daughter. She'd introduce her family by pointing out BD, Charles, and Momma.

Church got started, and when it was time for the choir to come marching in, Rev. Reason got up and made the announcement that they had a new choir director and pianist. He introduced Margaret, who was led to the piano, and he told the congregation they were in for some real good singing.

Margaret sat at the piano, turned her head over her left shoulder and nodded. Hank and Dexter were sitting right there in the front row, almost in arm's reach of the piano. They were both looking at their mother and knew that she was telling them they'd better behave. Mary and the rest of the family were sitting near as well. Not only was this Margaret's first introduction to the church's service, but it was also training for the boys.

Rev. Reason requested everyone to rise, and Margaret started to play. She brought the choir in on a marching theme, with the choir singing:

> We come this far by faith,
> Leaning on the Lord,
> Trusting in his holy Word,
> He never failed me yet.
> Oh, can't turn around;
> We come this far by faith.

It wasn't something that had been practiced, but it was a song everyone, including the congregation, could join in and sing. The choir marched in, singing proudly. Their robes were crisp and clean, and they held their heads high. Many of the choir members were smiling, and it was obvious they were happy to be there. The feeling was contagious, and many in the pews started smiling too.

Rev. Reason instructed everyone to sit down, and he took a seat at his throne. He didn't smile; he had a stern look on his face. As usual, it was a look of authority. He held his head high and looked over at the choir like they needed to get down to business. The choir remained standing, and Margaret began to play. They went over two of the selections they had rehearsed, and they sounded tight. The rest of the service went as planned, and Rev. Reason gave his sermon.

Rev. Reason's sermon was delivered just fine, but it had failed to ignite the people. The deacons had done their part in trying to cheer him on and stir up the crowd, but it just didn't work. After the sermon, the reverend announced the doors of the church were open, and he called for a selection from the choir. The deacons stood up behind their chairs, inviting new members to come forward. Margaret began to play.

"Shine on me," sang the choir. Everyone's attention was on the choir; they sounded great. "Shine on me," they continued with the chorus.

Again, it was Margaret's turn. "I heard," she sang, stretching out the I; "a voice," she dragged out the words, and it sent a piercing jolt out through the crowd.

If someone hadn't been paying attention at first, they were paying attention now.

She continued, her voice sounding like no other, "… of Jesus say …"

A jolt went through one of the mothers on the other side of the church. "… Come on," she continued, "to me."

Some amens could be heard now, and the deacons had now taken notice.

Margaret continued to sing, "And rest."

"Yes, Lord," someone yelled out.

Margaret continued, "Let the weary and worn lay down. Lay your head upon my breast."

Margaret sang through the second verse, and then it was time for the choir to sing the chorus.

The choir sang out with all their hearts, "Shine on me."

Margaret chimed in with the lead, singing along with them "Shine on me," her voice echoed and filled the church.

People began to shout and cry out, "Yes, Lord, thank you, Lord. Praise your holy name."

The church was on fire. Rev. Reason jumped up out of his seat and yelled uncontrollably to Margaret, "Sing it, Margaret!"

Women were rocking back and forth in their seats and men's legs were shaking up and down. An usher was shaking her head back and forth vigorously and stretching out one arm, "Thank you, Jesus," she shouted out.

The choir continued to sing, and they came to the part, "Let the Light," and they sang it real sharp, then dragged out "from the Lighthouse," and then back to the ending, "shine … on … me."

When Margaret sang out, "Ohhhhhh," that did it: the church came apart. Then a couple of choir members fell limp, and they had to be attended to by a neighbor or just let loose.

Margaret then paused the piano and sang without music; her voice filled the air. The song had gotten to her like it did so many times, and she began to testify and sing at the same time. She yelled out, "O God, you've been so good to me. You've brought me from a mighty long way. You've been there when I had nowhere else to go."

Hank and Dexter were sitting on the bench holding onto each other. Margaret played, and the choir jumped back in, "Shine on me."

By the time the song was over, six people, including one child, had come forward to join the church. Pastor Reason had gotten the result he was looking for. He went through the process of bringing in the new members. Some were coming by Christian experience, and others were to be baptized.

After the reverend finished, he went back up into the pulpit and asked the congregation, "Didn't I tell you that we were in for a treat?"

Shouts of "Amen!" filled the room.

"Isn't Margaret special?" he continued. "The Lord has truly blessed us."

Church service was over now, and everyone was dismissed after the benediction. People began to crowd around Margaret to say hello and shake her hand and welcome her. Dexter and Hank were holding onto her legs and pulling on her dress and clinging on.

The excitement was beginning to scare Hank a little. "Baba, Baba," he yelled as he pulled on her dress. Mary walked over to Margaret and reached down to try and pick Hank up, but he refused to let her. "Baba, Baba, picky up, picky up!" he shouted.

Margaret bent over and picked up Hank. She couldn't keep track of so many hellos and greetings. People kept asking, "Are these your boys?"

Margaret answered, "Yes, this is Hank, and this is Dexter."

People's inquiries always followed with compliments of, "They are so cute," and "They're so good looking."

Margaret always replied, "Thank you."

One member said, "They are so pretty, just like girls."

"Oh, well, thank you, but they're boys," said Margaret.

"Oh, I can see that, but they are so pretty. Look at all this hair. Just so curly and fine," said the woman, as she ran her hands through Dexter's hair.

One of the deacons, Deacon Dell, walked over to introduce himself. Most of the members made way for him to get to Margaret. He was a handsome man with bright skin, curly hair, and a friendly face with a slight moustache. He approached Margaret and said, "Hello, charming Miss, I'm Deacon Dell. I just wanted to say what a pleasure it was hearing you today, and I believe that the Lord has something dear in store for us here at First Union with you here."

"Well, thank you." Margaret blushed. Deacon Dell was smooth and polished; his clothes were tailor-made, and his shoes were so shiny, Dexter could see his face in them.

"I just want to say that, if there is anything that you need here at First Union, don't you hesitate to ask me. If Gussy can't get it done, I'll get it done," added Deacon Dell.

"Thank you, Deacon Dell; I really appreciate that. Everyone has just been so nice to me; I really like it here. Thank you again," responded Margaret.

Deacon Dell looked down and saw little Dexter looking at his shoes. He was looking at his reflection in them. "Hey there, little man. What's your name?" he asked.

"Dexter," he replied.

"And how old are you?" asked Deacon Dell.

Dexter got shy and cowered behind his mother. "Answer the nice man, Dexter," Margaret said as she nudged him.

"Almost three," said Dexter, holding up his fingers.

"Wow, almost three; you're a big boy," said Deacon Dell.

"Yeah, I a big boy," replied Dexter. Deacon Dell smiled and chuckled.

The deacon then directed his attention to Hank. "Now, who might you be?" he asked. Hank turned his head and looked the other way behind his mother. Margaret said that he was shy and still a baby. Deacon Dell then took two quarters out of his pocket and gave one to Dexter, and then gave Margaret one for Hank.

"Baba, I got money," yelled Dexter.

"Now you put that in your pocket, Dexter," Margaret instructed.

"All right," replied Dexter.

Rev. Reason then made his way over to Margaret and asked if she would meet him in his office. "Yes, Pastor," she responded. Mary took the boys, and Gussy walked her to the office.

Once in the pastor's office, Margaret had a seat, and then the reverend said, "Margaret, you were fantastic today, just like I knew you would be. I was very pleased, and I know the Lord was too. Our Lord touched many hearts today through your music."

"Thank you, Pastor Reason," replied Margaret.

"You know, Margaret, I mentioned to you that I have a vision for this church and for the choirs we plan to have. Right now, we have the Mission Chorus and the Senior Choir. Our membership is growing, and I want to add a few choirs. Eventually, I'd like to see a Men's Chorus, an Ushers' Chorus, a Young Adults' Choir and a Junior Choir for the children.

"Now, we'll take it a step at a time. But I guess what I'm saying is that, if you will help me, I can help you. The more you take on, the more money you'll make. Now, how does that sound to you? It's going to take a lot of work and rehearsals," said the pastor.

"That sounds good to me, Pastor. Praise the Lord. He knows we could sure use the money," Margaret replied.

"Good, that's what I wanted to hear. Now, how would you suggest we start?" asked the reverend. They briefly discussed some of Margaret's ideas, and then BD came to escort her back to the family and home.

Over the next couple of years, the membership at First Union Baptist Church grew and so did the choirs. Before long, Margaret was playing for the Senior Choir, the Men's Chorus, the Young Adults' Choir and the Ushers' Chorus. The only choirs that she didn't play for were the Mission Chorus and the children's Junior Choir. Being responsible for all these choirs meant more work and more time away from home. Because the Senior Choir sang on the first and third Sundays, they practiced almost every week on Thursday nights. The Young Adults' choir practiced on Thursday, just before the Senior Choir, two Thursdays a month. The Men's Chorus practiced twice a month on Monday nights, and the Ushers' Chorus practiced twice a month on Tuesday nights.

Duane was seeing less and less of his wife. He would be off working odd jobs, when he could find work. Many times he'd come home when Margaret was leaving for work and take care of the kids, which he loved to do. At times it would begin to wear on him. It seemed like Fridays and Saturdays were the only times he could spend with his wife. When Margaret was at home, she was reading the Bible to the kids, practicing songs on the piano for work, or cooking and cleaning.

For Margaret, Duane had to take a backseat to the Lord. For Duane, he felt he always came second and they never had any fun together. Most of his fun was either with the kids when he kept them while she was away or at those times when he'd get out of the house with his buddies. His friends didn't come around too often, because they knew that Margaret didn't want their kind of fun around the children. Margaret and Duane were growing further and further apart.

One Saturday, everyone was at home; the boys were playing with their toys, Margaret was on the piano, and Duane was doing some repairs around the apartment. Margaret was the first one to smell smoke. She mentioned it to Duane, and he said he could smell it too. Duane said it smelled like it was coming from the hallway, and went to open the front door.

When Duane opened the front door, he could see a haze of smoke hanging in the hallway. Then he heard someone yell for help. The voice was coming from across the hall in Wilbur's apartment. Duane ran to the door and knocked hard, calling out to Wilbur. Wilbur opened the door and said his kitchen was on fire.

Duane ran into the apartment and over to the kitchen, only to see that it was in flames. The fire already had reached the ceiling. He quickly ran back and told Margaret to grab their coats and go outside. He then grabbed Dexter but didn't see Hank because he'd gone into the bedroom because of the smoke. Ironically, Dexter had been playing with his toy fire engine and complained that he dropped it when his father picked him up. He let Dexter grab the toy and then went to get Hank, and they all hurried outside.

Once out on the sidewalk, Duane rushed to the corner and pulled the fire alarm. He came back and told Margaret to stay put with the boys and said he'd be right back. Duane ran back into the apartment building and banged on the downstairs apartments, advising all the tenants to get out of the house. He then went back upstairs and banged on the apartment door next to theirs, waking John up who was asleep. Duane quickly went back into their apartment to get any monies and clothes he could carry. The flames were now coming out into the hallway.

By the time Duane got back outside, the fire department's trucks were just pulling up. The firemen could see the flames coming from the front windows of Wilbur's apartment and immediately went to work, pulling out their hoses to douse the flames. One crew ran inside with a long hose, and one crew stayed in front, watering down the top front window of Wilbur's apartment. Little Dexter was on the sidewalk down on his knees in front of the apartment building, pretending to douse the fire with his little fire truck. He looked so cute, and you couldn't tell him that he wasn't fighting the fire. To him it was real. He was a fireman.

Because of the fire, the Vizinaus had to move. They moved to a small apartment in an alley on Elm Street, which was still in the Fillmore District, but near Scott and Golden Gate Streets. It was a dead-end street on a slight hill, where people would dump trash at the bottom of the hill. The Vizinaus' building was about halfway down the street. The apartment was a small flat but with a little more space than the previous apartment, and Dexter and Hank had their own room.

Mary did not approve of the apartment. She complained to Duane about all the trash at the end of the street and that there were some little black kids living at the end of the street who were always out playing near the trash. She told Margaret never to let the boys outside to play with those "bad little so and so's" down the road and complained that it was filthy down there, with watermelon rinds and spoiled food in the street.

One of the main things Duane liked about the new location was that it was right around the corner from Golden Gate Elementary School. Dexter had just turned five years old and was now ready for kindergarten.

Margaret and Duane bought Dexter his first tricycle, and Duane would take him outside to ride. Dexter would ride around the corner and watch the kids play in the schoolyard. Dexter liked to watch the kids through the fence and asked to go inside the schoolyard to play with the rest of the children. Duane told Dexter he'd be going to school soon and would be able to play with them then.

One morning, Margaret and Duane were in the kitchen, having a disagreement about the children. Duane wanted to take the boys camping before the end of the summer, and Margaret was saying that she couldn't afford to let them go because she needed them to help her get around.

Sometimes their voices got a little loud, but the conversation was civil. Eventually, their voices woke Dexter up. He was lying in his bed on his back and opened his eyes. He lay there for a moment staring at the ceiling. There were carvings in the moldings around the borders of the walls and ceiling. Dexter studied the detail of the carvings, making note of their consistency.

Dexter soon realized he needed to use the bathroom. He looked over; Hank was still asleep. He decided to get up. He sat up and went to stand but dropped immediately to the floor. He reached over to pull himself up on the bed and again dropped to the floor. He then realized that he was unable to stand because his legs were limp.

"Baba, Daddy, come here," Dexter called out. He heard no response but could still hear them talking in the kitchen. "Baba, Daddy, come here!" he yelled louder. Duane walked into the room to see Dexter sitting on the floor with his legs turned to the side, and he had a look of hopelessness on his face.

"What's wrong, son?" Duane asked.

"I can't walk, Daddy. I can't get up," answered Dexter.

"What do you mean you can't walk? Come on, let me see you get up," instructed Duane.

Duane watched as Dexter struggled to get to his feet only to see him slump back down on the floor. Duane then reached down and picked Dexter up and tried unsuccessfully to stand him up. Dexter's legs just went limp and were unable to support him.

"Daddy, I got to pee pee," Dexter told his father. Duane picked him up and carried him to the bathroom so he could go.

Margaret went to the bathroom door and asked Duane what was wrong.

"I don't know; Dexter can't walk," he informed her.

"He can't walk? What do you mean he can't walk?" inquired Margaret.

"He can't walk. He can't stand, and he can't get up," said Duane.

"Well, what's wrong with him? Why can't he walk?" asked Margaret.

"That's what I'm trying to find out," Duane snapped back at Margaret.

"Well, we need to get him to a doctor," said Margaret.

"I know, I know," Duane said, as though Margaret were irritating him.

Duane then picked Dexter up and carried him to the front room and sat him up in a chair. He then started to do an examination. "Do you feel this?" Duane asked, as he touched Dexter on his legs.

Hank was now awake and walked into the front room, wondering what was going on, and then realized he was hungry. "Baba, I'm hungry," he said. Margaret called Hank over to her, and then he led her into the kitchen.

"How about this, son; do you feel this?" Duane said, pinching Dexter's legs.

"No," Dexter answered.

Duane was puzzled. Dexter couldn't feel anything in either leg. Duane then tried again to get Dexter to stand, only to see him fall immediately to the ground. Duane put Dexter back in the chair and told him to stay put. Duane then called their family physician, Dr. Lad Paul Hite. Dr. Hite had become their physician when the family moved back to San Francisco from Los Angeles. He was recommended to Margaret by a fellow church member and had proven to be an excellent choice.

Duane explained what was happening with Dexter over the phone, and Dr. Hite started asking lots of questions. After Duane answered no to just about every question, Dr. Hite instructed Duane to take Dexter to Children's Hospital and said that he'd meet them there about noon. He also said he'd call the hospital to make them aware they would be arriving soon.

Doctor Hite was always on time; he met Duane and the family right at noon. A nurse and another doctor accompanied Dr. Hite. The doctors were amazed at how Dexter didn't appear nervous or frightened, and Duane explained that Dexter never seemed to cry when he got hurt. He said Dexter seemed unlike most kids in that respect.

It was true; whenever Dexter fell down or got hurt with a cut or bruise, the most he'd say was, "Ouch," and rub it, but he never cried.

Dexter sat calmly as the doctor inspected him. There were no visible signs of any trauma. He didn't have any reflexes below the waist, and his blood circulation was normal. The doctors were puzzled, so they ordered some x-rays and a blood test. Dr. Hite had to return to his office, but he told Duane that he'd call him with the results of the test. He recommended Dexter be kept in the hospital for observation and said they were welcome to stay with Dexter, or they could go home and the hospital would care for him once he was admitted.

Dexter was a smart child. He also had great listening skills and had heard and understood everything that was said. Right away he started to protest, "Daddy, I don't want to stay in the hospital. I want to go home."

"Don't worry, Daddy is going to be here," Duane responded.

Margaret and Hank stayed at the hospital until Dexter was checked in and given a room. He had a room all to himself. By this time it was later in the day, and Duane needed to get Margaret and Hank home. Duane tried to explain to Dexter that he needed to take Baba and Hank home but that he would return. Now was the time for tears. Dexter started crying in protest and begged his father not to leave. All Duane could do was reassure him that he'd return soon.

Duane, Margaret, and Hank left to catch the bus home. Dexter's room was at the front of the hospital building with a window that looked out onto Broadway Street. Dexter was able to maneuver his way into a position so he could see out the window, and he watched as his family left the hospital to make their way to the bus stop. Duane was holding Margaret by the elbow with one hand, and he had Hank in tow with the other. Dexter continued to watch them as they stood at the bus stop waiting for the bus. Soon the bus came, and he watched as they boarded. He began to weep.

Dr. Hite made it back to the hospital before Duane got back. It was a little after five in the afternoon, and he had finished all of his appointments. Dexter had cried himself to sleep and had just awakened from a nap. He was happy to see Dr. Hite who had a sucker and a balloon for him, which gave him a little joy.

Dr. Hite was a man with a lot of class. He was a tall, blond-haired, blue-eyed, white man, with a lot of charisma and charm. His hair always seemed to be combed perfectly, and his clothes were always crisp and clean. This was the first time Dexter had seen him in a suit, because he usually wore a smock in his office. Dr. Hite drove a white Corvette and sometime made house calls to the Vizinau home when needed. Whenever Dr. Hite came to the house, Dexter and Hank would run outside to look at the car, and Dr. Hite would always take the time to talk about the car with them. Dr. Hite also had a beautiful brunette assistant named Geri. She always had a treat for Hank and Dexter when they came to visit, and Dexter had a major crush on her.

When Dr. Hite walked into the room with the balloon, a smile lit Dexter's face. Dr. Hite gave him the balloon and the sucker and then asked, "Now, how's my little friend doing?"

"I'm okay, Dr. Hite; I don't hurt. I can go home now," answered Dexter.

Dr. Hite just smiled and said, "Well, we have to figure out what's wrong first, son. Let's take a look and see what we can find out."

There were some x-rays in an envelope on a table that the doctor was expecting. There was a note on them, which indicated that there were no physical problems seen. "Well now, let's take a look," he said. The doctor held up the x-rays over his head in front of the ceiling lights and peered over them. "Nothing wrong there!" he said. Dexter asked if he could see them. Doctor Hite held them up in front of Dexter so he could see and explained to Dexter what he was looking at.

Dr. Hite then looked around and saw another envelope, which he was also expecting. It was the blood test, and the results of that were negative too. He read the results and told Dexter, "Well, there's nothing wrong with your blood either." Dr. Hite was puzzled; he couldn't figure out what was going on with Dexter. He walked over to the bed, pulled up the crib gate, and asked Dexter to try and pull himself up and stand.

Dexter tried to pull himself up, to no avail. Dr. Hite then reached over the bed and tried to stand Dexter up, asking him to hold onto the bed and stand. This didn't work either. Dr. Hite sat him back down and said, "Dexter, we can't seem to find anything wrong with you. There is no logical reason why you shouldn't be able to stand."

Soon, another doctor came into the room and walked over to the bed and said hello to Dexter and the doctor. He and Dr. Hite began to talk and walked out into the hallway. They were brainstorming on what to do next. Both agreed they needed to do more tests and would begin scheduling them for the next day.

Dr. Hite needed to leave, so he said good-bye to Dexter who was now saddened because he was going to be alone again. A nurse brought him some coloring books and a few toys to play with in his bed. After Dr. Hite left, Dexter began to weep again and stare out the window. Soon a bus pulled up to the bus stop, and Duane stepped off onto the curb. This made Dexter cheer up.

Duane entered the room, and Dexter was excited to see his father. He immediately asked if he could go home. Duane told him, "Not yet," and asked if anything had happened. Dexter filled him in as best he could, for a five-year-old, and then Duane called for the nurse. The nurse updated Duane on what had transpired and what was now recommended.

Duane played with Dexter and colored some pictures with him until it was time to eat dinner. Duane then fed Dexter and stayed with him until he went to sleep. Once Dexter was asleep, Duane caught the bus home.

The next day, Duane, Margaret, and Hank arrived at the hospital early and walked into Dexter's room, only to be surprised to see Dexter jump up, yelling about how he could stand up again. He was jumping up and down in the bed and saying, "See, see, I can walk now. I'm all right, Daddy, I can walk. Can I go home?"

Duane was amazed. But Margaret said that she had prayed all night and there was a prayer chain going between her, her friends, and the church, and that God had answered their prayers. "It's a miracle," she said. "Praise God." She felt her way over to the bed and grabbed her son, held him, and began to pray.

"Thank you, Lord; thank you, Jesus. We asked for a miracle, and you gave us one, dear Lord. You are all powerful and almighty. Only God answers prayers. God can heal all things, all pains and ills. We thank you for this miracle, dear God, and we thank you for your son, Jesus Christ, who you gave for our sins."

Now she was holding Hank and Dexter tight, giving praise to the Lord. "Say 'Thank you, Jesus,' boys, say 'Thank you, Jesus,'" she told the boys.

Dexter and Hank were repeating after their mother, "Thank you, Jesus; thank you, Jesus; thank you, Jesus."

Margaret had tears coming down her cheeks, and they were all very happy.

Duane stood there in amazement, and a nurse walked in and asked what was going on. Dexter yelled out, "I can walk, I can walk. God healed me, and I can go home now." The nurse looked on as Dexter was running around the room.

The doctors still were not ready to let Dexter go home. They had no answers as to what had caused Dexter to be unable to walk, and they sure had no answers as to why he was able to now. As far as Margaret was concerned, it didn't matter, because it was not in their hands. But she still respected her doctor and did as he instructed. Dexter was kept in the hospital another night and released the next day. They were never able to explain what had happened to him.

The next Sunday, Margaret and the boys went to church. Margaret was playing the piano, and the boys were sitting on the bench within arms' reach, as they always were. When the doors of the church were opened, Margaret asked one of the choir members to escort her to a seat in front of the pulpit. She told Dexter to take her hand and instructed Hank to stay put. Margaret and Dexter took a seat in front of the congregation.

When it came time for Margaret to speak, she stood up to testify with Dexter in her arms. He was starting to get heavy, but she held him anyway. She began to tell the congregation about their ordeal. She explained how Dexter had awakened early one morning and couldn't walk; he'd been unable to use his feet or legs. She talked about how the doctors hadn't been able to explain what was happening to her son and how they hadn't known what to do. The church members were looking on in disbelief and sorrow.

She then explained how she had known what needed to be done, and that she needed to call on Jesus Christ. Soon the amens started. Margaret said she wanted to thank those church members whom she'd called upon to do a prayer chain. She explained how it was their prayers that had made the difference.

Margaret went on to say, "I don't know about you, but I know that prayer changes things."

"Yes, Lord," someone shouted. The church was starting to appreciate Margaret's message. "The doctors didn't know what to do, but I knew what to do. My God is a mighty God," yelled Margaret. "He knows how to answer prayers. I told those doctors they didn't have to worry any more, and that it was the hand of God who healed my son, and they wouldn't be able to figure it out. I tell you that God can heal all things, and I have seen it for myself. I just want to say thank you to all of you who helped me pray, and thank you, Jesus; thank you, Jesus; thank you, Lord."

Margaret was overcome with joy, and an usher had to assist her to her seat. She was crying with joy and happiness, and Dexter noticed that Hank was crying too. Then he began to cry. Hank grabbed onto his brother, and they held on to each other and cried.

Rev. Reason was standing in the pulpit, and he, like everyone else, was choked up. He began to speak. "When you have no one else to turn to, who do you turn to?"

There were shouts of "Jesus," "Yes Lord," and "Hallelujah," from the audience.

The reverend raised his hand and shook his finger in the air. "He's my Doctor when I'm sick. He's my Lawyer in a courtroom. He's my Water when I'm thirsty and my Food when I'm hungry." Then he yelled out, "He's my All and Allllllll!"

The congregation was on fire, and Molly was on the organ, playing in synch with the reverend.

With the Holy Ghost in Rev. Reason, he continued, "You don't know what I'm talking 'bout?" Sweat was beading on his forehead. He pulled out his hanky and wiped it away. "How many of you know that Jesus will fix it?" asked the reverend. Hands began to go up all over the church. "How many of you know that God matters, that God can change things?" asked the reverend with a voice of authority. The music of the organ was moving like a drum beat. "Ain't he all right? I said, ain't he all right?" The pastor demanded acknowledgment from the congregation. Rev. Reason couldn't stop now. God had touched his soul and many souls in the church. They had heard the testimony of Margaret, a blind woman with two small boys, who had been touched by the grace of God.

"I don't know about you, but I'm going to be with my Father one day. I know my soul is saved. Is your soul saved? Do you know Jesus Christ? Have you accepted Jesus as your savior?" asked the reverend with a thundering roar. People were crying and shouting and praising God.

"If you haven't accepted Jesus, it's not too late!" said the reverend "Will you come?" he asked, with his hand outreached. "Won't you come?" he asked again. "Will you come and ask him to save your soul? Will you come and ask his forgiveness? For your sins?" he continued. "It's not too late. Come! Come now! Come now, that your soul may be saved," appealed the reverend in a pleading voice.

Four people got up and walked to the front of the pulpit and took seats along with the others who had come before Margaret got up to speak. It was a great day at First Union Baptist Church. God had made his presence known to all of those in attendance. If there was anyone in the church that had not been touched by what had happened that day, they were either nonbelievers or not paying attention.

It was the end of summer, and school was about to begin. Dexter was now ready to enter kindergarten, and Annie and Margaret had taken him to buy some new clothes for school. Dexter was excited and was looking forward to playing with the kids beyond the fence that he used to watch from his tricycle.

Having the school just around the corner was a real convenience for the Vizinau family. Margaret or Duane could each take turns walking Dexter to school, or, if need be, he could even walk or run to school himself. Once Dexter crossed the narrow street in front of his house, there were no other streets to cross and no traffic. In the morning, there were many other kids walking to the school, and Dexter could be herded right along with them. Whenever his parents decided to let him go on his own, he'd run all the way to the school.

Dexter enjoyed going to school, and he was a good student. His mother and father had taught him to respect older people and how to behave. He was always very attentive and courteous. He also liked to share his things and never caused any troubles. The teacher really liked Dexter, and he became one of her favorite students.

Margaret and Duane were growing further apart. Duane wanted to do many things with the boys. He wanted to explore with them and to teach them the things that a man teaches boys. He wanted to go fishing and camping and hiking. But he wasn't able to do those things, because Margaret was always taking them to church.

It was frustrating for Duane, and he didn't know how much longer he could take it. Also, Margaret was not a very sexual person, and Duane had a strong sexual appetite. He wanted to listen to his blues and his jazz, but Margaret didn't want it in the house. It was the devil's music, she said, and she didn't want it influencing the boys.

Margaret too, had come to see that things were not working out between her and Duane. They were arguing a lot and never seemed to agree on anything. The two of them sat down to talk things over, and they agreed they needed to divorce. They agreed to stay together until after Dexter finished kindergarten so that Margaret could move to a more affordable location without interrupting Dexter's schooling.

Margaret and Duane coexisted until the beginning of the summer of 1957.

9

The More

Right after I finished kindergarten, we again moved. This time it was to the other side of the Fillmore, without my father. It would be almost two years before I'd see him again. He moved to Los Gatos, up in the mountains, and I missed him a lot. Hank missed him too, but I don't think he missed Daddy as much as I did. He was the baby and my mother's heart. Whenever she was near, he was content. I was the older brother and had a little different role to play.

The Fillmore was alive and vibrant in the fifties. It was a Mecca for black people. There were many black businesses scattered around the Fillmore in those days, and the circulation of the black dollar was bountiful. Black commerce was good! We had barbershops and beauty parlors, nightclubs and restaurants, dry cleaners and shoe stores. There were clothing stores, pool halls, grocery stores, and furniture stores— all owned and operated by black people, up and down Fillmore and Divisadero Streets.

Just as there were quite a few legitimate black businesses in those days, there was also quite a bit of illegal business going on. There were pimps and prostitutes, drug dealers and gamblers, hustlers and gangsters aplenty as well. Everybody had a hustle, and black people were making money the best way they knew how.

My mother tried to shelter us from all of the devil's deeds, but I could see it and soon was able to recognize it as well. It was the pimps who caught my eye the most. They were always dressed sharp, with sharkskin and silk suits, and they kept their hair real slick. Do City barbershop was famous for giving out the toughest processes your money could buy, and if you were a pimp in San Francisco, you had to have a process.

These cats drove Caddies that were boss. They had their women four and five deep when they rode around the neighborhood. They would be "leaning" with their shades on and profiling like they were on top of the world.

We had moved to 433 Waller Street, between Fillmore and Steiner, one block away from the intersection of Fillmore and the famous Haight Street. It was a busy part of town. Actually, I don't know too many areas in the city that weren't busy, unless you were out in the Avenues or the Ingleside districts.

The building we lived in consisted of three flats, one on top of the other. Ours was the bottom flat, which was one story up from the street level. There was a flight of winding concrete stairs in the front of the apartment building, which had a curving iron banister. We used to slide down that banister. The stairway led to a porch that had three front doors leading to each apartment flat. Our front door was the one on the left, and it entered directly into the hallway of our apartment. On the street level, there was a side door that led to a walkway past several storage rooms to the backyard. There were families with children living on every level, and we all became very close. All the children thought they were cousins of each other.

The middle door took you to a flight of stairs that took you to the third-story flat, which was where "Aunt" Lucy lived. Her daughter, who lived with her, had two children named Victor and Loretta. Hank and I used to play with them often.

The door on the far right opened to a flight of stairs that went two stories up. That was where the Grahams lived. Their children were named Eddie, who was about seven years older than I was; John, who was about my age; and Darlene, who was about two years younger than me.

I used to play with John from time to time, but somehow he and I always seemed to get into a fight. Hank played with Darlene. Eddie liked to tease us a lot, but I really liked him and didn't mind the teasing so much. I don't think Hank cared too much for it, though.

Our flat went straight back. The front door opened to a hallway, and there was a doorway immediately on the left, which was a living room. We called it the front room; it had three windows looking out onto the street. The two side windows were at an angle so you could see up and down the block. Hank and I would go and look out the window often.

The next room down the hallway was a dining room that served as my mother's bedroom. It had two sliding double doors between it and the front room. Farther down the hall on the right, under the staircase that led upstairs, was a small bedroom that was our room. Inside there were twin beds, one for me and one for Hank.

Continuing on down the hall, past a bathroom on the left, there was a fork in the hallway where you could enter through a door on the left to a room that served as a family room, or a door on the right that lead to the kitchen. On the far wall of the kitchen was a door that led out to a back porch, where we had a washing machine. The back porch was enclosed and had a back door leading to an enclosed stairwell that led down to the backyard. There was also a window next to the washing machine, with a clothesline just outside that ran to a pole on the other side of the yard. Whenever kids were playing in the backyard, water would drip down on them from the drying clothes.

By the time I was six years old, I pretty much knew how to get just about anywhere in San Francisco on the bus. Hank and I took our mother almost everywhere she needed to go. Usually I'd take the lead, and Hank would be in tow. I can remember times when the three of us would be waiting at a bus stop, and some person would walk up and ask another person for directions on how to catch the bus to some place. I'd run over, jump into the conversation, and say something like, "You take the 22 Fillmore bus and get off at Geary, and then transfer to the 38, and it will take you to Sears." The person would look down at me in amazement, and another person standing near would acknowledge that it was the right way to go.

We took our mother everywhere—to the bank to pay her bills, to go shopping, to the dentist, to church, and to get her hair done. Anywhere in San Francisco that she wanted to go, we took her there, on the bus.

It was an exciting time for a small boy in San Francisco; there was always a lot going on. Times were changing and moving fast. The cars coming out of Detroit were getting longer and lower, with chrome everywhere. I can remember checking out the cars in detail every time I saw a new one go by. I began to learn the different makes and models.

The music was changing too. The new sounds could be heard playing from car radios as they went up and down the streets, and it seemed like everybody was going somewhere fast, at the same time.

I was about to enter the first grade, and Hank was ready to enter kindergarten. My mother enrolled us in John Muir Elementary School. It was at the corner of Page and Webster, one block up from Haight Street, and about three blocks from where we lived.

John Muir was a rough school. It was just a few blocks from the Hayes Street Projects, and a lot of tough kids went there. I got into fights almost every day. My mother would send me to school dressed real nice, and I'd come home with my clothes torn and dirty. She could always find out if I'd had a fight or fallen when she prepared to wash our clothes. She'd ask me what happened, and I could never lie; I'd tell her the truth.

My mother was always calling or visiting the school, complaining about my fights and the torn clothes, but the school never did anything about it. Usually the fights would be because one of the kids from the projects didn't like what I was wearing or that I didn't live in the projects or because I was defending my brother.

Hank was a crybaby, and any time he got into any trouble or someone pushed him or hit him, he'd start crying and come to find me. Then I'd have to go and fight; it happened a lot. Finally, my mother went directly to the board of education and requested a transfer to another school. One thing about my mother was that she was educated and she spoke very good English. She knew how to get what she wanted, and she knew how to get it done.

Margaret wouldn't accept no for an answer. If she had a problem she couldn't solve, all she had to do was talk to a deacon or the pastor at the church. The church had political clout, and there were many prominent Negroes at First Union.

Dexter had gotten into a fight for the last time. Margaret pulled Hank and Dexter out of John Muir, and they took the bus down to the board of education offices on Van Ness Avenue. She wasn't getting anywhere with the people at the school, and she wanted her sons transferred.

When they arrived at the board offices, she was told to have a seat, and they made her wait. She waited for over an hour, and when someone finally came to assist her, it was a flunky. She complained about the school and the fighting problems, and she also complained that the boys were not learning anything there. The flunky told her, "I'm sorry, but there's nothing that we can do. We have a policy here that the children have to go to school within the same geographical district they live in."

Margaret wouldn't accept that answer and demanded to speak with the superintendent of schools whom she called by name. Margaret, knowing whom to ask for, and by name, caught the flunky by surprise. The flunky now needed to get rid of Margaret more than ever, because she felt that if she didn't, her superiors would think she couldn't do her job, which was to run interference.

The flunky stood her ground and refused to get the superintendent, saying that he was in a meeting and could not be disturbed. Margaret jumped up and said, "We'll see about this. Come on, boys, let's go." She grabbed Hank and Dexter by the hands, and Dexter led them down the hall and out of the building and onto the bus for the ride home.

When Margaret got home, she made a phone call to one of the deacons, told him about what was happening at the school, and said that she wanted to transfer the boys somewhere else.

The deacon asked, "How about if we talk to the school?"

"No, I want my boys out of that school," demanded Margaret.

The deacon said, "Fine," and he'd see what they could do.

When Margaret kept Dexter and Hank out of school the next day, she got a call from the school inquiring why they were not in attendance.

She informed the school that the boys would not be attending there anymore and that she was having them transferred to another school. The lady on the phone tried to explain to Margaret that it was the only public school the boys could attend because of where she lived. Again Margaret said, "We'll see about that," and hung up.

About an hour later, the phone rang; it was the superintendent of schools. He asked if she could come in to visit him. Margaret gathered up the boys, they said a prayer, and then they caught the bus back down to the board offices.

This time Margaret was cool and calm. She explained the situation, and the superintendent was very hospitable. He asked her to give him a day or so to work on it. The next day, she got a call from the superintendent who said that the boys could be transferred to Dudley Stone Elementary School. It was on Haight Street in the middle of the Haight Ashbury District, about a mile from her house. He told her that it would be easy for the boys to catch the bus at Haight and Fillmore, which would drop them off right in front of the school. It shouldn't take them more than twenty or thirty minutes to get there.

The superintendent said that he had talked with the principal of Dudley Stone and made him aware of the circumstances. He informed Margaret that she could enroll them the next morning and that she would be expected. He also told her, if she had any more problems, to feel free to call him directly. Margaret was elated and thanked the superintendent then hung up the phone. She called to the boys and told them they'd be transferring to another school, and she wanted to pray and thank the Lord. They gathered around in a circle and bowed their heads and prayed.

Dudley Stone proved to be a much better school for the boys. It had a very diverse student body, and it wasn't difficult for the boys to get to. They'd leave the house in the morning, walk around the corner, and catch the bus on Haight Street at Fillmore. They could take any of the four lines that stopped there—either the 6, 7, 71, or 72 lines.

Taking the bus each morning was an adventure for the boys. The buses were packed with all types of people—anyone from laborers to doctors and nurses going to UC Medical Center, high school students on their way to Polytechnic High, as well as gang members and beatniks heading to the Haight.

Hank and Dexter made a whole new set of friends at school. But even though the school was integrated, the ethnic races still pretty much stuck together. It was during this period that Dexter began to get a little interested in some athletic play. He played four square, kickball, and volleyball; Hank was totally the opposite and didn't like to play sports at all. Dexter made friends with many of his classmates. There were Alvin, Manuel, Melvin, and Samuel. Hank basically only had one friend, and that was Michael. There was another boy in Dexter's class named Hector whom he never really quite got along with.

Sometimes the boys would walk home rather than catch the bus. Margaret always made sure the boys had enough money to get them back and forth to school or get themselves a snack if they got hungry. When they walked home, it was usually because they'd spent all their money and no longer had enough to catch the bus.

Walking home was always an adventure. They could begin by walking around the edge of Yerba Buena Park that was about a block from the school, or they could walk through the park that was hilly and wooded. If they walked around the edge of the park, they'd continue down Haight Street, heading home. This would take them by Hector's house, which was at the corner of Haight and Scott Streets.

Whenever the boys walked through the park, they'd walk down Waller Street, straight home. Walking through the park was interesting because they encountered all the park animals, like squirrels, different kinds of birds, and sometimes snakes and lizards. Yerba Buena Park was also rather dark because it had tall trees that screened out the sun.

Every now and then, they'd come across some teenagers lying on a blanket away from the path, making out. The boys would stop and watch them and laugh and giggle until the couple either stopped or told them to go away.

Walking down Haight Street was also an adventure, because it was a main thoroughfare. There was always a lot of traffic, with many people too. The boys usually walked down the right side of the street, since Hector lived on the left. At times, Hector would be outside, and at other times, he wouldn't. Sometimes, when the boys walked by, Hector would see them and not say anything, but at other times, he'd cross the street and approach them.

"Hey, Dexter, Hank," Hector would shout from across the street. The boys wouldn't say anything, and Hector would dash across the street and approach them. "Do you have any money?" he'd ask.

"No," Dexter would answer.

"Let me see," Hector would say, trying to put his hand in Dexter's pocket. Dexter would pull away. Hector would then try to search Hank's pockets, but Dexter would pull Hank behind him.

"We don't have any money," Dexter would shout. "Leave us alone!"

At this point Hector would then do one of two things—either he'd turn away and leave, or he'd punch Dexter.

Margaret was a devout Christian who read and practiced the Bible. She also instilled in her children the teachings of the Bible. Because Dexter used to get into so many fights at John Muir, she made Dexter promise to try and walk away from fights when they transferred to Dudley Stone. Dexter was good at keeping promises.

Margaret taught her sons to turn the other cheek when hit and never start a fight. Their uncle Charles taught them to do what their mother told them, but if someone hit them a second time, they had to defend themselves. But Hector always hit only once. Dexter wanted to fight Hector really bad, and Hank wanted his brother to beat him up, but Dexter always heard his mother's voice in the back of his head when trouble came, so he did his best to avoid it.

Because Dexter and Hector were in the same class, eventually they became friends—not the best of friends, but they were on speaking terms, and Hector began to leave them alone. Although Dexter was ready to fight, he really didn't think he could win because Hector was more rugged, stronger, and quicker than he.

It was now 1958; Dexter was seven and Hank was six years old. Margaret didn't like to let the boys play outside, but the pressure was on. All the kids from upstairs were outside, just at the bottom of the stairs, and they kept waving to Hank and Dexter in the window to come out and join them. Victor, John, and Eddie, as well as Butch and Edward from around the corner, were all there.

"Baba, can we go outside and play?" asked Dexter.

"No, I don't want you outside," answered Margaret. "I can't keep track of you when you're out there," she added.

"Please, please, can I go outside? All the other kids are out there," begged Dexter.

Margaret was under pressure and being stressed by Dexter. Hank didn't really care if they went outside or not.

"If I let you go out, you have to stay in front of the house so that, if I call you, you can hear me," Margaret told Dexter.

"Okay, I'll stay right in front," said Dexter.

"Come on, Hank, let's go outside," he said to his brother.

"No, I'll stay here. I'll stay with you, Baba," said Hank.

"No, you go outside with your brother," Margaret told Hank.

"No, I don't want to go. I want to stay here with you," answered Hank.

"Oh well, fine, stay here," replied Margaret.

Dexter opened the front door, stepped out, and slammed it behind him and headed down the stairs.

Victor and John were huddled up with Butch from around the corner in front of the apartment building. "Hi," Dexter said as he approached them. "What are you doing?"

"We're starting a gang," said John.

"Yeah, we're starting a gang," added Butch.

Dexter's eyes lit up and he asked, "Boy, can I be in it?"

"Yeah, you can be in it, but you can't tell your mother; you can't tell anyone who's grown," said Victor.

"Okay, I won't tell anyone," answered Dexter.

"We have to come up with a name," said Butch.

Just then, a brand-new, shiny red '57 Chevy drove by with the windows down. They could hear music coming from inside. The boys stopped and looked.

"Shooby do wop, wop, wop. Shooby do wop, wop, wop. My heart is crying, crying, lonely teardrops, my heart is never dry." The music was blaring from the radio. "Just say you will, say you will."

"That's Jackie Wilson!" said John.

"Yeah, he's really cool, man," added Butch.

"Yeah man, he's the best. He's got a really cool process," said Victor.

Dexter was listening, but he really didn't know what they were talking about. He didn't know who Jackie Wilson was.

"One of these days, I'm going to get me a process," said John.

Butch chimed in, "Yeah, me too!"

Dexter said, "Me too!"

Butch looked at Dexter and said, "You don't need a process, silly. You got good hair."

Dexter paused and thought, and then said, "So, I can still get a process if I want to."

"No you can't; your mama won't let you," said Victor.

Dexter couldn't answer that.

"So what are we going to call the gang?" asked Butch.

They began to think. There were several teenage gangs in the area. There were the Trojans and the Barbarians and the Tyrants. Butch then made a suggestion, "How about the Junior Tyrants?"

"Yeah, the Junior Tyrants, I like that," said John.

"Okay, let's vote. Raise your hand if you like the Junior Tyrants," instructed John. They all raised their hands, and the Junior Tyrants it was.

They also each agreed to put in a nickel; they'd have the money on Monday after school. They also said that anyone else who wanted to join had to pay a dime, and everyone had to pay a nickel every month. One of the storage rooms in the basement served as a clubhouse.

The gang never really functioned as a gang. On a couple of occasions, someone stole some candy from the corner store, but it never got more serious than that. One day, Dexter stole some ice cream, and the storeowner told Margaret. Whenever Dexter or Hank got into trouble, she'd have them bring her a belt. Then she'd grab them with one hand and whip them with the other. The boys never ran; they'd just jump around and holler while Margaret held on to them and whipped. Sometimes, depending on how bad the incident was, she'd have them strip. Sometimes it would be a belt, and other times it would be an electric extension cord.

The Junior Tyrants acted more like a club than a gang. They probably numbered a dozen members at the most. They could never raise enough money to buy any jackets, so usually they'd just wear white T-shirts.

One day, one of the members ran into the clubhouse and yelled, "Spider Willie is around the corner on Haight Street." Spider Willie was a crazy man. He lived somewhere in the neighborhood, but no one knew where. He was a white man with a crew cut and had a deranged look about his face. He looked mentally disturbed. Every so often, a group of kids would tease Spider Willie and make him chase them. Dexter had once seen it happen while watching from the front-room window.

All the kids jumped up, ran from the clubhouse, sprinted across the street, then down the block and up Fillmore to Haight. Dexter and Hank were never supposed to leave the block, but they followed the kids anyway.

When the gang reached Haight Street, they looked down toward Steiner and could see about five other kids heading their way. They were running from Spider Willie, and he was walking fast and deliberate, trying to catch them. He was shaking his fist in the air and yelling, "I'm going to get you; I'm going to get you," and spit was running down the side of his mouth.

One of the gang members said, "Come on," and ran down the block toward Spider Willie to catch up with the rest of the kids. Someone picked up a bottle and threw it at Spider Willie but missed. He stopped and started yelling and shaking his fist. Suddenly, someone threw a small rock and hit Spider Willie in the head; it drew blood. Spider Willie grabbed his head, looked at his hand and saw the blood, and took off after the kids. Everybody started running. When they got far enough ahead, they stopped and yelled back, "Spider Willie, Spider Willie." When the kids hit Fillmore, they ran a few feet down the hill and waited until Spider Willie appeared. As soon as he appeared, they yelled out again and started running. Dexter and Hank were in the middle of the crowd, running and yelling along with the rest.

When the group hit Waller Street, they made the right and started heading up Waller. Spider Willie was gaining ground, and Hank and Dexter were falling behind; Spider Willie was beginning to catch up. Dexter and Hank broke off from the group and darted across the street to try and make it to their house. Instead of going up the steps to the front door, they went through the side door on the street level to go up the back porch and through the back door. They made it to the side door, ran through it, and slammed it behind them.

Spider Willie was dead on their trail. The boys were frightened now. They ran to the backyard and started up the back stairs to their place. Dexter grabbed for the doorknob, but it was locked. Hank started banging; they could hear the footsteps of Spider Willie coming up the stairs. "Baba, Baba, open the door. Baba, open the door. Help, help!" they screamed.

Spider Willie came up the stairs; he had turned the twist in the stairwell and was staring them both straight in the face. He yelled, "I'm going to get you! I'm going to tear you apart. I told you to leave me alone!" And he started to move toward them.

Just then, the backdoor opened; Margaret had a broom, and she started swinging. Spider Willie ducked, and the first swing missed him. But Margaret caught him on the way back. She was yelling, "You leave my boys alone. Go, go, get out of here!"

She had found her mark with that last connection, and she stayed on it. Spider Willie was on the defense and trying to block her shots. He didn't even realize that she couldn't see.

He yelled back at her, "You make them leave me alone. Make them leave me alone."

"Go, go, now," she yelled back as she pulled the boys in behind her and slammed the door. Dexter and Hank were screaming and hollering and crying their eyes out.

Margaret went to the dresser to get her belt and told the boys to take off their clothes. Then she decided to get an extension cord. Whenever Margaret got the extension cord, she was really angry. The boys hated it because it hurt more, and it left welts on the skin.

Hank and Dexter were already crying, and when Margaret went to beat them, they were hysterical. "Didn't ... I ... tell ... you ... to stay ... in front ... of the ... house!" Margaret said, bringing the cord down across their backsides with every word.

"Yes, Baba, yes, Baba," they cried as she beat their butts. "I won't do it no more, Baba," they both yelled.

The boys hollered and cried, and when they finished crying, they were sniffling, "sup, sup, sup." Margaret made them take a bath, put on their pajamas, eat, and go to sleep. Usually, Dexter would lie awake for a while when he went to bed, but Hank had developed a habit of rocking himself to sleep. On this night, Hank lay down, did a couple of rocks, and went right to sleep. Both the boys slept really well that night.

After the Spider Willie incident, Margaret decided that the boys needed more to do. She asked some of her fellow church members about daytime activities that her boys could participate in, and someone recommended the Boys Club. The Boys Club was not far from the school, so they could go there right after they got out of school. It was also a place where they could play during the summer. Margaret enrolled them in the Boys Club, and they often went there.

On some Saturdays, Annie would catch the bus over to Margaret's and take her and the boys grocery shopping. From Margaret's home, they'd catch the bus down to Fillmore and Geary where Annie loved to do her food shopping. She'd bring her own brown paper shopping bags with brown paper string handles and fill them with groceries.

Annie was sixty-four years old now, and her small frame was beginning to look frail. But she was stronger than she looked and was as sharp as ever. She wouldn't buy her groceries at one store either. When they went shopping, she had to buy her greens at one store and her potatoes at another. Then she'd go to Frank Ontario's to buy her fish. After that, they'd head over to the pharmacy where she'd buy ointments, and then over to another store to get her gin, and finally to another for her rock candy. Whenever Annie came to Margaret's to go shopping, it was an all-day venture.

Dexter and Hank loved their great-grandmother, and she loved them. She'd always tell them the same stories over and over. She'd talk about her father and how he used to be a slave in Mississippi and that, when they had moved to Arkansas, she took care of him when he got old.

Annie would say, "My daddy got old and gray, and he got to be too much for me to lift. So I called the white doctors to come out to the house to look at Daddy. They looked at my daddy, and then they said they wanted to put him in the hospital to be cared for." Then she'd continue, "I looked those doctors straight in the eye and asked them, 'Doctor, is it the hospital, or is it the poor house?' And the doctor looked at me and said, 'It's the poor—' and I cut him off; I said, 'Don't come back. My daddy done worked too hard and too long to die in the poor house.'"

Annie would explain how the doctor said, "Well, if that's how you feel, we'll send a nurse out here three days a week to help you take care of him."

Annie would then say, "You see, if you treat people right, they'll treat you right. Always remember to 'Honor thy mother and father, that thy days may be long.' This is the only verse with promise."

After shopping, they'd all head home on the bus, with Dexter holding onto Momma and Hank holding onto Baba.

That summer, Margaret began a full schedule of directing four choirs at First Union. She now had responsibility for the Senior Choir, Ushers' Chorus, Men's Chorus, and the Young Adults' Choir. She also started a singing group with Aunt Lucy who lived upstairs. They called themselves The Evangelist Singers of San Francisco.

To the boys it seemed like they were at choir rehearsal all the time. Most of their friends were either home watching television or still playing outside. Sometimes Margaret got someone to babysit the boys, but on most occasions she took them with her. They'd usually catch the bus to the church, and then someone would give them a ride home.

Margaret would sit at the piano, and Hank and Dexter would be sitting less than seven feet away on the front-row pew. If they got too loud, all she had to do was look in their direction, and if they continued, she was in vocal range to restore order. The choir members got a kick out of watching Margaret direct them, getting two boys, six and seven years old, to behave. Hank and Dexter usually had some kind of toy or coloring book to keep them busy, but it still wasn't always enough.

Margaret was enjoying doing the Lord's work, but all Hank and Dexter could hear was, "Shhhh. Sit down; be quiet and stay still." But then there were times when the music would get real good, and the boys would have to take notice; they'd begin to clap and sing along.

Sundays could sometimes be long and tiresome for the boys. They might start the day with Sunday school and then morning service; these two programs would go from 10:00 a.m. until 1:30 p.m. Sometimes there would be a special afternoon program too, like a musical or a visiting church, or they may be visiting another church for their afternoon program. On these occasions, they'd have dinner at the church around 2:00 p.m. after morning worship, with the afternoon program beginning at 3:00 p.m. Sometimes there was Baptist Training Union (BTU) that began at 5:00 p.m., then afterward, evening worship at 6:00 p.m. So sometimes they could be at church from 10:00 a.m. until 9:00 p.m. when evening worship ended.

Margaret saw that it was getting to be quite a bit for the boys, so she let them go to visit their grandparents after morning service. This was perfect for the boys, because they loved to go and visit Nanny (Mary) and Momma (Annie) every chance they could get. The boys had a whole different set of friends in the Bayview neighborhood where the Dillards lived. They could play outside or in the backyard, and sometimes Uncle Charles took them different places for fun. Nanny would always be cooking, and Granddaddy (BD) would be listening to the baseball game on the radio. Occasionally Momma would cook as well.

Annie spent most of her time sitting in her room in her rocking chair, watching television and dipping snuff. One Sunday, the family was sitting around the table eating dinner when Annie said, "They got a colored boy going to be on Ed Sullivan tonight."

Charles jumped in and said, "Yeah, Sam Cooke is going to be on."

"Nanny, can we watch it, please?" asked Dexter.

And Hank chimed in, "Please, Nanny, please."

Mary knew she was supposed to be ready to take Hank and Dexter home not long after dinner, but she knew that if the boys stayed long enough to watch Ed Sullivan, they'd have to spend the night. "Your mother is going to be looking for you tonight; you probably should go home," said Mary.

"No, she won't, she has to play tonight," answered Dexter. Mary had forgotten, so that meant that the boys would need to spend the night anyway.

"Boy, you don't know who Sam Cooke is anyway," said Mary, teasing Dexter.

"Yes, I do; he sings that song, 'You Send Me,'" replied Dexter.

After hearing Dexter's response, Mary said, "Now, how you know that song, boy? You know your mother would have a fit if she knew you knew about that music."

"I hear it all the time in cars riding down the street, and I was upstairs in John's house, and they were singing it and talking about Sam Cooke. That's how I know," replied Dexter.

Mary looked at Dexter and thought, "Um, smart boy." So she decided to let them watch it. "Okay, you can watch it," she told the boys, and they both celebrated.

That night, they all gathered around the black-and-white TV and watched Ed Sullivan. As the other acts were performing, the boys kept asking, "When is Sam Cooke coming on?"

Annie said, "Probably last. You know how they treat colored people. Ain't no different on Ed Sullivan." As the program drew near the end, Annie yelled, "Shhhh, be quiet. He's getting ready to come out now!"

Ed Sullivan walked out onto the stage and faced the audience. He began to speak and explain that he was sorry, but they had run out of time, and Sam Cooke would not be performing. Everyone in the room expressed their disappointment. "What? I don't believe this," said Mary.

Annie became angry and voiced, "You see, that's what I was talking about. Let this be a lesson to you boys. I don't care how much money you make or how famous you get, you still colored. They always let you know your place. Bastards, damn crackers, that's what they are, all of 'em. Ed Sullivan too!"

Uncle Charles was angry and expressed his disappointment too. It was time for the boys to go to bed, and it was a real letdown for everyone in the house. It served as a reminder that colored people were treated as second-class citizens in America. The next day, all the kids in the neighborhood were talking about what had happened to Sam Cooke. The boys were outside playing, and some grown people who were milling around talking about how racist it was started talking about white folks.

Dexter and Hank hadn't really experienced any form of racism that they could recall. They knew they were colored, but their father was white, and he always treated them well, and so did his friends. With all the talk about white people, Dexter began to think of his father; it was almost two years since they'd last seen him, and Dexter missed him very much. His father had called last year for his birthday and for Hank's birthday. He'd also called at Christmastime, but other than that, they hadn't heard from him.

Dexter soon became very sad. He felt like crying, but he didn't want anyone to see him. So he said he had to go to the bathroom. He stood up and walked into the house, went upstairs to the bathroom, and closed the door. He then went over to the toilet, closed the seat, sat down, and began to cry. He got down on the floor and cradled the toilet in his arms and wept. Dexter was moaning quietly and calling to his father, "Daddy, Daddy, please come back. Please."

After sitting on the floor for a little while, he got up and looked at himself in the mirror. He saw the tracks of his tears and knew he couldn't walk out of the bathroom looking this way, so he washed his face and then went back outside to play.

It seemed like the Lord had heard Dexter's prayers, because in a couple of weeks the boys were at home with their mother when there was a ring at the door. It was their father. They ran to the door, and when they saw that it was Duane, they fought to open the door. "Daddy!" they yelled.

Duane walked through the door wearing a scruffy beard. He picked up both boys, one in each arm, hugged and kissed them and almost cried. They were so happy to see each other. Margaret knew the boys had missed their dad, and actually, she had too. She was expecting him but hadn't told the boys. The last thing she wanted to do was say that he was coming and then have him not show, so she just waited to see.

What Duane didn't tell Margaret when he said he wanted to visit was that he wanted to bring the boys home with him for a couple of weeks. Duane knew that if he'd asked her over the phone, she'd have said no, like she used to when they were younger. He figured he'd ask her in front of the boys and gain their support. It proved to be a good idea, because when he brought it up, the boys rallied together and asked, "Can we go, Baba? Can we? Please?"

Margaret had never been without the boys since she and Duane had divorced. Not only was she very protective of them, but they were also essential to her ability to get around easily. It would be more difficult to get around without them. But she knew she couldn't be selfish, and he was their father. She had to give in to the pressure.

Duane took the boys to his home in the mountains of Los Gatos, about fifty miles from San Francisco. His parents had moved out of the house to another home in King City, so they let Duane stay in the little mountain cottage. It was a small place nestled in the forest, about a mile from Highway 17, down some twisting roads. There was a narrow trail that led down to a small lake that had a beach and a swim platform a few yards out from shore. It was a great place for the kids to play.

Duane spent all his time with the boys, playing and having fun. He took them hiking, and they also played at the beach during the day. At night they played games, and Duane taught them how to play chess and checkers. He also had a pet cat he had saved from the lab at the university, because the university was planning to put it under. The cat was part of a science project, and instead of walking like most cats do, it hopped like a rabbit. The boys thought it was the strangest sight.

One day, Duane and the boys were sunbathing on the lakefront. Duane got up and told the boys to watch him swim. He demonstrated how he was using his arms to pull through the water and how he was kicking his feet to push. He asked the boys if they saw and understood what he did, and they both said they did.

Duane then took Hank and Dexter, one at a time, into the water where it was just above their heads and held onto them to let them practice what he had shown them. They splashed their arms and kicked their feet while Duane pushed and pulled them around.

After practicing a few more times, Duane said to Dexter, "Climb on my back and hold on." Dexter mounted Duane's back as if going for a horseback ride, and Duane walked into the water until the water came above his waist, and then he began to dog paddle out to the swim platform. When he reached the platform, he helped Dexter climb onto it and told him to stay put. Duane then went and repeated the same process with Hank. Duane sat the boys on the platform and had them watch as he demonstrated again how to swim. Hank and Dexter watched him closely. Duane climbed onto the platform and grabbed Dexter and said, "Okay, swim," then threw him into the water.

Dexter hit the water and went under. He took a mouthful of water and began to splash his hands. "Hold your breath," Dexter could hear his father say as he and Hank looked on. Dexter held his breath and kept splashing.

Duane shouted, "Kick your legs and move your arms. Swim, come on, swim over here." Dexter started kicking and splashing his arms, and he began to reach for the platform. He made it.

Hank was scared and didn't want to do it, and he voiced his apprehension. Duane just grabbed him and threw him in the water. Hank was able to swim back to the platform too. "Good job, boys. You did great," Duane said, laughing. Next they got into the water and held onto the platform while Duane taught them how to tread water and how to dog paddle. From that day forward, the boys never feared the water, because they could swim.

In the evenings when Duane began to cook dinner, he'd put some records on the record player. Duane's taste in music was now changing to include the sounds of rock and roll. The boys were in the living room playing with a few small toys while the music was playing:

> I know a cat name Way Out Willie
> He got a little chick name Rocking Chilly
> He'd walk, and stroll, and Suzy Cue
> And do that crazy Hand Jive too
>
> Hand Jive
> Hand Jive
> Hand Jive
> Doing that crazy Hand Jive

The sounds of Bo Diddly had Hank and Dexter bopping their heads and tapping their feet while their father fixed their meal. Duane would put on Elvis Presley, and the boys would try to imitate Elvis, the way they'd seen him dance on TV.

Duane was getting a kick out of seeing the boys dancing, so he kept the music going. He put on "Hound Dog," "Blue Suede Shoes," and "Jail House Rock." Next, Duane put on Chuck Berry's record, "After School," and Dexter wanted to play it over and over again. He played it until Duane couldn't take it anymore.

Duane thought that, if Margaret knew what the boys were doing, listening and dancing to the devil's music, she'd have a fit, and he'd have a big fight on his hands.

Two weeks went by real fast, and Duane had to return his sons home to their mother. He'd had a great time with his boys, and they'd had a great time too. It was something that all of them really needed.

For Dexter, it was more than just a visit with his father; it was a time out from responsibility. When he and Hank were at home, it meant more work than play. But both of the boys missed their mother and were ready to go back home.

Not long after having returned from their visit with Duane, Dexter fell off his bicycle. Charles had given him the bike, but it was entirely too big for him. Dexter's arm was broken. He'd been trying to ride with Hank sitting on the back fender and had tried to break a fall with his arm. When he hit the ground and put his arm out, it popped. Dexter got up from the fall and his arm was limp. He told Hank to walk home, and he rode home on the bike using one hand. He got to the house and walked inside.

Margaret's friend Kiddo from the church was visiting. Dexter walked up to his mother and announced, "Baba, I broke my arm."

"Oh boy, come over here and let me see," Margaret replied. She reached down, felt his arm, and tried to raise it. The pain shot up Dexter's arm. Up to this point, he hadn't cried. But now, Dexter yelled out in pain, and Margaret quickly released it. At this point Dexter began to cry from the pain.

Kiddo examined the arm and noted some swelling. She recommended that Dexter be taken to the hospital, so Margaret said she'd take him to the doctor the next day. Dexter lay in bed all night in pain, and Margaret took him to Dr. Hite the next day. He had a fracture just below the shoulder of his right arm and had to be put in a cast for six weeks.

After the summer, the boys were back in school. They were now seven and eight years old. As the school year progressed, Dexter and Hank were beginning to read pretty well. Dexter was ahead of Hank in spelling and reading, not only because he was ahead of Hank in school, but also because he read more often for his mother.

Now that the boys were beginning to read, it was time for them to learn the Bible. Margaret wanted them to know the Bible in depth. So every Saturday, they'd hold Bible study and go over a scripture that she had assigned them during the week.

Margaret had a bookcase on wheels that housed all her Bibles. They were immense books of Braille, and there was almost one book for each book of the Bible. Most of these Bible books had hard cardboard covers that were covered in a burgundy vinyl. They measured about twelve inches by fourteen inches and could be up to five inches thick; they were very heavy. The titles were printed in gold lettering on the edge of each book and also printed with raised Braille writing. Inside there was no writing, only Braille.

One Saturday, Margaret called the boys into the family room where she was seated in her rocking chair with a Bible in her lap.

"Hank, Dexter, do you have your Bibles?" Margaret asked.

"Yes, Baba," they answered in unison.

"Hank, what were you supposed to read?" she asked.

"Proverbs 19 and 18," Hank replied.

"All right, let's turn our Bibles to Proverbs 19 and verse 18. It's in the Old Testament. Let me know when you've found it, and Dexter, you read the verse," instructed Margaret.

"Cha … Cha …?" Dexter was looking for help.

"Chasten," said Margaret.

"'Chasten thy son while there is hope, and let not thy soul spare for his crying,'" Dexter read slowly, one word at a time.

"Good, that's good, Dexter," Margaret praised.

"Now Hank, can you tell me what this verse means?" asked Margaret. There was silence; he couldn't answer. "Dexter, do you know?" she asked. Still silence. "All right, let's take a look at it together. You follow me and read." Margaret put both hands over the pages of her Bible. One hand found the place to start, as a guide, and then the other hand scanned across the lines to read.

"'Chasten thy son,'" she said. "That means to punish, like spank or get a whipping. It means to punish your children."

Hank and Dexter looked at each other; they were hoping they hadn't done anything wrong. Dexter pointed to Hank and asked silently, just moving his lips, "You?"

Hank shook his head no and pointed to Dexter, "You?" Dexter shook his head too.

Margaret continued, "'While there is hope.' That means, while there is still time. Time, as in, before you grow up! It means to punish your children for sinning before they grow up. Now, Hank, you read the next part."

Hank began to read, "'And let not thy soul spare for his crying.'"

"Can either one of you tell me what this means?" asked Margaret.

Hank and Dexter looked at each other, and there was silence.

"It means, don't let the crying stop me from punishing you."

This was some pretty strong stuff for Hank and Dexter. They didn't know what to think or where this was going. They just had the feeling that they had done something but didn't know what it was.

"All right, Dexter, now can you tell me what we just learned here?" asked Margaret.

"It means that you're supposed to whip us while we're small, because when we get big, we'll be too big for you to whip us," answered Dexter.

"That's right. Amen!" said Margaret.

"Okay, let's turn over to chapter 22 and verse 6 in the same book of Proverbs," instructed Margaret. The boys fumbled around a little, but they found it. "All right, Hank, your turn to read," instructed Margaret.

"But I read last time," said Hank.

"That's okay, you read anyway," said Margaret. Dexter sat there smiling. Hank looked at him a little angrily, and then Dexter stuck out his tongue, and Hank shook his fist back at him.

"Hank, go ahead, read now. Listen, Dexter, 'cause I'm going to ask you what it means," instructed Margaret. Hank stuck his tongue out at Dexter, because now he was on notice.

"'Train up a child in the way he should go, and when he is old he shall not depart from it,'" read Hank.

"All right, Dexter, what does it mean?" Margaret asked.

Dexter didn't know.

"It means that I have to teach you about what is good and what is bad, now, while you are little, so that when you grow up, you'll know what's right and what's wrong," said Margaret.

Margaret continued, "This is why I have to punish you and spank you. Baba doesn't like whipping you. It hurts me more than it hurts you, but I have to do it because God said I have to. I have to teach you how to be good Christian boys. That way, when you grow up, you can teach your kids. When we all leave this world, we can be together in heaven and live forever with God and with one another."

"Baba, you not going to die, are you?" asked Hank.

"Not anytime soon, son. Not if the Lord is willing. But we all have to die sometime. And when I die, I want to go to heaven. I don't want to go to hell and burn forever with the devil. Do you?" asked Margaret.

"No, not me!" said the boys.

"That's good, boys. I want you to grow up and be good strong men and know the Lord. Let's bow our heads and pray," said Margaret, and she led the boys in prayer.

One day, Dexter went outside to play with some of the other Junior Tyrants; Hank decided to stay in the house. There was a small store at the corner of Waller and Steiner. The little gang decided they wanted some ice cream, but they didn't have enough money to buy for everybody. So they decided to steal it. Dexter didn't want to go along with it, but he knew he had too. They devised a plan where one of the boys would walk to the back of the store and trip. When the storekeeper went to see what happened to the boy, the others would dart into the store and go to the freezer and get the ice cream. Just as they were about to leave for the corner store, Margaret called Dexter, and he had to leave his friends. He was never so happy for his mother to call him in. He had stolen before, and he regretted it. He also knew it was a sin, and he probably wouldn't get away with it. The gang carried out the plan and got caught.

Margaret had called Dexter into the house because she'd been informed that there was a woman who lived in the next block who was holding Bible classes for children during the day, three days a week. She wanted Hank and Dexter to go. "Ah, Baba, come on, I don't want to go to Bible class. We're already in church all the time. We want to have some fun," said Dexter, voicing his displeasure. Hank didn't say anything.

"You should be having fun in the name of the Lord. There are plenty of things you can do with God that are fun. Look, there are going to be other kids there, and I hear they play games and have all sorts of fun. Now, the address is 312 Waller Street. It's near the corner of Webster Street. I just got off the phone with Sister French, and she says they're just getting ready to start now, so she's expecting you. She'll call me and let me know when you get there. Here's ten cents each for dues," Margaret instructed the boys.

Dexter was really upset, but Hank didn't much care. They walked down the block and crossed Fillmore Street, taking their time getting to Sister French's apartment. When they got there, they rang the doorbell, and the door opened. Someone at the top of a long flight of stairs had pulled a handle at the top of the stairs that opened the door automatically. Dexter and Hank walked into the apartment and immediately noticed a peculiar smell. It didn't stink, but it wasn't a good smell either. It was the smell of scented candles burning.

At the top of the stairs, there was a short, dark-skinned, fat lady waiting for them, grinning. Both boys were immediately frightened of her. She had huge white teeth and salt-and-pepper hair. She had wide hips and a big butt, and when she walked, she waddled back and forth.

"Come on in, boys. You must be Hank and Dexter. I've heard a lot about you boys, and I know your mother is a good Christian woman," said Sister French. Hank and Dexter noticed that she had a belt in her hand. "Go on in there with the rest of the kids," she instructed, raising her arm and pointing the way with the strap in her hand.

The boys entered a small room where there were six other kids. They looked at Hank and Dexter as if to say, "Boy, you just don't know what you're getting yourself into," and they had scared looks on their faces.

The room had pictures depicting stories from the Bible all over the walls. There were crosses and crucifixes everywhere. Small seats and benches cluttered the room. Hank and Dexter took a seat. Sister French gave a Bible to each of them, told them where they were reading, and to open their Bibles and follow along. She then told a little girl named Diane to read out loud, and she instructed a little boy named Michael to pay attention.

Diane started reading the scripture, and everyone followed silently. Then, all of a sudden, "Whop," went the sound of a belt going through the air and finding its target. "Michael, that was the third time I had to tell you to pay attention. I mean, pay attention," said Sister French, as Michael began to cry. His mouth opened wide but there was no sound. The sting of the belt was so sudden that Michael couldn't get the sound out at first. Then he let it all out, "Wahhhh," he cried.

"Be quiet," snapped Sister French. "If you did as you were told and paid attention, then you wouldn't get into trouble. You got the devil in you, boy, and I pray each day to save you."

Dexter and Hank were new to this Bible class, but they soon became very familiar with the rules. Margaret sent the boys to attend Sister French's class as often as she could. Dexter was very careful to pay attention and not attract attention. But every now and then, Hank tested Sister French's patience.

One day, one of the other boy's mothers had reported to Sister French that her son was suspected of stealing at a local corner store. Sister French told the boy's mother that she'd find out the truth. She took a rope with a makeshift noose in it and threw it over the door. She then took the boy and put the rope around his neck, tightened it, and pulled it tight over the top of the door. The boy started crying, and Sister French said, "Repent. Repent now so that the Lord will save your soul. If you don't, I'm going to hang you, and when you die, your soul will go to the devil and burn forever in fire and brimstone. Repent. Repent now. Did you steal from the store? Did you?"

"Yes, I did it. Don't kill me. Please don't kill me," cried the boy.

Sister French then said, "Ask the Lord to forgive you. Ask him."

The boy was standing by the door with a noose around his neck, crying and sobbing, with tears streaming down his face. All the children looked on in fear. "Forgive me, forgive me, Lord," said the boy.

Sister French loosened her grip on the rope and opened the loop to take it off his neck. Although she'd never have hung the boy, she accomplished what she wanted to—instill the fear of God in him and the other children, and have them fear her.

There were times when Sister French was kind and gentle, but she could switch on you in the name of the Lord in a minute. Everyone was well behaved when they were in her house.

Almost a year had passed, and the boys hadn't heard a word from their father. Christmas had come and gone, and Dexter wondered where his father was and what he was doing, because he really missed him. It was Easter Sunday, and that meant the children in the church were putting on a special program. Margaret had Hank and Dexter practice a song for the program. They went over the song again and again.

The children's program was the first thing on the agenda for the morning service. First there was a play put on by the children, where they reenacted the crucifixion and the rising of Christ. The Junior Choir sang a song, and then it was time for the Vizinaus. This was the first time Hank and Dexter had gotten up in front of an audience to sing. Both of the boys had nice voices, and they both knew how to carry a note.

Margaret sat at the piano, and the boys stood next to her and faced the audience. Dexter and Hank were both smiling and trying hard not to laugh. Margaret started the introduction, and then the boys sang, "Yes, Jesus loves me; yes, Jesus loves me. Yes, Jesus loves me; the Bible tells me so."

They were so cute; Margaret and Annie had taken them shopping for some new clothes, and they were all dressed up and had fresh haircuts. Dexter was shy, being in front of all those people, so when he sang, he was not singing at the top of his voice. On the other hand, Hank loved being up front, and his voice wailed. Margaret was coaching the boys on, and she played deliberately with each word they sang. She was proud of the way they sang.

After church, several members approached Margaret to compliment her on her sons. One member said, "Margaret, your sons were wonderful. They sounded so nice. And that Hank, he has such a beautiful voice, and they look so handsome all dressed up. Girl, I tell you, when these boys grow up, they're going to break some hearts. Look at their pretty hair; I just want to put my hands through it," said the woman as she rubbed Dexter's hair. He began to blush. "Ah, he's blushing. You are so cute," she said.

Margaret thanked the woman. She loved to get compliments on her sons, and she received them frequently everywhere they traveled. More members were approaching Margaret. The boys saw Deacon Dell standing near the corner. "Hank, there's Deacon Dell," said Dexter, and they both took off running.

"Hi, Deacon Dell," yelled the boys, interrupting his conversation with another deacon.

Deacon Dell stopped and looked down and smiled at the boys and said, "Well, here's my favorite brothers. Boys, you sounded so good today. Hank, where did you learn to sing like that?"

Hank smiled and said, "From my mother."

"I bet you're right about that. Your mother is my favorite singer; yes, she is," said Deacon Dell.

Dexter and Hank stood there waiting. Deacon Dell had a quarter for them every Sunday. He reached into his back pocket, pulled out his wallet, then squatted down on his knees. "Now, I have a special treat for you boys. I'm proud of how you sang today and also how you take care of your mother. You boys keep on taking care of your mother, now, you hear me?"

"Yes, Deacon Dell, we will," answered Hank and Dexter.

Deacon Dell took two one-dollar bills out of his wallet and gave one to each of them. "Thank you, Deacon Dell," they yelled as they ran off to their mother.

That evening, Margaret had the boys take their baths, put on their pajamas, and get ready for bed. When the boys were ready for bed, she entered their room and had them get on their knees to say their prayers. Margaret kneeled down between both of them, and they all folded their hands. She told the boys to start. "Now I lay me down to sleep. I pray the Lord my soul to keep. And if I die before I wake, I pray the Lord my soul to take. Amen," the boys prayed in unison.

Margaret began to pray. "Dear Lord, Heavenly Father, I want to thank you, dear Lord, for giving me these two boys. If it weren't for them, dear Father, I don't know where I'd be. They're good sons, Father, and I just want to say thank you, Jesus." Margaret's throat tightened. "Lord, let us walk in faith. For without you in our lives, where would we be? Keep us in your heart, dear Father. Watch over us, and I pray that you stay with us throughout our travels," Margaret said as she cried. "All these blessings, we ask in your Holy Son, Jesus's name. Amen," she finished.

Margaret got up and dried her eyes and sat on the side of the bed. "Sons, come here to your mother," she said as she kept wiping her eyes and sniffing. "Let me take a look at you."

Hank and Dexter stood in front of their mother. She took them one at a time, placed her hands on their faces, and traced the outlines of their faces. She placed her hands on their heads and ran her fingers through their hair. She traced their heads and outlined them from the top of their heads down both sides to their ears and on down to their shoulders. She hugged and kissed each boy, one at a time. She then got up and walked out of the room saying, "You boys get into bed and go to sleep."

Hank and Dexter got into their beds and pulled up their covers then lay down to sleep. Margaret went into her bedroom and started crying. She walked over to her bed and fell to her knees. She cradled the covers in her arms and laid down her head. "O God, you know I never ever complain, Father. I don't know the reasons why you chose for me not to see, and I don't question them, Lord. But I pray that just for once, dear Father, I could see what my sons look like. If I could only see them once, Lord Jesus, just once, Lord, just once!" She stayed there on the floor, kneeling at her bed, and wept until she fell asleep.

In the boys' room, Hank had rocked himself to sleep, but Dexter was awake. He heard his mother's cries and listened to her prayer. Dexter was going on eight years old, and he'd come to know things were different in their family than most other families. He knew of his importance to his mother and of his responsibility. His father had told him how important he was to his mother every chance he could when he was younger. So did Nanny, his grandmother.

Not too often did Dexter feel sorrow for his mother; perhaps because she never felt sorrow for herself. But on this night, he did feel it; he felt sorrow. His mother's cries had touched his heart and brought him pain. Dexter began to weep. He turned over and silently cried and asked God, "Why, Lord, why?"

A few months later, the family went to church, and in the morning service, Dexter noticed that Deacon Dell was sitting in the church pulpit. He nudged Hank and pointed to Deacon Dell. Usually Deacon Dell was down in front with the rest of the deacons.

When it came time for the altar prayer, Rev. Reason got up and announced that Deacon Dell was now an ordained minister. The congregation displayed their happiness and acceptance with the usual, "Amen!" Next, the reverend said that Deacon Dell would do the altar prayer, and the next week he'd deliver the sermon. Usually, when the altar prayer took place, Dexter would lower his head and not pay much attention to what the preacher was saying. He wouldn't be praying either; he'd just let his mind wander. But he paid attention to Deacon Dell's prayer and thought it was a good one.

On this Sunday the Junior Choir was singing. Margaret didn't direct the Junior Choir, so she had to get up from the piano and move back and forth from the piano bench to the pew seat, between sets. Hank helped her move.

Dexter and Hank were still used to sitting within arm's reach of the piano, and this always gave them an up-front view of all the choirs. As the Junior Choir sang, Hank and Dexter watched, listened, and clapped their hands along with the choir. Some of their friends sang in the choir, and they looked like they were having a good time.

After church, Dexter asked his mother if they could sing in the Junior Choir. Margaret told them that they couldn't because they were not members of the church. In order to sing in the choir, they'd have to join the church. She also explained they couldn't join the church until their souls were saved, and they'd have to accept Jesus Christ as their savior. Margaret asked Hank and Dexter if they understood what she'd said, and they both acknowledged they did. Then she asked them if they knew what it meant. They both answered yes.

The next Sunday, the family went to church. Margaret had this Sunday off. It was the second Sunday, when the Mission Chorus sang, and Margaret didn't direct or play for them, so it felt a little strange to Dexter when they were not sitting in the front row. This meant grown people would be sitting in front of him. He couldn't see as well, and he felt hidden.

Margaret sat between the boys to keep them from talking and playing. Dexter had a small pencil with him and began to draw on the program document. Hank, sitting on the other side of his mother, started rocking back and forth. Rev. Reason stood up in the pulpit and introduced Deacon Dell as Reverend Dell and announced that he would be giving his first sermon. Rev. Dell then stood up and approached the podium. He asked everyone to bow his or her head and pray. Margaret and Hank bowed their heads and closed their eyes. Dexter bowed his head but kept his eyes open and scanned the room.

"Amen," sounded the congregation. Dexter was startled; he had been letting his mind wander again. He looked up and could see Rev. Dell slightly between the people sitting in front of him. Dexter moved up to the edge of his seat and sat up straight to strain and see Rev. Dell.

"What are you doing?" asked Margaret.

"Baba, I can't see; I'm trying to see," answered Dexter. Margaret let him be.

Rev. Dell was as sharp as ever; his suit was crisp and clean, and his shirt beamed a bright white. His hair was jet black and wavy. To Dexter, he could have been Clark Gable. He liked Rev. Dell, and he wanted to be like him. He was someone who everyone respected, and he always had money. Dexter listened to Rev. Dell's sermon, and this was something that he rarely did. Rev. Dell had a teaching style of preaching. He sounded more like a schoolteacher than a preacher. His words were crisp and clear, and he spoke like an educated man. Rev. Dell's sermon was about Job—a man who was the richest man in the world, and God had him lose everything to test his faith. It was a good sermon, and Dexter understood everything about it.

Toward the end of the sermon, Rev. Dell couldn't help but take it back to that old time religion. He fell right into the same tune most Baptist preachers did. He began with, "Just like Job, I want to know, do you have faith? Do you know the Lord? I don't know about you, but I know that God is on my side. Can I get a witness? Is there a witness in here?"

The congregation was getting excited. Margaret was fanning herself back and forth, and Hank was next to her, rocking. "Is your soul saved? Can you honestly say that you know the Lord?" asked Rev. Dell.

Rev. Dell continued, "I can say that I know the Lord. He's been my Rock in a weary land. He's been my Lawyer in a courtroom, my Doctor in a sick room." Suddenly, Dexter was getting excited and many people were up on their feet. Dexter couldn't see, so he stood up on the seat. Rev. Dell had taken off his jacket; he was sweating profusely. He looked like he was struggling to breathe. After each sentence, he'd gasp for air and heave back and forth with a roar. "Uhhhhhhh … ahhhhh … uhhhhhhh."

Rev. Dell continued, "God is by my side. He's here with me now and tomorrow. He's here, and he's there. God is everywhere. He's in me; is he in you?" Dexter was jumping up and down on the seat, and suddenly, it felt like a jolt of electricity went through him. He got a quick chill, and then felt a short shaking feeling all over his body. Just then, Rev. Dell called for people to come and be saved, saying that the doors of the church were open. God had touched Dexter; he knew that was the only reason he felt like he did. He had never felt that way before. When Rev. Dell reached out his hands to the congregation, Dexter got up and began heading down the row and down the isle.

Margaret felt what was going on and didn't try to stop Dexter or question him when he went to move past her. As Dexter went by, Margaret said, "Thank you, Lord." When Dexter passed Hank to go and join the church, Hank got up and followed.

The congregation started shouting, "Hallelujah, Hallelujah!" Rev. Reason was standing behind Rev. Dell, cheering him on. Soon a few more people came forward to join the church.

When Rev. Dell finished, Rev. Reason walked over to Hank and Dexter and waved for the secretary to stand off. The church was silent. He stood before the boys, opened his jacket and poked his belly out, and then said, "I know these boys! How many of you know these boys?" There were many responses in the audience. "Margaret, where you at?" Rev. Reason yelled out. "Somebody help Margaret come down here," he instructed. An usher went to the end of the aisle and escorted Margaret to the front of the church and over to Rev. Reason.

"I remember when I first saw these boys; they were at their mother's side. They are always at their mother's side. These are some good boys. I watch all the little boys and girls around here, and I know who's been good," said the reverend. Then he yelled out, "These are some good boys! Let's give these boys a hand for taking care of their momma," and the congregation started clapping their hands.

"Dexter, do you know the Lord?" asked the reverend.

"Yes," replied Dexter.

"Hank, do you know the Lord?" asked the reverend.

"Yes," replied Hank.

"Praise God," shouted the reverend. "Will you boys accept Jesus Christ as your savior?"

"Yes," answered the boys.

The reverend faced the congregation and said, "All in favor of accepting these boys as members of the First Union Baptist Church once they have been baptized, say aye."

The congregation confirmed, "Aye."

"Nays?" asked the reverend.

There was silence, and then the reverend said, "Ayes have it. Dexter, Hank, you boys will be baptized on the first Sunday," and he shook their hands.

On the first Sunday after the sermon, the choir moved out of the choir stand, and the deacons began removing sections of chairs to reveal a deep concrete pool. Someone pulled back a curtain that was hanging behind the choir stand to reveal a large mirror. A long cord keeping the mirror upright was released, and the mirror tilted forward, providing a top-down view of the pool.

Hank and Dexter were downstairs in the choir's dressing room, changing into casual clothes along with the other male baptism candidates. One of the sisters of the church came into the room with a stack of white sheets and began wrapping each candidate in the white linens. A deacon walked into the room and instructed everyone to bow their heads for prayer. After the prayer, they were told what the process would be. They walked out into the dining room and were met by the females. The group of candidates then formed one line and headed upstairs to the sanctuary. Hank and Dexter were in the middle of the group.

When the front of the line reached past the top of the stairs to the door entering the sanctuary, the line stopped. Hank and Dexter were standing in the middle of the stairwell waiting. They looked at each other and smiled. Dexter was a little frightened. He asked Hank, "Are you scared?" And Hank replied, "Uh huh."

They could hear the voice of one of the assistant ministers speaking, and then the music started. The choir started singing, "It is no secret, what God can do. What he's done for others, he'll do for you."

The line began moving to the edge of the pool. One by one, Rev. Reason spoke, and asked a few questions. He then put his hand over each one's face and nose, and he and another preacher tilted each person back then dunked him or her in the water.

Dexter was in front of Hank in the line, and as they got closer, he told Hank, "You go first."

"No, you go first," replied Hank.

"Come on, you go first," begged Dexter. Hank shook his head.

Dexter was now at the front of the line, watching the teenage girl in front of him get baptized. The reverend finished with her, and then reached up for Dexter. Dexter hesitated for a moment, and then took the preacher's hand and walked down the steps into the water; the water was cold.

Rev. Reason took Dexter and guided him to position. "Dexter, do you accept God into your life?"

"Yes," answered Dexter.

"Do you accept Jesus Christ as your savior?" asked the reverend.

"Yes," answered Dexter.

Rev. Reason then put his hand over Dexter's nose and mouth. He had a large hand, and if felt strong and forceful to Dexter. "I baptize you in the name of the Father, the Son, and the Holy Ghost," said Rev. Reason, and he tilted Dexter back until he was completely submerged. Dexter had closed his eyes when he went under, and then Rev. Reason pulled him back up out of the water. The whole process was over in less than two minutes. To Dexter, it seemed like it took much longer. It seemed as though, when the reverend put his hand over Dexter's nose and mouth and dunked him in the water, everything moved in slow motion. When he surfaced, he had a fresh, clean feeling.

The assistant guided Dexter over to the steps and past Hank as they prepared to baptize him. Dexter was immediately escorted downstairs to the dressing room to dry off and change clothes. He wasn't able to see his brother being baptized. Soon Hank entered the dressing room, and they were both smiling and giggling and talking about the experience while they dried off and dressed.

Now that the boys were baptized, they wanted to join the Junior Choir. Choir rehearsals were at noon on the second and third Saturdays, and the choir sang on the third Sunday. With Margaret's hectic schedule of choir rehearsals, shopping, paying bills, getting to the hairdresser, and such, the boys were always busy. They never really seemed to have much time to play.

Margaret was always an early riser. She would usually be up in the morning before the boys woke up, but on some occasions when she was really tired, she'd lie in bed and rest and let the boys take care of themselves.

One morning, Dexter woke up, got out of bed, and walked into his mother's room. Margaret was still in bed. He walked over to the bed; she was still asleep. Dexter reached up to the bed and tapped her. "Baba?" he said. Margaret didn't move; she continued to lie there, asleep. "Baba?" Dexter said, as he tapped her again. She still didn't budge. Dexter walked out of the room and went into the kitchen to fix some breakfast cereal.

Soon Hank woke up and walked into the kitchen and saw Dexter eating. He got a bowl and poured himself some cereal. A little too much came out of the box, so he scooped up some cereal in his hands and placed it back into the box, making even more of a mess. Dexter then poured him some milk. The boys finished eating, put their bowls into the sink, and went into their bedroom to watch Saturday-morning cartoons. After watching cartoons for some time, Hank went into his mother's bedroom to wake her up. Margaret was lying still with her mouth wide open; she was drooling.

"Baba," said Hank as he tapped his mother. There was no response. "Baba?" he said again, this time shaking her. Still no response. "Baba!" Hank hollered as he shook her. This time there was a moan, but she did not awaken. Hank ran into the room where Dexter was and told him that he couldn't wake up Baba.

Dexter tried to awaken his mother too, but she still wouldn't wake up. The most he could get out of her was a moan. Dexter ran over to the phone and called Mary. "Nanny, I can't wake Baba up. She won't wake up," Dexter told his grandmother.

"Dexter, take the phone over to your mother, and try to get her on the phone," Mary instructed Dexter. Mary listened on the other end of the phone to Dexter's attempts. "Dexter, Dexter," Mary was yelling through the phone, trying to get Dexter's attention. Hank was standing near and beginning to get scared.

Dexter picked up the phone and answered his grandmother. "Nanny, I can't wake her," he said into the receiver.

"Dexter, listen to me. You listen to me, you hear?" instructed Mary sternly. "After we hang up, I'm going to call the police. When they get there, go let them in and stay there until I get there. I'm on my way. Do you understand me?" asked Mary.

"Yes, Nanny," Dexter answered.

Hank was standing near and wanted to talk to Nanny. "Let me talk to her," he said as he reached for the phone, but Mary had hung up. "I wanted to talk to her," Hank complained to Dexter.

"She's calling the police, and they're coming over. We have to let them in and wait for Nanny," responded Dexter.

Hank stayed by his mother's bedside while Dexter went to the window and watched for the police. Soon, a patrol car pulled up out front; two policemen got out and walked toward the apartment building. Dexter ran to the front door and let the policemen in. "Where's your mother?" asked one of the policemen. Dexter showed them to his mother's bedroom.

The officer quickly checked Margaret for a heartbeat and to see if she was breathing. She had a heartbeat, but it was faint, and she was still breathing. He instructed his partner to go out to the patrol car and call for an ambulance. He then told the boys to go and put some clothes on and get ready to go to the hospital with their mother.

Hank was beginning to get scared and started to cry. "What's wrong with my mommy?" he cried to the officer.

"She's going to be okay. I need you to go and get dressed. Can you do that?" asked the officer.

"Yeah," Hank said, crying as he walked to his room.

Dexter's heart was racing as he got dressed. He was trying to rush, but it was slowing him down. He tripped over getting his pants on, and he couldn't get his shoes on because they were tied. He was getting scared now too and felt as though he was going to cry, but he held on. He looked at Hank who had sat on the floor and started crying. "Come on, Hank, you got to get dressed. Come on, let's get dressed," said Dexter.

"I want my Baba," cried Hank.

"Come on, get dressed," Dexter said, trying to hold back the tears. Hank finally began to dress.

The ambulance arrived, and the paramedics quickly checked on Margaret and transferred her into the ambulance. The police officer then instructed Hank and Dexter to come with them, saying they'd take them to the hospital with their mother. Dexter objected. "My grandmother is coming to get us. We can stay here until she gets here." The policeman told the boys they couldn't leave them alone, and they had to come with them.

Just then Mary arrived, and the police told her that the ambulance was taking Margaret to San Francisco General Hospital, emergency ward. They released the children to Mary and left. Mary and the boys then drove out to the hospital. When Mary and the boys arrived at San Francisco General, the emergency ward was a busy place. The administrator told them to have a seat and that someone would let them know about Margaret just as soon as they had something to tell.

It was the first time Hank and Dexter had been to an emergency ward. It was a long wait, and people of all walks of life wandered in and out of the swinging doors. They sat and watched as a Negro drunkard walked in, holding a rag on his bleeding forehead. He came through the door mumbling and cussing and started shouting for assistance.

Soon a Mexican woman who was about to deliver a baby walked in. Then a white man with a big naked belly, who had bloody sheets covering his lower half, was wheeled in on a stretcher. Someone asked what had happened and was told that the man had been stabbed. There was a teenage boy who had a broken leg and a little girl who was sick to her stomach.

Finally, a doctor came out and called out Margaret's name, looking for the family. Mary got up and went over to the doctor and told him that she was Margaret's mother. The doctor then informed her that Margaret had slipped into a coma. Mary's hand immediately moved up to her mouth in fright. He told her not to worry and that Margaret was coming out of it. He then told her that he suspected she was suffering from diabetes, but there were some additional tests that needed to be completed. He wanted to know if she had a family physician.

Mary informed him that Dr. Hite was her medical doctor. The hospital contacted Dr. Hite who wanted her transferred to Kaiser Hospital. Mary then went to check on Margaret, who was groggy but was coming around. After Margaret was stabilized, Mary took the boys home with her. The next day she went out to Kaiser Hospital to see Margaret. Mary decided to leave the boys with Annie.

The testing confirmed that Margaret had diabetes. Doctor Hite told Mary that Margaret would have to take shots of insulin every day from now on to maintain an active lifestyle. She'd have to watch her diet and change her eating habits. He wanted to keep Margaret in the hospital for a few more days to stabilize her blood sugar and to have her learn how to inject herself. Mary voiced her concern about Margaret's ability to take the shots on her own, but Dr. Hite assured her he was confident that she would be able to do it.

When Mary went in to see her daughter, Margaret was sitting up, eating fruit, and she appeared to be fine. Her hair needed combing, but otherwise, she looked her normal self, and she had a strong appetite. Mary and Margaret talked about Margaret's situation. Margaret didn't seem to be that concerned. She felt it was something that she'd have to deal with but that she'd be able to with the help of the Lord.

"That's all fine and dandy, but you have more than yourself to worry about," said Mary. "You have Hank and Dexter to think of. Those boys were scared to death when you got sick. If you keep getting sick, I don't know how it will affect them."

"I know, Mother, but I think Hank and Dexter will be able to help me. If I didn't have them, I think I'd have more to worry about," said Margaret. Mary acknowledged that Margaret was probably right.

"You know that the boys are pretty bright, and Dexter really knows how to be responsible. Hank is the baby, but as long as he has his brother, he knows how to be responsible too," continued Margaret.

"Yes, that's true, but, Naomi, you have to take better care of yourself. Dr. Hite says you have to give yourself a shot every morning, or you'll get sick. The boys will need to learn how to give you shots," Mary said, voicing her concern.

"Mother, they'll learn; I'll teach them," replied Margaret.

"I hope so," said Mary.

After having been out of the hospital for several weeks, Margaret had become comfortable injecting herself with the insulin shots. She sat down with Hank and Dexter and taught them how to administer shots to her. They learned how to take out clean needles, how to draw insulin from the small bottles kept in the refrigerator, and then how to inject her on the inside of her thigh. Dexter and Hank hated the whole process, but they understood why they needed to know what to do. They also had to learn to sometimes give their mother orange juice with lots of sugar when Margaret's sugar got low.

Over the course of the next couple of years, Margaret slipped into comas several times and had to be taken to the hospital by ambulance. After a while, it became easier for the boys to recognize the signs when their mother needed insulin, orange juice and sugar, or needed to go to the hospital. When it came time for one of them to inject their mother with insulin, the boys even argued over who was going to do it. In most cases it was Hank who injected.

10

Brighter Days

It was 1960 and Chubby Checker had America dancing and "twisting the night away." He exploded onto the charts with "The Twist," and everybody in America was doing the dance—white, yellow, black, and brown. Margaret was now thirty-four; Mary was fifty-one; Annie, seventy-one; Dexter, nine; Hank, eight; and Charles was sixteen. Mary often let Charles use her car, as long as he took Hank and Dexter along. She figured, if he had them with him, he'd stay out of trouble.

Charles would pick up the boys, and then go and get his girlfriend. Charles would ride them out to Golden Gate Park near Stow Lake, park the car, and tell Hank and Dexter to go and play. They'd leave the car and wait for Charles to start necking with his girlfriend, and then come back and sneak up on them. Charles would get angry and yell at them to go away, and the boys would leave for a while, only to return and disrupt them again.

Mary gave Charles strict instructions not to let anyone else ride in the car, so he'd make the boys promise not to tell Mary he picked up his girlfriend. The boys promised not to tell, but as soon as they returned home, Hank would run and tell Mary, and Charles would get a whipping. He was sixteen years old, and his mother was still whipping his butt.

Sometimes Charles took the boys to places where there were a lot of teenagers. He was an athlete and really popular; baseball was his game of choice. He attended Polytechnic High School. Dexter really looked up to his uncle Charles who was like a big brother to him. Charles taught him how to catch and throw a baseball, and they also practiced swinging with the bat. Baseball didn't interest Hank.

Charles took the boys on a picnic with a bunch of his teenaged friends. The boys and girls played music and danced the Twist and the Swim and had a great time. Hank and Dexter knew their mother felt this was the devil's music, but they enjoyed it anyway. If Margaret had known what Charles was showing the boys, she'd surely have disapproved.

Margaret changed hairdressers and began to let Molly style her hair. Molly lived on Spruce Street, about a block off Geary Boulevard, and she had set up a small salon downstairs in her home. One Saturday, Margaret and the boys took the bus over to Molly's so that Margaret could get her hair done. Hank and Dexter loved to go over to Molly's because they could play with Molly's son, Guy, who was about a year older than Dexter.

On this particular Saturday, Molly's house was full of people. Several of her relatives had come over to get their hair done, and they'd all brought their children with them. The children were running all over the house, having fun. Eventually, one of the teens in the house put Chubby Checker's record, "The Twist," on the phonograph, and the music was blaring. The kids were dancing and having a good time in the living room upstairs.

After Molly finished Margaret's hair, Margaret got ready to leave because she was annoyed by the music. As far as Margaret was concerned, they were playing the devil's music upstairs, and she wanted to get Hank and Dexter away from its influence.

Margaret called to Hank and Dexter from downstairs and instructed them to get ready to go. But the boys were not ready; they were having fun, and the kids upstairs were about to have a dance contest. Margaret again called for the boys to come but got no answer, so she asked Molly to take her upstairs.

Molly led Margaret up the stairs and into the living room. Chubby Checker was playing on the phonograph, and there were seven kids in the middle of the floor doing the twist. One of the teenagers would walk amongst the dancers and tap him or her on the head one by one to leave the floor.

Hank and Dexter were out in the middle of the group. Hank was twisting back and forth; his chubby belly looked a lot like Chubby Checker's when he did the twist. Hank was smiling, shaking his hips back and forth, and swinging his arms from side to side. Margaret asked Molly what was going on, and Molly said they were dancing. "What?" asked Margaret.

"Margaret, relax, they not doing anything wrong. Let them have a little fun," said Molly.

"I'll say," said Margaret, and she sighed with disapproval. But she was outnumbered, and she dared not stop the contest.

Soon the teenage judge walked over and tapped Hank on top of his head. "Ahhh," said Hank as he stumbled off the dance floor. The only ones left on the floor were Dexter and a young girl named Heidi. "Okay, we have two finalists. They have to dance for the winner. Start the song over," said the judge.

The song was started again, and Dexter and Heidi started twisting. Heidi looked so pretty with her sandy-colored hair bouncing back and forth. She was smiling and putting all she had into her dancing. Dexter was slim and lanky with a head full of curly hair. His smile looked as though it was stuck on his face.

The two dancers were swinging back and forth, hips twisting side to side. Then Dexter started going up and down. He twisted all the way down to floor, and the small group went wild. He'd seen one of Charles's friends do it, so he copied it. Heidi then started twisting and leaning forward, and then she leaned backward. Everyone started yelling and howling and laughing. Dexter copied Heidi and did what she did. Next, Dexter started doubling up on his twist. He'd twist double time, then normal, and then double time again. Finally, the judge stepped in and said that Dexter was the winner and raised his arm. Everyone was clapping and laughing and smiling. There was no prize; it was just a bunch of kids having fun.

Molly told Margaret not to punish the boys since they'd done nothing wrong. She said they were just having a good time, and she made Margaret promise not to say anything to the boys. Margaret didn't want to promise, but she did anyway.

The boys and Margaret were getting ready to leave when the doorbell rang. Margaret said to Molly, "That's probably Leon. He's coming to give me a ride."

Molly went to open the door and there was a tall gentleman in a suit and tie, standing in the doorway. "Hello, Molly," he said.

"Hi, Leon," Molly answered with a smile. Molly's smile was not a smile of delight, but a smirking smile, as if she'd heard a joke. She motioned for Leon to come in.

When Leon stepped through the doorway, he saw Margaret and said, "Hello, Margaret, are you ready?"

Margaret answered yes and told the boys to come so they could leave.

Hank and Dexter grabbed their coats and got ready to go. They were both curious about who the gentleman was and were looking at him as they got ready. "Hi there, Hank and Dexter. I'm Mr. Leon. I'm a friend of your mother's," said Leon to the boys, and he stuck out his hand to shake theirs.

Dexter looked at Mr. Leon's hand; there was something wrong with it. They each took turns shaking his hand, and somehow it felt funny to them. Hank and Dexter were slow to respond, so their mother told them, "Speak up when grown folks talk to you."

"Hi," answered the boys in unison.

Hank kept looking at Leon. He thought he recognized him. He then turned to Dexter and said, "I've seen him at the church. He's a preacher." Dexter looked at Leon, and his mind took him back to the church. He had remembered seeing Leon sitting in the pulpit. He also remembered seeing him talk with his mother, but at the time he hadn't thought anything of it.

Dexter picked up his mother's purse and handed it to her, and then he went to take her arm so he could guide her. Leon stepped in and said, "I'll take her out, son." Dexter then stepped away so Leon could guide his mother.

Many people, including men, had come to pick them up and give them rides in the past. In most cases, the person picking them up would lead Margaret, and the boys never gave it much thought. But, for the boys, this time seemed different. There was something about this man that let them know it was a different situation.

Leon was a tall, thin man. He stood about six feet, two inches tall and weighed about 175 pounds. He was a brown-skinned redbone Negro. His head was bald with a ridge of hair growing around the sides and back. He took a few strands of hair and combed it over the top, as if to hide his baldness. He had deep wrinkles on his forehead and face, and there were bags under his eyes that made him appear tired.

Leon was wearing an old baggy suit with wide lapels. It looked like something out of the forties. It was in good shape, made from a nice wool gabardine material, but it was old. Leon also had a hat in his hand; he placed it on his head when he stepped outside. On his feet he was wearing a pair of Stacy Adams knobs with sheer socks. His shirt was white and starched with a wide necktie as old as the suit, but it was clean.

Leon led Margaret out to the car, and the boys followed. Outside at the curb was a 1957 blue Plymouth with white stripes on the sides. They walked over to the car and Leon opened the door to let Margaret slide into the front seat. Leon then went around and opened the back door for the boys to hop in.

Once inside the car, the boys looked around; the car was a mess. On the dashboard there were a couple of empty paper cups with coffee stains on them. Next to the cups was a large old Bible that had little pieces of paper sticking out from between the pages, and some pages were folded. The floor in the backseat was covered with papers and debris, along with some old, greasy overalls. There were also a couple of two-by-fours and a large hook with a wooden handle on it. Dexter reached down and picked up the hook to examine it. "What's this for?" he asked.

"I use it at my work to grab large crates so I can move them," answered Leon. Dexter didn't understand what Leon was talking about. Leon was looking in the rear-view mirror and saw Dexter's expression.

"I'm a longshoreman," said Leon. Dexter still didn't understand. Leon then said, "I work at the shipyard, unloading the big ships when they come in." Now Dexter understood. He remembered seeing a movie on television where there were people unloading ships at a dock.

Dexter took the hook and held it up, made an ugly face, and went "Argh," toward Hank, playing like he was a monster.

Hank cried, "Stop."

Leon said, "Dexter, put it down now; don't play with it." Dexter put down the hook and sat back in his seat.

Dexter began to tell Leon how to get to their house, but Leon said he knew where to go. The ride was quiet on the way home; the boys sat back and watched the scenery. Leon drove down Geary Boulevard, past First Union to Divisadero Street, made a right, then continued up to Waller Street where he made a left to their house.

"That's where we live," said Hank to Leon.

"I know," replied Leon.

The boys looked at each other in the backseat as if to ask, "How does he know?"

Leon found a parking space just down the block, where he parked the car. Hank opened the back door and jumped out. He went to open the front passenger door for his mother, but Leon jumped out and said, "I'll get it, Hank." Hank kept trying to open the door, but it was locked. "Hank, I'll get it," Leon said firmly. Leon grabbed the door handle and gently moved Hank back out of the way. Hank didn't care for Leon's assistance. He moved back out of the way, and Leon assisted Margaret out of the car and up the steps to the front door.

Margaret reached into her purse, felt around, and took out the keys. She opened the door, walked in, and Leon stepped in behind her. He was coming in. There was no, "May I?" or anything like that. Leon walked inside like he belonged there, and Hank and Dexter immediately felt violated.

"Hank, Dexter, go to your room and watch TV," ordered Margaret.

"Baba, I'm hungry," complained Hank.

"Dinner will ready in a little while," replied Margaret. Dexter didn't say anything; he just walked to their room, turned on the TV, and sat on his bed. Hank followed closely behind.

Hank sat on his bed and pouted then turned to Dexter and said, "I don't like him."

Dexter looked at Hank and said, "I'm hungry. I wonder what's for dinner."

Margaret and Leon were now in the kitchen, and Hank was trying to eavesdrop on their conversation. "What's he doing here?" asked Hank.

"It's probably nothing; he just gave us a ride," answered Dexter.

Hank responded with, "I don't think so. I think he likes Baba."

Dexter's mind then drifted to thoughts of his father. "I wonder where Daddy is. I wonder what he's doing. I miss him. I wish I could see him," said Dexter, thinking out loud.

"I don't know. I miss Daddy too. I wish he were here," replied Hank.

Dexter lay across his bed and looked at the TV. He then grabbed the basketball his uncle Charles had given him and cradled it in the bed with him. The television was on, but neither one of the boys was watching it. Hank kept trying to listen to what was going on in the kitchen, and Dexter just kept thinking about his father.

In a little while, Hank decided he was thirsty, so he walked out of the bedroom, went into the kitchen, and announced his thirst. "I'll get it. Margaret, you just relax," Leon said, as he went to the refrigerator.

"What would you like, Hank?" asked Leon.

Hank went over to his mother. "Baba, when are we going to eat?" he asked.

"I thought you said you were thirsty?" asked Margaret.

"I am," replied Hank.

"Well, he asked you what you wanted; answer him," Margaret instructed.

Hank looked at Leon, still clinging to his mother. "I'm sorry, what did you say your name was?" asked Hank.

"Leon, Mr. Leon," he replied.

Hank was being sarcastic; he knew Leon's name. He just didn't care for him, and it was his way of letting him know.

Leon then said, "Hold on, Hank, let me turn over the fish." Leon went over to the stove where he was frying fish. Hank looked at Leon, open-mouthed. This man was cooking in their kitchen, and Margaret was sitting at the table, relaxing.

"Baba, I thought you were cooking," Hank said to his mother.

"No, not today. Mr. Leon volunteered to cook for us. Don't you think that's nice of him?" asked Margaret. Hank looked over to Leon, still clinging to his mother; he didn't respond.

Margaret decided not to push it and let Hank be. "You get yourself something to drink, but don't drink too much. I don't want you spoiling your appetite. Dinner will be ready in a moment."

Hank poured himself some milk and then went back to his room.

"I don't think he cares for me," Leon voiced to Margaret.

"Oh, he's just the baby, and he always wants his mother. He's a sweet boy. You'll see, once you get to know him," replied Margaret.

Once in the bedroom, Hank told Dexter, "He's cooking dinner."

Dexter sat up on his bed. "He's what?"

"He's cooking dinner. He's frying fish," answered Hank.

"What?" said Dexter in disbelief. He got up from his bed and moved over to the doorway so he could look into the kitchen. He saw Leon's back over near the stove. Leon then moved over toward Margaret and gave her a kiss on the cheek, and Margaret blushed. Dexter saw this and whispered, "Oh! He kissed her. He kissed Baba."

"He what?" asked Hank as he moved over to try and see. But by the time Hank got there, Leon was back at the stove with his back to them.

Hank got angry, and Dexter sadly said, "I want my daddy back," and threw himself across his bed and cuddled his pillow. A tear came to his eye. He laid his head on his pillow to try and doze off. Hank moved over to his own side of the room, sat on his bed, and angrily folded his arms. He then lay across his bed, turned over, and began to rock back and forth.

After a few minutes, Margaret called out, "Hank, Dexter, it's time to eat." Dexter was almost asleep, and Hank was still rocking to ease his anger. They got up and washed their hands, went into the kitchen, and sat at the table. The food was good. Actually it was great. Margaret was eating and picking out the bones. "Um, this sure is good."

"Thank you. I caught this fish yesterday," replied Leon. Dexter looked up when he heard that. He'd never been fishing and had always wanted to go.

"You caught this fish?" asked Dexter.

"Yes siree, I caught it yesterday out in the bay. Me and my friends went out on the boat and caught them," replied Leon.

"What kind of fish is it? I never had this fish before," said Margaret.

"Perch," answered Leon.

Dexter looked at Leon as he was eating, and he noticed the hand again. There was something crooked about it. "What happened to your hand?" asked Dexter.

"Dexter, that's rude. You're supposed to say sir," Margaret corrected him.

"Oh, excuse me, sir. Uh, sir, Leon, what happened to your hand?" Dexter asked.

Hank was now staring at the hand too as Leon answered, "I was unloading a crate of bananas off a ship down at the docks, and one of the crates fell on my hand and crushed it."

"Does it hurt, Mr. Leon, sir?" asked Dexter.

"No, the doctor fixed it up so I can use it. I just can't straighten out my fingers all the way. But I can grab with it," answered Leon.

Hank was staring at the hand. The middle knuckle was set higher than the rest of the knuckles, and the middle finger was set below the rest of the fingers. There was a big dot in the middle of the back of the hand where there was a scar that looked like a permanent scab. Hank shivered at the sight of it; it looked hideous.

They finished dinner, and then Hank washed the dishes while Dexter dried. Afterward, the boys took their baths and got ready for bed. Margaret and Leon went into the family room where Margaret played on the piano what she'd be playing the next day in church. Leon read his Bible, and the boys watched Amos and Andy on television until it was time to go to sleep.

The next morning, Leon came to pick up Margaret and the boys to take them to church. Leon led Margaret out to the car. Hank and Dexter fought to open the car door for their mother, but Leon opened it for her, and then he unlocked the back door for Hank and Dexter to climb in. This time the car was clean inside, and the boys immediately noticed it.

As they rode through the Fillmore on the way to church, Dexter looked out the window at the sights and sounds of the city; Hank sat with his legs together and his hands folded in his lap while he rocked back and forth in his seat. As Leon was driving, he noticed Hank rocking. He thought to himself that the behavior seemed a little unusual. However, he quickly dismissed it.

It was Sunday morning, so the radio broadcast was either gospel music or church service. KDIA either broadcast live from a local church, or the deejay played gospel records. It set the tone for the day.

Leon drove down Divisadero, made a left turn onto Geary Boulevard, and pulled up in front of the church. There was no place to park, so he slowly turned the corner onto Baker where he found a space at the side of the church. Rev. Dell just happened to be standing outside talking with one of the deacons and noticed Margaret in the car with Leon. Leon had a look about him that said, "She's with me."

Leon parked the car and got out. Hank jumped out of the car and went to open his mother's door, but it was locked. He kept pulling on the latch, but it wouldn't work. Leon walked over, gently moved Hank out of the way, and unlocked the door to let Margaret out. Rev. Dell watched as Leon helped Margaret out of the car and walked her into the church through the garage door to the ladies' room. Hank and Dexter took off to play with the other children at the church.

Once Margaret was out of earshot, Rev. Dell walked over to Leon and said, "Leon, what are you doing?"

"What do you mean, what am I doing?" responded Leon.

"Are you dating Margaret?" asked the reverend.

"Why?" Leon asked.

"Look, man, you'd better be real nice to Margaret. She's a good woman; she has those two boys to look after, and she doesn't need any foolishness. I'm just a friend looking out for her," said Rev. Dell, voicing his concern.

"Shit, man, err, I mean shoot, man. I got good intentions with Margaret. I know she's a good woman. I bet a man that I'd be right by her. You don't need to be worried," responded Leon as he started walking backward away from the reverend, heading back to the basement where Margaret was in the ladies' room. Rev. Dell stared at Leon, giving him a stern look to let him know he meant what he said.

Leon walked through the garage into the dining hall and headed toward the ladies' room. Molly walked out and almost stepped into him. "Hey, Molly, how you doing?" asked Leon.

Molly smiled at Leon, anticipating that he'd be asking about Margaret. "I'm fine, Leon; what are you looking for?"

"Well, ah, I was just wanting to make sure Margaret wasn't going to need my help," Leon offered.

"I don't think so, Leon. I think she'll be fine. One of the choir members will bring her upstairs. You can run along," responded Molly.

"All right, I was just checking. You know, you look real nice today, Molly," said Leon.

"Thank you, Leon," Molly answered, kind of smirking, then turned and walked off.

Leon watched Molly as she walked off; he was looking at her behind. He thought to himself, "Um, boy, she sure got a body on her." He caught himself, realizing what he was doing, and then glanced around to see if anyone had seen him looking at Molly. Sure enough, a couple of the sisters that were cooking in the kitchen were looking right at him. Noticing how they were looking at him, Leon shaped up, stretched out his neck, straightened his tie, cleared his throat, and walked off. One of the sisters just shook her head and returned to her cooking.

Morning worship was now in session, and both the Senior and Junior Choirs were providing the music. Both choirs marched in and took their places after the deacons had opened the service with an old-time hymn. Hank and Dexter were seated in the back row of the Junior Choir, located in the side choir section to the right of the pulpit. Margaret was seated at the piano in order to lead the Senior Choir seated behind the altar in the main choir stand.

Once the altar call was completed, it was time for the collection. Rev. Reason stood before the congregation and began to speak. "'Will a man rob God? Yet ye have robbed me. But ye say, wherein have we robbed thee? In tithes and offerings. Ye are cursed with a curse: for ye have robbed me, even this whole nation. Bring ye all the tithes into the storehouse, that there may be meat in mine house, and prove me now herewith, saith the Lord of hosts, if I will not open you the windows of heaven, and pour you out a blessing, that there shall not be room enough to receive it.'"

Rev. Reason talked about the reasons to tithe, and then instructed the congregation to follow the ushers. Margaret played, and the choir sang:

> You can't beat God giving
> No matter how you try,
> The more you give
> The more he gives to you,
> Just keep on giving
> Because it's really true
> That you can't beat God giving
> No matter how you try.

The congregation was led in sections down the aisles and past the deacons to the plate in front of the altar. It was almost time for the Junior Choir to walk past the plate. An usher instructed the choir to stand. Rev. Reason turned and looked toward Leon who was sitting in the pulpit and instructed him to pray over the money once it was all collected.

When Leon approached the podium, one of the girls looked over at Hank and then tapped him and said, "I hear that's your new daddy."

Hank pulled away from her touch and responded, "Uh uh, that ain't my daddy."

Dexter heard and saw what happened and told Hank to be quiet. He then looked up at Leon at the podium and had to move with the line. As the choir walked by the collection plate, Dexter stared at Leon as they passed. Hank was pouting, and Dexter forgot to put his money in.

As Leon blessed the tithes and offering he tried to put a little preaching spin on it. Everyone's eyes were closed and heads bowed. One of the boys, standing near Dexter, started snickering and whispered, "Please bless my bald head," and several of the other kids started laughing. It was so funny that Dexter had to laugh too, but Hank just got angrier. "Shhhh," came from the direction of an usher. After the prayer, they were all seated.

Richard, the Junior Choir director, exchanged places with Margaret at the piano and instructed the choir to stand for their selections. They sang, "I've got joy, joy, joy, down in my heart." While they sang, Dexter's eyes were fixed on Leon who was seated in the second seat from the end of the pulpit, directly in front of the Junior Choir.

Dexter stared at Leon's head and noticed the overhead fluorescent light was shining right on top of Leon's slick, bald head. He burst out laughing and quickly put his hand over his mouth to try and contain it. When Dexter snickered, a couple of the other boys seated in his row started to chuckle, and Richard gave them a very concerned look. The boys straightened up, stopped laughing, and continued to sing.

After church, the Junior Choir was in their choir room changing out of their robes. While disrobing, Dexter looked over at a boy named Junior and said, "Man, that was funny. Bless my bald head! I couldn't stop laughing. Did you see the light shining on his head?" Junior was laughing with him, but Dexter noticed Hank was angry.

"Hank, what's wrong with you?" asked Dexter.

Hank was visibly upset. "He ain't my daddy."

"Ah, come on. You know he's not our father. Don't be so upset. Come on, let's go find Baba," Dexter said pulling on Hank.

The boys walked out of the choir room. Margaret was standing directly across the dining room in front of the ladies' lounge. Leon was standing next to her, holding onto her arm to lead her. Dexter and Hank walked over to their mother, and Hank moved in between Leon and Margaret, then took her by the arm and interrupted Margaret's conversion. "Baba, come on, let's go."

"Hank, wait a minute. You see I'm talking; you know better than to interrupt," Margaret said. She continued her conversation with one of the church members while Hank held on. Leon noticed how Hank had become territorial and decided to let him have his way.

After Margaret finished her conversation, it was time to leave, and Hank led his mother outside and up the hill toward Leon's parked car. As they walked, Dexter noticed Rev. Dell and called for Hank to come with him to go and visit Rev. Dell. Hank wanted to go, but that meant he would have to let his mother go. He looked at Mr. Leon who motioned for him to go. He looked at his mother, glanced at Rev. Dell where Dexter was, then decided to release his mother and ran to meet Dexter and Rev. Dell.

Rev. Dell greeted the boys, who shook his hand. He then squatted down to chat with them. While he chatted, he reached into his pocket for two quarters and glanced over at Margaret and Leon. Leon was standing at the car and opening the door for Margaret to enter. Leon then glanced over at Rev. Dell and noticed that he was handing money to the boys while watching him. The two men looked at each other, and then Leon nodded his head. Rev. Dell responded with a nod and motioned for the boys to return to their mom. He then looked on as the boys piled into Leon's car. Rev. Dell continued to watch as Leon walked around to the driver's side to get in. Leon looked back and nodded again at Rev. Dell who responded with a nod.

Summertime in San Francisco could get cold and windy. But in the Fillmore, the weather was usually sunny and comfortable. The Fillmore had some of the best weather in the city. The fog would roll in during the evenings but would burn off by noon, giving way to nice, comfortable, sunny weather.

Hank and Dexter spent most of their days catching the bus up Haight Street to the Ernest Engle Boys Club at the entrance to Golden Gate Park on Page Street. At the boys club, they played billiards, ping-pong, and bumper pool, and participated in some arts and crafts activities. Usually they brought a pair of swimming trunks for a swim in the swimming pool. Many times they ventured into Golden Gate Park and explored its vast gardens, trails, lakes, ponds, playgrounds, and meadows. It didn't take long for them to come to know just about every inch of the park.

The boys club was having a two-week camping trip to a boys camp in Mendocino County. Dexter wanted to go, but Hank really wasn't interested. Dexter talked his mother into letting them go; Margaret felt she could use the break.

Dexter had a fondness for animals and critters, a feeling he got from his father. He'd had pet hamsters, rabbits, turtles, lizards, and frogs. At that particular time, he had a pet white rat, which he wanted to take with him to camp. Margaret didn't care if he took the rat, because she knew she wasn't going to be able to care for it while they were away.

Mary arrived to take the boys to the boys club for the bus ride to the camp. When Dexter walked out carrying the small cage with the white rat inside, his grandmother suggested that he not take it. But Dexter put up such a fuss, he was allowed to take it.

Craigmont Camp was a great place for boys. Everything was there for boys to enjoy. They could swim, play games, and participate in many activities. On the third day of camp, the counselors announced that they were all going on an overnight hike, and they'd sleep out under the stars. The hike was about five miles each way. There were trails that went through meadows, around creeks, through forests, and along steep hills. At times, it got pretty challenging, but the boys endured. Hank occasionally complained, but Dexter helped him along. They hiked until it got dark.

After nightfall, the group set camp and started several campfires. They roasted marshmallows and hot dogs, and several kids traded ghost stories. After the stories and eating, it was time to bed down. Everyone climbed into his sleeping bag, and the fires were put out. Dexter lay in his sleeping bag and looked up at the stars. He couldn't remember seeing so many stars in the sky. At first, it seemed as though they were in pitch darkness. But then he noticed, with the moon shining bright, he could actually see at night.

Next to Dexter lay Hank. He was in his sleeping bag and was rocking back and forth. Dexter noticed that Hank was crying silently. He reached out to his brother, tapped him, and asked, "Hank, what's wrong?"

Hank was sobbing as he turned over to face his brother. Dexter could just make out Hank's face in the moonlight. Tears were streaming down his face. "I want to go home. I want my Baba. I don't like it here." He looked scared.

"Aren't you having fun?" asked Dexter.

"No, I want to go home," replied Hank.

The boys had tried to call home from a pay phone before they left for the overnight hike, but Margaret wasn't at home. They hadn't spoken to their mother since the day they arrived when they called to say they'd made it okay. Dexter tried to comfort Hank and told him they'd call their mother as soon as they got back to base camp the next day. Hank said okay and turned back over and rocked himself to sleep.

The next morning, Dexter was the first to wake up. He noticed he was feeling itchy, and he started to scratch. Then he noticed the itch felt more like stings or bites. He sat up and unzipped his bag. There were large red ants crawling all around in his sleeping bag and on him too. He jumped up and shouted and began to brush himself off. In a moment, several other boys jumped up and did the same because they had the same problem. Dexter then looked around and noticed they were in the middle of a field with cattle grazing no farther than a hundred feet from where they'd set camp, and there were cattle droppings everywhere. Suddenly, camping didn't seem so much fun anymore. He quickly changed clothes and crushed every ant he could find.

On the way back to the main camping lodge, the boys encountered lots of wildlife. They came across a bobcat, a fox, eagles, and rattlesnakes. Whenever they encountered a lizard or horned toad, Dexter would try to catch it. When the boys arrived back at the lodge, Dexter hurried to his bunk to check on his white rat. When he arrived, the cage was empty. His rat was gone; someone had released it. He searched everywhere, but it was too late. The rat was gone.

Hank was getting impatient; he wanted to call his mother, so the boys walked down to the phone booth. Dexter dialed the number and listened to the ring. After the third ring, Margaret answered the phone.

"Baba, it's me, Dexter,"

Hank grabbed the phone away from Dexter and cried into the phone, "Baba, I want to come home." Dexter tried to calm Hank and told him to stop crying. He could hear his mother saying no, that they should stay at the camp.

Hank's cries began to get louder and uncontrollable. Margaret wanted to speak to Dexter; she told Hank to put him on the phone. Dexter took the phone and Margaret started questioning him about their activities and if they were having a good time. Dexter explained that he was having fun, but he kept looking at Hank who was crying, with tears flowing down his cheeks, looking genuinely sad. Hank was crying for his mother, expressing that he wanted to go home.

Hank said he wanted to speak to Baba, and he continued crying. While watching his brother cry, Dexter suddenly became sad and homesick too. Hank's crying became contagious, and so Dexter began to cry as well. Dexter then got on the phone and asked to come home.

So the next day, Mary and Margaret drove out to Mendocino County to pick up the boys. Hank was ready to go, but by then, Dexter wanted to stay. Margaret decided to make both the boys come home.

As the summer continued, the boys stayed busy with church, singing in the choir, Bible school, rehearsals, and the boys club.

It had been two years since the boys had seen or heard from their father. Then one day, the doorbell rang, and there he was. Duane's hair was beginning to thin, and he had grown a beard. In his arms was a small cage, and inside was a snake; it was a king snake, long and black with white rings. Excited, Hank and Dexter jumped up and down, climbing on their father, trying to get a look. The snake was wide-awake, and its tongue flicked in and out of its mouth.

Margaret was not too fond of the idea of the kids having a pet snake, but she knew it would break their hearts if she objected. Plus, she was used to the way Duane had been with animals, and she knew it had rubbed off on the boys, especially Dexter. He was always bringing home some kind of critter he'd caught in the park.

Duane had come to take the boys away for a couple of weeks to visit his parents who were living in King City. Dexter was ready to go, but Hank, as usual, wanted to stay home. But Margaret told Hank that he had to go, so the boys were off.

The first week, Duane took the boys camping. Duane brought along a girlfriend, and they drove down the coast to Big Sur. It was a great trip with lots of swimming, sleeping in tents, hiking, and learning about the forest. Duane knew everything about the plants, animals, trees, trails, and the stars. He knew the names of just about every kind of rock and stone, and he and the boys collected samples and labeled them. Duane tried to teach the boys as much about the outdoors as he could while he had them.

Duane and the boys caught snakes, lizards, frogs, and turtles, and Duane taught them what species they all were. The boys had a good time, and Duane loved every minute of it too.

One night, as they were about to turn in, Hank reminded Dexter they had to pray. It was something their mother had taught them to do every night, but they had gone a few nights without saying their prayers. "Come on, Dexter, we have to say our prayers," Hank said as he got on his knees.

Dexter said, "I don't feel like praying right now."

"Shh, God will hear you. You better get on your knees and pray. Now you have to ask him to forgive you," responded Hank.

Duane saw what was happening, but he didn't want to be an influence in the matter. Dexter then said, "Daddy doesn't pray, do you, Daddy?"

Duane had to think about how he was going to respond to this. Hank then asked, "Why don't you pray, Daddy? Don't you believe in God?"

"Dexter, Hank, I don't know what I believe in. I believe there is something that's greater than us. But I don't know what it is. I can't say whether it's God or not. I've been reading about Buddha, which is a god that the Chinese believe in. I meditate sometimes, which you could say is like praying. I can't tell you what to do or believe in. But you should listen to your mother and do as she says. One day, when you are grown, you'll be able to make up your own minds. That's what I did," Duane said.

"Well, I know there's a God, and I'm going to pray," said Hank.

"Dexter, you'd better pray too," instructed Duane.

Dexter got down on his knees, and the boys said their prayers together. "Now I lay me down to sleep, I pray the Lord ..."

The next week, they headed back to the cabin in Los Gatos to spend the night before heading to King City. The next day, they headed out for the long drive. King City was a small town in the central valley, a farm town with a large garlic factory. Duane's parents had moved there and stayed on a lot that was about an acre. The lot had a small church on it with some living quarters attached, which was where they lived. There was also a small barn, and they had a few animals. They also had two Chihuahua dogs that they loved and treated like children.

Duane's parents, Muriel and Henry, were running a ministry in the small town. The church was a Kingdom Hall for the Jehovah's Witnesses, and Henry was the leader of the congregation, the overseer. Henry also worked at the garlic factory. Hank and Dexter knew their grandparents, and they were excited to see them, but they'd never really spent a lot of time with them. This was a chance for them to really get to know Grandmamma and Grandpapa and to meet some of the other family members.

The boys were able to meet their aunt Dawn, Duane's sister, and their cousins, Mikey and Duana. Everyone made them feel like family and embraced them with love and comfort. Just like Duane, his sister and her children had dark hair, which they got from Henry (Grandpapa). Muriel (Grandmamma) had blond hair and blue eyes, but the Native American in Henry was dominant in their children.

Hank and Dexter were now nine and ten years old, and they had come to realize that the world was not just black and white, but that the world was made up of all types of people. After all, they were growing up in San Francisco, one of the most diverse cities in the world.

One thing they did realize and were regularly reminded of was that they were Negro. They would be with their father who'd introduce them to someone as his sons, and there would always be that puzzled look on the person's face, as if to say, "But those are Negroes," or even in some cases, "… niggers." But, as far as things went with the family, family was family, and everyone in the family treated them as such.

That Sunday, there was service in the Kingdom Hall. Henry introduced his grandsons to the congregation and then led the service. Hank and Dexter had their own Bibles with them; they opened their Bibles and read along when scriptures were read. The boys knew a lot about the Bible. Their mother had taught them well, and church was almost all they lived for. Margaret had had them memorize the names and order of all the books of the Bible by the time they were seven and eight years old. The parishioners in Henry's congregation were impressed by how attentive and studious the boys appeared to be.

That evening, while sitting around the living room, Muriel asked Dexter to bring her his Bible. Dexter took her his Bible, and she held it in her hand. It had a zipper on it, and on the end of the zipper was a cross. Muriel grabbed the cross and showed it to Dexter. "Do you know what this is?" she asked.

"It's a cross," replied Dexter.

"Yes, but what does this cross mean? What does it symbolize?" she asked him. Hank sat close by and watched.

Dexter said, "Jesus died on the cross for our sins."

"Yes, he died on a cross, and we use the cross as a symbol that he was killed on the cross. How would you like it if someone killed you on a cross, and everyone took around a cross to celebrate your being killed?" she asked.

"I don't know," replied Dexter.

Muriel grabbed the cross and yanked it off the Bible. "No!" Dexter shouted as he reached for his Bible. "My godmother gave me that Bible. She's going to be mad that you took off my cross," said Dexter.

"Well, you shouldn't be celebrating that Jesus died," she replied. Grandmamma had thrown the cross on the couch next to her. Dexter grabbed it and walked out of the room and went into the bedroom. He was angry and hurt. Hank walked in behind him and announced that he was ready to go home. Dexter said, "Me too."

The next day, Dexter and Hank were playing outside, and Hank was chasing a rooster. He'd been told on more than one occasion not to chase the rooster, but he wouldn't listen. At one point, he cornered the rooster, and then fell to the ground near the rooster. The rooster then jumped up on top of Hank and pecked him on his nose. Hank jumped up and ran into the house, crying. His nose was bleeding, but when he went to Grandmamma, she scolded him for chasing the rooster. She cleaned up his cut and sent him back outside.

The next day, Hank's nose was swollen and red; it was infected. Hank was now more than ever ready to go home. The boys called their grandmother, Nanny, instead of calling their mother. They knew that Margaret might try and make them stay.

Dexter dialed the number while Hank sat near. "Hello?" Mary answered the phone.

"Nanny, we're ready to come home," said Dexter.

"What's wrong? What's wrong with you?" asked Mary. Mary had a love-hate relationship with white folks. On one hand she loved them, and on the other, she didn't trust them. She'd say things like, "White folks are nasty," or "You can't trust white folks."

Dexter began to tell Mary about the Bible situation just as Muriel walked into the room. "Who are you talking to?" she asked.

"My grandmother, Nanny," replied Dexter. Muriel stopped short and walked out of the room. But she stood near so she could listen.

Again Dexter started telling Nanny about the cross. When he said a rooster had bitten Hank, Mary yelled, "What?"

Hank heard his grandmother yell through the phone, and he grabbed the phone from Dexter. He then said to his grandmother, "Nanny, a rooster bit me, and my nose is all swollen and red, and it hurts. I want to come home. Come pick us up."

"I'll come and pick you up first thing in the morning. Let me speak to Muriel," instructed Mary.

Mary got on the phone with Muriel, and she let her have it. Hank and Dexter could hear her loud voice through the phone. Muriel was embarrassed because Mary also intimidated her. She knew Mary from the few times they'd met, and she knew Mary was a strong, Negro, no-nonsense kind of woman. Muriel also knew her son, Duane, would be upset if she got into a confrontation with Mary. The best thing for her to do was be cooperative. She told Mary that she'd have the boys ready. The boys could hear Nanny say, "You do that!" and Muriel hung up the phone.

Muriel became really passive and nice to the boys after she got off the phone. She began to try and entertain them and show them love. The boys really did love Henry and Muriel, but they were ready to get back to the city. The next day, Mary didn't get there until late afternoon. She had calmed down, but she still had some attitude, especially after she saw Hank's swollen red nose. Muriel was being very courteous and accommodating.

Duane wasn't around when Mary arrived, because he'd left the boys to visit with their grandparents for a few days. Muriel told the boys that she'd tell their father good-bye for them. They said thank you and piled into the car. BD was at the wheel; he hit Highway 101 and headed north. As soon as darkness fell, Dexter and Hank fell fast asleep in the backseat. When they woke up, they were at their grandmother's house.

Summer break was about to end, and soon the boys would have to be back in school. Each year they'd get new clothes for school and maybe a new suit for church. Whenever it was time to go downtown and shop, it was also time to dress up. Margaret would have the boys put on some slacks and dress shoes, along with a nice shirt and sweater. In many cases, she'd have them dress alike.

Margaret was in her bedroom getting dressed, and the boys were getting dressed in their room. Hank had picked out the clothes he wanted Margaret to wear, along with shoes, handbag, and jewelry. He rushed to get dressed so he could help his mother dress up. He loved to comb her hair and assist her with her makeup. Margaret loved the attention that Hank gave her in these moments. She'd sit on her stool in front of the dresser mirror, and Hank would make a fuss over her. When he added lipstick to her face, he'd get so close to her that she could feel his breath on her face. It was always the perfect moment to steal a kiss from her baby boy. Hank would voice a little complaint, "Baba, you got lipstick on me." Margaret would just laugh, and then grab him and kiss him all over his face.

Once they were dressed, it was time to leave. Margaret would have Dexter check how much money they had. She only had fifty dollars in her pocketbook, so they needed to go to the bank. They stepped out the door, and Margaret pulled out her folding cane. Hank began leading his mother down the stairs to the sidewalk, and Dexter made sure the door was closed and locked. Dexter then jumped down the stairs and positioned himself on the opposite side of Hank. They headed down Waller Street to Fillmore and then on toward Haight Street.

The bank was at the corner of Haight and Fillmore Streets. The tellers knew Margaret and the boys very well. They waited in line for the next teller, and then walked up to the window. Hank and Dexter's heads were just about level with the counter where they could grab onto it and stand on tiptoe to have a good look at the teller and the money.

"Hello, Margaret," said the teller.

"Oh hello, Jamie. I didn't know that was you," responded Margaret.

"What can I do for you today?" asked the teller.

Margaret felt for her savings book and held it out in front of her for the teller to take. She then said, "I'd like to withdraw two hundred dollars, please."

Hank and Dexter let out a "Wow," and looked at each other like they were about to get some candy.

"Sure, we can do that for you," said the teller as she verified the funds.

The teller then counted out the cash in twenties for Margaret while Dexter looked on and counted along.

After Margaret received the money, she pulled the fifty dollars out of her purse, separated the two twenties from around the ten, then placed them with the other twenties as Dexter and Hank looked on. "Would you break this ten for me? We need to catch the bus, and I don't have any change," Margaret asked the teller. The teller then gave Margaret back one five and four one-dollar bills, three quarters, and five nickels. It was a nickel each to ride the bus. Margaret then asked Dexter which one was the five, and she folded it separately from the ones, and then folded the ones.

Once Margaret had the money in her purse, she asked the teller, "Is there a desk or table I can sit down at for a moment?"

"Sure, you can use the small desk over there," said the teller as she pointed it out for the boys.

"Thank you," replied Margaret.

"Take us over to the table, sons," instructed Margaret. They approached the table, and the boys helped Margaret sit down. She then took the folded twenties out of her purse along with a writing pen. "Dexter, I want you to take this pen and write the letter D on the front of each of these twenty-dollar bills. Put it right next to the face," Margaret instructed.

Dexter took the pen and wrote the letter D on each of the bills, and then gave them back to his mother. Margaret folded the bills together and put them back in the small money pouch in her purse.

Once they left the bank, Margaret and the boys took the bus on Haight Street and headed downtown. First, they stopped by The Emporium and got some new shoes for the boys. On the second stop, they went by the City of Paris department store where Margaret got some makeup. They shopped at the White House department store, and Hank picked out a hat for his mother. Next, it was time to visit Bonds department store on Post Street to buy a few pairs of shirts and pants and some sweaters for the boys.

After spending quite a bit of time in Bonds, they were loaded down with shopping bags. Margaret always had one last stop to make before heading home. She wanted to go by Woolworth's and get some candy for her and the boys. Woolworth's had the best selection of candy in town. There was a display case that was a whole aisle long, full of all types of candy. You could buy it by the piece or by the pound.

Margaret and the boys stepped over to the counter, where they had to wait because the clerk was helping someone else. A white man walked over to the other side of Dexter and stood at the counter to be waited on. When the clerk was done with her customer, she looked and saw Margaret and the two boys, and then went over to the white man and said, "May I help you?"

Margaret began to speak, but the white man cut her off. She quickly realized what had happened and interjected, "Excuse me, Miss, but we were here first."

The clerk was aware all along that Margaret and the boys had been standing at the counter before the man had arrived. She looked at the man, and he said, "Yes, they were before me. You go ahead and take care of them."

"Thank you," said Margaret, turning to face the direction of the man.

"All right, what would you like?" asked the clerk, with a negative attitude. This type of negative attitude did not faze Margaret; she had encountered it before, and she knew this wouldn't be the last time.

Margaret ordered some corn candy for the boys, some chocolate turtles and large candy-cane sticks for herself, and then she decided to get some rock candy that she'd later give to Annie. After she was finished with her order, the clerk went to the register to ring up the charges. She came back to Margaret and announced, "That will be one dollar and seventy-six cents. Margaret knew she had a couple of twenties left and wanted to break one. She reached into her purse and pulled out a twenty-dollar bill and gave it to Dexter to hand to the lady.

The clerk went to the register and came back and counted the change back to Margaret. "Okay, that's two, three, four, five, and five is ten."

"Excuse me, Miss, but I gave you a twenty-dollar bill," Margaret said firmly.

"Uh uh, no, you gave me a ten," replied the woman.

"I'm sorry, but you need to go back and check again, because I gave you a twenty-dollar bill," Margaret said sternly and a little louder.

"No, Missy, I know what you gave me. You gave me a ten," said the smart-alecky clerk.

Hank looked at the lady and started to get angry. "My mother gave you twenty dollars. You're trying to cheat us," he said loudly. The ruckus was now starting to draw attention.

"Miss, you need to get the manager, because I'm not leaving this store until you give me the rest of my money," Margaret shouted.

The man standing next to Dexter decided to leave. Dexter was starting to get uncomfortable because people were looking at them because they were causing a lot of commotion.

"I don't need to get the manager, because I know what you gave me," said the clerk again.

Just then another woman, who was also a clerk behind the counter, but at the other end, came over to see what was going on. She inquired of her co-worker, "What's the problem?"

The first clerk then said, "This gal thinks she gave me twenty dollars, when she gave me a ten."

The woman was now disrespecting Margaret. "I am not a gal, and I'm sure if you look in your cash register, you will find a twenty-dollar bill, and it will have the letter D written on it next to the face on the front of the bill," Margaret said confidently.

Just then, the manager walked up and inquired quietly of the two clerks what the problem was. The second clerk informed the manager what the problem was. They went to the register, and the manager pulled out the twenty-dollar bill that was on top. He looked at the twenty-dollar bill and saw the D written on the front next to the face. He then looked over to Hank and Dexter who were both watching him and were aware that he'd seen the D.

The manager was burning up with anger at the clerk who'd tried to cheat Margaret. She stood there, gasping and ashamed, because she knew she'd been caught. The manager apologized to Margaret and the boys and gave her back the whole twenty dollars and told her to keep the change and the candy. He also informed her that it would never happen again. Margaret accepted the man's apology, and then she and the boys left the store. Dexter flagged down a yellow cab, and the family headed home.

11

A Time for Adventure

The next day, Dexter wanted to buy a small mouse to feed his snake. The closest pet store was on Haight Street near Ashbury Street. Margaret gave the boys enough money to buy a mouse, get something to eat, and catch the bus. But the boys also wanted to buy some candy at a candy and toy store near the pet shop, so they decided to walk all the way up Haight Street to save some money.

Walking up Haight Street was always an adventure for the boys. There was always something to see or do. On the Fillmore end of Haight Street, there was a lot of commerce. There were a few stores, a church, some bars and restaurants, a bookstore, a pharmacy, and some knick-knack shops.

Heading toward Ashbury Street, it became more residential until you passed Yerba Buena Park and the school they attended. Once you hit the intersection of Masonic, Haight Street once again became a really busy place. It was bustling with traffic and commerce. Just about every kind of store or shop you could imagine was on Haight Street between Masonic and Stanyan Street, the entrance to Golden Gate

Park. There was plenty for the boys to see or even to get them into trouble.

Hank and Dexter had come to know every block of Haight Street. They knew every storefront and what was housed there. Sometimes they'd plant themselves outside an establishment, watch people as they came and went, and also watch what was going on inside.

There were coffee houses that beatniks would frequent and read poetry and listen to jazz. These places always reminded Dexter of his father. Duane loved jazz, and he had a look that was similar to the beatniks' the last time Dexter had seen him.

There was a liquor store that had a magazine rack sitting out in front of it on the sidewalk. The boys would go over to the store, and Dexter would scan the magazines on display. Some of the magazines had covers with explicit pictures of scantily clothed, caricatured women, depicting the images of stories inside. They were magazines with titles like Stag, Men, and Man Magazine. Hank really wasn't interested in the magazines, so he'd just stand nearby and wait. Sometimes Hank would scan a MAD magazine. Dexter would look inside the store and wait to see when the cashier got busy. When a customer approached the counter, Dexter would pick up one of the magazines to see the women inside. The cashier would yell out at them, and Dexter would quickly put the magazine back on the rack, and the boys would run off.

Before heading to the pet store, the boys stopped by the candy store. It was a small shop, dark and cluttered with toys and shelves of candy. They had just about any type of candy you could want. Hank purchased some Dot candy with little dot droppings of candy in different colors attached to long strips of paper. He'd peel a dot off the paper and eat it. Dexter purchased a Winner sucker. It was a sucker that came in purple or red, which, when unwrapped, if there was a paper strip over the sucker, you won another one for free.

The boys had some extra change that their mother had given them when they left to go shopping, so Dexter purchased some itching powder and some sneezing powder. Hank purchased a fake turd.

The next stop the boys made was the pet shop. Dexter purchased a small mouse to feed the snake, and then they petted the puppies and kittens and left to head home. Hank and Dexter were tired and didn't feel like walking home, but they had spent all of their money. Dexter decided they should try to sneak a ride on the bus. Hank objected, but Dexter told him not to worry. The boys went to the bus stop that was in front of the liquor store and waited for a bus, positioning themselves close to the magazine rack so it wouldn't appear to the bus driver that they were waiting.

First a 71 bus line came, and there were not very many people on it, so they had to wait. Soon the 72 bus line came; Dexter looked toward the driver, who was a white man. The driver looked Dexter directly in his eyes momentarily, and then put his attention back to pulling up to the curb to pick up passengers. There were several people on the bus that were standing in the rear waiting to get off, and there were also several passengers waiting to get on.

When the bus pulled up to the curb, the driver opened the front doors, and people began departing. The back doors to the bus opened, and Dexter said, "Come on, Hank," and they darted for the back door.

People were departing down the steps of the back door to get off, and Hank and Dexter were kneeling down and climbing up the back steps to sneak onto the bus. Once they got on the bus, Hank grabbed a seat, which was the only one vacant, and Dexter stood holding onto a rail.

"Hey, you two!" yelled the driver. "Get off my bus," he demanded angrily. Dexter and Hank scrambled off the bus.

"Damn," Dexter complained. He was tired, and his feet hurt, and he didn't want to walk home. "Let's wait for another bus," he told Hank.

Hank again objected, but Dexter overruled. They stood back from the bus stop and waited for another bus. This time the 7 line bus came. It was a trolley bus that had two long poles attached to the top that drew electric power from twin cables that hung from poles up and down the street.

Dexter again looked at the driver as he approached. Once again the driver glanced at him; this time it was a Negro driver. The bus pulled up to the curb, and the doors opened, and then people began to depart.

"Come on, Hank," said Dexter, and they ran for the back door. Again they kneeled and crawled past the people departing from the back. This time, the bus was packed, and there was nowhere to sit.

The boys quickly moved all the way to the back of the bus and stood between people to hide.

This time, no one said anything, and the bus pulled off and headed down Haight Street toward Fillmore. When the bus reached Steiner Street, the boys got off and walked around the corner to their home.

When the boys got home, they were tired from the day's adventure. Dexter went out onto the back porch where the cage with the snake was kept. He went to open the top of the cage to drop the mouse in and noticed that the top was ajar. Dexter looked inside the cage. There was no snake. He must not have locked the cage properly the last time he handled the snake. He tried to think back to when he'd last played with the snake but was sure he'd locked the cage.

"Hank, come here," Dexter called out. Hank ran out onto the back porch. "The snake is gone."

Hank put his hands up to his mouth in shock. "What are we going to do?" asked Hank.

"Let's look for it," instructed Dexter.

Dexter and Hank began to search the house; Margaret noticed that something was up with the boys. "Hank, Dexter, what are you boys doing?"

Dexter looked at Hank, trying to figure out what to say. "Ah, I don't know," answered Dexter.

Now Margaret was really curious. That kind of an answer spelled trouble. "What do you mean, you don't know? Come here. Come to me now," she demanded. "What are you doing? What happened? You tell Baba, and don't you lie. What did you do?"

Dexter told her how he'd gone to feed the snake but found that the snake was wasn't there and said that they were trying to find it. Margaret was upset, but she wasn't angry. She instructed the boys to continue looking for the snake. They looked but couldn't find it.

After dinner, Margaret told the boys to get undressed and get ready to take a bath. Hank and Dexter went to their rooms and undressed while Margaret ran the water. When the water was ready, the boys were in the room, naked, waiting to get into the tub. Margaret walked into their room with an electric extension cord in her hand.

"What do you think you're doing, sneaking on buses? Huh? Answer me. What do you think you're doing?" asked Margaret.

Hank and Dexter were stunned; how did she know? "Now, didn't you sneak on the bus? Didn't you?" asked Margaret. There was silence. "Answer me, and don't you lie to me. Don't you ever lie to me," she demanded.

"Yes, Baba," Dexter answered nervously as Hank began to cry.

"I'm sorry, Baba," Hank cried. "I'm sorry. I won't do it again."

"I know you won't," said Margaret. "Dexter, come here. Come here," Margaret ordered. The boys never ran from their mother when they were going to be whipped. They were always obedient and took their punishment.

Dexter walked over to his mother and gave her his hand. She grabbed his hand and began to whip. Dexter kept jumping and trying to make her miss. He also was trying not to cry. Margaret kept striking until she began to connect and the blows were whipping across Dexter's legs with a fierce sting. Still, he bit his lip, refusing to cry. Red welts started to pop up across Dexter's legs and rear end. He jumped, and Margaret missed. She took another swing, and the tip of the cord whipped across Dexter's penis. This time he hollered and started crying and yelling, "I'm sorry, Baba. Baba, I'm sorry. I won't do it again."

Hank stood nearby, watching. He was bawling his eyes out, and he hadn't even been touched yet. Margaret released Dexter and called Hank over. He started apologizing and begging and crying even more. He gave his hand to his mother, and she raised the cord and began to whip. Hank hollered so loud, the neighbors down the block could probably have heard him. Upstairs, Lucy and Victor and Loretta could hear the spankings taking place. Above them, John and Eddie could hear. Everyone in the building knew Hank and Dexter were in trouble and were being punished.

After the whippings, Margaret told the boys to go and take their baths. Dexter got in the tub, sobbing.

"Shut up, and be quiet," Margaret shot out at him. She was angry, and she wanted them to know it. She kept on talking from different parts of the house as she moved about. "Don't you know you can't go anywhere in this town where somebody I know won't see you?" she muttered. "God don't like ugly. He knows I'm trying to do the best I can with you two boys. When you do wrong, he's going to let me know. Don't you ever do anything that I'd be ashamed of. If you do, I'm going to find out, and I'm going to tear your hides up," she shouted from the kitchen as she began washing dishes. "Do you hear me?" she asked.

"Yes, Baba," the boys muttered.

"Do you hear me?" Her voice got louder.

"Yes, Baba," the boys shouted.

Margaret was well known in the Baptist church community around San Francisco. She had sung in front of just about every large congregation in the city. Her choirs followed the pastor from church to church, participating in musicals, revivals, Men's Day, Women's Day, and all kinds of special events.

Margaret performed at Third Baptist Church, Evergreen Baptist Church, Mount Zion Baptist Church, Friendship Baptist Church, and Providence Baptist Church, as well as many others throughout the Bay Area. Everywhere she went, the pastors asked her to do a solo. Most of the time, she sang "Shine on Me." Because of her performances, she became known as the blind woman singer with two little boys, and due to Margaret's notoriety, many people knew the boys when they saw them.

In this case, the bus driver had recognized Dexter and Hank when they snuck onto his bus. It was because of Margaret that he'd let them go. But when he got off work, he called one of the sisters he knew at First Union and informed her of what had happened. She, in turn, called Margaret and informed her of what the boys had done. Dexter and Hank now understood that their mother had eyes everywhere, and they needed to be good, or at least they'd better keep a sharp eye out for people who might know their mother.

A few days after the bus incident, Margaret was going to have her hair done. Leon had offered to take her, so she decided to see if she could get someone to watch the boys. Margaret called Annie, who agreed to sit the boys.

It was rare for Margaret to leave the boys alone and unattended. There had been one occasion when she was unable to get anyone to watch the boys. She needed to go Christmas shopping without the boys, because she didn't want them to see what she was getting for them. Normally, Hank and Dexter didn't mind being left alone while their mother went out, but on that occasion, when Margaret had gone out alone, Dexter had strongly objected, and he was a nervous wreck the whole time she was away.

Hank and Dexter loved their great-grandmother Annie. Even though she was now seventy-two years old, she still had lots of energy. She was small and petite and appeared fragile but was actually strong, physically and mentally. When the boys were small, they used to climb up on her, and she'd cross her legs so they could ride her foot, like a pony. But they'd also grown to treat her carefully. As far as Annie was concerned, if they got out of line, they could still be whipped. Annie had given them their share of spankings when they were younger, and they knew she wouldn't hesitate to get a strap if they got into trouble. Plus, Annie had many times told the story about her taking care of her father when he got old and sick and she'd kept him out of the poor house. They knew that when Annie came over, she'd tell it to them again.

Annie had no problem catching the bus wherever she needed to go. To get to Margaret's, she only needed to catch one bus from Potrero Hill. She could leave the house and walk up the hill on Missouri Street and catch the 22 Fillmore bus in front of Mr. Munter's dry-goods store. The 22 bus came by frequently, so she never had to stand and wait very long.

Dexter and Hank were eagerly awaiting Annie, so when she arrived and rang the doorbell, the boys went running to the door. "Momma," they yelled out as they ran. She could hear them, and see them running through the sheer curtains on the glass front door. Dexter and Hank opened the door, and Annie was showered with their love. She loved it.

She walked into the apartment and down the hallway to the kitchen; she had a brown paper shopping bag in her hand. Leon was in the kitchen, sitting at the table. "How do, ma'am?" he said.

"Howdy, Mr. Leon," she answered. Annie walked over to the refrigerator and put in some fruit she'd brought with her. She then walked back down the hall and entered Margaret's room. Margaret was putting on her dress and called for Hank to come and give her some assistance.

"Neelmah, how you doing, child?" Annie asked.

"Oh, Momma, I'm doing all right. How are you? Are you getting ready to move?" asked Margaret.

Annie sat on the bed and got comfortable. "Child, I'll never get used to moving. I don't know why we're moving in the first place. I'm fine just where we are. That's Mary's foolishness. Always talking about how she needs more room, wants a garage, bigger kitchen. Ever since we moved out here from Little Rock, she just gets more citified every day."

Margaret didn't respond; she just smiled at what Annie was saying. Mary and BD had purchased another home in the Bayview district. Many middle-class Negroes had moved there from the Fillmore. The Bayview had newer homes that were more modern, and most of them had garages where one or two cars could fit. There were also many Negroes who worked in the naval shipyard who'd settled in the community. The Bayview district also lay in the foothills of Hunter's Point, which was a major housing project development that housed many of the city's low-income Negroes. It was also an area plagued with crime.

What Annie had yet to understand was that Margaret was going to move into the house on Missouri Street and rent it from her mother! Margaret hadn't yet told the boys they'd be moving. She saw no point in telling them until it was about time to move.

Margaret and Leon were about to leave, and Annie called out for the boys. Hank and Dexter came running. She reached down into her shopping bag and pulled out an empty coffee can. She reached into her purse and pulled out an empty canister of snuff. "Now, Hank and Dexter, I want you to go down to the corner store and take this here empty snuff can with you. Tell the man behind the counter that you want a can of snuff just like this one. Now make sure it's just like this one." She then pulled the money out of her small pocket purse and gave it to the boys along with a dime for each of them. "Make sure you come right back home," she added.

The boys took off for the corner store, and Leon and Margaret left for her hair appointment. Annie went into the family room and positioned Margaret's rocker in front of the TV. She went into the kitchen and poured herself a glass of water, and then planted herself down to watch some wrestling on television. When the boys returned, she took a drink of water, then took her teeth out and put them into the glass. Hank and Dexter stood before her and watched the ritual. She then opened the small container of snuff, pulled out her bottom lip, and tapped a portion between her bottom gums and her lip. She sat the coffee can down on the floor and sat back in the chair. She then told the boys to go and play but not to go too far.

Hank and Dexter asked Annie if they could go into the backyard; she thought that was a good idea and gave her okay. Dexter ran to his room to get some toys, and Hank headed for the back door. Suddenly, Hank yelled out, "Dexter, I see the snake."

Annie didn't know what was going on, but she knew she'd heard the word snake. Dexter came running down the hall toward the back porch and almost knocked Annie down, trying to get to Hank. She caught herself by grabbing the doorway and looked at Dexter as he asked Hank, "Where?"

Hank stooped down and pointed to the pipes under the sink. Dexter crouched down and looked and saw the snake curled around the pipe, resting.

"I'll get it," said Dexter as he began to slowly reach for the snake.

"Boy, get back away from that thing. Don't you touch that snake! If that thing bites you, you'll die for sure," Annie shouted.

"No, Momma, it's not poisonous; it's a king snake," replied Dexter.

"Boy, I said get back," she yelled, and she grabbed Dexter and pulled him back away from the snake.

Annie looked around and saw a broom. She grabbed the broom and moved to beat the snake, but Dexter grabbed the broom from her. "No, it's my pet snake. My daddy gave it to me. Stop, no, stop!" yelled Dexter.

Hank just stood back and watched the action.

"Boy, I said get back, and I mean get back," yelled Annie.

Annie commenced to beat the snake with the broom. The snake was caught by surprise and tried to get away, but it was too late. Annie used that broom as if she'd had experience with this kind of stuff. She beat the snake until it began to bleed and became limp. After it was obvious the snake was dead, she instructed the boys to go back into the house, saying she'd have Leon get rid of it when he and Margaret returned.

Annie had the boys come into the family room for a lecture. She told the story about the woman who came home on a cold winter day and saw a snake, near frozen, in her walkway. She told them how the lady had said, "Oh, look at the poor snake, all frozen stiff. Don't worry, I'll take you inside and warm you up and take care of you." She told them how the woman put the snake in her bosom to warm it up, but that, after the snake thawed out, it bit her. The woman asked, "Why did you bite me when I was trying to take care of you?" The snake replied, "You knew I was a snake when you brought me in."

"Boys, you can't trust a snake. I don't care what nobody says. They are all poisonous," Annie told them.

Dexter wanted to dispute it, but he knew it was no use. Annie was old and set in her ways, and there was nothing he could say to change her mind, but he was clearly upset about losing the snake for a second time. Annie then began to preach to them.

"Look here, Dexter, I don't like you not minding me. I got a good mind to whip you. You need to obey me when I tell you something. The Bible says, 'Honor thy father and thy mother that thy days may be long.' This is the only verse with promise."

Hank and Dexter just stood there and nodded their heads. They could have recited it themselves. They must have heard it a hundred times, and it wouldn't be the last time they'd hear it.

"I should whip you, boy. The Bible says that I'm supposed to whip you. It says, 'Chasten thy son while there is hope. And let not thy soul spare for his crying,'—Proverbs 19 and 18. I should spare not the rod and chasten the child," she said. "I'm going to let you go this time because your daddy gave you that snake. You go on and play now and think about what Momma done told ya," she instructed.

Annie went back into the family room and sat, thinking about Duane. "Boy, that Duane, he was something else. Actually, white folks is something else. Taking snakes for pets, and all."

One day Hank and Dexter were at the boys club; Hank was downstairs playing bumper pool while Dexter was upstairs in the arts and crafts center, making a clear plastic heart-shaped charm to wear around his neck. Hank was getting hungry, but they only had enough money to catch the bus home. Dexter knew he didn't want to walk all the way home, and he didn't want to sneak on the bus.

Dexter thought for a moment and had an idea on how they could get some money. He and Hank and another boy left the club and headed for the entrance to Golden Gate Park at Stanyan and Haight

Streets. There was a pond at the park where people threw coins in, like a wishing well.

"Okay, this is what we're going to do," said Dexter. "There's not much money in here, but there's more at the Japanese Tea Garden. We can get enough money here to get inside there, and when we get inside the Tea Garden, we can get more money."

It was a great idea! So the boys took off their shoes, rolled up their pant legs, and waded out into the pond and started collecting coins. After they'd collected enough for admission into the Tea Garden, they dressed and hiked their way over to the garden.

The boys paid their way in, and then worked their way over to one of the goldfish ponds where there were lots of coins. "All right now, we have to be careful, and we have to move fast. Go for the quarters and half dollars. Fill your pockets with as much as you can, and be ready to run when they come," said Dexter.

Hank stayed at the water's edge and served as a lookout. Dexter and the other boy took off their shoes and rolled up their pant legs. They sat next to the bank until the coast was clear, and then jumped in. They scooped up coins and filled their pockets, all the while getting wet. After a few minutes, a tourist asked what they were doing. Dexter replied that he'd dropped his keys and was looking for them. The tourist then said he'd go to get some management. At that point, the boys jumped out of the water and grabbed their shoes, and then ran to another section of the garden where they put on their clothes and left quickly.

After splitting up the money, they went to get something to eat and visited the toy store. When the boys got home, Leon was there, and he noticed the few new toys and several items of candy the boys had. Leon went to alert Margaret. "Margaret, how much money did you give the boys today?"

"Not much; just enough to go to the boys club and get something to eat," answered Margaret.

"Well, they have a bag full of candy and a few cheap toys, and they just went into their room," Leon informed her.

"What?" said Margaret, sounding concerned. "Dexter, Hank, come here," she yelled. The boys walked slowly into the kitchen where Margaret and Leon were. "Where did you get the money to buy those things?" asked Margaret. The boys began to stutter and mumble. They didn't have an answer. "Go to your room. I'll deal with you later," she instructed.

Hank and Dexter knew they were in trouble again. They hadn't counted on Leon being at the house and seeing them. They sat around and tried to come up with a reason why they had the money to buy the things they had. "Hank, you say that you found the money and that we wanted to bring it home but we were hungry," said Dexter.

"No, Baba will get me if I say that," said Hank.

"No, she won't. Not if we were hungry and found it. There's nothing wrong with that," Dexter said convincingly.

"But it's a lie, and Baba don't like lying," answered Hank.

"But she won't know it's a lie. Come on, just tell her that! Whatever you do, don't say we got it out of the pond," said Dexter, and Hank finally agreed.

Later that evening Margaret confronted the boys. "Where did you get the money?" she asked. Hank said he found it. When she asked him where he found it, he didn't have an answer, so she knew he was lying. After she couldn't get a straight answer out of Hank, she had him bring her a belt.

Margaret whipped Hank, and he cried and screamed. Dexter went into the bedroom because he couldn't watch Hank being whipped. But he couldn't take the sounds of Hank's cries either, so he started to cry. Hank was taking a beating because of him, and he felt real bad about it. When Hank came into the bedroom, Dexter was crying. They both hugged each other and cried, and Dexter said he was sorry and would never ask Hank to lie again.

Mary

Charles Dillard Sr. (BD), and Mary

Margaret and Duane

Margaret and Hank
Musical program photo

Mary, Annie, BD and Mother Cole (BD's Mother)

Margaret and Leon

Dexter and a friend

Dexter, top row second from left. First grade, class picture.

Dexter's baby picture.
Mary cut the woman out of the picture.
She was a friend of Duane's.

Charles with Dexter's children
Duane and Michelle (Mimi)

Margaret presented with an award.

The Evangelist Singers of San Francisco (Margaret is on the left).

Hank, 12 years old.

Dexter, 13 years old.

Charles

Mary, Dexter, Cynthia and Lady

Duane and Mimi

Dexter, Annie, and Hank

Duane about 1976

A presentation to Margaret

Margaret

Dexter 92'

Dexter 04'

Margaret early teen

12

Potrero Hill

In 1961, my grandmother, Mary, purchased and moved into a house at 1530 Thomas Avenue in the Bayview district. I was ten years old, and Hank was nine. We then rented and moved into her house on Missouri Street in the Potrero Hill district. Potrero Hill was a lot different from the Fillmore. For one thing, it was quieter, and the weather was sunnier and warmer. Our house was on a steep hill. The hill was so steep that cars couldn't park parallel but had to park perpendicular to the sidewalk.

Unlike Waller Street, where the majority of the children on the block were Negroes, the Missouri Street block had children of all backgrounds and color. The transition from Fillmore to Potrero was an easy one, because we already knew all the neighbors and kids, since Hank and I used to go over to Nanny's house almost every Sunday. Hank and I transferred to Daniel Webster Elementary School after the summer; this was my fourth school since kindergarten.

Charles was now seventeen years old, and I really looked up to him as a big brother. He was a baseball player and very athletic; he did his best to teach me the game of baseball. Although he'd visit our house often, Hank and I still had no father figure in our lives. Leon just didn't seem to be cutting it in that respect.

Leon came over to our house all the time, but he seemed too old and set in his ways to really spend the kind of quality time with us that we needed. He was now fifty-three, and my mother was thirty-four. Because Leon worked as a longshoreman on the docks at night, he often slept days.

Charles had been driving for a couple of years, and he'd purchased a 1959 Chevy Impala. It was red with a black stripe on the side. He had raised the rear end and put some cheater slicks and mag wheels on it to hop it up. My grandmother let him buy the car because he'd talked her into buying a new Pontiac Grand Prix, and she'd caught him drag racing it.

On Thursday nights, teenage kids drag raced their cars on Carroll Street, not far from Nanny's house. Nanny got a call from a friend who told her that Charles was down on Carroll Street, racing her car. She grabbed a belt and told BD to drive her there in their second car.

When Nanny arrived on Carroll Street, there were hopped-up hot rods all over the place. The kids would meet at Tick Tock's drive-in burger joint on Third Street to plan out the races. They'd travel in twos and head down to Carroll Street where there was a long straightaway that stretched for more than a quarter mile. People would line the streets on both sides and watch the races take place down the middle of the street.

Nanny went looking for Charles with her belt looped over her shoulder. When she finally found Charles, he'd taken the stock wheels off her car and put some racing tires on it, getting it ready to race. She grabbed hold of Charles and started letting him have it. Everyone laughed at Charles, while he kept yelling, "Mother, no, no, Mother, no!" He was seventeen years old, and it took him quite a while to live that down. But as soon as he got his own car, he was able to save some face.

In the Potrero Hill district, living on a steep hill proved to be a lot of fun. We'd build a body for a go-cart out of a plank of wood, a couple of two-by-fours, some nails, and some nuts and bolts. We'd use large ball bearings for wheels and an old kitchen seat pad for a seat. We'd take some rope and hammer each end of it to each side of the front axle for steering. Then we'd nail down a pair of old shoes or slippers to each side of the front axle for brakes, so we could place one foot over each slipper and press the slipper down onto the pavement to slow down or stop.

There were three and a half blocks of steep hills on our street, and the block we lived on was in the middle. Below our block was a hill equally as long and steep as ours, and above was another one of the same steepness and length. The next block above that one was about half the length.

We'd take our go-carts to the top of the hill, and one boy would be placed at each intersection to stop traffic, if necessary, when we crossed them on the way down. Three or four of us would line up side by side on our carts and wait for the signal from the boys at the intersections below. It was four blocks straight down; the fifth block leveled out so you could coast to a finish. The first one to cross the last intersection at the bottom of the hill won.

Looking back on this, I realize now that it was really crazy and dangerous to do what we did. Crossing those intersections could have resulted in some dangerous accidents, not just for the riders, but for the lookouts as well, because they'd run out into the street and flag down the cars to have them stop as we passed.

Crossing Sixteenth Street was the most dangerous because it was a main thoroughfare, and the 22 bus line traveled that route. Soon things became more dangerous because we started building skateboards. We'd take a small wooden board and get a metal skate that we'd take apart, making two wheeled pieces. We'd then nail one piece to each end of the board. Once the board was finished, we'd go to the top of the hill and ride the skateboard all the way down to the bottom of the hill. We didn't have any brakes or anything that could help us stop. If we wanted to stop, we had to jump off.

Not long after that, someone got the great idea to manufacture skateboards with quality materials, including rubber wheels and a rubber stopper on the back for brakes. But the new ones in the store just didn't seem as daring as the ones we made.

Just before we moved to Missouri Street, someone from the recording industry heard my mother sing on the live evening broadcast from First Union on radio station KDIA. They contacted her and asked her if she was interested in making a record. Of course she was very interested, so they cut a record deal.

My mother made several recordings, including "I'll Search Heaven for You" and "Shine Heavenly Light." She also sang "Sing a New Song" as the featured soloist with her singing group, the Evangelist Singers of San Francisco, under the recording label, Reid's Religious Gems. I don't know how many of the recordings were sold, but I do know that it seemed as though everyone in the church community was praising my mother because of the records, and many said they had purchased the records.

My mother must have done well with the recordings because, when we moved to Missouri Street, she purchased a new piano—a Yamaha upright that I still have today. It seemed like we were doing pretty well, because Hank and I were getting new clothes and lots of fun toys. We needed for nothing and whenever we didn't have choir rehearsal on the weekends, Hank and I received money to venture out somewhere.

Sometimes Hank and I caught the bus downtown and went to the movies. We'd go to the Fox Theater, the Paramount, Lowe's, or Saint Francis Theater and catch the latest flicks. Baba never worried about us, because she knew that we knew our way around town.

San Francisco was a great place to explore as a child. If we weren't in Golden Gate Park or at the boys club, we might be at Fisherman's Wharf, at the Junior Museum, or maybe at the Aquarium. Sometimes Charles picked us up and took us with him and his various girlfriends; it seemed like he had a different girl every time he came by to get us.

Not long after we moved onto Missouri Street, Baba had us spend a weekend at Nanny's house, because she and Leon were going to Reno. When they returned, they announced that they were married. I was happy for my mother, and Hank seemed to be happy as well. Leon and Margaret became Mr. and Mrs. Leon Evans. Once they were married, Leon moved in, and once Leon had moved in, his family was around our house all the time. Leon was from a large family. He had at least three brothers and a sister, from what I can remember, and he had nine children from a previous marriage, or marriages.

Leon was close to his family, and we welcomed them as though they were our own blood. Often, on Sundays after church, Leon would drive over to his children's house and bring them food and money.

They lived on McAllister Street near the corner of Baker in an old Victorian house. Leon would park, or double-park, in front of their house, walk up the stairs, and go inside. Our stepbrothers and sisters that were close to my and Hank's ages would come running out to greet us.

At times, I didn't think that my mother cared too much for some of them, probably because she felt they were tough and streetwise and would be a bad influence on us. As far as Hank and I were concerned, they were no different than we were because, although we hid it from our mother pretty well, we were somewhat streetwise too. But Baba had provided us with a very strong Christian upbringing, and so she felt we knew better about some things.

Soon Leon moved his mother (Big Momma) in from Texas. She was old, senile, short, and very large. Sometimes when Leon wasn't home, my mother had to help her get to the toilet. She was much too heavy for my mother to lift, so Baba would call for Hank and me to assist, but she still weighed too much for us. It seemed as though we'd never make it on time, and Big Momma would cut stool all over herself and anything else that was in the way. It was a mess, and it stank, and I hated it. I didn't hate her, but I hated the mess she made, because we had to clean it up. Big Momma didn't live very long with us. She passed on, and we buried her in Richmond, California.

Leon's brother, Uncle Beale, lived in the Sunnydale projects near the Cow Palace on the southern end of San Francisco. He always wore a riverboat hat and smoked cigars. Once a week, Uncle Beale would come over to our house and play dominoes, smoke, and drink beer.

Three of Leon's sons were much older than Hank and I; they were grown men. The oldest was Brother, and he was close to my mother's age. He was average height with a slim build and dark brown skin. He had a large, wide nose and large, puffy lips. Brother had the biggest and most powerful arms I'd ever seen on a man. I used to have him hold one arm up so I could swing on it.

Brother had a drinking problem, and he drank all the time. For the most part, he could handle his liquor pretty well and function too. But I could tell that he'd had his moments from the battle scars on his body and face. He was in more fights than I could imagine, but he was also one of the sweetest and most caring people I ever met.

221

I can remember several occasions when Leon had to bail him out of jail for one reason or another. Usually it was for drunkenness or fighting. Brother was no criminal but was just another Negro man with heavy burdens and bad luck.

Next, there was Heldred, and he was a smooth operator. Heldred drove a shining pink Lincoln Continental and kept himself sharp as a tack. He always had a pretty woman with him, and it seemed like he didn't have a care in the world. When Heldred came around, I always wanted to ride in his car. I thought it was so neat because it had an electric rear window that I always had him roll down for me.

Then there was BC. It seemed like BC was Leon's right-hand man. Whenever Leon needed anything done, he could count on BC to do it. If I had to describe someone that BC favors, I'd have to say it would be James Brown. He was short and stocky, very muscular, dark skinned with a bumpy complexion, and had processed hair.

BC and Leon were always working on their cars together. It was from hanging around them while they worked on cars that I gained knowledge of auto mechanics.

Leon's other children were his daughters, Eunice, Greta, Hattie, Janice, and the twins, Sandy and Mandy. Leon's family was a tight-knit family who, like most families, sometimes fought each other but stuck together. If you messed with one, you messed with them all, and believe me, you didn't want to mess with them. Hank and I went from having just each other to having nine brothers and sisters. Although they didn't live with us, they were very much a part of our lives, especially the brothers.

Leon was a preacher man on Sundays, but during the week, he was just like any other man. He smoked and drank and swore. His favorite pastime was sitting around playing dominoes with his brother and his sons, drinking beer, and smoking cigars or cigarettes. At first, it seemed as though they were over at our house pretty often. But Baba could only take so much of that kind of activity, so as time went on, it became less frequent until it finally ceased.

Living in Potrero Hill was very nice, but I missed the Fillmore. While living in the Potrero, I can remember ...

One day, Leon and BC were in the front of the house working on BC's car. Dexter was down the block playing cowboys and Indians with Anthony, the Italian boy who lived next door, and Sonny, a blond-haired, blue-eyed white boy who lived down the block. Hank was across the street, playing house with a couple of young Negro girls who lived on that side of the street.

Dexter and his friends were hiding behind porches, trashcans, and anything else they could find, shooting cap guns at each other. Every now and then, one of them would act as though they were shot and dying.

After playing cowboys and Indians, the boys took a break and were sitting around talking. Sonny looked across the street and noticed that Hank and the girls were sitting in a large empty cardboard box. The box looked like a box a refrigerator might have been shipped in. Inside they were playing with a toy oven and a tea set. Hank was pretending to cook, and the girls were pretending to sip tea.

Sonny looked over at Dexter and said, "Your brother's a sissy."

Taking offense at this comment, Dexter stood up and replied, "He is not."

"Yes, he is. He's always playing with the girls," shouted Sonny.

Angrily Dexter shouted, "You take that back."

"I will not. He's a sissy. He ain't nothing but a punk," shouted Sonny.

Dexter stood up and looked at Sonny, and then looked over at Hank. Hank was pouring imaginary tea for the girls. Dexter got angry at what he was seeing and was embarrassed by Hank's actions. He looked back at Sonny and said, "Forget you, punk," and turned to walk away.

Sonny then stood up and approached Dexter and punched him in the chest. Dexter wanted to punch him back, but Margaret had always taught him to walk away from a fight, so he stormed off.

Dexter was unaware that Leon had seen the whole thing. Leon didn't hear exactly what was said; it was the shouting that had drawn his attention to the boys.

As Dexter approached the house and started up the front stairs to the porch, Leon called out to him to come over to where he was.

"You let that boy hit you like that?" Leon asked Dexter.

"Baba told me not to fight anymore. She said I have to turn the other cheek," replied Dexter.

"Boy, don't you ever let me see you walk away from someone hitting you like that. You got to stand up for yourself. It's just you and him. It ain't like you're outnumbered or anything like that," said Leon.

Dexter looked down the street. Sonny's attention was on his brother, Jimmy, who'd come outside to play.

"You better get back over there and finish that fight. I don't care if you lose or win. You just stick up for yourself. And if you don't, you gonna have to fight me," instructed Leon.

Dexter looked back at Sonny again and took off running. He caught Sonny by surprise and connected with a right cross on Sonny's jaw. It knocked Sonny back, but he quickly gained his ground, and he and Dexter began boxing. Dexter had taken boxing lessons at the Police Athletic League gym near the school and was fresh with his technique.

Sonny wanted to brawl, but Dexter maintained his guard. He had his hands up in front of his face, and Sonny was trying to punch him, but Dexter was blocking his punches. Dexter's position forced Sonny into boxing rather than a street fight. Dexter punched Sonny in the face with a jab, and Sonny tried a body punch but couldn't get through. Dexter was doing a peek-a-boo and kept connecting with some quick jabs to the face and body.

Leon and BC came down to coach Dexter on.

"Hit him, Dexter," BC shouted.

"Get 'im, boy," Leon chimed in.

Dexter was hyped up because he had some cheerleaders now. Sonny had his hands up in front of his face, and the boys were circling. Hank was still up the block and across the street in the cardboard box, totally unaware that his brother was fighting.

Soon the boys were circling, and no one was taking any shots; they were getting tired. Dexter saw a clear shot to the face, swung with a left hook, and caught Sonny on the nose. Sonny's nose began to bleed, and then he began to cry.

"I'm going to get you," cried Sonny.

Just then, Sonny's father came outside and called to him, "Sonny, come here! Stop it! Stop that fighting, right now! Didn't I tell you to not get into fights?"

Sonny ran up the front stairs of his house to his father. Sonny's father looked at Leon and yelled, "What's going on here?"

Leon looked up at the tall, slender white man, standing on his porch. He had blond hair, blue eyes, and he was neatly dressed with a fine leather belt and slacks, dress shoes, and a white open-collared shirt. His hair was combed with a part on one side and was nice and neat, without a hair out of place.

"Your boy started a fight with our boy, and our boy finished it," Leon shouted back at Sonny's father.

Sonny's father took a long look at Leon and BC. He saw Leon was wearing some old dirty coveralls and had some sweat across his forehead. His strong arms and huge, greasy, dirty hands hung down so low, they looked like they almost reached his knees. He then took a look at BC who was wearing a short-sleeved shirt that was rolled up to where he kept his cigarettes, exposing his large, muscular black arms. BC's process was a couple of weeks old, and several hairs were sticking up out of place because he'd been working on the car with Leon. They both looked intimidating and dangerous. The expression on their faces seemed to say, "Okay, now what?"

Sonny's father motioned for his sons. "Come in the house, boys." He then grabbed them as they approached, turned, and walked through the front door of his home and slammed the door behind him.

Leon put his arm on Dexter's shoulder and turned to walk back up the hill to their house. Leon then said, "Dexter, don't you ever let me see you walk away from a fight. If I see you walk away from a fight, I bet a man you'll have a fight with me. You understand me, boy?"

"Yes, Mr. Leon, I mean, Dad," responded Dexter.

"What were you fighting about anyway?" asked Leon as Dexter climbed the steps to go into the house.

"He called Hank a sissy," responded Dexter, and he turned and kept on moving.

Leon and BC looked at each other then looked for Hank. He was still across the street in the cardboard box with the girls. They shook their heads and returned to working on the car.

225

It was the end of the summer, and the boys were now going to Daniel Webster Elementary School. The school was about three blocks from their house, straight up Missouri Street. It was a well-integrated school, much like Dudley Stone, only it had many children attending who were from the housing projects farther up Potrero Hill. Like the kids from the projects at John Muir, they were hard and tough, and the fifth-grade girls who lived in the projects were pretty fast.

Many kids coming from the housing projects in San Francisco had filthy mouths. Coming from the Fillmore, Dexter was used to hearing a fair amount of cursing, but it didn't compare to what was coming out of the mouths of the kids from the Potrero Hill projects. During recess, Dexter was sitting on a stoop in the play yard. Nearby, he overheard a couple of girls chanting a song, "Put your foot on the rock. Shh ah, shh ah. Then you stick in the cock. Shh ah, shh ah. If that don't do. Shh ah, shh ah. Then stick on through. Shh ah, shh ah."

Dexter sat up and looked to see who was singing the song and saw two girls from his class. One of the girls was named Margie, and she lived in the projects. Margie was short with dark skin. She was beautiful. Her hair was always nice and neat, and she was always dressed very well. She had skin that was always clean and shiny, and she had sexy bowl legs.

Dexter always noticed Margie; actually he had a crush on her, but she never knew it. Although they were in the same class together, she didn't even know he existed. Margie was ten years old, and she had a boyfriend named Junior who was around thirteen who used to come around the school to see her. Junior already had a reputation as a "hood." He was always getting into fights, and he was always in trouble with the police for stealing. Juvenile Hall became his second home.

Because of Junior, there was no way Dexter would even give Margie a hint of his affection of her. She was from the projects, and he had sense enough to know that the projects spelled nothing but trouble, and trouble was something he always tried to avoid. Margie was the first girl Dexter had a crush on. There was a cute little light-skinned girl at the church that he used to play with, and liked, but not the same way he liked Margie. He'd watch her in school and dream about her at night, but she would never know.

Not all of the kids from the projects were bad or troublemakers. Hank and Dexter made friends with several of them, but they were never allowed to venture into the projects. So they'd venture out into other areas of the Potrero. One of the areas they liked to go was down by the railroad tracks. They'd throw rocks, play around the tunnel, and catch frogs in a small marsh near the tracks.

While down by the tracks, Dexter found a small shelter directly under one of the overpasses. He later returned and set up a small camp there. He stocked the shelter with some blankets and candles, along with a few snacks. One night he snuck out of the house to spend the night there. It got very cold, and every time a train rode by, the candles would blow out. So he had to sneak back into his house. Once back home in bed, he noticed Hank was still fast asleep; no one ever found out about the adventure.

Along with their new brothers and sisters came new aunts, uncles, and cousins. Brother had a son named Leon Jr. who lived across the bay and who was about the same age as Dexter. One weekend, Leon Jr. came over to spend the weekend, and Dexter and Hank took him to the movies. They caught the bus downtown and went to see Bye Bye Birdie. They had such a good time at the movie that they couldn't stop talking about it while they headed home. The thing that most impressed the boys was the music.

Times were changing, and so was the music. The blues had given way to rock and roll, and rock and roll was giving way to pop and soul music.

When the boys were really young, Margaret rarely let them listen to any music other than gospel or children's music. She had tried to teach them that rock and roll, blues, and jazz were the devil's music. But as the boys got older, it became harder for her to keep it out of their reach. So she began to loosen up. It was either loosen up or fight with them all the time. She felt if she constantly fought with them, it could put a wedge between her and her sons.

Hank and Dexter had received a record player as a gift, and they began to spend their allowances on 45-record singles. They listened to radio station KYA and heard popular and soul music hits, but they both had different tastes in music. While Dexter loved to listen to the sounds of artists like the Four Seasons, Gene Chandler, Elvis Presley,

Sam Cooke, and the Beatles, Hank enjoyed listening to female artists singing songs like "Soldier Boy," "Two Lovers," and "It's My Party, and I'll Cry If I Want To." The older the boys got, the more different from each other they became.

Margaret, Leon, and the boys stayed in the house on Missouri Street for about two years between 1962 and 1963. Leon worked overtime, and Margaret sold out all of the records she'd produced, so they soon had saved enough money to purchase a home.

In the summer of 1964, the family moved from Potrero Hill to the Ingleside district in San Francisco. This area was informally called Lakeview, and they lived in a house on Geneva Avenue, which was on the northern border of the district.

Lakeview was an area where many Negroes who were considered upper middle class were moving. The homes in Lakeview were a little newer than the homes in the Bayview district, which was where many middle-class Negroes also lived. Unlike the Bayview district, which had two housing-project developments (Hunter's Point and Doublerock), Lakeview had none.

The transition from the Fillmore to Potrero Hill had been an easy one for the boys, because they'd moved into their grandmother's house. Since they had always visited there on the weekends, they already knew most of the kids in the immediate area as well as many in their school. But the transition to Lakeview was a little more difficult, because they didn't know any of the kids in the area.

Hank was the first to make friends with someone. He met a boy named Mallory and introduced him to Dexter. Dexter thought that Mallory was an odd name for a boy, but he liked Mallory, and they began to play together and have fun.

One day, Mallory came over to the house to play. They were out in front of the house—the area that Margaret had them limited to, because she didn't want them wandering off into unfamiliar territory.

"Where are you from?" Mallory asked Dexter.

"The Fillmore," answered Dexter.

"The Fillmore?" responded Mallory.

"Yeah, the Fillmore. We lived on Waller near Fillmore Street," said Dexter.

"The Fillmore is pretty tough," said Mallory.

"Yeah, my bother was in a gang," said Hank. "And he can fight too," he added.

Mallory looked at Dexter and asked, "What gang were you in?"

"The Junior Tyrants," answered Dexter. Mallory took Dexter at his word and didn't take it any further.

The boys kept playing, and then Mallory grabbed Hank by the head and put him in a headlock. "Come on, let's wrestle," he yelled.

"No," cried Hank, trying to break loose.

Dexter grabbed hold of Mallory and said, "I'll wrestle you," and pulled Mallory to the ground.

Hank backed up and watched Mallory and Dexter wrestle. Dexter eventually got on top of Mallory. "Say uncle," he said squeezing Mallory tight. Mallory struggled and tried to break loose but couldn't; Dexter had him pinned down pretty good. "Say uncle," Dexter commanded again.

"Uncle," said Mallory, and Dexter let him go.

Dexter and Mallory then played handball with a foursquare ball against the house for a while until Mallory had to leave.

That evening, Leon wasn't home, so it was just going to be Margaret and the boys. Margaret was in the kitchen, and the boys were in the bathroom washing their hands, getting ready for dinner, when the doorbell rang.

Hank and Dexter ran downstairs to open the door. When they opened the door, Mallory was standing there with another boy.

"Hey," said Dexter to Mallory.

"Hey, Dexter, I want to show you something," said Mallory as he motioned for Dexter to step outside.

"This is my friend, Andy," Mallory said, pointing to the other boy.

"Hi," said Dexter to the boy.

"I hear you think you bad. I hear you think you can beat my ass," said the boy to Dexter.

Without waiting for a reply, Andy drew his right arm from behind and connected squarely with Dexter's jaw. The force of the boy's blow knocked Dexter off his feet.

The hit took Dexter totally by surprise, and as he tried to gain his composure, Margaret yelled down from the top of the stairs, "Dexter, what's going on down there?"

Dexter knew if his mother thought there was going to be a fight, she'd either come downstairs and get involved or maybe call the police. If Leon were there, he'd force him to fight. But his mother always told him to walk away from fights.

This was not the time to try and prove himself. He was in a new neighborhood, and he was from the Fillmore. It could bring on more trouble if he took this guy on, especially if he beat him. "No, Baba, everything's all right," Dexter responded to his mother. Then to Andy, he said, "No, man, I didn't say I could beat you up. I don't even know you. I don't want to fight you, man."

"Oh, all right, it's cool then. It's cool. I'll see you around," said the boy as he and Mallory turned and walked away.

It was the first time Hank had seen Dexter actually back away from a fight since they used to avoid Hector back in the Haight. Hank got angry and wanted to get back at Mallory because he felt Mallory had been the one who started it. Dexter told him to leave it alone, because they were in a new place and needed to be careful. Hank angrily agreed, and things went back to normal.

Unlike the Fillmore and the Potrero districts, Lakeview was cold in the summertime. The fog would roll in from the ocean and create a cloud cover that burned off on some days, and on others, hung on all day. Evenings were cold and wet.

On the weekends after church, Hank and Dexter would still go over to their grandmother's house, and since it was summer, sometimes they'd stay overnight. Annie would watch them while Mary and BD were at work on Monday. One Sunday in late August, the boys were playing outside, and Margaret had come over for dinner. It was a nice sunny day in the Bayview. One of the neighboring children had a small transistor radio, and the deejay was talking about a new music sensation. No one was really paying too much attention. The music began to play:

> Everybody say yeah,
> Say yeah,
> Say yeah, yeah, yeah,
> Clap your hands just a little bit louder,
> Clap your hands just a little bit louder.

A harmonica wailed, and all the kids ran over, gathered around the radio, and began to snap their fingers and clap their hands. "That's Little Stevie Wonder," said one of the kids. Hank and Dexter hadn't heard the song before but had listened along with the others. The song was jumping. Then another kid said, "Yeah, he's only twelve years old, and he's blind." That's when Dexter really began to pay attention. His mother was blind and was also a singer and a musician. As far as he was aware, the only other blind singers and musicians were Ray Charles and the gospel group, the Five Blind Boys.

The deejay came on and confirmed what the kids had said, and Dexter ran into the house to his mother. "Baba, guess what? There's this little boy, and he's twelve years old, and he has a song on the radio, and he's blind. The song is so good; you should hear it. I want to buy it. Can I buy it? Huh, huh, can I buy it?"

"Well, I guess so," replied Margaret.

Dexter ran outside and was so excited he was going to buy the record that he was going to tell the others. But most of the boys had moved across the street where they were about to play a game.

Dexter walked across the street and asked the boys what they were about to do. They were about to play a game called "King of the Mountain." In the front of the house where they'd decided to play was a small concrete partition about eighteen inches high, ten feet long, and about twelve inches wide. One boy would stand on one end of the structure, and the others would line up behind each other on the other end. One by one, each boy in the line would challenge the boy on the other end and try to make him fall. Whoever succeeded in throwing the king off the structure would take the place as king.

After several challenges, one boy named Ray who lived in the next block stood out as the strongest and the best. Ray was short, stocky, and strong, with big hands like a man. His hands had fat fingers and wrinkles like an old man, even though he was only about thirteen years old.

Everyone decided to start the game over again, and Ray took his place on one end of the partition, waiting for a challenger. All the other boys lined up at the other end, one behind the other. Since Dexter was late getting in line, he took the last position. There were five boys ahead of him. Hank was still in the house and probably wouldn't play anyway.

One boy took one step out toward Ray to challenge him. This time, Ray did not wait for the boy to meet him half way. Ray yelled out, bent his head down, and rammed the boy back into the rest of the boys; they all went falling down on top of Dexter. Just as Dexter hit the ground and the weight of the five boys toppled on him, he heard his arm snap with a pop. Dexter was familiar with what had happened, because he'd been in this position before. His arm was broken. It was the same arm and in the same place he'd broken it five years before.

After everyone climbed up off Dexter, he got up and announced, "My arm's broke." He wasn't crying, and he wasn't feeling a lot of pain, not yet anyway. He held onto his dangling right arm with his left one.

Ray walked over to him. "Let me see," he said. He reached for Dexter's arm and tried to raise it. That's when the pain hit.

"Oh no, don't, don't," yelled Dexter. He then turned and walked across the street and up the front stairs into the living room where his mother and grandmother were sitting and chatting.

Dexter walked into the living room and again made the announcement, "My arm's broke."

"What? Boy, come here! Your arm ain't broke. Let me see it," said Margaret.

Dexter moved in front of his mother, and Margaret felt for his arm and tried to raise it. The pain shot up to Dexter's skull. "No, no, stop!" he yelled, and Margaret released it.

Margaret turned to Mary and said, "Mother, ask Momma if she has some Camphorpheque to put on Dexter's arm, and give him some aspirin. I'll take him to the doctor tomorrow. You might as well take us home now."

Just like the time before, Dexter had to wait until the next day to go to the doctor and had to endure the pain all night. The next day, Margaret took Dexter to Dr. Hite's office near Union Square on Post Street. Doctor Hite in turn sent them to a building at 450 Sutter Street for some x-rays. On 450 Sutter Street was a building that housed many doctors and medical specialists. It was nicknamed "450 Suffer."

The x-rays confirmed that Dexter had broken his arm a second time in the exact same place, and he had to wear another cast; only this time, his arm was positioned up, straight out, and bent at the elbow to the left in front of his chest. It covered his whole upper torso. It was unlike the last time when he'd worn a cast with his arm down and tucked across his belly. The cast was awkward and uncomfortable, and because it was a second break, the doctor told Margaret to bring him back for a checkup in two months.

The next month, Dexter started his new school, James Denman Junior High School, in a cast. Hank was admitted to San Miguel Elementary School, which was right next door. Hank was entering the low sixth grade class, and Dexter was entering the low seventh grade class. After about two months, Dexter's checkup showed that his arm had not yet completely healed, so the doctor made him wear the cast an additional two months. Dexter had hoped his cast would be coming off so he could go back to school as normal, but he had to wait.

One day while sitting in class, another teacher walked into the classroom and whispered something to Dexter's teacher. There was a shocked look on the teacher's face as she raised her hand to cover her mouth. She nodded to the other teacher who then turned and left the room. The teacher then made the announcement that President Kennedy had been shot. Everyone was dismissed and told to make their way home.

Dexter left the school and walked the half mile or so home. When he arrived home, his mother was in the garage washing clothes and was not aware that the president had been shot. Dexter walked into the house and yelled out to his mother. When she answered, he went into the garage and informed her that the president had been shot and the school had sent him home.

Margaret was shocked with the news. She and Dexter went upstairs to turn on the television, and soon Hank walked through the front door. The story was being televised on every station, and soon it was announced that President Kennedy had died. Margaret began to cry, and Hank and Dexter tried to console her. Soon Hank too began to cry, and Dexter began to weep. They huddled together and wept. It was tragic news, and the world and the family took it hard.

Negroes felt a fondness for President Kennedy that hadn't been seen in quite some time. These were trying times for Negroes, and especially so in the South. Jim Crow was alive and well in the South, and even though racism wasn't as much "in your face" in the North, especially in California, there was evidence of it being shown on television all the time.

People were speaking out against racism and starting to take action. In church, the preachers brought it up often. Although the boys were not exposed to much hatred, they did have a few encounters. When they first moved to Lakeview, Margaret had given them some money to go and get haircuts. The boys didn't know where to go to get a haircut, but they remembered seeing a barbershop on Geneva and Mission Streets at the bus stop.

The boys walked into the barbershop and sat down in the seats where patrons wait to be served. The barber looked over at the boys with hatred in his eyes. It was a look they'd never noticed anyone give them before.

"What in the hell do you think you're doing?" asked the white barber.

"We want to get a haircut," Hank replied.

"We don't cut your kind of hair here. Get the hell out of here," said the barber.

Hank and Dexter got up and walked out and could hear the white barber say to one of the other barbers, "Goddamn stupid-ass niggers."

Margaret and the boys watched more of the news on the assassination, and soon it was again time to pray. She and the boys stood in a circle, and Margaret prayed for the president's family. She prayed for the country and for the Negro race. Next she preached to the boys about how these were the signs of the last days in time, and how they needed to be close to the Lord so that, when the day of reckoning came, they would all enter into heaven. She made the boys promise they'd meet her in heaven after death. Hank and Dexter both promised.

Over the next six months, Dexter tried as much as possible to keep a low profile. It was difficult because the cast covering the top half of his body with his arm positioned bent out in front of his chest was very noticeable. He sat in the back of the room at school, kept to himself, and didn't make too many friends.

Dexter had been wearing the cast for so long because, after his four-month checkup, his arm still had not healed. The doctors decided to operate. They broke his arm a third time, took bone chips out of his hip, and put them in his arm. This time, he was in a cast for almost an additional four months. It seemed as though he spent his whole twelfth year in a cast.

Hank graduated to James Denman Junior High after having finished at San Miguel Elementary, so now both boys were back in the same school.

Over the next few years, things began to change rapidly—socially, economically, and politically. President Johnson waged war against Vietnam, and young men over the age of eighteen were drafted and shipped off to war. Just about every Sunday, some young man in the congregation would be standing before the pews in uniform, asking for prayers, while he was about to go into service for his country.

The music scene was changing, and the San Francisco Bay Area now had two AM radio stations that featured soul music; they were KDIA and KSOL. Motown was taking the country by storm with the new Motown sound. Martha and the Vandellas' "Heat Wave" had kicked things off, followed by the Supremes with "Baby Love."

White pop music also began to change with the influx of British groups; this had a profound impact on children. The Beatles had come on the scene with their shaggy hairstyles, and many white boys began to let their hair grow.

Television was also changing, and kids were being provided with more programming. Shows like The Flintstones and Bewitched now provided later evening entertainment for children and teens. Another popular show that was drawing a large teen audience though it was intended for adults was Star Trek. Shows like Batman kept the nation's children's eyes glued to the tube.

Sex was becoming ever more and more prevalent in movies, television, and advertising. Dresses were getting tighter, necklines lower, and hairstyles outrageous.

James Bond was the new big-screen lover, with his trick gadgets, fast cars, and fine women. But I Spy was the hit spy series on television, and Negroes had themselves a new hero in Bill Cosby.

Dexter sometimes flipped through his uncle Charles's Playboy magazines and often saw clips of Bill Cosby in different settings, all dressed up and being the man of the party, surrounded by white folks, and even more so, white women.

Times were changing for sure, and Margaret was trying to keep a tight grip on Hank and Dexter, but the music, television, and the changing of the times were having their impact on them as well. They started to let their hair grow, and before long, they were wearing pompadours or "fluffs" as they were called in the Negro community. Fluffs were hairstyles with the hair grown out and up, above the forehead. The sides and back were either cut close or combed back. Many kids in school were trying to be cool, and the longer the fluff, the cooler you were.

To be cool, you also had to dress cool. Dexter got a job as a paperboy and began spending his money on clothes. Girls now became a major focus, and he had to look cool and hip to attract them and to fit in.

Soon Dexter was wearing silk and satin shirts with ruffles around the cuffs and ruffles along the front buttons. Tight, iridescent and sharkskin slacks hugged his tall, skinny frame, and high-heeled Spanish boots made him appear even taller.

Although Dexter was becoming a real cool cat, he had lost a lot of his toughness. After having broken his arm twice in the same place, the doctors had warned him that a third break might be cause for amputation. That really shook him up, so fighting was something he always wanted to avoid, and there was always a lot of fighting going on at James Denman Junior High School.

James Denman was right next door to Balboa High School. "Bal" had a reputation as a tough school, although it was not a bad school scholastically. Its population was around 70 percent Negro, and it was one of the best athletic schools in the city and the Bay Area. Bal had a direct impact on Denman. Many of Denman's students had older brothers and sisters who attended Balboa. Bal was a fighting school, and there were rivalries not only between them and other high schools in the city, but also within different factions in the school.

Although the schools were integrated, kids generally stuck to their own kind. Negroes played with Negroes, Italians played with Italians, and Mexicans played with Mexicans. But many times, minorities mingled together.

The Italians had no problem dealing with the Negroes. Although they were in the minority, there was no way anyone could tell them they weren't as tough or as cool as any nigger. So in most cases, the Italians were accepted by the Negro kids as cool.

Most of the white kids stayed clear of the Negro kids. If one white kid got into a fight with a Negro, he wouldn't stand a chance. Just as a fight would get going between a white kid and a Negro kid, another Negro kid would come up behind the white kid and hit him in the back of the head. The next thing you knew, the white kid would be bombarded with hits from as many as seven or eight other Negro kids.

Several of the Negro kids at Denman formed a gang. They called themselves the Centurions, and they wore black and white on the days they'd have meetings or confront rival gangs. Dexter knew many of the kids in the gang and was friends with many of them. However, he managed to stay away from them as a group and never got into trouble with them. Having the broken arm the first year there and not having grown up with the kids at Denman probably spared him the peer pressure. He'd gone through that in the Fillmore and had had his share of gang moments.

Instead of choosing to become close friends with gang members, Dexter chose a few boys who also were outside of the gang circle. Homeroom 55 was the class Dexter stayed in from the seventh through ninth grades. In his class was a boy named Alfred who didn't live far from him. Al was tall and slim like Dexter, very handsome, light skinned, with a baby face, and was a genuine all-around nice guy. Al also had a younger brother named Bernard who was in Hank's home room, and that gave them even more in common. Bernard, like Hank, was shorter and plumper than his older brother.

Like Hank and Dexter, Al and Bernard had strict parents—not necessarily from a religious position, but just in wanting to keep a tight reign on their boys. Hank, Dexter, Al, and Bernard began to hang out together, and soon Al introduced Dexter to Clifford who was in a different homeroom. Cliff was in a class for bright, intelligent, and gifted children. It was homeroom 210. The kids in homeroom 210 were in the high tenth percentile in terms of IQ, and Cliff was a consistent straight-A student.

At thirteen years of age, Dexter, Al, and Cliff were the same height, build, and frame. They were about five feet, ten inches tall, thin, and lanky. Al and Dexter were light skinned, and Cliff was dark skinned. Like Dexter and Al, Clifford came from a strict family. His father was a preacher who kept an even tighter reign on his children than Al or Dexter's parents did on them.

For example, Hank and Dexter were allowed to go outside and play almost every day, as long as their homework and chores were done. They were allowed to venture out into the neighborhood but were always given a time that they had to be back home. They were almost always allowed to have their friends come and visit at their house.

Al and Bernard were allowed to play outside only on a few days and usually could not venture more than a block from their home. When they were allowed to come out, it never was for very long. It was seldom that Al and Bernard were allowed to have their friends visit at their house.

Clifford, on the other hand, was very seldom allowed to play outside and would often watch, and sometimes talk with, his friends from the front window. He was never allowed to have any of his friends visit. His family didn't even have a television set in their home because they thought it broadcast nothing but the devil's programming.

Another boy in Dexter's homeroom was Mattock Jade. Mattock was the tough guy. He had a bad mouth, was short, stocky, and rock solid. His arms were very muscular for a thirteen-year-old, and his hands were the size of a man's. He had brown skin and a wide nose, and he had a handsome, hard look about him. Mattock and Dexter soon became the best of friends.

Mattock's family consisted of his father, one brother, and six sisters. His mother had passed away sometime after she gave birth to the twin boys. This left Mattock's older sister Celia the responsibility of being the mother of the group.

Because he had eight children to take care of, with no wife, Mattock's father worked very hard to provide for his family. He worked at the airport and often worked double and triple time to make money. So Mattock pretty much did whatever he wanted to do. He just needed to be home whenever his father arrived.

At twelve and thirteen, Hank and Dexter were given a lot more freedom from religious activities. They were still required to read the Bible and participate in home Bible study sessions, but because Leon was now a part of the family, he had the main responsibility of getting Margaret to and from church or choir rehearsals. If Leon couldn't take her because of his work, a choir member would pick her up and bring her home. On these occasions, Hank and Dexter were allowed to stay home, but they couldn't have any company.

During the summer, Margaret would try to find some sort of Christian activity for the boys. Up the street from the house on Geneva Street was a Seventh Day Adventist church that had a Vacation Bible School. Margaret enrolled them in the school for the summer. But the boys often put up a fuss and many times wouldn't attend, so she finally took them out and enrolled them in the Boy Scouts.

Hank and Dexter enjoyed the scouts because they met a new set of friends, and they were kept busy with a lot of indoor and outdoor activities. The only thing Hank didn't like was when they went on overnight camping trips.

Dexter was proactive about his participation in the scouts and soon moved through the ranks from troop leader to assistant senior patrol leader, a rank that was second highest in command. Hank was satisfied to be a troop member. The Boy Scouts troop met above the Balboa Park Police Station, not far from where the boys lived. Often, after scout meetings, the boys visited the police station and made friends with the officers. A few years later, this station came under assault by the Black Liberation Army (BLA), and a police sergeant was killed at his desk.

Balboa Park also had an indoor public swimming pool where the boys visited and often swam, especially during the summer. Because Hank and Dexter had learned how to swim at an early age, they were better swimmers than most of their friends.

Next door to Margaret's home was a private school named Lick-Wilmerdean. It was an all-boys school and had a mostly white student body. There was a small football and baseball-training field, which came right up to their backyard fence. At the opposite end of the field, near the back entrance to the school, was a basketball court.

Al, Clifford, Mattock, and Bernard sometimes came over to Dexter and Hank's house where they'd hop the backyard fence and play basketball on the school grounds. It was the perfect place to play ball where they wouldn't have the hassle of trying to play at the few crowded playgrounds that were in the area. The school was closed during weekends and the summer, so no one would ask them to leave. It was as if they had their very own practice field.

By the time Dexter reached fourteen years of age, his arm had recovered and was almost back to normal. It was finally the same size and thickness as his left arm, and he was getting his strength back. He began to be more active in sports, especially basketball. Hank was now thirteen and still had no interest in any sports.

Girls were now a major topic of discussion with Dexter and his new friends. Although he wasn't a very popular figure among the girls at school, he was very popular with the girls at church. On the other hand, Hank didn't seem to have much interest in the girls.

There were a few girls at Denman that Dexter was fond of, but he never felt as though any of them were interested in him. Plus, one day he overheard a conversation between a few of the girls in class. They were sitting in the back of the room talking about the boys they liked and thought were cute; then he heard one of the girls say, "What about Dexter? I think he's cute," and another girl responded by saying, "He ain't cute. He's just light skinned with good hair."

Upon hearing that, Dexter just thought to himself, "Damn, that's cold." It crushed any thoughts about even trying to approach any girl in his class. Just as it was during the times of slavery, it was still a time when, like whites, many Negro people were color conscious and prejudiced.

The Bay Area seemed like a long way away from the constant struggle of Negroes in the South. It had become a place that was more diverse than any other place on the planet. People could live wherever they wanted to live and go wherever they wanted to go, as long as they could afford it.

But the voices of the struggle were beginning to come through loud and clear via the media. Martin Luther King Jr., Malcolm X, and Stokeley Carmichael were constantly fighting for justice for the Negro people. Not only was the struggle being fought in the South, but voices trying to bring about a change were also heard in places like Chicago, Detroit, and Cleveland.

Malcolm X was assassinated, and all kinds of theories emerged as to why it was done. Negro people were angry and hurt by the loss of such a great leader. The anger was felt all over America. It was felt in the work place, in the churches, and in the schools. Soon Dexter also began to take more notice of racial injustice.

Although Dexter gained an interest in basketball, he knew he was not skillful enough to participate on any school teams. Denman was a very competitive school with lots of talent. Some of the kids had been playing on teams since the age of seven or earlier. They were making moves and taking shots that were hard to conceive. The school was full of show offs; some were just faking it, but a good many were very good.

Denman Junior High School had rallies to boost the school spirit before games; the school band would play while the cheerleaders worked hard to get the students hyped. The school had a great music department, and Dexter had taken up the clarinet and played for a while in the school band.

By this time, Margaret had pretty much given up on trying to steer the boys away from the music of the times. Dexter had a small transistor radio with an earphone, and he'd lie in bed at night and listen to Sly Stone on the radio station KSOL. Sly was one of the most popular deejays on radio in the Bay Area. His show was creative and unique. He played the hits and gave the lowdown on what was happening with the artist. The show was poppin'!

After playing a hit like "Cool Jerk" or a Temptations hit like "Get Ready," he'd have dedication time. People would call in and dedicate the next song to their friends. Boys would call in and dedicate a song to the girls, and the girls would call in and dedicate a song to the boys, and just about every caller would dedicate to the same people at the end of their dedications as if they all knew the same people.

"All right, next caller, this is Sly Stone. You got a dedication?" Sly would say.

"Yeah, ah, I'd like to dedicate to my cousin, Joe, and, ah, my main man, Fred, my girl, Judy, and, ah, let me make a dedication to, ah, Willie Popcorn, A Natural Woman, and Five Hundred Percent More Man," the caller would say.

"Okay, next caller. Who is this?" Sly would continue.

"Oh, is this Sly? Is this really Sly Stone?" a female caller would ask.

"Yes, baby, this is Sly," he'd answer.

Then would come a scream from the woman in the background. "Oh, Sly, Sly, I love you."

Sly would interrupt her, "Ah, baby, you got a dedication?"

"Yes, Sly, I'd like to make a dedication to my boyfriend, Bobby, and my best friend, Shirley, and also to Fillmore Slim, A Natural Woman, Willie Popcorn, and Five Hundred Percent More Man." The caller rambled the names.

These so-called friends-in-common were local San Francisco characters who were considered "cool" to know.

After the dedication, Sly would put on another hit. Sam and Dave would be blaring through the radio with "Hold on! I'm coming!" Then some character of Sly's creation would come on the radio and say, "Let me have a tall glass of buttermilk." At the close of every show, Sly would put on Ray Charles's hit, "Let's Go Get Stoned" as he walked out the door of the studio. The recognition of soul music during this time period was fun and exciting. It was an expression of the greatness of a people on the move.

That same year there was a big basketball game that was going to take place between Denman and Benjamin Franklin Junior High Schools. Basically, it came down to a game between Lakeview and Fillmore.

Denman was having a rally to get ready for the game, and it was rumored that Sly Stone was going to make an appearance. On the day of the rally, the auditorium was packed. The cheerleaders had gotten the crowd all hyped up, and everyone was feeling the school spirit. The principal came out and made the introduction, "And now for a real treat—boys and girls, Sly Stone!"

Sly walked out on stage of the school auditorium, and the crowd went wild. Girls screamed and jumped up and down when Sly came out dressed in some slacks, a wide open-collar shirt, and high-heeled boots. He was holding his guitar, and his brother, Freddie, also had a guitar. There was also another person on drums. Sly got the crowd pumped up by asking them which school was number one. Then he asked what was the number-one radio station, and the crowd hollered, "KSOL!"

Sly began to play and sing, "I wanna take you higher, higher, higher." It was an early version of a song that, in later years, became a hit. The event was a special one that the student body boasted and bragged about for the remainder of the semester.

That next year, Sly officially came out with his new band, Sly and the Family Stone. At the time, Sly set a precedent for being the first truly integrated soul/rock group. It was racially integrated with blacks and whites, and men and women. Sly Stone was a pioneer of music who had a profound effect on the new direction of soul.

13

It's a New Day

In the spring of 1966, the City of San Francisco made Leon and Margaret an offer they couldn't refuse. Highway 280 was being developed and a freeway exit was planned that would allow cars to exit onto Geneva Avenue at the exact location where their home was. So they sold the house to the city and purchased a newer and more modern home on the other side of the hill at 147 Orizaba Avenue. Early that summer they moved into the home, which was still located in Lakeview.

Along with the new home, the family purchased new furniture. Leon purchased a newer used car because he had a policy of never buying a new one, and things seemed good economically for the family. In spite of the good things taking place, it was not a very happy family.

Margaret was becoming more demanding of Leon, and he was becoming disenchanted with the marriage. Leon's passive nature was no match for Margaret's strong and independent character. She was a strong woman and was much like her mother, Mary, who also was a very strong woman.

Mary was the dominating figure in her household, and Margaret was greatly influenced by her. Whatever Mary wanted BD to do, he did, no questions asked. It could be the middle of the night, and if she wanted some ice cream, she'd say, "BD, I need you to go to the store," and BD would get right up and go. He never talked back, he never complained, and he did what he was told.

After they were married, it didn't take long for Margaret to move into the position of boss, and Leon hated it. Nothing Leon could do would allow him to be what he thought the man of the house should be. He and Margaret were always at odds. If Leon came in too late, Margaret would drill him. When Leon wanted sex, she'd deny him. If he had somewhere to go, he had to take her where she needed to go first, and if he had any money, she wanted it. It became a very dominating situation for Leon.

Hank and Dexter would hear them argue and close their bedroom door. If things got too heated, Hank would let Leon know that he couldn't talk to his mother like that. Dexter was a little more sympathetic to Leon and felt somewhat sorry for him. Leon would get frustrated, go down into the garage where he hid his stash of alcohol, and drink. He'd get drunk and then want to talk with Dexter, whom he knew would listen.

"Dexter," Leon would yell from downstairs in the garage. "Dexter, come here, boy," he'd yell again. Dexter would be lying across his bed, trying to watch television or listen to the radio. He'd hear Leon calling him and would let out a sigh, because he knew what was in store. Dexter would slowly get up out of bed and go downstairs. At the bottom of the stairs, the door leading to the garage would be wide open, and there, next to his fishing boat (which was cluttered with junk), Leon would be staggered, drunk, and smelly.

"Come here, boy," he said on one occasion, motioning for Dexter to approach him. Dexter entered the garage and stood before Leon who went into his ritual statements, "You know, you're a smart kid. You're gonna be somebody when you grow up. I can tell." Leon then placed his arm around Dexter's shoulder and said, "You know Margaret; I love that woman. I bet a man I'll kill anyone that try and put a hand on her.

I'll do anything for that woman. But she treats me so bad. I don't know what to do. I can't tell if I'm coming or going."

Dexter just stood there and nodded his head, not saying anything. He felt sorry for the man because he recognized his mother was sometimes hard for Leon to deal with. She was a good Christian woman with an education and skills. Leon wasn't highly educated and was no match for her wit. But Dexter loved his mother, and he and Hank had taken care of her for several years before Leon came along. What could Leon possibly expect him to say? Nothing, he could say nothing. He just stood there and listened and nodded his head.

"Listen to me, Dexter. When you grow up, you're going to appreciate what I'm telling you. I bet a man you will," Leon continued, his breath reeking of liquor.

"You make sure that, when you get married, you marry a woman that's going to love you and serve you and do what you want her to do. You hear me, boy?" asked Leon. Dexter just nodded his head. "You hear me, boy?" Leon wanted an answer.

"Yes, Dad," answered Dexter.

Dexter was the only one of the boys that called him Dad. Hank called him Mr. Leon. "Can I go now, Dad?" asked Dexter.

"All right, you can go. You're a good son. You're going to thank me one day. I bet a man you will," Leon mumbled as Dexter walked away.

After Dexter left, Leon turned and went scrounging around in his fishing boat for another bottle. When he found a bottle of bourbon, he unscrewed the cap, turned it up, and took a large swig. Next he grabbed his old, thick, shabby Bible. He pulled up a chair, slouched down in it, then opened up his Bible.

Leon thumbed around the Bible until he found a passage he wanted to read. Once he found what he was looking for, he stood up and read the verse out loud. Margaret, Hank, and Dexter could hear him reading downstairs.

"If you would, please open your Bibles with me to the text, John 4, verse 9." Leon was speaking to an imaginary audience. He continued, "Follow with me, if you will."

Leon was talking to himself. In the hallway downstairs was a mirror that hung directly across from the doorway leading into the garage.

Leon was standing just inside the doorway to the garage, and he was looking at himself in the mirror.

Leon read aloud, "Then saith the woman of Samaria unto him, How is it that thou, being a Jew, askest drink of me, which am a woman of Samaria?" Leon was drunk and practicing for a sermon he'd never preach. Rev. Reason hadn't asked him to preach in almost three years, but nonetheless, every Sunday he sat up in the pulpit ready to go.

Margaret closed her door. Hank got out of his bed and closed the door to his and Dexter's bedroom. Dexter turned up the television, but they could still hear Leon downstairs preaching, drunk.

After about fifteen minutes, Leon got warmed up, and they could hear him shouting, complete with the inhaling and exhaling between phrases, "Ah ummm, ahhhhh, I know the Lord. Ahhhhhhh, I know him for myself, ahhhhhh, he brought me from a mighty long way."

Dexter was trying to watch TV, but the sound of Leon kept coming through. Dexter sat up in his bed and shook his head. "Damn, he's such a hypocrite. He's down there, drunk as a skunk, preaching," Dexter said to Hank.

"All I know is, he better not ever put his hands on my mother. He won't know what hit him," responded Hank.

That Sunday was the first Sunday of the month, and that meant it was communion service in the evening. First Union was packed with people who came to partake in the service. The lights were out, candles were lit, and the deacons were passing around the grape juice and crackers that symbolized the blood and flesh of Jesus Christ. The choir was singing:

> I know it was the blood
> I know it was the blood
> I know it was the blood
> For me.
>
> One day when I was lost
> He died upon the cross
> And I know it was the blood
> For me.

Rev. Reason then stood before the congregation and recanted the words of Jesus during the last supper. In unison, the congregation ate the crackers and drank the juice.

After the service, Leon was driving home and Margaret was sitting in the front passenger seat. "I have to go by and see my kids for a minute," Leon told Margaret.

"All right, if you must," replied Margaret. She never got in the way of him and his children; she knew not to cross that line.

Leon drove over to McAllister Street and pulled in front of the old Victorian house where the majority of his children lived. He double-parked and honked the horn. Dexter leaned down to look past Hank to the top of the stairs and saw someone peek out a window curtain. A moment later, the front door opened, and out came Leon's girls, running.

They ran over to the car, and Margaret rolled down her window so they could speak with their father. Hank also rolled down his window. Leon talked to the girls and asked them how they were doing, and then reached into his pocket and pulled out a wad of money. The girls were jumping and moving around so, it looked like they had to go to the bathroom. Hank was smiling and teasing them outside of his window, while Dexter was holding his hand over his mouth, trying not to laugh.

Leon gave each of the young girls some money and instructed them to give some to their older sisters who remained in the house. The girls said thank you and ran up the stairs and into the house, waving back at Hank and Dexter as they disappeared. Leon started up the Chrysler and headed down McAllister Street.

As they were riding, Dexter was sitting slouched down in his seat with his legs spread wide open, peering out onto the street as they rode through the Fillmore. He looked over at Hank who was sitting with his legs together, leaning over to one side with his hands clasped together, resting in his lap.

As Dexter stared at Hank, he started to think back on the many times he'd seen his brother sitting like that, and it had never really bothered him before. The difference was that they were older, and it bothered him now. Hank was sitting in a manner that girls did.

Dexter kept looking over at Hank, and the more he looked at him, the more he got upset. Eventually, Hank felt Dexter staring at him. So he looked back at his brother and asked, "What are you looking at?"

Dexter sat up, reached over, and grabbed Hank by one knee, and whispered, "Stop sitting like that. You sit like a girl."

Hank whispered back, "Leave me alone."

Dexter became angrier and whispered more loudly, voicing his discomfort with his brother. "Stop sitting like that." And he gave him a shove.

This time, Hank shouted back, "Leave me alone."

Margaret was in the front seat and heard what Dexter said. "You boys stop that. I don't want you fighting."

"But he's sitting like a girl. He's always sitting like that, and the kids tease him," responded Dexter.

"Well, he ain't a girl, so you leave him alone," shouted Margaret. "Do you hear me, Dexter? Do you hear me?" asked Margaret.

"Yes, ma'am," answered Dexter. He looked over at Hank who stuck out his tongue at him. Dexter then punched Hank on his thigh, and Hank punched him back. Dexter paused, then lightly punched Hank back to get in the last lick, and it turned into a tapping session for the last lick.

Whenever the family went to church evening services, Leon would stop by Kwik Way Diner to buy some coffee for himself and some hot chocolate and french fries for the boys.

As the car approached the intersection of Webster Street at Golden Gate Avenue, Leon had to make a stop for the traffic light. Dexter looked out the window and saw a woman standing on the corner. She stepped off the curb and crossed in front of their car. She was wearing a longhaired wig, tight-fitting clothes, a short skirt, and high-heeled shoes. Her face was covered with makeup, but in spite of the makeup, she was an attractive woman.

As the woman walked by, she looked into the car and winked at Leon as though she knew him. Leon smiled and nodded his head, and then drove across the street into the parking lot of the diner. Dexter turned around and watched the woman as she crossed the other crosswalk. She then walked down the block, past the diner parking lot and disappeared.

Going to Kwik Way after church on Sunday evenings was a ritual, and as Dexter got older, he began to take notice of his surroundings. He had come to recognize that this was a "Ho Stroll." Up and down Webster Street, there were prostitutes walking the street, selling tricks. On more than one occasion, Leon parked the car, bought his coffee, got some chocolate and french fries for Hank and Dexter, handed them their food through the car window, and then took a quick walk down the block out of sight.

Now that Dexter was getting older, he began to see things more clearly. When Leon came back to the car, got in, and drove home, Dexter's suspicions were aroused. After they arrived home and everyone got settled, Leon went outside, got back into his car, and drove off. Dexter had a pretty good idea where Leon was headed. He climbed into bed and thought about what he'd seen. In his mind he was thinking, "Leon is a trick." He wondered if Hank had checked things out. He quickly decided that Hank didn't have a clue. For a moment, Dexter wondered if he should say or do anything. He finally decided not to do anything.

Since moving to the southern edge of Lakeview, Dexter was now closer to Mattock, so they began to hang together much more frequently. Mattock soon introduced Dexter to a boy named Raul who lived just down the street from Mattock, and the three of them became really tight. Raul was a smoker, and soon Mattock and Dexter began to smoke as well.

One summer day, Dexter, Raul, and Mattock were sitting around Mattock's house, and their conversation turned to Mattock's uncle Frank who was living there. Frank was in his room, toward the back of the house past the kitchen, and he was drunk. He had gotten up early that morning and started drinking Hamm's beer.

The boys decided to visit the back room and have some fun with Uncle Frank. When they entered, they found him drunk and cussing. Frank started capping on (insulting) Mattock, and Raul and Dexter laughed at the things he was saying. Mattock tried to cap back on Uncle Frank, but Frank was an old-timer, and Mattock was no match for him.

Uncle Frank finished a beer and threw the empty can over to a trashcan that was full of empty cans, and missed. He then reached down by the side of his bed and grabbed another beer from a six-pack carton he had stashed there. There were three cans left. Raul asked Uncle Frank if he could have a beer, and Frank replied, "Hell, no. Go buy your own, little muthafucka."

Dexter and Mattock were laughing at Raul, because Frank had capped on him. It was clear that Frank wasn't going to give them any beer, so they decided to leave and let Uncle Frank be.

The boys went back into the living room and sat back on the sofa and lounge chairs, bored. Raul said, "Damn, that beer sure look good. I wish I had one right now."

"Ah, you don't drink," said Dexter.

"I do too," replied Raul.

Mattock then chimed in, "I could out-drink both of you."

"I never had a drink," said Dexter.

Raul and Mattock laughed and teased Dexter for never having had a drink of alcohol.

Suddenly Dexter had an idea. "Hey, I know where we can get some liquor!"

"Where?" Mattock and Raul both asked.

"My stepfather has a whole bunch of it stashed in his fishing boat stored in our garage. We can go there and take some. He won't say anything about missing it, because he ain't supposed to be drinking. He acts like I don't know he drinks. Because he's a preacher, he doesn't drink in front of me. He just drinks a beer every now and then when his family comes over for a game of bones. So he hides his hard liquor and takes his nips out of my sight. So, if he doesn't drink, then he can't ask me about it," Dexter reasoned.

Mattock and Raul looked at each other and said, "Let's go."

When the boys arrived at Dexter's house, Margaret was upstairs napping, and Hank had gone over to one of his friends' houses to play. The boys went into the garage, and Dexter climbed up into the small fishing boat. It was cluttered with junk. He fumbled around and found a blanket covering two cases full of alcohol. There was a mixture of quarts in each case, with vodka, gin, bourbon, whiskey, rum, and brandy.

Dexter grabbed bottles of gin, bourbon, and rum; put them in a brown paper shopping bag; and then they headed back to Mattock's house. When they arrived at the house, Celia, Mattock's older sister, and his sister Melanie were gone. Only the younger kids were home.

They went into the kitchen and took some glasses out of the cupboard. Dexter didn't know how or what to drink, so Raul said, "What you got to do is sip it. You can put it over ice and mix some soda or juice with it if you don't like the taste. I'm going to have mine over the rocks. That's with ice and nothing else; it's what my father drinks."

Just then, Mattock interrupted and pushed Raul aside and said, "Hell, I don't need no glass. I can drink it straight out the bottle." He reached for the rum, twisted off the top, swung his head back, and began to gulp. He brought down the bottle and let out a big, "Ahhhhhhh," as he wiped the excess off his lips.

Raul poured himself a gin over ice, and Dexter poured bourbon over ice. Next the boys went into the living room, put on a Temptations album, sat back, and sipped. Mattock kept his bottle with him.

Soon Mattock's siblings, Troy, Karen, and Rita, walked into the room. Troy happened to walk in just when Mattock had his bottle turned up while taking another gulp.

"Oh, I'm gonna tell," yelled Troy, who was about three years younger than Mattock.

Karen chimed in, "Daddy's going to kill you." She was about two years younger than Mattock.

The boys decided that maybe it was time to leave, so they quickly exited the house. They walked across the street, and then headed down the block to the basement of Raul's house. When they arrived at Raul's, he fixed Dexter and himself another drink; Mattock still had his bottle, which was now half empty.

Raul had a pool table in his basement, so he and Dexter decided to shoot some pool, but there was one problem—Mattock! Raul and Dexter had been sipping on their drinks, and they had a nice buzz going. But Mattock, who was chugging down his liquor, was now drunk. He was sloppy drunk, belligerent, and obnoxious.

Dexter and Raul were trying to play a game of pool, but Mattock kept swearing and trying to grab the pool cues. When he couldn't get the cue sticks, he kept messing with the balls to disrupt their game.

"Fuck you, muthafuckas, ya'll can't play shit anyway. I can kick both your asses. If I can't play, you ain't playing. Shit," Mattock said as he reached for the cue ball.

Raul moved to get in the way of Mattock and pushed him aside. "Muthafucka, sit your ass down," he said, as Mattock went flying back and fell on his ass.

"Ow," yelled Mattock, and he tried to get back on his feet, but he could barely stand. Raul and Dexter tried to get back to playing and sipping on their drinks, but Mattock somehow got back on his feet and leaned across the table again to disrupt the game.

Raul moved over toward Dexter; he had an idea. "Let's tie his ass up!" said Raul.

Dexter smiled and snickered, agreeing that it was a good idea. While Mattock was slouching over the pool table, Raul went over the plan with Dexter. He told Dexter to jump Mattock from behind, and he would tie him up.

"Hell, nah, you jump him. Shit, he's too damn strong for me," Dexter cautioned.

Raul thought about it and agreed. Raul knew Mattock would put up a strong fight. He also knew he had the height advantage on Mattock, and his strength was a pretty good match too. There was no way Dexter would be able to hold Mattock down.

Mattock was slumped over on the pool table almost asleep. Dexter grabbed the rope; Raul crept up behind Mattock and grabbed him.

"Hey," Mattock yelled and began to struggle.

Raul had a good grip on Mattock, locking his arms to his sides. Dexter moved toward Mattock who threw his leg up and kicked.

"Muthafucka, let me go, goddamn it. Shit, let me go!" Mattock shouted, his speech slurred.

"Get his feet—tie up his feet," yelled Raul as he lifted Mattock up off the ground.

Dexter was buzzed, and he started laughing. The humor of the situation was making it harder to tie Mattock up. He finally got a loop around one foot and then the other. Like lassoing a cow, he quickly tied up Mattock's feet. Mattock was strong as an ox and putting up a good fight. But Raul maintained his hold, and Mattock began to tire from the struggle. Dexter made a loop with the other end of the rope and got it around Mattock's neck and moved it down around his shoulders until finally it was around his arms. Quickly, Dexter and Raul had completely restrained Mattock.

After having gotten Mattock good and tied up, they moved him out of the way and laid him, tied against a pillar, to rest. Mattock complained and cussed and slurred a little bit longer until finally he was asleep. Raul and Dexter played a couple of games of pool and continued to sip on their drinks. Dexter didn't care for the taste of the bourbon but wanted to be cool, so he didn't complain. Mattock was knocked out and was snoring through his wide nose, with his slobbering mouth wide open.

They looked at Mattock and began to laugh. "That muthafucka stomped on my foot while I was holding him," said Raul.

"Yeah, asshole almost kicked me in my nuts," said Dexter.

"Let's kick his ass," said Raul.

Dexter busted up laughing. He was laughing so hard, his eyes were tearing at the thought of it. "Yeah, let's kick his ass." He and Raul were pretty high and were feeling no pain.

Raul moved in close to where Mattock was seated on the floor, tied against the pillar. Dexter moved in and stood next to Raul. Raul then took the pool cue and gently poked Mattock in the side with it. He then put the tip of the cue under Mattock's nose and began to tickle it. Mattock flinched and wiggled his nose. The two of them stood over Mattock and started to laugh.

Raul then took the tip of the cue and poked Mattock a little harder in the side. This time Mattock complained in his sleep. "Ow," he grumbled.

Dexter reached down and gently slapped him across the face. "Ow!" shouted Mattock in his sleep.

They started laughing uncontrollably. Because they were both high, it was hard for them to contain themselves. When they regained their composure, they started punching and kicking Mattock who cussed and complained with his eyes closed. He tried to open his eyes, but they were so tight and red, he couldn't keep them open. All he could do was lie there and get his ass kicked. They weren't hitting Mattock hard enough to hurt him, but they hit him hard enough to be able to say they whipped his ass, and hard enough for Mattock to know it.

It was getting late; Raul's parents would soon be coming home from work, and they needed to get Mattock back to his house.

Dexter and Raul untied Mattock, who was now out cold. When they tried to raise him from the floor, he was a dead weight. Mattock was short and stocky, and his body was rock solid. Raul took one side and Dexter took the other. They lifted him to his feet, and each took one of Mattock's arms and wrapped it around their shoulders. It was a steep slope from the basement's garage doors up the driveway to the sidewalk. Dexter and Raul struggled to make the climb.

When they finally reached the sidewalk, Mattock groggily came to. "What, what?" he said, puzzled and still drunk.

Dexter and Raul tried to make their way quickly down the street.

"Nah, let me go," Mattock complained as he fought and struggled to get free. He fought himself out of their grasp and fell to the concrete sidewalk, face down, bumping his face.

Raul and Dexter reached down and tried to get Mattock back on his feet. They noticed that Mattock's nose was bruised and a little swollen, but it wasn't bleeding. Again they tried to make it down the block. It felt like Mattock was heavier than a ton of bricks, and carrying him became laborious. People in the neighborhood were gawking and checking out what was happening. Older people were pointing at them from across the street. Kids, riding by on their bikes, were laughing and pointing at Mattock.

Finally, they made it to the intersection. They still needed to get him across two crosswalks to make it to Mattock's house, which was directly in front of the trolley car stop a few feet from the corner. They stopped to catch their breath and began to pull Mattock to his feet. Once they had him on his feet, they draped his arms around their shoulders and stepped into the street.

Mattock and Raul lived on Broad Street, which was where the M trolley car traveled. It was also the end of the line. The trolley cars were like long buses that traveled on train tracks. All along the streets above the train tracks hung electric cables that provided power to move the trolley cars, transferred through long extension poles that connected the trolley cars to the cables.

Just as Raul and Dexter were crossing the tracks, Mattock came to again and tried to fight his way out of their grasp. He fell to the ground and laid stretched out over the tracks. Just then, a trolley car approached, and the driver noticed the kids blocking the tracks, and rang the trolley bell. He pulled up just in front of them and stopped the trolley. The driver stuck his head out the side window of the trolley and yelled at the boys to get off the tracks. Dexter and Raul were exhausted. They were sweating and huffing and puffing, trying to get Mattock home. He was laid out on the tracks, asleep in the middle of the street.

Again, they pulled Mattock up to his feet, but they just couldn't hold on. Finally, they looked at each other, reached down, both grabbed an arm, and pulled, dragging Mattock out of the street so the trolley car could pass. Once they were in front of the house, they needed to get Mattock up about a dozen steps to get him into the house. Raul grabbed one arm, Dexter took the other, and they dragged him up the steps—thump, thump, thump, thump. "Ow, ow," Mattock complained as they dragged him across the wooden steps.

Dexter opened the front door to Mattock's house, finding his sisters, Celia and Melanie, were home. Celia was livid, and Melanie said, "Daddy's gonna whip his ass when he gets home."

Raul and Dexter got Mattock into the hallway where they wanted to leave him on the floor. They also wanted to get out of there before Mattock's father got home. When they tried to leave, Celia stopped them. "Ah nah, hell nah, you're not going to leave him there. Take him up to his room, and put him in his bed."

Mattock's bedroom was on the second floor, up about twenty narrow stairs. Dexter and Raul had no option but to get him up the stairs into bed. They were totally exhausted, and their arms were hurting from all the lifting. As they pulled Mattock up the stairs—thump, thump, thump—he mumbled and complained, and his brothers and sisters laughed with every bump.

That evening, when Mattock's father came home, Mattock was still asleep and drunk. His father took off his belt and whipped Mattock while he cried out in his sleep. Mattock was put on punishment for a week after that. Leon never said anything about the missing liquor, because he wasn't supposed to have it. Dexter never could stand the smell of bourbon again.

Earlier that summer, the News Call Bulletin newspaper was looking for paperboys to deliver morning papers. Dexter heard of the opportunity and asked his mother if he could work a route. Margaret knew Dexter was responsible enough to hold down a job, and it would be a great opportunity for him to get a start in the job market.

The newspaper route was Dexter's first job. He was used to working hard because, prior to this job, he'd taken many odd jobs around the neighborhood—gardening, washing cars, cleaning up garages, or whatever he could do for money. Hank occasionally accompanied his brother.

Sometimes, Dexter and Mattock went to the nearby golf course and got caddy jobs, carrying bags for golfers. They never knew if they'd be able to caddy or not. Sometimes the management would let them, and other times they wouldn't. Mattock's father had a set of golf clubs, and sometimes, at the end of the day, after having done a couple of caddy jobs at the course, the management let them play a few holes. Even though they had watched many games played, no one ever took the time out to explain the game to them. So they didn't know what they were doing when they tried to play.

Because they were getting older, Dexter and Hank had a lot more responsibility in keeping the house clean and doing chores around the house. Their grandmother Mary and their uncle Charles also paid the boys to work around their homes, performing different chores. With the weekly allowances they received from Leon and the extra money they received from the odd jobs, they always had enough money for their needs.

Hank and Dexter were also generous with their money. Even though the district they lived in was a middle-class neighborhood, many of the children living there lived below the poverty level and didn't have basic needs met. If one of their friends didn't have bus fare or didn't have money for a movie or snacks or whatever, the boys never thought twice about covering the expenses for their friends. Margaret had done a fine job of teaching them to share.

One of Dexter's obligations regarding his paperboy job was that he had to take his brother with him. The route was a morning delivery route that required Dexter to rise at 4:30 every morning. Also, the route was in the immediate vicinity, which made it convenient. Hank didn't last on the job for too long. He was tired of getting up so early in the morning, so Margaret decided to let him stay in.

Dexter had a wind-up alarm clock that he set at night so he could wake up on time. He'd rise in the morning and rush to put his clothes on, then walk three blocks up the street to meet the delivery truck. The driver would throw out the bundles of papers for the three or so boys waiting to get started. He'd then give them each a handful of rubber bands to hold the papers together once the boys had folded them.

Dexter would sit on the ground and, one by one, fold each paper and place a rubber band around it, then stuff them all into his canvas carrying sack. There were large pockets on each side of the sack that had a large hole in the middle where the carrier could stick his head through, supporting the weight of the load on his shoulders.

After stuffing the papers in the sack, Dexter would lift the heavy sack over his head and begin to walk his route. When he approached his customers' homes, he'd throw the papers onto their porches or walkways. He always had to be on the lookout for dogs that early in the morning. Many people let their dogs out then so they could get some exercise, and many times the dogs traveled in packs. On several occasions, Dexter had to run and jump on top of a car to escape being attacked by the packs. He'd be on top of a car, yelling and kicking at the dogs until they ran off, either to chase a cat or find somebody else to chase.

Dexter would finish his route around 7:30, then return home and go back to bed. Many times, Leon would be coming in from the shipyard, ready to get his rest too. The house would be fairly quiet so they could all rest. A little later, the boys would eat, complete their chores, and then leave the house so that Leon could continue to sleep.

During this time, Margaret usually planned out the evening's meal, read her Bibles, or practiced her music. When she practiced her music, Leon would sleep downstairs. The boys would hop on their bikes and go and track down their friends. Summertime was a great time for adventure. Sometimes the boys played together; at other times, they split up to play with their different friends.

Dexter usually started out by going over to Mattock's house. He was always welcome in the Jades' residence. Most of the time, Mr. Jade wasn't there. Mattock had to finish up his chores before he was allowed to leave. Sometimes Mattock had money, and sometimes he didn't. If he did, that was great. If he didn't, that was no problem, because Dexter usually had some.

They'd take off on their bikes and ride to pick up Raul, Alfred, and Clifford. Once the friends all got together, they'd try to decide what to do. It all depended on how far Alfred and Clifford were allowed to go. Dexter, Raul, and Mattock could go almost anywhere as long as they were back at a set time.

Alfred and Clifford were often limited geographically. But sometimes they'd stretch the limit by asking if they could go over to Hank and Dexter's house. Their parents respected the Vizinau household, so they'd often say yes. If their parents said yes, the boys took that to mean anywhere on the other side of the hill.

The Vizinaus' house on Orizaba Avenue was at the foot of one of the steepest hills in Lakeview, and the block where they lived was where the hill flattened out. This block was also a gateway to a wooded community in San Francisco, near the border of Daly City. Orizaba Avenue intersected with the beginning of Brotherhood Way, which traveled down a roadway lined with religious synagogues and temples set in a forest setting. The foot of Brotherhood Way dead-ended at Lake Merced, which was about a mile from the Vizinau home.

Lake Merced offered fishing, boating, hiking, and other activities. The boys often went there to fish, skip rocks, ride their bikes, catch turtles and frogs, chase ducks, and just have fun. Not far from the lake were the San Francisco Zoo and Ocean Beach. Many times, the boys also visited the zoo or the beach.

One summer day, Dexter placed phone calls to Mattock and Clifford, asking them to come over for some fun. This time, Al wasn't able to make it. The boys were sitting around the living room, trying to decide what to do. Hank walked into the room, carrying a large golden key. The key was close to two feet long.

Mattock jumped up from the couch and snatched the key out of Hank's hand. Hank protested, "Give me that key back."

"Hey, what's this key go to?" asked Mattock, dangling the key in front of Hank, teasing him to try and take it back.

"That's my mother's key," Hank snapped at Mattock.

Margaret was in the kitchen and heard what was taking place. "Dexter, bring me that key," she shouted from the kitchen.

Dexter rose from the couch, moved in between Hank and Mattock, and reached out for the key. Mattock gave up the key, and Dexter went into the kitchen where his mother was washing some greens.

"Now, take it and put it in my dresser," instructed Margaret. "I don't how it got out of my bedroom in the first place."

"Yes, ma'am," responded Dexter.

Clifford, being curious about what the key represented, inquired of Dexter what it was all about. He explained that, before he was born, Margaret was given the key to the city by the City of Berkeley, but that he didn't know why. Clifford didn't question it any further.

"Let's go down to the lake," suggested Dexter. Everyone agreed, so they left the house, mounted their bikes, and headed down Brotherhood Way.

Hank was always trailing behind, so they'd ride for a way, then stop and wait for Hank. While they waited for Hank, Clifford turned to Mattock and said, "When we get to the lake, let's sneak up on the ducks hiding in one of the marshes and scare them." Mattock and Dexter agreed.

Once Hank caught up, the boys took off again. When they arrived at the lake, they got off their bikes and worked their way down the bank of the shore, quietly heading toward a cove of high grass where they knew ducks often hid.

Quietly, they moved forward, one at a time, crouching and hiding behind boulders as they headed toward the ducks. They got into position and scoped out a group of ducks that appeared to be a family, bathing, grooming, and feeding in the brush. "Shhhh," said Dexter to the others, and just as he was getting the words out, Clifford jumped out, ran ahead of the others, and yelled, "Ahhhhhhh!" He ran and jumped and flapped his hands like a scarecrow, and the birds took flight.

Clifford had a large rock in his right hand; he reached way back, then let the rock fly. The rock soared through the air and connected with an adult male mallard that was about twenty-five feet up.

The duck let out a loud quack, and the rock fell into the water. The duck flapped its wings wildly, and then spiraled downward and fell into the water. The boys stood at the shore and watched in horror as the poor duck flapped about in the water with its head submerged, unable to lift it. Slowly, the flapping got weaker and weaker until it finally stopped, and the duck was dead. It had drowned from a broken neck.

There was silence and sadness. They knew they'd been wrong and that it had been a senseless killing. Clifford stood by the shore with his head hanging low. "I didn't mean to kill him," he confessed. "I only meant to scare them. I didn't want to kill one," he said, looking around for some acknowledgment.

"Why did you have to throw a rock? And such a big one too?" asked Dexter.

"I don't know; I just grabbed a rock. I didn't mean to kill the duck. I'm sorry," Cliff said.

The boys looked at the dead duck, still floating in the water with its head dangling underwater, trying to figure out what to do. "Get the duck," said Dexter to Cliff.

"Nah, I'm not going in that water," responded Cliff.

"Well, we can't just leave it there," Dexter stated.

"Why not? What are we going to do with it?" asked Cliff.

Dexter pondered and didn't have an answer. He almost suggested they bury the duck, but then decided that sounded ridiculous. He pulled out his packet of Kool cigarettes and put one in his mouth. He pulled out his bicycle lighter, lit the cigarette, and took a long drag. Dexter exhaled the smoke, then pulled the cigarette out of his mouth, took a long look at it, and said, "These things make me sick. I don't know why I smoke them anyway."

He threw the cigarette on the ground and stepped on it to put it out. "Here, you can have them," Dexter said as he handed them to Mattock. "Come on, let's go."

The boys hopped on their bikes and rode to another part of the lake.

To this day, Clifford feels sorry about the duck incident.

That summer, First Union Baptist Church was having their annual picnic at Alum Rock Park in San Jose. The picnic was held at Alum Rock Park every year. It was a great park in the foothills of Mt. Hamilton where there were lots of entertaining things to do. There were hiking trails, a creek, a small animal zoo, and an indoor swimming pool, as well as areas for baseball, basketball, and tennis. It was an exciting place where the young and old could have a good time.

Hank and Dexter always had a great time at the picnic. Their favorite activity was swimming in the pool. Margaret usually sat on a bench near the church members who were cooking, or she'd lie out on a blanket and sunbathe with Molly. The boys usually wandered about through the canyon, taking in as much fun as they could. But they were no longer little kids; they were becoming teenagers, and Dexter's interest was changing to girls.

Although there was a core group of kids in the church that grew up together and were close friends, Dexter really didn't have any serious interest in the girls in the choir. He and the girls in the choir flirted and teased each other, but when it came down to it, they were all just friends.

During the late afternoon, when the picnic was beginning to wind down, Dexter was waiting for the homemade ice cream to be ready so he could enjoy some. While he was waiting, there were a few girls around his age playing around the swings near the same area.

These girls went to First Union but were neither part of the core group that sang in the choir nor on the Junior Usher Board. These girls weren't there every single Sunday, but they'd show up maybe once or twice a month.

There was one girl in particular that caught Dexter's attention. She was fourteen, the same as Dexter, only soon he'd be fifteen. Dexter had seen her at church many times, but they'd never spoken to each other. She was dark-skinned and had the prettiest smile Dexter had ever seen. Her teeth were bright white and were as straight as the keys on a piano. Her eyes were hypnotic; they were slanted and looked like they were sleepy. They were "bedroom eyes," and when she batted them, they could put any boy into a trance. Dexter got caught up in that trance. He couldn't help but stare at her.

One thing that Dexter never did was approach a girl without some kind of signal. A girl had to give him a look or a smile or something to let him know it was okay to come over and talk. If he didn't get that, he wouldn't move.

Dexter sat on the bench next to the ice-cream maker where a grown-up was churning. The adult asked him to pour on some salt, but Dexter didn't hear him, "Young man, hello, young man!" shouted the man. "Would you please help me by pouring on some rock salt?"

"Huh? Oh yeah, sure," responded Dexter.

Dexter stood up and went to grab for the salt but wasn't paying attention to what he was doing and instead grabbed a bag of potato chips.

"No, boy, the salt. Right there, the salt," said the man, continuing to churn.

"Oh, okay, I'm sorry," said Dexter as he exchanged the bag of potato chips for the salt.

"Come on, boy, pay attention," demanded the man. Dexter then kept his attention on the ice-cream mixer and began to pour.

Dexter asked, "How much longer before it's ready?"

"Oh, about twenty minutes or so," answered the man. Then he added with a sly grin, "Boy, you better watch yourself; you're going walk into a wall or something, looking at the girl like you doing."

Dexter blushed and acknowledged what the man had said.

Dexter got up and moved to another area and sat on a bench closer to where the girl was swinging. This way, Dexter could get a closer look at her. He watched and checked her out from head to toe.

Her hair was nice and neat and had been straightened, cut, and curled to just above shoulder length. It was frosted with a reddish-blonde tint. She was wearing a grass green, flower-print dress that was form fitting from the neckline to just below the bust-line and then flowed out, somewhat like a Hawaiian muumuu. The dress was short and came to just above the knees.

She had beautiful legs that looked muscular and strong, and they glistened in the sun from the oil or lotion she'd applied. Her skin was a pretty, dark, chocolate brown, but she had a case of acne, and her face was a little bumpy. In spite of the poor complexion, her beauty still came through.

Because of the way the dress fit her upper body, it was obvious that she had developed well and probably had a C-cup bra size. The shortness of her dress revealed her thighs as she swung on the swing. After a closer look, Dexter could see that she was wearing a pair of tight spandex black shorts under the dress.

It didn't take long for the girl to notice Dexter looking at her. She thought he was cute and glanced over his way and smiled. It was a wide and bright smile. That was all Dexter needed; he got up from his seat, walked over, and sat in the swing next to her.

"Hi," said Dexter.

"Hello," she replied.

"I'm Dexter. What's your name?"

"Joy."

"Hi, Joy, nice to meet you," responded Dexter with a smile.

There was a brief pause, and then Dexter said, "I've seen you in church before."

"Yes, I've seen you too. You're Miss Margaret's son," responded Joy, returning the smile.

This caught Dexter by surprise. She had one up on him, because she knew more about him than he knew about her.

"Your mother and my mother know each other. Sometimes they talk on the phone," added Joy.

Now she really had him stumped. Dexter thought he knew all of his mother's friends, and especially those she talked with on the phone. Evidently he didn't know as much as he thought he knew. But then again, Margaret was always full of surprises.

Sensing that the ice cream was about done, Dexter offered, "Would you like some ice cream?"

"Sure. Is it ready?" asked Joy.

"I think it is. I'll go and get us some." Dexter got up to walk over to where the man was churning. He took two steps and stumbled on a rock but quickly caught himself. He turned toward Joy. "I'll be right back."

Joy smiled and giggled and said, "Okay." She thought he was cute.

Dexter came back with the ice cream, and he and Joy sat and chatted until Margaret was ready to leave. They decided to become friends and exchanged phone numbers.

Soon Leon walked over to where Dexter was and announced that it was time to leave. "How do, young lady," Leon said, acknowledging Joy and tipping his cap before he turned and walked away.

As Leon drove up Highway 101 heading north toward San Francisco, he looked in the rear-view mirror and noticed Dexter staring out the window. "I see you met you a new friend," said Leon. "She looks like a fine young lady."

"Yeah, she's nice," answered Dexter.

Margaret heard this and jumped into the conversation. "What young lady?" Before he could answer, she continued, "Dexter, you need to concentrate on your books and not on girls. You're too young to be thinking about girls."

"Margaret, the boy is fourteen, and almost fifteen years old. Of course he's gonna start talking to girls. What do you want? Him to grow up like a sissy?" Leon asked.

"Baba, she's just a friend, that's all," said Dexter. "She says you know her mother and that you two are friends."

"What's her last name?" Margaret asked.

"Dell, Joy Dell," answered Dexter.

"Oh, Sister Dell's daughter. Yes, I know her. She's a nice girl. I know her mother very well," said Margaret. "Well, that doesn't change a thing. You just stay focused on your education."

That night, Dexter called Joy, and they talked on the phone for about an hour. Dexter asked her if she'd like to go to the movies the next weekend, and Joy asked her mother if it was all right. It was, and so it was set. It was Dexter's first date.

Dexter waited until Leon was around to ask Margaret if he could take Joy to the movies after choir rehearsal on Saturday. Surprisingly, Margaret said it was fine, only that he had to take Hank along. Dexter agreed to take Hank along, but he wasn't very happy about it.

That Saturday, after choir rehearsal, the boys walked to Joy's home. She lived with her mother in an apartment on Bush Street at the corner of Broderick. The apartment looked out onto the intersection from the second floor. They picked up Joy and took the Sutter Street bus downtown to the movie theater.

While en route to the theater, Hank and Joy had a good time talking. Joy liked Hank, and she thought he was so cute and sweet. Hank was a funny guy, always playing around and making jokes. He kept Joy laughing. It was a fun ride, and by the time they arrived downtown, it seemed as if they'd been friends for a while. Dexter wasn't so upset anymore that Hank had tagged along.

Hank, Dexter, and Joy went to the Paramount Theater on Market Street to see The Seven Faces of Doctor Lau. They paid the entry fee, purchased some snacks, and walked into the dark theater to find seats. Dexter wanted to go over to the opposite side of the theater and sit in the right column of seats in the back row on the very end. Hank took a seat two rows ahead of them. Dexter had already schooled him on what to do.

Joy was very comfortable with Dexter. On the way to the theater, Dexter had taken her by the hand on a number of occasions; she enjoyed the softness of his touch. Dexter was equally comfortable with Joy. They'd spoken on the phone for hours and talked about many things. She had a good sense of humor, and he was able to keep her entertained without any effort.

While enjoying the movie, they shared popcorn and laughed during some of the funnier scenes of the movie. Every now and then, Dexter would look at Joy, or she'd look at him, and their eyes would meet. After a while, the attraction became overwhelming, and Dexter wanted to kiss her, and Joy also wanted to be kissed.

Dexter had learned how to french kiss about a year earlier. One day when he'd been over at Mattock's house, the subject of kissing came up. Celia had asked Raul if he thought he was a good kisser, and eventually the topic focused on Dexter. Dexter confessed that he had never french kissed but had only kissed girls with his mouth closed. Celia volunteered to teach him, and Dexter accepted.

Celia had Dexter stand up in front of her, then she put her arms around the back of his neck and firmly kissed him on the mouth. Because Celia was kissing him in front of all the other kids, Dexter tried to act as if it were natural to him. But Celia's mouth felt wet and foreign, and she had her tongue darting around the inside of his mouth. It was very uncomfortable, and there was no emotion on his part. When she parted lips with Dexter, she asked him how he'd liked it. He lied and said it was great. Then she asked him if he wanted to do it again. "Nah, that's all right, I think I've got it," answered Dexter.

Initially, Dexter thought that the way Celia kissed him was nasty. But it didn't take very long for him to begin to enjoy it with the right girl. Eventually, he kissed a few other girls, including a couple in the choir. By the time he met Joy, he knew how to kiss a woman, and he knew how to make sure she enjoyed it.

During the movie, Dexter and Joy's eyes met a few more times, and the desire to kiss overcame both of them. First, Dexter eased his arm around Joy's shoulders, and she responded by moving closer and laying her head on his.

Joy had just had her hair done, and the scent of her hair and perfume began to get him aroused. He started rubbing Joy on her shoulder and stroking her arm. Then he kissed her on her head. When Dexter kissed her on the head, she moved her head up to look at him in the face. Their faces were inches apart, and they looked into each other's eyes, then kissed. The kiss came softly, affectionately, and naturally.

Joy then moved to sit more upright and in a better position. She placed her hand on Dexter's chest, and the touch of her hand sent chills through his body. He took her in his arms and kissed her passionately and purposefully. Joy responded by opening her mouth wide to receive him. They kissed long and strong until both were breathing and moaning passionately. When they finally broke apart, each of them knew without saying that she was his girl, and he was her boyfriend. Dexter asked her if she would be his girlfriend, and she accepted. They kissed again, and Joy lay in his arms to watch the rest of the movie.

Joy and Dexter continued to kiss and neck throughout the movie while Hank sat two rows down and watched the movie. After the movie, they caught the bus back to Joy's house, and then the boys took the bus and trolley back to Lakeview.

Dexter was love struck and called Joy as soon as he got home. Unbeknownst to him, Margaret had received a phone call from Joy's mother, letting her know when they left her house. When Dexter got on the phone, Margaret knew he was calling Joy. Plus her hearing was much better than the average person's. She could even hear through walls.

After a few minutes, Margaret decided it was now time to put Dexter in check. She picked up the phone and said, "Dexter, it's time for you to take your shower and get ready for church tomorrow. You need to tell your friend goodnight."

"Damn," Dexter thought to himself. "Okay, be off in a second," he answered.

"Now. I mean now," Margaret said.

"All right, bye, Joy," Dexter said, frustrated.

Joy replied, "Good night."

The next morning, Dexter had to sing in the choir. Joy came to church with her girlfriend that day, and they sat where she could see the choir, and she and Dexter flirted with their eyes during the whole service. After service, they both found each other and flirted some more, and then went their separate ways.

Dexter was now fifteen years old and entering Balboa High School, while Hank was still at James Denman Junior High. Margaret and Leon had settled into the new home, and the excitement was beginning to wear off. They argued often, and Hank and Dexter would retreat to the sanctity of their bedroom. Even though the house was a three-bedroom house, Hank and Dexter still shared a room with twin beds. It was a comfortable bedroom, large enough to accommodate both of them, but occasionally, they'd fight over the phone or the television.

The boys were still very close and, for the most part, didn't argue much. They usually got along and cared for each other with a strong brotherly bond. Dexter was always there for Hank, and Hank was always there for Dexter. Only at school were they apart. Where Dexter was, Hank was usually nearby. At fifteen, Dexter was about six feet tall, and at fourteen, Hank was about five feet, eleven inches.

They were handsome young men. Dexter was slim, weighing about 129 pounds, with broad shoulders. Although he still wore his pompadour hairstyle, he'd cut down the front of it so that it wasn't as much of a fluff. The light spots on his face, which were from a slight skin condition, were gone, and so were his buckteeth, which Hank used to tease him about, calling him "rabbit."

Because Dexter was the oldest and had had a lot of responsibility from a very early age, he'd also developed good habits. Although he didn't like getting up early in the morning and would rather have slept late, he always set the clock next to the bed and arose when it was time to rise.

Hank was pudgy and had a round belly. He always outweighed Dexter by a few pounds and had a healthier appetite. Although Dexter was a good-looking young man and was more handsome than Hank, Hank was prettier; actually he was beautiful.

Dexter's hair was fine and wavy. Hank's hair was fine and curled in large locks. Dexter's skin was a nice golden tan and was a little brighter than Hank's. Hank had more red in his skin and could be considered more of a redbone. His coloring probably came from his Indian grandfather, Henry. Dexter was more of a light-skinned Negro, like a mulatto. He probably got his coloring from his Swedish grandmother, Muriel. They were often mistaken for Latinos. But when someone got to know them, there was no question they were Negroes. Hank and Dexter didn't interact with white people often, even though San Francisco was a very integrated place.

While at James Denman Junior High, Dexter made friends with a white boy named Ricky. He really liked to play with Ricky, and they shared some good times together. But many times, when he went over to Ricky's house, the other white kids in the area would remind him that he was a Negro. One day, one of Ricky's friends called him a nigger, so he had to fight; eventually the boy apologized.

Once Dexter was enrolled at Balboa High School, he lost track of Ricky and stuck to his own kind. Mattock, Raul, Clifford, and Alfred were his running crew; they were his "ace boon coons," and he trusted them with everything.

Most of Hank's friends were girls. He did have one male friend, a boy named Michael, who lived around the corner on Sadowa Street. Often, when Hank visited Michael, he'd ask Dexter to come along, and Dexter sometimes agreed.

In 1966, soul music was more popular than ever. Soul music, pop music, and the British music invasion had replaced rock and roll as the music of choice for America's young. Most young whites were into the Beatles and the Rolling Stones, while most young Negroes preferred the Motown sound and Watt Stax music. Somehow, the Beach Boys managed to hold their own, while Motown managed to bridge the gap between the races and develop a crossover appeal.

But there was a new brand of music that was rising throughout America that began to incorporate a message of social consciousness and mental enlightenment.

Music started to become a vehicle with which to protest and express opinions. Young white people were letting their hair grow long, and the look and makeup of the Haight Ashbury district was rapidly changing. Psychedelic music and folk-rock emerged on the scene, and terms like "acid," "far out," "right on," "groovy," "turned on," and "out of sight" were often heard.

Posters began to pop up all over the city, announcing concerts by the Grateful Dead, Big Brother, and Holding Company. Bob Dylan was singing about "Rainy Days" and "Like a Rolling Stone."

The majority of the Negro music was still focused on love and partying. The Temptations were the number-one male group with hits like "Get Ready" and "Ain't Too Proud to Beg." Smokey Robinson was a lyrical genius to many singing groups, plus he had his own superstar singing group, The Miracles. The Supremes were the number-one female group, with a string of hits like "Back in My Arms Again" and "You Can't Hurry Love."

Stevie Wonder dropped the "Little" from his name and was blowing up the charts with his hits, "Uptight" and "Blowing in the Wind." James Brown was proclaimed the King of Soul and would keep a party rocking with "I Got You," "I Feel Good," and "Papa's Got a Brand New Bag." When his hit, "It's a Man's World," hit the radio waves, he'd taken soul to a level that was out of sight.

Demonstrations against the Vietnam War were beginning to take place around the Bay Area, and young white people were beginning to wear their hair long in protest of "the establishment." They began to camp out in Golden Gate Park and to smoke marijuana openly.

Soon the term "Black Power" surfaced. The Black Panther Party was born across the bay in Oakland, and young Negro men and women were now preaching that Negroes were no longer Negroes but were black and should be proud of it.

Challenges to civil injustice and racism in the South were at an all-time high, and the news constantly carried stories about it. Then an event happened in San Francisco that, for Dexter, brought the struggle home. A riot broke out in San Francisco in the Bayview district, near his grandmother's house. A white policeman had shot and killed a black youth, and images of the riots on Third Street were being played out on the television.

Dexter sat close to the television and watched as black people he knew and loved threw rocks and bottles at police on the streets where he often visited. He felt angry and wished he could be there to fight.

Balboa High School was a proud and high-spirited school. It was a school that was a top contender in football, basketball, and track and field. The school's top athletes were ranked among the highest in the state, and the school's rallies were highly charged and united. Generally, the kids in school tried to get along, but there was a group of troublemakers that kept things on edge.

The school was over 60 percent black, the majority of them coming from either Lakeview or the Sunnydale housing projects, as well as a few from the Bayview district and the Double Rock housing projects.

The thugs on campus began something secretly called "White Boy Day," which was every Friday. They'd target a small group of white boys or a specific white individual, isolate them, then jump them and beat them down. Usually they targeted those who were timid and weak.

These were cowardly acts; the thugs never targeted any of the white boys from the Excelsior district, because they all stuck together. If you fought one of them, you'd have to fight them all. But at the same time, the Excelsior group never seemed to come to the rescue of any of the other white kids that lived out of their district.

Dexter never participated in any of these activities. He also never did anything to stop it. He knew why it was happening, so he understood it. But he also knew that, if he did try to intervene, it would be over for him because, although he didn't hang out with the kids who caused the trouble, he knew each and every one of them, and they left him alone. Dexter wanted to keep it that way.

One day, while Dexter was catching the 29 bus to go home, several of the troublemakers boarded the same bus. He was sitting about halfway toward the back of the bus with Mattock and Clifford. The Kidrey boys, Monkey, the Black brothers, and a couple of others took seats in the back of the bus.

There was a white boy, around fourteen years old, sitting in a seat with his back to the bus's back-door exit. Dexter was sitting alone on his seat, which sat two, and Mattock was sitting in the seat across from him and was also sitting alone. They were facing each other with one leg on the floor and one leg on the opposite seat.

Dexter and Mattock could see what was about to take place. Clifford had gotten off at his stop on Howth and Mt. Vernon Streets.

271

There were two more stops before the Plymouth Street stop, which was where Dexter and most of the others were going to get off.

When Clifford got off the bus, one of the Kidrey boys moved over next to the white boy, blocking him in so he couldn't escape. Monkey reached up and pulled the cord for the driver to stop at the next stop. As the bus slowed to make the stop, the rest of the group got up and lined up behind each other as if they were about to get off. The white boy sat in his seat, reading a book, totally unaware of what was about to happen.

When the bus pulled over to the curb and stopped, one of the Black brothers stepped on the first step to open the back door. He then reached back and rammed his fist into the back of the white boy's head, then jumped off the bus. The force of the blow pushed the boy's head forward, and he instinctively grabbed the back of his head. Suddenly, there was a blow to the left side of his head, close to his ear, which also came from behind, delivered by the other Black brother as he exited the bus. The white boy tried to make a move to get out of his seat. But one of the Kidrey brothers pinned him in and began punching him in the side, making him drop back into his seat. Kidrey then jumped up, raised his foot, and stomped the white boy's head into the window, cracking it.

Dexter sat there watching, feeling disgusted by what he was witnessing but knowing there was nothing he could do. Suddenly, Mattock sprang up, leaped into the air, and as he came down, smashed the boy across his nose with his massive fist, and then jumped off the bus. Dexter was disturbed, but not surprised, by what Mattock had done.

Everything happened so quickly that, before the bus driver knew what was happening, the thugs had gotten off the bus and run down the street. Once the group had gotten off the bus, Dexter got up and approached the boy to lend a helping hand, but the boy rejected his offer and told Dexter to leave him alone. He had a bruise on his forehead, and his nose was bleeding.

When the bus driver, who was black, approached the boy to assist him, the boy told the bus driver that he was all right, so the driver went back to his seat and continued to drive. Dexter got off at the next stop, and instead of waiting for the next bus to carry him over the hill, he decided to walk.

Once over the hill, Dexter decided to stop by Mattock's, since it was on the way home. When he arrived at Mattock's, Mattock was laughing and bragging about what they'd done. Dexter told him that it was fucked up; the boy hadn't done shit to anybody. Celia overheard the conversation and came into the room and got into an argument with Mattock. Mattock walked out of the house. Dexter sat there for moment, and then went home.

Tensions between blacks and whites were getting heated, and things would get worse before they got any better.

14

The Concepts

It wasn't long before the trio of Raul, Mattock, and Dexter began to recognize that they could all sing. So they began to sing and harmonize together. Soon they decided they should become a singing group. Raul would sing first and second tenor, Dexter would sing second tenor and baritone, and Mattock would sing second tenor, baritone, and bass. They needed a name for the group, so after much debate, they came up with the name, the Concepts.

After the group was formed, they needed to start scheduling practices. Dexter didn't want to practice at his house because he didn't feel his mother would approve because it was so-called devil's music. They couldn't practice at Raul's house because, although his mother thought they were cute, Raul's father thought it was foolishness, and that Raul needed to focus on developing a trade.

Mattock's house was the logical choice since his father was always away at work and his older sister, Celia, didn't care. Also, Celia liked Dexter; she thought that he was the sane one and that he was cute. She didn't care for him in a boyfriend-girlfriend kind of way, but she thought that he was nice and clean and wholesome and a good influence on her brother, Mattock.

Singing groups were being formed all over the Bay Area, and several popped up at the school. The Temptations was the group that was setting the trend in soul music, so The Concepts practiced all their songs. They started out singing the older tunes that were easy to sing. They usually began practice by tuning up to "Farewell My Love."

Mattock had a great voice; it was strong and hard. He could sing lead and background; he had a great baritone, an okay second tenor, and a good bass. But whenever he sang bass, he'd have to turn his neck and lower his chin down toward his chest to get the really deep low notes. Sometimes Dexter and Raul had to stop singing because they couldn't help but laugh when Mattock had to go through all those contortions to get down low. Nonetheless, he could hit the notes.

The group sang and harmonized close together, in each other's faces, damn near kissing. When a lead part came, they'd break apart and move back while the lead sang. When it came time for the background to sing again, they'd huddle together again. Mattock would turn his neck, stick his chin on his chest, and Raul and Dexter had to try really hard not to laugh.

After warming up with "Farewell My Love," they'd sing another song by the Temps to tune up:

> I love you (all together)
> Ba do Ba do Ba do (Mattock singing
>   bass, chin down)
> Oh Oh Oh Oh (all together)
>
> I love you (all together)
> Ba do Ba do Ba do (Mattock)
> Baby, baby, baby, don't you know (all
>   together)
> That I love you (Dexter)
> So (Mattock), So (Dexter), So (Raul),
>   So (all together).

Once they got warmed up, it was on to the harder songs. "Ain't Too Proud to Beg" and "Don't Look Back" were their favorites. They always finished with "Old Man River," so Mattock could show his bass-singing talent.

Mattock could sound just like Melvin Franklin of the Temptations, and he loved to get to the part where he could speak out the words, "Tote that barge, lift that bail." Mattock would curl his head and press his chin to his neck and sing something you couldn't understand, "And you laaaaa Ang-ng-gelll-lll."

If they didn't start laughing, the group would continue in unison, "Doom, doom, doom," then harmonize, "Ohhhhhh."

Mattock would half-straighten up and sing, "I gets weary," and so on.

The group sounded good, and they sang everywhere they went. It didn't matter who was or wasn't listening, they'd sing. Walking to school, they sang; going to play basketball, they sang; on the back of the bus, they sang. Everywhere they went, people—blacks and whites—complimented them on their singing.

One day in the spring of 1967, Dexter got home from school and heard that the Black Panthers had stormed the State Capitol Building in Sacramento. He turned on the television and saw Bobby Seale with a group of brothers behind him, all carrying guns. He was talking about the right to bear arms, the right to defend yourself, and how the black community was not going to stand by and let the police practice genocide on an oppressed people.

"Damn, these brothers ain't playing." Dexter was sitting in front of the TV, talking to himself. "They're not bullshitting. These brothers are bad!" he thought. After watching the events that took place, Dexter sat and began to think about the struggle. He wondered about what he was doing, which was nothing. For now he'd let things be, but he'd remain conscious of it all.

Local young black singing groups and bands were performing at dances in the Fillmore and other parts of the city. Hank and Dexter wanted to go to these parties, but they always had to be home by dark. Then their break finally came.

Margaret always listened to the religious radio stations. In fact, it was the only kind of radio she listened to, day and night, every night. While listening to the radio station KEAR, she heard about a weekly event that took place on Saturday nights that focused on Christian youth. They had games, skits, panel discussions, guest speakers, and singing, along with other activities for teenage Christians to participate in.

Margaret was looking for something to get the boys into, to keep them on the straight and narrow path. She felt they were beginning to get caught up in the ways of the world, and she was right. She was concerned for her growing boys. Although she couldn't see what they were up to, many of her friends tried to keep her informed about anything regarding the boys that seemed out of place. If she did receive a call, she wouldn't hesitate to bring the issue before her sons and confront them on it.

Hank and Dexter weren't aware that their mother was in constant prayer about them. They knew she prayed for them in a general sense, but she'd been praying for some specific guidance in these trying times. Hearing about this program for youth was an answer to her prayers.

Margaret called and inquired about the program. It was called Youth for Christ, and it took place every Saturday night, beginning around 8:00 p.m. at the War Memorial Building, next door to the San Francisco Opera House, and across the street from City Hall, in the Civic Center.

When Margaret approached Hank and Dexter about the program, they thought it was great. Hank was interested for the right reasons, but Dexter was thinking, "Yeah, we can get out of the house, go to the event and make an appearance, and then cut out and go to the parties."

Margaret called and arranged for someone from the organization to meet the boys when they arrived and get them acquainted with the group.

Everything was set. The boys would leave the house around 7:00 p.m. on Saturday night, catch the bus downtown, and then walk to the event. Dexter called Mattock and Raul and told them about the plan. Mattock was to find out where the parties were going to be, he and Raul would drop by the Christian event and make an appearance, and then they'd all split the scene and go to the party.

One Saturday night, the boys dressed semi-casual, and when Mattock and Raul arrived, they watched out the kitchen window for the 26 Valencia bus to cross the overpass on Brotherhood Way, a few blocks down the street. When they saw the bus cross the overpass, they left the house and ran across the street to catch the bus as it arrived on Alemany Boulevard. It was a good way to wait for the bus because they didn't have to stand out in the fog and wait for too long. But they had to be fast to make sure they didn't miss it.

The 26 Valencia made its way all the way downtown to Fifth and Mission Streets. From there, they could either walk through the Tenderloin district to the Civic Center or catch another bus. The boys decided to walk through the Tenderloin.

The Tenderloin was the armpit of San Francisco. The worst of the worst was in the Tenderloin. There were junkies, drunks, drug dealers, prostitutes, pimps, and hustlers, all trying to make a buck by taking advantage of any sorry soul that happened to venture by.

The boys were not afraid to venture into the Tenderloin. Even though they were young, they'd seen just about everything growing up in the city. Therefore, walking through the Tenderloin was an adventure in itself; there was no telling what they might see.

As they walked up Turk Street, they passed several bars, cafés, bookstores, liquor stores, and so on. People were begging on the street; prostitutes were walking their turfs while pimps were driving around in Cadillacs. Hustlers were gambling on the sidewalk or trying to run a Murphy on some lonely tourist. Others were trying to sell hot merchandise.

As the boys traveled up Turk Street, at about midway between Jones Street and Leavenworth, they reached a bar that was appropriately named the Trapp. Just as they were about to cross in front of the entrance, a woman stepped out, with a man close behind her, and blocked their way—only the woman was not a woman, he was a man—a white man, dressed like a woman. The boys stopped dead in their tracks.

This was the first time the boys had ever seen anything like that. The "female" man was wearing a tight, sequined, strapless dress, which showed the cleavage of his large breasts. He was about 6' 3" tall, with blond hair and a mole painted above his lip. He had a large nose that stuck out from his face, and he had an Adam's apple the size of New York. His hands were massive, and the white high-heeled shoes he wore looked like a size fourteen.

"Oh, excuse me, boys," he said, in a deep voice, trying to sound like a woman. "Oh, you're cute," he said, pointing at Dexter. He then turned and stumbled off because he'd had too much to drink. The man with "her" followed closely behind.

The boys were dumbfounded and turned to look inside the bar; it was full of men dressed up like women. There were also men in there who looked normal; they were sitting around the bar, drinking, and flirting with the drag queens.

"Damn, you see that shit?" said Raul. "Owe," he continued, as he let out a big laugh.

The boys stared into the bar and began to tease and point and laugh. Mattock yelled, "Fucking sissies," and they all began to run.

They ran up the street and crossed Leavenworth, and then they slowed down. They couldn't stop talking about what they'd just seen. They talked and laughed and joked about it until they reached the auditorium.

Margaret had given the boys the name of someone to ask for, and when they arrived at the auditorium, they found the person and he introduced them to a few folks. To the boys, it seemed like a group of rich, spoiled, Christian white kids having a boring time. They were very nice and pleasant to the boys, but the boys felt totally out of place. Hank and Dexter were used to a good gospel time, but the songs these folks were singing had no beat or rhythm.

They stayed for about an hour, until approximately 9:00 p.m., and then they split and went over to the California Hall, which was within walking distance on Polk Street at the corner of Turk. When they arrived at California Hall, the party was just getting started, and they all agreed they'd leave at 11:30 p.m. The party was great, and they danced, drank some spiked punch, and then left right on time.

The plan worked like a charm. They arrived home around 1:00 a.m. Margaret asked them about the service, and they said they'd enjoyed themselves and wanted to go again. Margaret was happy they'd enjoyed themselves. She said, "Praise God," and told them they could go back again in a couple of weeks.

Dexter got a summer job as a gardener. The job was with the City of San Francisco's Recreation and Parks Department. Dexter had applied for a summer job though the Youth for Service program, which was set up in the Bayview district on Third Street to help inner-city youth obtain summer jobs.

In the beginning, Dexter was stationed at Funston Park in the Marina District, along with several other boys. He was a hard worker; he followed instructions very easily, and never had to be told twice what to do. A supervisor recognized Dexter's skills and abilities, and decided that he'd benefit more from a job that would give him more direct training and experience than he'd get working with a group.

Dexter was transferred to a job assisting the groundskeeper who maintained the grounds around Coit Tower, on top of Telegraph Hill. The Coit Tower gig was one of the best jobs for youth in the department. Being a landmark for the city of San Francisco, it was a high-profile place of interest.

On one particular day, Dexter's supervisor informed him that the television series I Spy was going to be filming on the grounds, so some of their routine chores would have to wait until the next day. As the film crew moved in and set up for a fight scene, Dexter took a break and watched.

Bill Cosby and Robert Culp took up positions by the concrete barrier that protected people from a steep drop down the wooded terrain. Bill and Robert stood by the barrier, talking with two other men. Next a fight broke out. "Cut," yelled the director, and two doubles that looked just like Bill and Robert, stepped in and took over from the beginning of the fight scene. The men swung at each other, and one went over the side of the barrier falling down the terrain. "Cut," yelled the director again.

They went over and over the scene, trying to get it right. After a while, it was boring to watch, and Dexter had to get back to work. He was scheduled to clear out some weeds that were down a path just below where they were filming. Dexter left his observation point, went to the tool shed, grabbed some tools, and walked down the path with his trash container on wheels to the site he needed to clear. He took the rake out and laid it on the ground out of harm's way. Next he grabbed the sickle he used to clear the brush. "Whack, whack," went the sickle as Dexter began to cut through the tall grass and weeds. "Whack, whack," it continued.

"Hey, you down there," someone yelled from up above. Dexter stopped and looked up. It was Mr. Cosby. "Can you cut down that racket? We're trying to get some work done up here," yelled Bill.

Dexter was surprised to hear Bill Cosby talking directly to him. "Sure can, Mr. Cosby," Dexter said waving back at him.

"Thank you," replied Bill.

Dexter packed up and called it a day since there was nothing else he could do. It was an easy day's work with full pay. He came back and finished up the next day. The gardening job continued through the end of the summer.

When the summer ended, Dexter returned to Balboa as a junior, and Hank entered the school as a sophomore. Over the summer, they'd grown their hair into "naturals" (Afros). The hairstyle had become very popular and had become a symbol of black pride. Hank and Dexter's hair was high and long on their heads, while being soft and fluffy.

Since Dexter made his own money over the summer, he could pick out and buy his own clothes. When he returned to school, he wore slacks instead of pants, and most of his slacks were made of wool or silk. He purchased a few nice Italian double-knit sweaters and a couple of sport coats, along with a few new suits. Dexter also purchased several pairs of dress shoes, which replaced the tennis shoes he sometimes wore.

Margaret was still paying for Hank's clothes, so Mary picked out most of the clothes he wore. Dexter wanted to be sharp and clean. He was in a singing group and wanted to look the part, just like the Temptations. Soon he became one of the best-dressed young men on campus.

Many times, Dexter wore dress shirts in a variety of pastel colors, and the majority of them had high-boy collars. He'd take them to the dry cleaners and have them use extra-heavy starch so that the collar would stand tall and stay in place. He and Mattock would compare collars by popping them with their middle fingers to see whose collar was the stiffest. The two of them would get dressed and meet up at one of their houses then profile in the mirror to see how cool they were. They'd strike a pose, pop their collars, and put their hands on their chins with one arm down to their sides, and profile. They just knew they were so cool.

Even though Dexter and Mattock had a habit of capping on each other, they also used to compliment each other. They'd stand at the mirror while profiling and talk about how sharp they were.

Dexter would say, "Ah, nigga, you clean! You a clean muthafucka!"

Mattock would come back with, "Ah, muthafucka, you sharp as a tack, cleaner than a broke-dick dog, nigga!"

"Nah, nigga, you sharper than the president," Dexter would claim.

Mattock would appeal, "Sharper than the president?"

Dexter would reply, "Yeah, muthafucka, sharper than the president. And you know the president is a sharp muthafucka."

They'd laugh and slap each other five and be ready to go on the prowl. Copping girls was a favorite pastime of Dex and his buddies. It wasn't long before Dex began to see and date other girls besides Joy. He was still going steady with Joy because she was his main squeeze, but he couldn't resist a pretty face. If he got a smile from a girl with a pretty face, that was his invitation, and he'd go for it.

It wasn't long before he was talking and making friends with girls all over the city. He wouldn't approach any of the girls in his own school because he didn't want to be tied down. It was also his way of keeping Joy from finding out about anyone else. She might know somebody at the school, and when a boy went steady with a girl in the same school, everyone in school knew about it.

There were guys in the school, especially the jocks, who walked around holding hands with their girlfriends and being the ideal couple, looking so in love. All the girls would see them and say things like, "Oh, don't they make a cute couple?" Dex didn't like that kind of situation and wanted no part of it. It was cool when he was with his girl, but on a day-to-day basis, day in and day out, all the time with the same girl? No, not if he could help it. He didn't care how fine the girl was. To Dexter, those cats that behaved like that were lame; they were the squares.

15

Far Out!

One Sunday, Margaret and the boys were at church. Leon was sitting in the pulpit while Margaret was at the piano. Hank and Dexter had taken seats in the back row of the church because they were planning to walk out when the preaching began. Gone were the days when they sat next to the piano so Margaret could watch over them.

They sat and listened while the choirs sang and the announcements were made. When it came time for the pastor to preach, they quietly stood up, held up one finger, and then walked with a bent posture out the front door. This was something that had become habit as the boys got older.

They'd walk outside, join a few other kids, and walk one block up Geary Boulevard to the Cable Car Diner where they'd buy some hot chocolate and french fries. Once there, they'd sit on the benches outside of the diner and eat and chat, and then they'd go back to the church and enter just before service let out. They did it like clockwork every Sunday, unless they were singing in the choir.

On one particular Sunday, the boys stepped outside and ran into three friends who often visited the church. Dexter asked them if they wanted to walk up the street to the diner, and the friends agreed to go along. So they gathered together and crossed the intersection at Baker Street then began to hike up Geary Boulevard.

As they walked up Geary, they engaged in some idle chitchat. After they passed about five or six houses, one of the boys stopped walking and pointed to the house they were passing, and said, "Look." When the rest of the boys looked up to see what their friend was pointing out to them, they saw, through the window of an old Victorian house, a group of white people dancing around.

It was a group of hippies, and they were having a party early on Sunday morning. They were twirling around and jumping up and down, waving their arms and hands through the air, and wearing silly grins on their faces as if they were in a daze.

The boys stood on the sidewalk and continued to stare until one of the white women noticed they were watching them from the sidewalk. Suddenly the white woman, who was wearing a headband and a tie-dyed flowing dress, stepped in front of the window and waved her hand at the boys. The boys waved back.

A tall white man walked over next to the woman, put his arm over her shoulders, and motioned for the boys to come inside and join them. The boys looked at each other, trying to determine which of them he was gesturing to. Dexter looked back at the man and put his finger on his chest in a gesture, asking if the man was referring to him. The white man nodded his head, acknowledging the invitation.

The woman left the man's side then came through the front door and said, "Come in, come in and join the party."

Dexter stepped aside to let the others walk ahead of him as they all entered the house. Once Dexter entered the house, the tall white man approached him and stuck a joint in his mouth, without asking, and said, "Here, smoke this!"

Several kids in the neighborhood had tried to get Dexter to smoke weed but he had refused. He was afraid of drugs. When he'd been in junior high school, several of the students had taken up sniffing airplane glue. They'd get a brown paper bag and put a small amount of glue inside the bag and inhale the fumes. It would give them a rush, and they'd walk around like they were drunk and out of control; this frightened Dexter.

On one occasion, an older brother of one of Dexter's friends had overdosed on the glue and received permanent brain damage. He was ruined for life and would never live a normal life again.

These incidents made Dexter very afraid of any drugs so, up until this point, he'd always refused. This time though, things happened so quickly, and the joint was already in Dexter's mouth, that he just began to smoke.

"Hi, I'm Sarge," said the white man.

"I'm Dexter," he answered.

"Welcome to my home. Let me take you on a tour," said the man, as he put his arm around Dexter's shoulder and began to lead him away from the rest of the group.

Sarge didn't seem threatening to Dexter, and he was aware that hippies were free spirited, so Dexter let the man lead him away.

As they entered a hallway, he looked back and scanned the room to see what the others were doing.

Two of the boys were sitting on pillows on the floor, smoking weed, another was dancing with a white girl, and Hank was standing by the mantle over the fireplace, chatting with another white woman.

Psychedelic music was playing all through the house and there were people everywhere. People were milling about, smoking weed, and the smell of incense and candles was coming from every room. It was a commune, and Sarge was their leader. Dexter had heard about communes, but he'd never seen or been to one. Tie-dyed sheets and blankets were used as curtains, covering the windows to block out the sun. Black lights fixed to the ceilings caused fluorescent posters to glow. The posters were hung on the walls, which were painted black.

"This is a place where people are free to be what they want to be, no matter what race or color. You're welcome to come here anytime," Sarge told Dexter.

Dexter was feeling stoned; it was a feeling he'd never felt before. When Sarge spoke to him, he stared back at Sarge, whose eyes were all aglow and his teeth were shining bright from the effects of the black light. It had a surreal effect on Dexter. He was in a different world, a world like no other that he'd ever experienced.

Sarge led Dexter downstairs to the basement where there were blankets and sheets hanging from the ceiling, forming partitions to create tiny makeshift rooms. There were pillows and mattresses forming cots on the floor of every little cubbyhole. There must have been at least thirty people living in the house.

As Dexter and Sarge passed by one cubbyhole, there was a couple on the floor, making love on a mattress, where anyone passing by could see. Dexter's eyes became wide when he saw the short, small, slender, brown-haired man mounted on top of a very large, heavyset, blonde woman.

The little man had a huge penis and he was plowing it in and out of her. She was moaning and scratching his back; her legs were wrapped around his waist as she pulled and pushed, trying to receive more.

"Yes, yes, more, more," she moaned.

"You can join in if you wish," said Sarge.

Dexter was shocked; his mouth fell open and he looked at Sarge, thinking about what he'd said. He looked back at the couple on the floor and shook his head replying, "Nah, that's all right. Thanks anyway."

Dexter stood there, watching for a moment, and began to become aroused. "Come on, let's go back and join the others," instructed Sarge.

Dexter was in awe of what he'd seen, plus he was also stoned. They went back upstairs and, as they entered the front room, a woman approached Sarge. "This is our woman, Sunrise," said Sarge as he introduced her.

Dexter wondered if he'd heard Sarge correctly. "Did he say our?" he thought.

Sunrise stepped in front of Dexter and planted a big kiss directly on his mouth. Dexter's eyes got wide and they darted about, scanning the room as the woman was kissing him. She finally let go of Dexter with a big "Muah." Dexter took a deep breath and exhaled. It was becoming too much.

One of the boys that came with Dexter was sitting on a pillow on the floor, and there was a large, overweight, white woman sitting on his lap. One of the other boys was sitting on a lounge chair, leaning back and listening to the music, with his eyes barely open; he was stoned. Hank was dancing in the middle of the floor with a cute oriental woman; he was also stoned. The third boy was standing near the mantel, tapping on it like he was playing drums; he was stoned too. They were all stoned! Everyone in the house was stoned out of his or her mind.

"Damn, we've got to get back to church," Dexter yelled. "Come on, guys, we've got to go."

Dexter told Sarge thank you and said he'd had a good time. "Wait, hold on a second," said Sarge. Dexter paused, and Sarge walked across the room to a large wooden wine barrel that sat in a corner. "Come here, Dexter," Sarge said as he motioned to Dexter.

He lifted the top off the barrel and exposed his stash of marijuana. The barrel was full to the brim. Next to the barrel were some plastic baggies; Sarge took one, then grabbed a handful of weed and stuffed it into the baggie and said, "Here, take this!"

Dexter's eyes widened in surprise. "Wow, thanks!" he said as he tried to stuff the baggie into the pocket of his pants. But the baggie was too big, so he then decided to stuff it inside his suit coat's outside pocket.

The boys left the commune and headed back to church where the service was still going on. They entered the church and found a row where they could all sit together. After they sat down, one of the boys started to giggle. Soon another began to giggle, then another, and another. It became contagious, and the boys couldn't stop laughing.

They were all high for the first time in their lives, and they all had the giggles. "Shh," instructed an usher, directing it toward the boys. Dexter put his hands over his mouth and tried to regain composure. "Shh, keep quiet," the usher instructed again.

Finally, the boys gained control but it was difficult to maintain. Unbeknownst to everyone in church, the five boys were sitting there stoned out of their minds. That day marked a time when Hank and Dexter embarked on a journey that would change the course of their lives.

In the afternoon, when Dexter returned home, he called up Mattock and Raul and told them to come right over. When they arrived, they went into the boys' room and Dexter shut the door behind them. Dexter walked over to the desk, opened the drawer, and then pulled out the baggie stuffed with marijuana.

Dexter and Hank told Mattock and Raul about their adventure that day. Mattock said he wished he'd been there, and that he'd have jumped on the woman having sex.

"So what do we do with this stuff?" asked Dexter.

Raul said, "I know what to do with it. We need to go to the store and buy some Zig Zags so we can roll up some joints."

"Yeah, I can dig it. Let's go to the store and cop some papers," replied Dexter.

So the boys left the house and walked to the corner store and purchased some Zig Zag cigarette papers.

When they returned to the house, Raul said, "Okay, now we need some newspaper." Dexter went downstairs to the garage and returned with the newspaper and gave it to Raul. Raul took the newspaper and spread it out over Dexter's bed. He took the baggie and poured the marijuana onto the newspaper. The weed, complete with stems and seeds, spilled out onto the bed. There must have been about two and a half ounces.

Raul took the Zig Zags out of his shirt pocket and then Mattock quickly grabbed them out of Raul's hand.

"I know what to do. Watch me!" Mattock snapped.

"Fool, you don't know what you're doing," Raul snapped back.

Hank, Dexter, and Raul watched as Mattock tried to roll a joint. But Mattock's hands were big and cumbersome. Although he was only sixteen years old, he had the hands of a grown man, with thick, fat, and stubby fingers. Mattock pulled one sheet of paper from the packet, then grabbed some weed and tried to sprinkle it onto the crease of the paper. He then tried to roll a joint but the paper tore apart. He then took another strip of Zig Zag and tried again. This time the stems poked a hole through the paper as he tried to roll.

Raul snatched the Zig Zags away from Mattock, "Idiot, I told you that you couldn't roll it. Watch me and learn; I've seen my brother do it many times." Raul took two sheets of Zig Zag papers and wet one side then glued the two sheets together to make one. "First, you have to clean the weed to get out all the stems and seeds," Raul said. He sifted through the weed and separated the leaves from the debris. He then took two fingers and gently placed a small portion of weed in the crease of the folds on the papers. As the other three looked on, Raul gently rolled the joint from the center out, explaining his movements as he went along.

"Now, that's a joint," Raul said, holding up his work of art. It was almost perfect. The boys each took turns rolling joints, and soon they opened the front windows and fired one up and began to smoke. Margaret was in her bedroom asleep, with her door closed, and Leon had done his usual exit after they'd returned home from church, so he wouldn't be home for a while.

With the boys' bedroom door closed and the window open, the smell didn't travel into the hallway. They sat on the bed and smoked and rolled up the whole stash. When they'd finished, they had about 180 joints. Dexter gave Mattock and Raul ten joints each and they left and went home.

The next morning, Dexter rose, got dressed, and headed for school ahead of Hank. When he arrived on campus, he walked over to the corner store and stepped a few yards around the corner into the driveway of a house, where he knew kids went to buy joints. Within ten minutes, a student walked by, looking to buy a joint. No dealers were there, so Dexter sold the boy a joint. "Twenty-five cents," said Dexter. The student didn't hesitate, and he gave Dexter the money. The next thing you knew, there was another, and then another, until soon he was drawing a small crowd of students waiting to score.

Dexter sold his joints for twenty-five cents each. He sold them during breaks, at lunchtime, and after school. By the end of the day, he was almost sold out, except for a few he decided to keep for himself. Dexter had over thirty-five dollars in his pocket. "Shoot, that was cool," he thought.

This was the beginning of something big for Dexter. He was now in business for himself; he was an entrepreneur. The next Sunday, Dexter went back to the house on Geary Blvd. to visit the commune. This time he went alone, and when he left the house, Sarge did the same thing. He filled a baggie with marijuana and gave it to Dexter without asking for a dime, and again, Dexter rolled up the whole bag, went to school, and peddled it all.

The following Sunday, when Dexter returned to the house, it was completely empty; there was no one home. The place was deserted; there wasn't a soul in sight. "Damn, what am I going to do now?"

Dexter thought to himself. "I wonder what happened," he continued. He stood back and examined the house, noticing that even all the furniture was gone. He peered through the windows and saw there were no more posters or sheets and blankets adorning the walls or windows. He walked away with his head bowed, pondering his next move.

That evening, Dexter was watching the news on television when a report came on about a drug bust in San Francisco earlier in the week. The police had raided a commune on Geary Boulevard and arrested its leader, who was a San Francisco police officer on suspension from the department.

Sergeant Sunshine was a beat cop who walked the Haight Street beat. He always wore a flower in his cap, and the local hippies gave him the nickname, Sergeant Sunshine. He was on suspension for smoking a joint on the steps in front of City Hall to protest the marijuana laws.

"Damn, that's the guy who gave me the weed. Wow, what a trip. Far out!" Dexter said out loud, as he watched the news. "What am I going to do now?" he asked himself. He only had a few joints left, and he needed to cop. Only now he'd have to pay for his inventory. It was a good thing that he hadn't spent the money.

He figured that he'd go to school the next day, and then he'd figure out what he was going to do. He did know one thing: he didn't want to buy from any of the brothers. They were a pain in the ass and too full of game; it would be a hassle, and worse, they might try and rip him off.

In the two short weeks he was dealing joints, Dexter had learned a lot. He learned the terminology and knew how weed was packaged and sold. He also learned which white boys and Mexicans on campus smoked and sold weed. After giving it much thought, Dexter decided that he'd approach a couple of Mexican brothers.

He approached a Mexican named Sanchez, who in turn told him to check with Harvey. This was good news for Dexter because he had known Harv since the seventh grade in Denman. They'd been in the same homeroom together and had both played on the basketball team. Dexter played for the 120s and Harvey played on the 112s.

Dexter located Harvey and approached him, "Harv, can I speak with you for a moment."

"Yeah, Dex, what's going on?" answered Harvey.

"I need to buy a lid," (one ounce) said Dexter.

"Dex, what are you doing? I didn't know you smoked weed. I thought you were kind of square to do that sort of thing," responded Harvey.

"Well, I started selling joints a couple of weeks ago, but I lost my supplier. It's a long story," answered Dexter.

"Okay, Dex. It's ten dollars a lid. How many do you want?" asked Harvey.

"Two, I'll take two," Dexter requested.

"Okay, meet me back here in fifteen minutes," said Harvey as he walked off.

Dexter returned in fifteen minutes, and they completed the transaction. He quickly put the lids in his pocket and went directly home after basketball team practice. When Dexter got home, he took out his stash and right away noticed that the weed was a different color than the stuff he'd had before. It was a dark reddish color. It was Panama Red! He'd heard about Panama Red, that it was some of the best stuff.

Quickly Dexter rolled up a joint, went into the back yard, and fired up the joint. He took a drag, and immediately choked on the smoke. Cough, cough, cough. "Damn, this shit is strong." Dexter said to himself. By the time he stopped coughing, he was already loaded. One hit, that's all it took. He went to his room, rolled up the joints, and the next day he went to school, back in business.

Dexter's business began to thrive, and it soon got to a point where Dexter would no longer market to strangers. He had developed his own clientele and only sold to people he knew. Whenever he sold out, he'd go to Harvey and re-up.

"Dex, you've been going through this stuff pretty fast, man. You mean you've been selling it all in joints?" asked Harvey.

"Yeah, in only a few days, that's all it usually takes," responded Dexter.

"Cool, that's cool, Dex," said Harvey.

"I'll tell you what. We don't have too many brothers with us, so I'm gonna do you a favor. I'll front you a quarter-pound; it will cost you thirty dollars and we'll see how it goes," Harvey informed Dexter.

"Cool, right on! That's cool, Harv," responded Dexter.

"All right, Dex, you meet me back here in a half hour. I'll be right back," Harvey said, as he turned and walked away.

"Cool, thanks, Harv," Dexter said, as he turned and walked in the opposite direction.

Harvey was a smooth Mexican. He was short and real handsome, with jet-black hair, which he wore in a pompadour. He was always dressed sharp, and he sometimes hung with the brothers.

Harvey returned with a brown paper bag in his hand. He handed it to Dexter and said, "You call me when it's gone." Dexter took the bag, and they shook hands and parted ways.

When Dexter got home, he opened the bag; this time the weed was a different color again. This time the buds had two colors. They had an olive green center to them with gold tips on the leaves; it was Acapulco Gold! Like the Panama Red, Dexter had heard about the gold, but hadn't yet had any.

As Dexter sat on his bed to begin packaging, he paused and began to think about everything he was experiencing. He knew that he was in the mix now, and that he had the Latin connection. It was a direct line!

A lot had happened in a short period of time. Dexter pondered over what had transpired—what was happening, where things were going, and what it all meant. The times were changing, and he was changing right along with them. He'd heard so many bad things about drugs, but this marijuana thing seemed harmless. He began to think, "Is this what they were saying was so bad? I don't see the harm in it. This seems much better than drinking to me. Hell, they acted like you'd lose your mind and couldn't function if you smoked a joint. It was all a lie."

Things began to get wilder and crazier in San Francisco in 1967. The Haight Ashbury district had become a circus. Occasionally, Hank and Dexter traveled there just to visit, or maybe to check things out and see what kind of weed was circulating there. The place had turned into a tourist site, complete with tour buses riding down the street, with people from the Midwest or overseas peering out the windows, pointing and quacking at the hippies they saw on the street.

Hippies were everywhere; they were crashing on the streets, in the park, or wherever they wanted to lie. They were turning on and tuning out. The drug scene had gone from people using mild drugs, like marijuana, to experimenting with dangerous psychedelic drugs, like LSD. Many people were hallucinating, and some were even hurting themselves.

Incense filled the air and psychedelic shops sold all kinds of paraphernalia for doing drugs. Black lights and posters, depicting everything from protesting the war to peace signs or free love, were on sale at every corner.

The Haight Ashbury was really a sight to see. Street artists were selling their wares up and down the street, while others sat on a stoop or stood on a corner and played folk music, trying to raise some cash. Every now and then, the police would have some young lady under arrest for exposing her breasts in public. The cops would try to cover her up, while she'd keep taking her clothes off.

Dogs freely walked the streets, unleashed, with their masters. Sometimes even the dogs were stoned, from hippies blowing marijuana smoke in their faces. Many dogs wore scarves around their necks, and some were painted like mosaics with collages of colors.

While in the Haight, Hank and Dexter purchased a few posters, a couple of black lights, and some fluorescent paint in different colors, to decorate their bedroom. They went back home and transformed their closet into a smoke-out room. They covered the walls of their closet in black paint then painted collages of peace signs, stars, spirals, planets, and mazes. They hung posters on the walls, above and behind their beds. They also hung black lights in the bedroom and in the closet.

Whenever they wanted to smoke a joint, they'd close their bedroom door and light incense, then either go into the closet or open the window and smoke by the window.

One evening, Mattock and Raul came over to Hank and Dexter's house and they all sat around in the bedroom getting high. Not long after Mattock and Raul left, the doorbell rang. Dexter ran to the window and saw that it was his grandmother, Mary. "Oh shit, it's Nanny," he yelled out to Hank. The smell of marijuana was still fresh in the room.

Hank and Dexter both went downstairs to open the door. Mary was standing there, smiling like she always did when she saw the boys. Dexter buzzed open the gate, and Mary walked into the house and began to climb the stairs.

When she reached the top of the stairs, she stopped.

"What's that I smell?" she asked as she sniffed.

"Oh, we were burning some candles in our room," answered Dexter.

Mary paused in front of the boys' room then opened the door and the smoke rushed out and hit her in the face. "That ain't no incense! That there is that damn weed! I know that smell. Mrs. Benton's son smokes that there stuff and she's always complaining about it," said Mary, busting Hank and Dexter.

Margaret was in her room with her door closed, resting. "Naomi. Naomi, come here quick. Naomi, come here I say," Mary shouted.

Margaret rose from her bed and walked down the hall. "Mother, what did you say?"

"Lord, these boys are hooked on dope. They're smoking that weed. I know what it is because Mrs. Benton's son smokes that stuff. Lord, I hope these boys ain't hook on no dope," Mary said voicing her concern.

"What?" Margaret said, sounding shocked, as she approached from down the hall.

"Hank, Dexter, where is it? Bring it here, let me see it." Mary instructed.

Dexter had a shoebox where he kept his personal stash. He kept his inventory elsewhere in the crawl space above the closet. Dexter went and got the shoebox and gave it to Mary.

Mary took the shoebox from Dexter and opened it up and looked inside. There were a few rolled joints, a little loose weed, an empty matchbox, rolling papers, a rolling machine, a small pipe, and some stems and seeds. "Is this it, is this all?" asked Mary.

Dexter bowed his head and answered, "Uh huh."

"Boy, look at me and answer me when I talk to you. You still ain't too old for me to whip," Mary snapped.

Margaret was in the background, saying, "My God, Lord Jesus."

Dexter straightened up, "Yes Nanny," he answered.

"Hank, is this all?" Mary asked.

"Yes Nanny," he answered.

Mary went on to lecture the boys about the danger of drugs. She told Margaret that it was probably too late because all the kids were doing it. And she was right! Mary told the boys they were on punishment, and that Dexter couldn't drive her spare car for at least a month. That really hurt Dexter because when he turned sixteen he got his driver's license, and he often used his grandmother's second car to go on dates with girls.

Mary then noticed that Margaret was a little lethargic. She was on the border of having an insulin reaction, and she could easily slip into a coma if it wasn't checked. Mary instructed Hank to make his mother some orange juice with about five teaspoons of sugar.

As Margaret was getting older, her diabetes was acting up more frequently. Hank and Dexter had to watch her more closely because she had a reaction about every two or three months. At least once a year, they'd have to call for an ambulance, and she'd be admitted into Kaiser Hospital for treatment.

Mary now complained to the boys about not watching their mother more closely. This made the boys feel really low because they knew what she was saying was true. From that day on, they stayed more on top of their mother's care. One of the reasons they had slipped was because Leon had taken on more of a monitoring role since he'd come into the picture. But he often worked late and wasn't always home. So the boys had to step up their care for her.

The episode with Mary didn't change anything in terms of the drugs. It seemed like everyone in school was getting high, and even more dangerous drugs began to enter the campus. Kids were popping pills, and some of the dealers were selling all kinds of stuff. They were selling Reds, Blues, Yellows, and Bennies. Some of the white boys were dropping acid, and every now and then, someone would have a bad trip on campus. The faculty was puzzled as to how to deal with the problems. Drugs had become a major problem in the schools and in society. Pretty soon, patrol cars were a common site on campus.

Dexter graduated from selling joints and matchboxes to selling lids and half-lids. Every now and then, he might sell a quarter-pound. He still carried a few joints for a quarter and some matchboxes for five dollars. But it wasn't long before he stopped selling the small stuff.

He still carried some extra joints for his own use or just to give away. It kept the thugs, gangsters, and bullies off his back. If they asked him if he had anything, he'd reply with, "What you want?" If they wanted anything more than a joint, he'd say that he could get it for them, but that he didn't have it with him. Usually they wanted it right away, so they'd keep moving. If they wanted to buy a joint, he'd say, "I don't sell joints," and he'd just give them one, and they'd say thanks, and move on.

It was a process that worked. It kept him out of conflicts and fights and from getting robbed. They just left him alone.

Dexter was also usually with his crew, and most of the thugs knew that Mattock and Raul had no problem taking on a fight, so there would seldom be any trouble. What Dexter didn't realize was that his mother had the angels watching over him.

It wasn't long before all of Dexter's friends began smoking pot. Al, Clifford, Mattock, and Raul all smoked regularly. Mattock also sold a little bit, and Dexter kept him supplied.

The times were changing quickly. Being teenagers in the sixties was challenging. It was hard to tell what the future held.

16

Lord, Why Forsake Me?

The war in Vietnam was escalating and young black males were being drafted and sent to the front lines to fight in a war and nobody even knew why it was being fought. There were more and more protests taking place, and young people were rising to the occasion to make their voices heard.

Race riots were breaking out all over the country. During the summer, Detroit and Newark were the worst of the worst. Black people were rebelling against the system, and Cassius Clay had announced that he was changing his name to Muhammad Ali. Dexter was a big fan of Clay, and so were most of the young black people in school. He'd followed all of Clay's fights and was trying to understand what Cassius was putting down.

Dexter knew that Ali was a close friend of Malcolm X, but he really didn't know much about the Nation of Islam, only that the Muslim brothers wore suits with bow ties and sold The Final Call newspapers that he never read. He also knew that the Muslim brothers had taken over the Temple Theater on Fillmore Street, which was where his grandmother had taken him to see the movie, Imitation of Life. He was about six or seven years old at the time. That was an experience he'd never forget because he cried like a baby during the funeral scene.

The Muslim brothers intrigued Dexter, but the pastor at church always spoke against them. He said they didn't believe Jesus Christ was the Son of God, and that you had to know Jesus in order to save your soul. For these reasons, Dexter pretty much stayed clear of the Muslim brothers. Plus, they didn't eat pork, they kept their women covered up, and another main reason, they didn't smoke weed!

Ernie Terrell, who was scheduled to fight Cassius, refused to call him Muhammad Ali. There was so much controversy that fight fans were getting into arguments about it. Leon had gotten into an argument with a white man at the gas station about it.

Leon kept saying, "Let the man be called whatever he wants to be called. What business is it of yours?"

Next the white man said, "It just causes problems and stirs up trouble with you Negroes. It ain't American."

Leon went off, "Ain't American? We ain't American. We not free; you people don't want us here."

"That's the problem with you folks, you don't appreciate nothing," said the white man.

Leon wanted to fight the man, but Dexter grabbed him by the arm and said, "Come on, Dad, come on. You don't want to fight with him," so they got into the car and drove off.

Dexter and Leon went to see the fight on the big screen at the Civic Auditorium in downtown San Francisco. The Auditorium was sold out and was filled with mostly black and white fans, as well as some Mexicans. Most of the white folks were rooting for Ernie, and the blacks and Mexicans were pulling for Ali. A few young whites were pulling for Ali, and some conservative blacks were pulling for Ernie, but for the most part, the crowd was cut right down the middle.

Ali stood for more than just his religion. He was a symbol of black pride, and it meant a lot to many black folks that he come out a winner. There was a lot on the line.

The fight started; Ali came out floating and stinging. When Ernie hit the ground, Ali stood over him and yelled at him, "What's my name? What's my name?"

The crowd went wild, and black people in the auditorium started chanting, "Ali, Ali, Ali." It felt good; it was a joyous and prideful occasion, and Leon and Dexter celebrated and jumped for joy.

Ali had won, which to them meant blacks had won. It seemed funny to Dexter how there were two black men in the ring but only one seemed to represent blacks. Many white people were angry and upset because Ali had rubbed their hatred in their faces.

Not long after the fight, Ali refused the draft and was stripped of his title and denied the right to fight. The boxing commission's actions depressed many black people, and the move became a symbol of oppression. But the people were proud of Ali because he didn't break under the pressure. He stood up for what he believed in, and the black community supported him.

As time moved on, Dexter began to read The Berkeley Barb and the Black Panther Party's (BPP) newspaper. These newspapers were the voices of the struggle, and carried columns about what injustices were taking place in the community.

The Berkeley Barb provided him with information on the politics of the war, and The BPP Newspaper provided information on the civil rights struggle and the black revolution.

In 1968 Rev. Reason died, and First Union Baptist Church was looking for a new pastor. When the new pastor, Rev. Henry Davis, came in, he wanted to make some changes.

Margaret had been Rev. Reason's favorite choir director, and he always called on her to bring the Holy Spirit into the Lord's house. Almost immediately, however, Rev. Davis cut back on the work Margaret was doing. Understanding what was taking place, she decided that it was time to leave.

Margaret had no problem finding another job. Her reputation was impeccable, and there was always a congregation looking for a choir director who was entertaining, consistent, and experienced. Right away, she found a job at Paradise Baptist Church in Lakeview, not far from the house.

Hank and Dexter didn't feel at home at Paradise Baptist Church. They had been raised in First Union, and it was the only church home they knew. Since they were both teenagers, Margaret felt they were old enough to make their own decisions, so she allowed them to continue their membership at First Union. Occasionally, Hank and Dexter visited Paradise to see their mother perform.

The boys also continued to visit the Youth for Christ programs occasionally on Saturday nights in downtown San Francisco. They'd walk through the Tenderloin and talk with the prostitutes and tease the drag queens, but something began to happen and change with Hank.

He wasn't really into smoking weed very much because it brought him down. What he did start to partake in was dropping pills occasionally, along with drinking alcohol every now and then. These activities didn't appear to be habit forming, but his behavior began to be rebellious.

Leon could never say anything to Hank without getting into an argument. Whenever Leon tried to chastise him, Hank would respond with, "You ain't my daddy," or "You can't tell me what to do."

Margaret would get angry at Hank and tell him he was being disrespectful. But Hank really didn't have any respect for Leon and he was totally aware that he was being disrespectful. He just didn't care.

One day, Margaret told Hank that he was on punishment for talking back, and Hank stormed out of the house. He'd never done anything like that before, and Dexter was becoming concerned. Dexter planned on having a talk with his brother when he returned home. But Hank didn't return that night. He didn't return home the next day either. He had run away!

That evening, Mary called over to the house and asked Dexter if he knew where Hank might be. He told his grandmother that he had no idea where his brother was. Mary voiced her concern; she was worried about him. She suggested that she'd come over in the morning and the two of them should go out and search for him. Dexter agreed that it was probably a good idea, and they could probably track him down. Early the next morning, Mary drove over to Margaret's house and picked Dexter up, and then they went off looking for Hank.

The first thing Dexter wanted to do was check with Hank's friends to see if any of them knew where he might be. They headed to Michael's house, one of Hank's best friends. When they questioned Michael, he said had no idea of where Hank might be. But Michael's mother said that she'd talked with Hank on several occasions, and that he'd shared some things with her about how he was feeling. She said that Hank was having some growing pains and that he wasn't very happy at home. She wasn't really clear about what she meant, but Dexter was aware that Hank had become very close to her and often confided in her.

The next place they visited was a friend of Hank, named Laron. He was a relatively new friend of Hank and lived on Broad Street. Laron told Dexter that he'd heard from him, but that Hank hadn't told him where he was staying. He did say that something Hank had said led him to believe that he might be in the Tenderloin.

Dexter thought that this might be the break they were looking for. He went back to the car where Mary was waiting, and they headed downtown to the Tenderloin.

"The Tenderloin, why would he be in the Tenderloin?" asked Mary.

Dexter sat in the passenger's seat and began to ponder. With a blank stare on his face, he answered, "I don't know."

As Dexter and Mary traveled downtown, Dexter started to think back to the times when he and Hank had walked through the Tenderloin with Mattock and Raul on their way to the Youth for Christ events. All that was in the Tenderloin were drunks, hustlers, pimps, prostitutes, and drug dealers. "Could Hank be turned out on hard drugs? Was he a junkie now?" Dexter wondered to himself.

Mary got off the freeway at the Seventh Street exit and headed toward the Tenderloin. They crossed Market Street, and approached Leavenworth Street and made a right, which went straight through the heart of the Tenderloin.

"Nanny, let's drive around the neighborhood for a while and see what we can see," Dexter said to his grandmother.

They rode around and circled several blocks, trying to see any sign of Hank. They drove down Eddy Street, then Ellis, and Turk, then over to Jones Street, and down O'Farrell Street. As they rode around, Mary was looking at the characters on the street.

It was a seedy place, and the people looked desolate and shady. There were drunks lying in the street; junkies were hanging out on the corners, begging for change; and hos were walking the streets, looking for tricks—and it was the middle of the day. On just about every other block, someone was having an argument. "My God, what would he be doing down here? Lord, help us. Please, Lord, let us find our boy," cried Mary.

Mary was driving down Mason Street, and Dexter had her make a right onto Turk Street. As they approached Jones Street, Dexter said, "Nanny, park over there," motioning for her to turn onto Jones and park on the opposite side of the street. Mary pulled the car over and parked at a parking meter. "I'll be back; you wait here," Dexter instructed Mary.

Dexter had seen someone he knew. It was a hustler who'd grown up in Lakeview. He was several years older than Dexter, but Dexter knew him, and he knew what he was. He had also burned Dexter and Mattock a few months earlier by selling them some bunk weed at Tree's Pool Hall on Fillmore Street, during a time when Harv was having a dry spell. Dexter also knew that the guy would recognize him from the neighborhood, and that there'd also be a good chance that he'd know Hank was his brother because Hank and Dexter were usually together.

The hustler was walking down Turk Street at a fast pace, so Dexter had to run to catch him. He ran down Turk Street then zipped out into the middle of the street, into traffic, to cross the street and catch up. When the hustler happened to look back and see Dexter running across the street, and that he was looking directly at him, he became jittery and had an anxious look on his face.

"Say, blood, let me holler at you for a minute," yelled Dexter, as he approached him. The hustler stopped and backed up to a wall, then put his hand in his jacket as if he had a gun.

He was about the same height as Dexter, but was much thinner, only weighing about a buck thirty. He was jet-black with an oily face; he had yellow teeth and red eyes to match. He was dressed neatly, with a double-knit sweater and silk slacks. On his feet, he wore a pair of alligator shoes. He needed to have his process done, and there were a few hairs sticking out of place. Dexter was thinking, "Man, they don't wear processes anymore," when he looked him up and down.

"What do you want?" the hustler asked apprehensively.

"You know me?" asked Dexter.

He took a second and stared Dexter up and down, then recognized him. "Yeah, young blood, you're from Lakeview," he acknowledged.

"Do you know my brother?" Dexter asked.

He smiled and said, "Yeah, I know him. He's the sissy."

"Yeah, yeah, I know. Have you seen him?" asked Dexter.

"Suppose I did, what's in it for me?" asked the hustler.

"Man, I ain't got time for games. Either you seen him or you haven't," replied Dexter.

The hustler pondered, and looked up and down the street, then looked back at Dexter, and quickly scanned him up and down again. Dexter was dressed to kill, and he looked like a hustler himself. He looked down at Dexter's shoes and saw he had some half-gators on.

"Okay, young blood, I saw him. Last night he was at the bar around the corner with this so-called pimp. This cat is new in town but he's weak; calls himself Kansas City Red. He's staying in the fleabag hotel in the next block, just up from the corner. I don't know if your brother is there, but that's who he was with last night," the hustler told Dexter.

"Thanks, man, I appreciate it. I owe you one," Dexter said, and he handed him a matchbox of weed.

"Don't worry about it, young blood. Good luck," he shouted, as Dexter ran back to the car where Mary was waiting.

Dexter was beaming with the news. He ran over to the car where Mary was waiting, and told her he had a good idea where Hank was.

"I'm going to go over there to that hotel," Dexter told her as he pointed to it. "If I'm not back in twenty minutes, go and get the police and bring them to the hotel. Don't make a move before that; just give me twenty minutes. Got it?" asked Dexter.

"All right, I'll wait here. Dexter, you be careful," Mary answered, with a worried look on her face.

As Dexter trotted off down the street, Mary watched him in the rear-view mirror. She thought about Hank and Dexter and how they were when they were the two little boys who cared for their mother. It seemed like it was just yesterday.

But time had gone by so fast and things had changed. Dexter seemed to have grown overnight and he was turning into a fine young man. But, when she thought about Hank, he was still the baby. He was always the sweet one who loved his mother so much. She sat there patiently and prayed.

Dexter walked down the block, crossed the street, and then continued to the hotel. He walked through the front door, which entered into a small hallway with a counter on the right. The attendant was standing behind the counter. "May I help you?" the attendant asked.

"Yeah, I'm looking for a Kansas City Red," Dexter stated.

"We don't have anyone named Kansas City Red registered here," answered the attendant smartly.

"Look, my brother is in your hotel with a pimp, and he's a minor. Now, all I want to do is get my brother out of here and go home. You know whom I'm talking about. So if you don't let me in here and tell me what room he's in, I'll come back with the police. I'm sure you don't want any trouble. I'm not trying to cause any trouble; I just want to get my brother and leave," Dexter said, looking the attendant directly in the eye.

The attendant looked back at Dexter and scanned him up and down. He could see that Dexter was a young kid. But he also noticed how he was dressed. "This kid ain't no square," thought the attendant. He thought about what Dexter said, and he didn't want any trouble. So the attendant said, "He's in room 302. We don't want any trouble here." Dexter didn't respond as he turned and headed into the hotel. He took the stairs up to the third floor.

Once Dexter reached the third floor, he walked over to the door numbered 302. He put his ear to the door, trying to listen. He could hear some talking but couldn't understand what was being said. He heard someone inside the room that sounded like Hank, but he still couldn't understand what was being said.

Knock, knock, knock. Dexter banged loudly on the door to shake them up. There was silence and no answer. Knock, knock, knock. He banged again and then announced, "Answer the door. I know you're in there, the front desk told me you were."

"Who is it?" asked a voice inside.

"I come for my brother. Open the door." Dexter ordered.

"I don't know who your brother is; he's not in here," answered the voice inside.

Again, there was silence.

"If you don't open the door, I'll be back with the police, and I'm sure you don't want that. I just want to get my brother and go home. You need to open the door," Dexter instructed.

There was another moment of silence, and then there was the sound of the lock turning. Dexter watched the doorknob as it began to turn and then the door opened slowly.

The first glimpse that Dexter's eye caught was the sight of an overweight, fat and burly, high-yellow, freckle-faced, older, black man with a red process, opening the door. Dexter's eyes then glanced downward, and just past him, and, sitting on a messy bed, was Hank. Dexter looked at Hank; he was dressed in a woman's see-through blouse that was unbuttoned and tied in a knot around the midsection. He had a scarf tied around his neck, and he had women's makeup painted heavily all over his face. His hair was pressed and fashioned in a woman's hairstyle. He was also wearing his bell-bottomed blue jeans and tennis shoes. Their eyes met; Hank had a look of anger and distrust on his face.

Dexter was shocked at what he was seeing. He was hurt and disgusted too. "Come on, let's go," Dexter commanded to his brother.

"No, I'm not going back home," responded Hank.

Dexter remained calm, but sternly told Hank, "Come on, let's go. I'm not leaving without you. I'm not going to fight with you, but I'm not leaving without you. So you might as well get your things and come with me."

Dexter could feel that Hank was going to continue to resist, so he said, "Nanny's outside, and if I'm not back with you in about five minutes, she's coming in here with the police."

Dexter knew that this was going to put pressure on the so-called pimp, so he looked in his direction. Red was now getting nervous. The situation was beginning to get out of hand. Red looked over to Hank and said, "What are you waiting for? Get your shit and go!"

Hank was angry, but he gathered his belongings and followed Dexter downstairs. When they got outside, Dexter walked ahead of Hank. He was ashamed. Hank walked behind him, and followed him up the street to the car where Nanny was waiting. Dexter wouldn't look at Hank or say anything to him, and Hank saw that he was upset.

When they arrived at the car, Dexter opened the back door and Hank climbed in. Dexter then opened the front door and hopped in the car. Mary looked back at Hank and then exclaimed, "Lord Jesus, what on earth?"

Dexter cut her off short, "Nanny, don't say nothing. Just drive."

As they drove across town, Mary was having a hard time controlling herself. She kept fidgeting and rubbing her head. She wanted to say something, but she bit her tongue. She'd shake her head, and then she'd shake all over. "Do you need me to drive?" asked Dexter. "No, I'm all right." They made the rest of the ride in total silence.

When they pulled up in front of the house on Orizaba, Dexter was hoping that none of the neighbors would see Hank going into the house, but there was no such luck. One of the girls next door was standing outside in front of her house, along with another girl from across the street. They both watched as the three of them got out of the car. When they saw Hank, their mouths dropped in amazement. Hank just held his head high and sashayed his way into the house.

When Margaret heard the front door open, she got out of her bed and went and stood at the top of the stairs. Hank climbed the stairs with an attitude and walked right by his mother. She felt him walk by and sensed that it was Hank. "Humph," she muttered as he walked by. Hank took a seat on the couch in the living room. Mary climbed the stairs, sounding as if she were exhausted. She took a seat on one of the cushioned armchairs in the living room. Finally, Dexter climbed the stairs, kissed his mother, and sat down on the couch opposite to where Hank was seated.

"Naomi, I don't know how to say this," Mary spoke out, and then paused. She only called her daughter Naomi when things were serious. "Lord, help me," she continued. "Margaret, we found Hank downtown, and he's all dressed up like a girl. He's wearing makeup all over his face, and he's wearing lipstick."

Margaret was shocked; she didn't know what to say. She raised one of her hands to her mouth then said, "I don't understand. Hank, why are you doing this, and why did you run away?"

Hank was visibly upset. He tried to gain his composure to speak, then tears started to develop in his eyes, "Baba, I'm gay," he said. Then he continued, "I was born a boy on the outside, but on the inside, I'm a girl."

"Don't say that! You're not a girl, you're a boy," yelled Dexter.

"I've been this way all my life. I used to fight it, but now I know what I am. It's what I was meant to be. I'm gay," responded Hank.

306

"Who's been teaching you such things?" asked Mary. "It's the devil, that's what it is. How would you know about these things?"

Dexter, feeling frustration and disgust, cried out, "You're not gay. My brother is not gay, why are you doing this?" Dexter hadn't cried in a long time. He actually thought he'd forgotten how to cry. But tears came to his eyes and he began to cry now. "No, no, not my brother."

Deep inside, he knew Hank was right. Ever since they were old enough to talk, kids always teased Hank and called him a sissy. He walked like a girl and he talked like a girl. He even sat like a girl. Now Hank was admitting it, and it was painful, and it hurt. Dexter never dreamed it would come to this.

"O God, dear Lord, my Father, why have you forsaken me? I've tried to do my best with my boys. Is it my fault? What did I do? How did I fail you, Lord?" Margaret began to cry out.

She was standing and looking up to the heavens with her arms stretched out. "Haven't I done the best that I could do? Didn't I try to raise them as good Christians?" She began to call on the Lord, "O God, dear Jesus, Satan has entered this household, my Father. Help us, dear Lord. Cast out the demons that have taken hold of this house, dear Father." She began to choke on her words; her voice was cracking, and she started to cry out loud.

Hank was crying, Dexter was crying, and so was Margaret.

Mary got up and started down the stairs. She was shaking her head and mumbling. What was going to become of her family, she was thinking. This was the devil's business; he was tearing the family apart. She went outside and got into her car and drove home to tell BD and Charles the news—Hank was gay! "It must be the drugs," she kept thinking. "It's got to be the drugs. They've got Hank's mind all messed up."

Margaret turned and walked into her room, kneeled down beside her bed, and began to pray. She was crying and calling on the Lord for some guidance. Hank stood up, walked out of the living room and into his bedroom, and then closed the door behind him. Dexter sat on the couch and got himself together. He contemplated what he wanted to do. He sure didn't feel like going into his room and dealing with Hank. He decided he needed the company of a female, so he made a few phone calls then left the house.

The next Monday, when Hank returned to school, he didn't come out in full drag, but he wore a little make up and had his hair styled like a girl. He also wore a scarf around his neck and had a hankie hanging out of his back pocket.

As it turned out, there were a few other gays in the school. After a couple of weeks, it seemed that Hank had gotten them all together and they'd all decided to come out of the closet. There were six or seven of them, and they began to parade around the campus in a group, showing off. They were proud to be gay and wanted everyone to know it, especially the boys!

When someone started to tease them, they'd do what they called, "read them." Hank would put his hand on his hip, shake his head from side to side, and snap his finger in the air while he "read them." He'd say something like, "I'm more woman than your momma could ever be. She wishes she was as much woman as I am, and you wish you could have some of this!" Next he'd wave his arm, give a snap of the fingers, then twirl around and swish away.

Most of the time, people laughed and thought it was a joke. They thought it was the funniest thing they'd ever seen. But sometimes, if it was the wrong person, he'd take offense and want to fight. That's when the group would band together, and they'd all get loud and give a major "reading." They'd walk off together, slapping five and shouting, "We read him!"

It was a difficult time for Dexter. Many of the students approached him and said things like, "What's wrong with your brother?" or "If he was my brother, I'd beat his ass."

Dexter would reply with, "I tried that. It didn't work. He's just gay, and that's the way it is."

For Dexter, the main problem wasn't just the fact that Hank was gay, but that he was a "flaming queen," and to him, it was embarrassing. He thought, "If Hank would just tone it down some." But Hank didn't care. He was enjoying being out of the closet, and the fact that he had a crew made it all the easier for him.

Whenever Dexter wanted to go somewhere, like to a party or a girl's house or somewhere with his crew, Margaret would make him take Hank. One day Dexter wanted to go and hang with his friends.

"Ah, Baba, do I have to take him with me?" complained Dexter.

"Yes, you do. He's still your brother," instructed Margaret.

"Damn, this is fucked up," Dexter thought to himself.

Mattock and Raul came by to pick Dexter up, and Hank stepped out the door all made up in makeup.

"Damn, we got to take him with us?" Raul complained.

"Yeah, my mother won't let me go unless I take him too," Dexter tried to explain.

"Shit, everybody's going to think we're all faggots," Raul said, being upset about the situation.

Hank flared up, "I ain't no faggot, I'm a woman, all woman, baby, and don't you forget it."

"Yeah, blah, blah, blah," Raul responded.

"You know you wish you could have some of this," Hank replied, snapping his fingers.

Raul and Mattock didn't complain too much because they knew Hank as well as they knew Dexter. He'd been their friend before he said he was gay, so in the end, he was still Hank.

But Hank didn't like the name Hank anymore. He wanted to be called "Terri." It didn't work with Dexter or his crew. No matter who he thought he was, to them, he was still Hank, and that's what they were going to call him.

This was in 1968, and the gay movement hadn't happened yet in San Francisco. To be gay was a shameful thing and 98 percent of gays were still in the closet. There was no Castro district with all the gay bars, nor a SOMA district with the leather bars, nor any of the gay bathhouses. Being gay was just something that was never discussed openly.

17

Power to the People

San Francisco was alive with music. Times were changing, and so was the music scene. The music out of San Francisco was having a profound effect on the recording industry because it was setting new trends.

On the white scene, Bill Graham was gearing up to capitalize and exploit the industry, and in the Mission District, Carlos Santana and a group named Malo were putting the Latino community on the map.

Posters were plastered all over the city promoting events at venues like the Fillmore, Winterland, the Polo Fields, the Village, and Bimbo's, among others.

Dexter's group soon began to come together. One evening, the Concepts were standing out on the corner of Broad and Plymouth, singing in the fog. It was cold and wet, and the fog was so thick that the dewdrops were collecting on the overhead power lines and large drops of water were falling to the ground like rain.

Mattock, Raul, and Dexter were all bundled up and huddled together, practicing the Miracles' song, "Oh Baby Baby." Raul sang the lead because he was a stronger first tenor than Dexter. While they were practicing, a young man who was walking by stopped when he heard the group singing.

The young man was a familiar face in the neighborhood and at school. He couldn't help but be noticed because he was extremely handsome. He was short, with an athletic build; his skin was a light golden-yellow color, and he had soft green eyes. He wore a large sandy-colored Afro that came to a point in the middle of his forehead, forming a widow's peak. Dexter had also noticed that he was always around Latino girls.

The boy wasn't shy; he walked up to the group and asked if he could sing with them. The group looked at each other for agreement and said that he could join in. The boy asked if he could sing the lead. Dexter and Mattock looked at Raul, and he said it was all right. Mattock counted off and the group started to sing. First, the background started with, "Oh Oh Oh, Baby Baby, Oh Oh Oh, Baby Baby."

The new guy started singing the lead, "Mistakes, I know I've made a few." His voice was smooth as silk; it was a much smoother and clearer sound than Raul's. He sounded almost as good as Smokey himself.

Raul, Mattock, and Dexter looked at each other and smiled, then continued the song all the way through to the end. When they finished, they all celebrated how good they sounded.

"Hey, man, you sound great!" said Raul.

"Ah, man, we were smoking," added Mattock.

"Yeah, blood, what did you say your name was again?" asked Dexter.

"Cary, Cary Rousseau," he answered.

"Rousseau, what's that, French?" asked Dexter.

"Yeah, my father's Creole," answered Cary.

"Cool, my name is French too," responded Dexter.

"Say, brother, are you in a group?" asked Raul.

"No, my brother's in a group, but they don't have any room for me," Cary answered.

"What group is that?" Mattock asked.

"The Marcels," answered Cary.

"That's Ray Sterling's group; we know them," said Dexter. "Who's your brother? Jonnie?"

"Yeah, that's my brother," answered Cary.

"You two don't look alike," said Dexter.

"We have different fathers," responded Cary.

"Oh, okay. You live on Lobus Street?" asked Dexter, knowing where Jonnie lived.

"Yeah, on Lobus Street," answered Cary.

"You want to be in our group?" asked Raul.

"Sure," Cary answered.

"Cool. Meet us right here tomorrow night at 7:00 on this corner," said Mattock.

They all gave each other the brothers' handshake and parted ways. Cary was walking up Plymouth and yelled back at Raul and Dexter, who had crossed Broad Street, "What's the name of the group?"

"The Concepts," Dexter yelled back.

There were plenty of black singing groups and bands in the Bay Area, and especially in San Francisco. There were always dances and shows taking place somewhere where the groups could perform. Local promoters kept them busy.

The singing groups and bands ran the full gamut of styles. There was the female group named French Toast—three of the finest sisters around. Another female group was the Sisters of the Ghetto, in which one of Dexter's fellow choir members, Sheila, performed as a lead singer. They were a soul-stirring group with lots of energy.

The band named The TCBs was the backup band of choice for many singing groups and promoters because they could perform a first-class show on their own. But the best band around, other than the major recording groups, was Granny Goose and the Soul Chips. They were a large band with about a dozen members, complete with a horn section, and backup singers, doing steps. Granny Goose was the lead singer, and he could sing and dance just like James Brown. He was also good at singing ballads. Their percussion section was tight, and Gary Green, one of the baddest drummers in the city, led the percussion.

The Whispers were by far the best male vocal group in the Bay Area. They hadn't made it big-time yet, but they had a string of local hits and received major rotation on the local radio stations. You could catch them almost every other week at the Dragon-a-Go-Go in Chinatown. The Whispers also did a lot of headlining for many of the smaller dance and show venues. A couple of hits by the Whispers,

"It's a Great Day" and "The Time Will Come," were favorites of the Concepts and the Marcels.

Many times, the two groups practiced together and sang the same songs. If one of the groups was missing a member, they could fill in for each other.

Music was always a part of Dexter's life while growing up because his mother and father were both musicians. So, when he became a teen, singing in a group was a natural thing for him to do.

As well as the Whispers, there were a number of other local groups that were doing their own recordings. There were the Ballads and the Natural Four. The Ballads would perform at a show, and when they sang the tune, "God Bless Our Love," the show would get turned out. Women would just lose their minds.

The Natural Four had a brother in the group with a gigantic Afro. He had to have had the largest Afro in the world. When the MC came out to introduce the group, one by one, the members would come out on the stage. The brother with the Afro would come out last, and the women would go wild. The crowd would get so hyped; nothing else in the world mattered. It was out of sight, far out, and right on!

The Concepts didn't get many gigs, mainly because they didn't have a manager to guide them. There were several other groups at Balboa High who had managers and were always performing and getting gigs.

The Promatics were the closest thing locally to the Temptations because they were a group of five. The Marcels, Cary's brother's group, always got gigs because their manager not only managed them, but also promoted and produced many shows. This guy was also a pimp who lived in Lakeview and had two women living with him. Eventually, he put the Concepts on a venue with the Marcels.

The Marcels had a routine they did, with a string of hits by the Intruders. Ray was the lead singer, and his voice sounded exactly like the lead singer of the Intruders. The Marcels would sing all their hits— tunes like, "Together United," "Me Tarzan, You Jane," "Cowboys and Girls," and "Love Is Just Like a Baseball Game." The routines they did were tight, and their steps were choreographed and timed perfectly.

Being in a singing group had its benefits, and the main benefit was girls. Dexter was still seeing Joy, and he was still in love with her, but he was ready for sex and she wasn't. Mattock had a girlfriend named Ellie, and he had begun to have sex with her often, and it was putting pressure on Dexter. He was now sixteen, and Joy was fifteen. Dexter began to make a real effort to have sex. Any girl who even looked like she was interested in him and was good looking, he'd try to get at. But he got nowhere.

One day Mattock told Dexter that Ellie had a friend named Brenda who lived in the Hunter's Point projects, and that he and Ellie sometimes cut school and went over to her house and engaged in sex. He said that Brenda would be in her bedroom, having sex with her boyfriend, while he and Ellie would be in her brother's bedroom, enjoying sex. Dexter listened to Mattock intensely and just imagined what it was like.

Mattock continued and said that Brenda had broken up with her boyfriend; this sparked Dexter's attention. Mattock went on to tell him that his girlfriend, Ellie, had told Brenda about Dexter and that she wanted to meet him.

Dexter got excited, for this was great news for him. "What's she look like?" he asked Mattock.

"She's all right. She's not the finest girl around, but you'll want to do her. She has some nice titties," answered Mattock.

"Cool, so when we gonna do it?" asked Dexter.

"I don't know. I have to talk with Ellie, but I'll tell her to set it up right away," answered Mattock.

Ellie and Brenda set things up for that Monday. Dexter would have to cut school, and he'd never cut school before. He was rarely even absent because he very seldom got sick. On the few occasions that he did stay home sick, the school never called, and all he had to do was bring a note. He always wrote the notes himself because Margaret couldn't write, and the teachers were aware of this, so they always accepted Dexter's notes.

Monday morning, Mattock and Dexter caught the bus to Hunter's Point. When they arrived at Brenda's house, Ellie opened the door and invited them in, and they took seats in the living room. Brenda came out from another room, and Ellie introduced her to Dexter. Dexter smiled and said hello, and Brenda smiled back.

Dexter thought Brenda was nice, just like Mattock had said. She was about 5' 5" and weighed close to a hundred pounds. She was on the slim side, with a nice caramel brown-skinned complexion. Her skin was smooth and creamy; her eyes were wide and brown in color; and her eyebrows were very thick and bushy, almost touching. She had a broad nose, which was cute and pug, almost like a button. Her lips were large and puffy, and the red lipstick she was wearing made them look juicy and kissable. Dexter liked what he saw. She was wearing a robe, and Dexter knew she was naked under the robe. The thought of this got him excited, and his nature began to respond.

Brenda moved to where Dexter was sitting and sat on the couch next to him, and then positioned herself to face him, crossing one knee. She placed one hand on Dexter's thigh and asked if wanted something to drink. Her thigh was exposed and Dexter could catch a subtle glimpse of between her legs. Her touch on his thigh immediately started an arousal in him and caused a chill, almost curling his toes. He told her that he and Mattock had brought some Ripple wine and a six-pack of Spur malt liquor. He said that he wanted a Spur and also wanted to smoke a joint. Although he and Mattock had already smoked one on the way over, he wanted to smoke another one.

The four of them sat around and chatted while they got loaded. Dexter was excited with anticipation and almost couldn't believe he was going to get this girl. Brenda was summing up Dexter and liked what she saw. She was thinking that he was cute and tall, and was wondering about what was between his legs. She was only fifteen, but she was already experienced and knew what to do. She also knew what men liked. Her ex-boyfriend used to give it to her all the time. It was not lovemaking; it was sex, just pure sex.

After they were stoned, it was time to get busy. Dexter leaned over to Brenda and kissed her on the mouth. She responded by parting her lips with a big juicy kiss and a moan. She tasted great, and she thought he was delicious. Brenda was in control of this situation, so she stood up and reached for Dexter's hand to lead him into the bedroom. When she arose, her robe partially fell open to expose her breasts and her pussy. When Dexter saw that, he was like a kid in a candy store, and he was now as hard as penitentiary steel.

They walked into her bedroom, where she took off her robe and climbed into the bed. She threw back the covers and lay naked, on display, waiting for Dexter. Her body was nice and slim, but not skinny. Her breasts were a full C-cup and she had large dark brown circles around her nipples, which were larger than a silver dollar. The hair on her stomach was soft and gentle. It became dark, bushy, and thick as it traveled down to her pussy.

Dexter stood in front of her in excitement. He was aware of his actions and tried to be cool. But it was difficult because of his anticipation. When he took off his underwear, his young teenage penis stood straight out like a tree branch on his skinny frame. He'd never had sex before, but he didn't want her to know it. He climbed onto the bed, moved close to her, placed his arm around her waist, pulled her near, and then kissed her passionately on her luscious lips.

Brenda responded by raising one leg and moving it to straddle Dexter's thigh. He responded by moving his leg in between hers. His hand then moved to her bottom, where he could cup it. She had a nice firm and round ass. Dexter rubbed it, and she loved the feel of his touch. They both moaned in enjoyment. While they continued to kiss, Dexter's hand moved down from the divide of her behind to the lips of her vagina. It was moist and wet, and she was ready to receive him.

He then mounted her, and when she opened her legs to receive him, his penis penetrated easily. He then slowly began to pump and grind. As his hands began to explore and caress her body, the intensity began to increase. He fondled her breasts and kissed and sucked on them passionately. She responded by moaning and rubbing her fingers through his fine hair. She began fondling his head as if she were feeding him, as he kissed her breasts.

The lust and passion grew as he started to hump her like a jackrabbit. He was pumping and grinding and pumping and grinding until there was no feeling of lovemaking; it was purely sex. She lay under Dexter and let him give her all he had, and she loved it. Her moans and soft-spoken "yes" made him even more excited and confirmed that he was doing well.

After about thirty minutes of slowing down, grinding, then speeding up, and pumping over and over again, Dexter was drenched in sweat. He finally stopped and turned over to lie on his back. They lay in bed and chatted for a while, and then she got up to bring him another Spur malt liquor. Dexter drank his brew, smoked another joint, and mounted her again. After another session, they both took a nap, and when they woke up, he mounted her again and continued for a third session. The missionary position was all they did, all day.

About three o'clock, Dexter and Mattock left and caught the bus home. They walked through the neighborhood to go to the bus stop. Mattock was a little nervous about being in another turf, but Dexter told him not to trip. He knew folks in the area; his grandmother lived not far from there, and the Bayview was like his second home. They got on the bus and talked about girls and screwing and laughed and joked on the bus all the way back to Lakeview.

A couple of weeks later, they did it all over again. Brenda had told Ellie that she liked the way Dexter made love and she wanted to see him again; Dexter gladly obliged.

Later that evening, the fellas were singing with the Marcels, and Mattock and Dexter soon began to talk about screwing that day.

Jonnie said, "Brenda? Brenda Biddle?"

Dexter answered, "Yeah, Brenda Biddle."

"Oh yeah, she got some good pussy, real hairy pussy. I fucked her. Big sexy dark circles around her nipples!" said Jonnie.

"Damn, yeah that's her," answered Dexter.

"Oh yeah, I used to fuck her; she got some good pussy," Jonnie added.

Dexter began to think to himself, "Ain't this a bitch. Bitch is fucking everybody." He let it go and they continued to sing. About a week later, after having left Brenda's house again, Dexter and Mattock were on the bus heading back to Lakeview. They were sitting in the back of the bus and a black teenage girl was looking at Dexter. He noticed her stare.

"What's your name?" she asked.

"Dexter," he answered.

"You're Brenda Biddle's boyfriend, right?" she asked.

"Nah, she ain't my girlfriend. We're just kicking it," Dexter answered sharply.

"Oh, excuse me. That ain't what I heard," she said smartly.

Dexter looked over and Mattock and said, "Damn, man, she's going around telling people I'm her man and shit. I got to stop fucking her."

Mattock cracked up, but Dexter had attitude. After that, he never slept with Brenda again.

It wasn't long before many of Margaret's friends began to find out about Hank. The boys went to church one Sunday, and even though Hank wasn't in drag, it was evident that there was a change in him. For one thing, his hair was styled differently and his eyebrows were plucked and shaped. He looked very much like a girl.

That evening, Margaret received several phone calls from her friends. Some were just being nosy, but others had a genuine concern. The calls kept coming, and after a while it became difficult for her, continually informing people that Hank had claimed he was gay.

"Margaret, how you doing, girl?" said the caller.

"I'm not doing too good right now," answered Margaret.

"I know, I understand. I saw Hank today, so I can understand your problem. Girl, I'm praying for you and him," said the caller.

"Thank you, that's just what we need. The more people we get to pray on this matter, the better it is. I just don't know what to do," said Margaret.

"Child, I know you don't," responded the caller. "So what happened? Why this and why now? I knew that Hank was a sweet child, but I never thought anything like this would happen. You know I love those boys."

Margaret began to break down. Her voice was trembling as she spoke, "I don't know why. You know I've always tried to do my best with these boys. I'm starting to wonder if it's my fault because I ran their father off. Maybe if I'd stayed with him and tried to work things out, this wouldn't have happened," she confessed.

"No, no, you can't blame yourself. You did the best you could do, and you did a fine job with those boys," responded the caller, trying to provide Margaret with some support.

Margaret was distraught. The guilt was overwhelming her as she took on all the blame. Crying out loud, she began to explain why she felt this had happened. "Duane wanted to take the boys and do things with them that boys do, and I wouldn't let him. We fought over it many times. I was stubborn and selfish. Duane tried to tell me, he tried very hard. But I wouldn't budge, and I kept the boys with me. It's all, my fault. I know it is. O God, what have I done? Why didn't I understand? O God, why? Why, dear Lord? Why?" she cried uncontrollably.

Margaret's friend could feel her pain, and listening to Margaret's sorrow began to impact her too. Holding the phone in her hand, Margaret let her arm drop down onto the bed. She held her other hand over her eyes and cried in deep sorrow.

At this point, Margaret became distant from the caller and was consumed with guilt. "Margaret! Margaret!" yelled the caller into the phone. "Listen to me! Margaret, are you there?" The caller continued to yell as she heard Margaret crying out loud on the other end.

"Listen, Margaret, are you there?" the caller asked again.

Margaret could hear the voice calling to her from the small speaker on the phone's receiver. She regained a little control and raised the phone to her ear, "Yes, I'm here."

"Maybe it's not too late. Maybe there's something that you can still do," said the caller.

Margaret began to listen up, and she stopped sobbing. "What? What can I do?" she asked.

"Margaret, I've been doing some reading. There are many people in the medical field that feel that this sort of thing is a mental situation that can be treated," informed the caller.

This got Margaret's attention, and she began to listen attentively. "Margaret, I think Hank should see a psychiatrist," suggested the caller.

"Maybe you're right. Maybe that can help," responded Margaret, feeling a glimmer of hope.

"Well, it sure can't hurt," said the caller, with some encouragement.

"No, it can't hurt," responded Margaret, feeling some comfort.

"I know a psychiatrist, and he's a Christian, and he's seen this type of thing before. I gave him a call and talked with him about Hank. He thinks that he might be able to help," said the caller.

This was good news to Margaret because it gave her some hope. She was at an end and didn't know what to do, but she felt she needed to do something. Margaret was thinking about Hank and how God was looking down on him. Homosexuality was a sin and condemned by

God. If Hank became a homosexual, then his soul would be lost. She hadn't discussed with him that aspect of what he was doing because she was too hurt and Hank was so defensive. She just wasn't able to carry on a conversation with him anymore.

"Can you have him call me?" Margaret asked.

"Sure, I'll call him right now and give him your number," answered the caller.

"Thank you, dear. You don't know how much this means to me. I just didn't know what to do," said Margaret.

"Don't you worry about this; it's not over yet. God can work miracles. You've seen his work before, and so have I," the caller said encouragingly.

"You're right, it's times like these that you have to have faith," replied Margaret.

Margaret got off the phone and felt much better. She decided to go into the living room and sit at the piano. But first, she went downstairs to her Bible rack and thumbed over the Braille covers to find a book. "Hebrews!" she said, as she stopped at the book. Margaret pulled the book out and went back upstairs then sat on the piano bench. She opened up the Bible to Hebrews 11:1 and read aloud, "'Now faith is the substance of things hoped for, the evidence of things not seen.'"

"Yes, Lord, that's it," she murmured to herself.

She ran her fingers on down the page until she came to another verse. She again read aloud, "Hebrews 11:6, 'But without faith it is impossible to please him: for he that cometh to God must believe that he is, and that he is a rewarder of them that diligently seek him.'"

After reading the scriptures, Margaret began to pray, "Dear heavenly Father, my God and Redeemer, you are almighty, my Lord. All things are within your power, dear Lord."

The boys' bedroom was right next to the living room, so Hank was able to hear his mother praying. Dexter wasn't at home.

Margaret continued, "Dear Lord, you know how much I love thee, Lord. I've been through a lot in my lifetime, Father, and you have always made a way when there was no way. My God, hallelujah!" she yelled.

Hank was used to hearing his mother pray, so he was only half paying attention to what she was saying.

Margaret continued to pray, "I come to you in your Holy Son, Jesus Christ's name, dear God. I come to you with a bowed head and a humble heart." Margaret's voice began to break, "My son, Hank, is in need of your service, dear Lord." She began to cry, "Hank is my baby. Dear God, I don't know how I have failed you, Lord. I've tried so hard to raise him in your way, dear Father."

When Hank heard his name he jumped up and went to the door and began to listen.

"I need you to touch him, dear Father. Have your way with him, O Lord. Heal him from the hands of the demon, dear Father. The devil has his hands wrapped around him, dear Lord, and he won't let go," she cried and pleaded as she prayed.

Hank became angry, then opened the door and ran downstairs and out of the house. Hank wasn't angry that she was praying for him, but he was angry because she wasn't accepting the way he was. He wanted to keep God out of this.

Margaret heard Hank walk out of his room and leave the house, and her prayers got louder. She began to call on God, and she wasn't crying anymore.

She began to pray with conviction, "My God, you are a mighty God. No one in heaven or on this earth has more power than you, my God. Reach down and touch my son, dear Father. Satan, I rebuke you in the name of the Father. And touch Dexter too, dear Lord. He needs you right now, dear Father. We all need you right now, dear Father. Oh, I know you can work miracles, dear God. You can make a way out of no way. Come into this household, my God, and cleanse this house, my Father. Wash it white like snow. I want to thank you, dear Lord. Thank you for being with me all these years, dear Father."

Margaret's praying began to subside, and she was beginning to tire. So she finished the prayer with, "All these blessings we ask in your Holy Son, Jesus's name. Amen!"

Margaret set her Bible down on the piano bench next to her and pulled the bench up to the piano. She thought about what song she'd play. She decided on an old spiritual. She raised her hands and found her position on the keys. "What a friend we have in Jesus," she began to play and sing.

She sat there and played the piano and sang, all alone. But then again, she wasn't alone. God was with her!

Dexter was out and about in the neighborhood. He was making a little change as he moved about from here to there. He was planning to go and visit one of his girlfriends across town in the Fillmore, but decided to stop by Clifford's house first.

Clifford lived on the other side of the hill on Mt. Vernon. Dexter was deciding if he was going to walk or catch the bus. He'd just left Mattock's house and walked across the street to the bus stop on Plymouth Street. He looked down Plymouth and there was no bus in sight, so he decided to walk.

After walking about a block, he crossed Farallones Street and looked back and noticed the bus was coming. It was another block to get to the next stop, so he took off running. He made it to the corner of Plymouth and Lobus just in time and climbed on the bus when the driver pulled over for him.

When Dexter walked to the back of the bus, he saw an old friend of his, Jerry Garr. Jerry had been the senior patrol leader in the Boy Scout troop that Dexter had been in. Dexter was second rank under Jerry; he was the assistant senior patrol leader. When Dexter sat down, they both said hello, but then Jerry had to get off at the next stop because he lived near the top of the hill. So they each said good-bye, and Jerry asked Dexter to give him a call. Dexter said he would, but he knew he'd probably never get around to it. When Jerry got off the bus, Dexter thought to himself, "Jerry's as gay as Hank is. He's fruity as a jail bird."

Many kids called Jerry a sissy, just like they did to Hank. He had many ways and mannerisms like Hank had. He was taller, but he even had the same build as Hank. He was a little pudgy, and he swished when he walked. He laughed like a girl, he talked like a girl, he moved his hands like a girl, and he acted like a girl.

Dexter wondered why he hadn't come out of the closet yet. Surely he knew that Hank had; after all, they both went to the same school. Dexter recalled that Jerry was a cheerleader at school, and he thought to himself, "Why would a guy want to be a cheerleader?" It just didn't seem like a manly thing to do.

Dexter and Jerry had been good friends when they were a little younger, and they'd had some good times together in the Boy Scouts. Even though Jerry was like a big sissy, Dexter had never let it bother him or even given it a second thought. He respected Jerry for his leadership ability and his skills. Jerry was a good scout and Dexter learned much from him. Sometime a few years later, Jerry committed suicide, and Dexter never found out why.

The bus traveled over the hill and down to Grafton where Dexter got off. It was only a few blocks up Grafton to Clifford's house, so he decided to walk. He rang the doorbell to Clifford's house and stepped back from the door to look up at the front window. Cliff's younger sister, Dierdre, appeared in the window to see who was at the door. When she saw it was Dexter she yelled out, "Bernard, it's Dexter."

Clifford's family called him Bernard, after his father. Dexter rarely called Clifford to let him know he was coming by, because Cliff usually couldn't have company anyway, so he'd just show up.

Clifford opened the door and stepped into the doorframe, pulling the door close to him. "Hey, what's happening? I can't come out," said Cliff.

"I know you can't come out. You can't never come out," Dexter answered, and they both chuckled.

"Damn, you're clean, Dex. Man, you're always sharp. You're the sharpest brother I know," said Clifford.

"Yeah, except for maybe Gary at school. He's pretty sharp too," Dexter responded.

"Yeah, but he's spoiled. His mother pays for all his clothes. You buy your own shit," Cliff said, as he caught himself and covered his mouth. He didn't want his mother to hear.

"Where you going?" asked Clifford.

"Ah, I'm going over to this babe's house in the Fillmore, named Rockette. She goes to Cathedral. I've been trying to get at her, but she won't let me. Damn, she's fine. She likes me but just as a friend. I can't get anywhere with her," said Dexter.

"Man, Dex, you got girls all over town. You a bad brother, man. I'm just glad I know you. You and Al be killing 'em," exclaimed Clifford.

Dexter said, "I wonder if Al's home. I'm gonna stop by there."

"You know he's there. He's just like me; he can never go anywhere. Only he's always faking it," said Clifford.

"Yeah, we should call him Hang-'em-up-Al 'cause he's always hanging ya up," Dexter said, laughing.

"Yeah, Hang-'em-up-Al, I like that! Let's call him that," Clifford replied, laughing too.

They both laughed and talked about Al some more behind his back. They always enjoyed doing that. Capping on Al behind his back was funny to the two of them because they both loved him. Al's ears should have been burning.

"Man, I been hanging with Mattock and I been getting some pussy, boy," Dexter told Cliff.

"What? Damn! Where?" Clifford asked with excitement.

"Over in Hunter's Point. I was knocking it out," Dexter said, laughing.

"Damn, was it good?" asked Clifford.

"Man, Cliff, it was great," responded Dexter.

"But I found out Jonnie, Cary's brother, had hit it. So I ain't touching it no more," said Dexter.

"The one who sings with Ray?" asked Clifford.

"Yeah," answered Dexter.

"Anyway, I got to split," Dexter finished up.

"Okay, Dex, later," said Clifford.

"Later," Dexter said, handing Cliff a joint as he left.

Dexter and Clifford didn't realize that Clifford's mother had heard the whole conversation. She didn't say anything to Clifford when he came back into the house, but after a while, she called up Margaret to tell her what she'd heard. When she made the call, Clifford overheard his mother. He wanted to warn Dexter, but he had no way to warn him.

"Margaret, how you doing?" Mrs. Westbrook asked.

"Well, I'm doing about as well as I can be," answered Margaret.

Mrs. Westbrook didn't know about Hank yet. "I'm calling you because Dexter came by here, and I overheard his conversation with Clifford," she said, sounding concerned.

"What did they talk about?" asked Margaret, feeling curious and a little nervous.

"Margaret, you're going to have to keep an eye on that boy because he's really going after the girls. If he's not careful, he's going to get into some trouble. You know, a lot of these young girls are growing up so fast today. They see a good-looking boy and right away they want to pull their skirts up. You don't want your son to be coming up with kids too soon. Margaret, you better have a talk with him. I'm telling you, you mark my word," said Mrs. Westbrook.

Margaret was relieved. It wasn't as bad as she thought it was going to be. Actually, she was glad that Dexter loved the girls after what she was going through with Hank. The whole time Mrs. Westbrook was speaking, Margaret was just answering "Ah huh. Uh huh."

"Well, I just thought you ought to know. I'll pray on it for you," said Mrs. Westbrook.

"Thank you, Sister Westbrook. I appreciate it. You take care now," answered Margaret as she hung up the phone.

Just after Margaret hung up the phone with Mrs. Westbrook, the phone rang again.

"Hello," she answered.

"Mrs. Vizinau?" asked the voice on the other end.

"Yes, this is Mrs. Evans," Margaret answered, correcting him.

"Oh, I'm sorry I thought this was Mrs. Vizinau," he responded.

"It is, only my name has changed. It's Evans now," she informed him.

"Oh, okay. Hello, this is Dr. Latham," he informed her.

"Hello Dr. Latham, I've been expecting your call," said Margaret.

"Yes, I've heard about your son. I'd like to meet him. I think that I may be able to help him," said the doctor, offering his services.

"Yes, I'd like for you to see him as well. I've been at odds on what to do," answered Margaret.

Margaret and the doctor continued to chat briefly. She provided the doctor with some background information, and then they arranged a time and date for Hank to have a visit. The next thing she needed to do was to get Hank to agree to go.

When Hank arrived home, Margaret called him to her room and told him that she needed to speak with him. Hank had calmed down by this time, so he entered her room and took a seat on her bed. She told him that she understood how he felt and that she'd prayed about it. She said that although she understood his feelings, she had a hard time accepting it. She also told him that she loved him very much, no matter what, and that he was always her baby boy. Hank became a little teary when he heard his mother speak of her love for him. He loved his mother very dearly, and he felt sorry about the pain he was causing. But at the same time, he knew who he really was and felt that she'd have to come to understand it.

Margaret told Hank that she wanted to help with this transition he was going through and wanted him to see a doctor. At first he objected, but Margaret was very civil and reasonable in her request. She was still his mother, and he was still her child. So he agreed to go.

Hank paid a visit to the psychiatrist, and it was a pleasant session. The doctor was able to get Hank to talk freely and Hank felt comfortable. The doctor convinced Hank that he could trust him, and that he felt he'd be able to help him.

After the visit, the doctor contacted Margaret and told her that Hank had some serious problems. He said he was convinced that Hank actually thought he was a woman trapped inside a man's body. He told Margaret that this was a common problem in dealing with homosexuals.

The doctor then went on to inform Margaret that it was going to take some time, and that he'd need to see Hank on a regular basis. He went on to say that the problem was a mental problem and that only through therapy would Hank begin to realize that he was not a woman, that he was a man who liked men. The doctor felt that if he could get Hank to recognize that he was a man, he could begin to help him function like a man. He also told her that Hank was going to need the entire family's support. Margaret agreed and felt good about what the doctor told her. They scheduled another appointment then Margaret hung up the phone.

A few days later, Dexter walked into the house with Mattock, Raul, and Cary. They'd been out practicing their singing and came by the house so that Dexter could pick up some of his stash. Once in the house, they climbed the stairs and entered the living room. Hank was there with his friends, Jerome, Genie, and Laron. They lived in the neighborhood and they were all gay, and when they saw the boys coming in, they began to cackle like hens.

Dexter led his buddies to his bedroom. As they passed each of the boys, they said their hellos or nodded with acknowledgement. Hank's crew, being all flirty, responded with long, drawn-out Helloooooooos and Hiiiiiiiiiiis.

When Dexter and the fellas went into the bedroom, Dexter closed the door behind him. Raul was the first one to speak. "Shit! Damn, Dex, they're going to be hanging out at your house now."

Mattock said, "Muthafuckas better not say shit to me. Let one of them touch me. I'll be fresh off a nigger's ass."

Cary didn't say anything.

Dexter stayed focused and grabbed his stash and said, "Come on, let's go!"

Just then Margaret called out from the kitchen, "Dexter, is that you?"

"Yes Baba," he answered.

Margaret came out of the kitchen with her pocketbook in her hand. "Dexter I want you to go to the store," she instructed.

"Ah Baba, can't Hank go?" asked Dexter.

"I asked you," she said sternly.

"All right, what do you need to get?" asked Dexter.

She answered, "I want you to go and get me some Uncle Ben's rice and some orange juice."

"Okay," said Dexter.

Hank and his friends were seated in the living room; Dexter and his friends were standing in the entryway to the living room at the top of the stairs. Everyone was quiet as they watched Margaret reach into her purse and pull out her pocketbook.

As she began to pull out some bills, a nickel coin slipped out of the bills and hit the floor then rolled about a foot away. Margaret immediately went right to the nickel, bent down, and picked it up. Everyone looked at Hank and Dexter in amazement. But Hank and Dexter were not fazed by it. They'd seen it done before, many times.

When Dexter and his friends were outside, Raul said, "Man, I thought your mother couldn't see."

Dexter answered, "She can't."

"Well, how did she know where that nickel was?" Raul asked.

"She listened to it and could hear where it stopped," said Dexter.

"Damn, that's a trip," Mattock added.

"That's why I say we can't whisper in my house because she can hear everything we say," added Dexter.

"Well, I got it now. You won't hear me doing any whispering," said Raul.

"Me either," added Cary.

The boys walked to the store with Dexter, and on the way back, they ran into some girls in the neighborhood. So while his friends chatted with them, Dexter ran home to deliver the rice. Dexter took the rice into the kitchen where Margaret was preparing dinner and told her where he was setting it.

"Okay, bye, I'll be back later," Dexter told his mother.

"Dexter, come here," she instructed.

Inside, Dexter was thinking, "Damn, I got to go," but he stopped and turned and approached his mother. "Yes, Baba?" he inquired.

Margaret stood in front of Dexter and reached out until she felt his arms. "Let me look at you!" she said, thinking of what Mrs. Westbrook had told her on the phone. Gently she traced the frame of his body, making note of how much he'd grown. He was fast becoming a man. He was sixteen years old now, and she was proud of him. Slowly, Margaret's hand began to touch his face. She traced his forehead and around his eyebrows and then felt his nose and touched his lips. Her hand then moved to his ears and his cheeks and chin. Next her hand went to the top of his head and felt his soft bushy hair. She smiled the whole time she explored his face. "Okay, now give me a hug," she asked Dexter.

Dexter became sad, and as he hugged his mother, tears began to form in his eyes.

He knew what she was doing. He knew she was wishing she could see him, just once.

"I love you, son," she said.

"I love you too, Baba," answered Dexter. He turned and ran past Hank and his friends so they wouldn't see his tears. Once outside, Dexter quickly wiped away his tears and ran off to meet his friends.

A couple of days later, Dexter got a call from his Uncle Charles. Charles said he wanted to see him, so Dexter agreed to meet at Nanny's house on Sunday. Charles was married now and had a daughter, whom everyone in the family referred to as Lady.

Ever since Hank and Dexter were small boys, Charles had played a key role in their lives, especially after the boys' father, Duane, had left. Dexter in particular looked up to Charles as his big brother. He idolized Charles and wanted to be just like him. But now Dexter was growing up and had become a teen. He was developing into his own person.

Charles always felt that he was more like a father figure to the boys. But he really wasn't old enough to take on that role. There were times when Charles chastised Hank and Dexter. But those days were quickly disappearing, only Charles didn't know it.

Charles and his lovely wife, Cynthia, purchased their first home on Bradford Street in Bernal Heights in San Francisco. Dexter often visited his uncle and watched him work on his racing car. Charles was always into auto racing.

That Sunday, Dexter met Charles at Mary's house. When he walked into the kitchen, Charles said, "Let's go for a ride." That was cool with Dexter, because in 1964, Charles had purchased a brand-new Mercury two-door Cyclone. It came stocked with a 289 Cobra engine. Basically, it was the same car as a Mustang Shelby Cobra 350 GT, only in a different body.

Charles had modified the car by adding dual-exhaust headers and a racing cam. He'd replaced the four-barrel carburetor with dual quads (two four-barrel carburetors); raised the rear end and put some cheater slicks on the rear wheels, along with some American racing mags on all four; he'd also added a posi-traction rear end. To say the car ran like a bat out of hell is an understatement. It had over four hundred horsepower, and if you weren't careful, you could break your neck when he pulled off at a light. The car was Charles's everyday car, and he worked on it continuously. On the weekends, he often put it on a trailer and hauled it out to Freemont Raceway, where he'd compete in drag races. Several trophies proudly adorned his living room.

Dexter often accompanied Charles to the racetrack where he'd work as part of his pit crew. He'd help to change the tires and put slicks on the car for the races. Occasionally, Dexter was able to ride in the passenger seat during a race. For him, this was one of the most exciting parts of his life.

As they left the house, Charles yelled out to Mary, "Mother, we'll be right back."

Mary said, "Don't take too long; dinner will be ready soon."

He and Dexter both chimed in, "All right, we won't be long."

Charles asked Dexter if he wanted to drive.

"Sure," said Dexter, who ran around to the driver's side.

Charles opened up the passenger door and got in, then reached over to let Dexter in. Dexter slid into the seat and looked out over the hood. The hood had a large scoop on it to cover the dual quads. The car was painted British racing green with a cream-colored interior, and the fenders were flared to accommodate the large, wide cheater-slick tires.

Dexter turned the key and stepped on the gas. Blammmmmmmm, roared the engine. He stepped on the gas again. Blammmm, Blammmm, went the engine. Dexter was excited. He'd only driven a clutch a couple of times. First, he stepped on the brake then released the emergency brake; he put his foot on the clutch and grabbed the Hearst link shifter to put the car in first gear; he took his foot off the brake, moved it over to the gas, then gently eased off the clutch while giving a little gas. The car jerked forward and died.

Charles laughed and walked Dexter through the process nice and easy. Soon Dexter got the hang of it, and off they went.

"Let's go down by Candlestick Park," Charles suggested.

"All right," said Dexter, and he turned to go the back way, through the neighborhood, since it wasn't far from Mary's house.

When they reached the park, Charles instructed Dexter to go and park in the empty parking lot. After they parked, Charles reached into the backseat and brought out a box of records. In between the seats was what appeared to be a metal box. Charles revealed that it was a small portable record player. Dexter was impressed and thought it was cool.

Charles picked out a record, put it through a slot in the front of the player, and the music started to play, in stereo. "Groovin' on a crowded avenue. Groovin' couldn't get away too soon. Oh no, no, no, no."

The music sounded good.

"That's the Young Rascals," said Charles.

"I know, that came out last year," Dexter said in a curt way.

Charles looked at Dexter like he was a smart aleck, and, actually, Dexter was. Especially when it came to something he really knew a lot about, and he knew a lot about music. After all, he was a singer!

Dexter smiled at Charles and thought it was funny because Charles was always late when it came to stuff like that. A movie would come out, or a new singing group, or something else, and Charles would find out about it and try to tell Dexter. Dexter would smile because he usually already knew.

He'd think to himself, "Charles, you're late! That came out three or four months ago." But he never wanted to bust Charles's bubble, so many times he'd let it ride. It was something that he loved about his uncle.

The two of them sat and listened to the music, and then Charles pulled out a joint. Dexter's eyebrows rose in surprise, and he thought to himself, "Charles?"

"You know what this is?" asked Charles.

"Yeah, it's a joint," answered Dexter.

"Well, last year mother told me she caught you smoking some weed. She asked me not to say anything to you about it at the time. But I thought it was finally time for us to talk about it," explained Charles.

"Okay," answered Dexter.

Charles fired up the joint and took one hit and coughed. He handed it to Dexter, and he took a hit—no cough. Dexter thought to himself, "Skunk weed." Before Charles could get started into his sermon, Dexter pulled a baggie out of his jacket. Inside were about a half-dozen joints and a couple of matchboxes of weed.

Charles was surprised, but he tried his best not to let on that he was. Dexter took out one of his joints, pulled a bicycle lighter out of his pocket, and fired up the joint.

"Here, hit this," he said, as he passed the joint to Charles. Charles took one hit on the joint and began to cough uncontrollably.

Dexter laughed. "Gold," he said.

The two of them sat, smoking on the joint and chatting. Charles was trying to tell Dexter about the challenges of growing up. Next they talked about Hank. They both admitted that all the signs had been there, and that Hank had been feminine all his life. Dexter expressed his disappointment but acknowledged that Hank was still his brother no matter what.

Charles and Dexter continued to chat. Charles inquired about Dexter's education and encouraged him to do the best he can. Dexter always paid attention to his uncle when it came to his advice. He knew that Charles was educated, smart, intelligent, and a good example to follow. The only problem was Charles couldn't be around enough to give it.

After they finished chatting, they drove back to Mary's for dinner.

That Thursday, Hank and Dexter were walking together from school. They took their time and weren't talking very much. Dexter was still not comfortable with Hank's new mannerisms and look.

As they got to Geneva and San Jose Avenue, Dexter decided he wanted to stop by the Donut Time coffee shop and pick up a little something to nibble on. Hank was walking a little behind.

"Hank, let's stop by Donut Time."

"My name is no longer Hank; I'm Terri," Hank snapped back to Dexter.

"Nah, you ain't. You're Hank, and to me you'll always be Hank. I don't care what you call yourself; you're still my brother, and you're still Hank."

He wasn't making much progress with Dexter, but he added his wishes anyway, "Well, I wish you wouldn't call me that, and I wish you'd get used to me being me, because this is who I am."

Dexter dismissed what Hank was saying and just said, "Come on," as he stepped off the curb to cross the street. Hank followed.

Dexter stepped up to the counter and ordered a jelly donut. Someone came into the shop and announced that Martin Luther King had been shot. Dexter grabbed his donut, and he and Hank quickly left the store. As they walked toward home, the news was spreading on the street like wildfire.

Hank and Dexter began to hurry, and Dexter's mind began to wander. "Damn, this is messed up. This is really messed up. Now they've gone and killed our leader. He stood for nonviolence and now he's dead. There's going to be a war. I know it. Black people are not going to stand for this. They're going to be rioting in the streets; I just know it!"

Dexter began to feel angry, and as he passed white people on the street, he looked at them and felt disgust. He wasn't feeling hatred; he was just angry and wanted justice.

When the boys arrived home, Margaret was listening to the radio, and the news was just being broadcast that Dr. Martin Luther King Jr. had been shot. Margaret was feeling sorrow and began to talk to herself. She decided to go into her room and pray. Hank went into the bedroom and turned on the television, where they were broadcasting information about what had happened.

Because the incident had just recently happened, the anchorman was providing news as it was being handed to him. He'd say one thing and then have to come back and change the story. The truth was they really didn't know exactly what had happened. But they had to say something to keep you glued to the tube.

Slowly, the information began to come out. Soon they made the announcement that Dr. King was dead. Hank's hands went up to cover his mouth, and he began to sob and cry out loud. In the rear of the house, Margaret began to call loudly on the Lord and had a talk with God. To her, it felt as though the end was near, and these were the signs of the times. The devil was busy, and corruption and sin were taking over the world.

President Johnson came on the television, asking people not to become violent, because that wasn't what Dr. King had stood for. Next the "I've Been to the Mountaintop" speech was broadcast, which Dr. King had just delivered a few days before.

At first Dexter became sad, and then he began to get angry. He stood up and walked out of the bedroom and headed downstairs, taking deep breaths as he walked. He opened the gate then walked over to the telephone pole and leaned against it. He looked around the street and everything appeared normal. People were traveling to–and–fro and going about their business. The cool air felt refreshing as he breathed in and out. He looked up into the sky; nighttime was falling, and the stars were beginning to come out.

Looking out into the heavens, Dexter thought the earth seemed like such a small place. Things that he once didn't think about, or even care about, were now burdens on his mind. So many bad things were happening in the world and around him that he began to question his faith. "Is there really a God?" he questioned.

Dexter looked up to the sky, and he was reminded that the universe was immense and that the earth where he lived was just a small speck in a massive space.

"Wow, look at that; there must be a God for only a God could create that," his doubt had quickly passed. He then called out to God, "Dear Lord, what's going to become of this place? What's going to happen? Please watch over us, God. We need you now more than ever. Amen!"

Dexter knew how to pray when he wanted to, but it wasn't often that he prayed. When he'd been a young boy, Margaret had made Hank and him pray every night. As he grew older, though, he didn't pray much. Hank continued to pray; he had talks with God often.

Later that evening, just as Dexter had thought, black people were rioting in San Francisco. They were rioting in every major city in America. The images of looting and burning seemed to ensure that a race war was inevitable. Dexter complained as the news came in and out during normal broadcasting.

"This is messed up. This injustice has got to stop. They can't keep us as an oppressed people. They don't want us to have anything!"

Over the next few days, the assassination was all that was talked about on the street and in school. It lay heavy on the minds of Americans, and it was a depressing time. Then, before Dr. King was even buried, more bad news hit the airwaves. Across the bay, in Oakland, there was a shootout with the police and the Black Panthers. The police had raided the BPP headquarters, and Bobby Hutton was shot and killed, and Eldridge Cleaver was taken into custody. The incident sparked outrage in Oakland.

The Black Panthers were claiming that the shooting was an assassination and that the pigs were out of control and practicing black genocide. It was the first time Dexter heard the term "Off the pigs," and the police being referred to as such. The Bay Area was probably the most diverse place on the planet. But at that time, to Dexter and many blacks, it seemed as though it was only black and white.

A few days later, Margaret attempted to get Hank to attend another session with the psychiatrist. Hank rejected her attempt and refused to go. He began to argue and eventually became loud. Margaret was trying to be strong and forceful and not accept no as an answer. Soon Hank was so upset that he stormed out of the house and didn't return.

When Hank failed to return home, Margaret decided to call the police and report him missing. She then contacted the psychiatrist to inform him about the events that had taken place. The doctor suggested to Margaret that if and when Hank returned home, she should call him. He also suggested that, if the police picked him up, she should do the same. The doctor explained to Margaret that he felt Hank was terribly ill and in such a mental state that he needed ongoing therapy and monitoring. He said that he felt Hank needed to be admitted into a hospital for treatment.

Margaret was in despair and at her wit's end. Her diabetes was bothering her, and Hank was worrying her so much that she just didn't know what to do. Admitting Hank into a hospital was not something that she really wanted to do. But Hank was uncontrollable and rebellious. Finally, she agreed with the doctor.

When Hank arrived back home, Margaret called the doctor. He told her not to alarm Hank, and that he'd come to pick him up and have the necessary paperwork for her signature. The doctor arrived with two assistants, and with only a little resistance, the doctor left with a sobbing Hank. They took Hank to the Napa State mental institution and admitted him for treatment.

Dexter was not home when they came for Hank. When he arrived home, Margaret informed him that Hank had been taken away and was being admitted to Napa State mental hospital.

"The crazy house?" asked Dexter.

"Yes, son. The doctor feels that it's the best thing for him, and they can better serve him there," said Margaret.

"But Baba, he's not crazy, he's just gay," Dexter said with frustration.

Dexter became sad and depressed at the thought of his brother being locked up. The two of them had been together all of their lives; they were never apart. Also, Dexter knew that Hank always depended on him to help him in tough situations. He knew Hank would be lonely without him there, and he began to have visions of Hank locked away in a cell, calling for him or calling for Margaret. Dexter thought about the times Hank had cried when they were away from home and he'd become lonely. He wished that he were there now to comfort Hank, and he felt helpless to give him the support he needed. Dexter went into his room and lay down on his bed. He looked at the empty bed where his brother always was. He then turned onto his stomach, grabbed his pillow and put his face in it, and cried.

Although Hank had turned fifteen, he was still Dexter's little brother, the brother whom he'd always protected and fought for. He thought about the time that Hank took a whipping for him, and about the time they went to camp and Hank cried so much because he wanted to go home. He thought about how when he saw Hank cry, he began to cry, and they'd both cried together.

Dexter missed those times when he and Hank had been close, and felt sorrow about how this whole gay thing was coming between them. He walked into the living room and looked at the portrait on the fireplace mantle of the two of them when they were about five and six years old. He looked at his face, and Hank's face, and how they were both smiling and looking happy. A lump began to form in his throat and his mouth was dry. Again he began to cry, and as he cried, he again talked to the Lord, "Why? Why, God? Why do these things have to happen?"

Dexter turned and walked into his room and took out a joint to smoke. He looked at it and then decided to pass on it. He put the joint back in his desk drawer and lay back in the bed and stared at the ceiling. He decided to call a girl he'd met, a Mexican girl named Milvia. He'd met her at the bus stop on Geneva and Mission.

Dexter called Milvia, and they began to chat. He let her in on the fact that he was feeling down and wondered if he could see her. Milvia told Dexter that Santana was playing at the Carousel Ballroom that weekend and that she wanted to go. Dexter thought it was a great idea, and they set a date for that Saturday night.

Margaret said it was okay for Dexter to go to the concert, and Mary agreed to let him use her second car. It was a 1959 Chevy four-door that was white with a blue interior. When Saturday night came, Dexter dressed in his purple wool gabardine slacks with a purple, double-knit, mock-tee sweater, which had a white embroidered border around the neck. He also dressed in his purple pimp socks, white belt, and white loafers. He topped off this ensemble with a white straw panama hat. With his Afro combed out underneath the brim, he was ready to go.

Dexter was excited about going to see Carlos Santana because he was rocking San Francisco like no other Latino band had ever done. The blend of Latin music along with the rhythms of rock, jazz, and soul were so original that his performances were almost spiritual. Dexter had seen him once at an outdoor concert in the Mission district at Dolores Park. One of his classmates had a brother who was in the band. David Brown played the bass, and Dexter had been to his house, visiting his sister, Diane. He felt privileged to have seen David practice and to have been inside his home. This gave him a special emotional connection to the group.

Milvia was the first girl that Dexter had dated who wasn't black. He was interested in the Latino girls, and he was excited about the date. When he arrived at her house, she was in the window and motioned to stop him from going to the door. She opened the window and told him to wait in the car around the corner, and she'd meet him there.

When she got into the car, she told him that if her father knew she was going out with a black guy, he'd have a fit, and she wouldn't be able to go. She also said that her sister was going to join them, and her sister's boyfriend would meet them at the front entrance to the concert.

Milvia's sister got into the car, and she and Dexter were introduced. They were all charged up in anticipation of a great evening. Dexter fired up a joint, started the car, and took off toward the freeway. They then headed for the Carousel Ballroom, which was soon to become Fillmore West.

When they arrived downtown, they met Milvia's sister's boyfriend. Right away, Dexter noticed they were stoned. He was also a black brother, so he and Dexter hit it off right from the start. He had a bottle of wine and suggested they walk around the corner and drink it before going inside. The four of them walked around the corner, where Dexter fired up another joint, and they passed around the bottle of wine until it was completely gone. It was time to go inside. Dexter grabbed Milvia by the hand and led the way into the concert. Milvia's hand felt good in his, and she followed him as though they'd been together for years. Dexter liked that!

The line going into the ballroom was crowded, so Dexter positioned Milvia in front of him and then embraced her as they began to push and move forward. Once inside, the music from the band that was performing was blaring, and there was a light show of psychedelic images flashing about the room. It was the strangest mix of people Dexter had ever seen. There were hippies and Latinos, along with Ivy-Leaguers, whites, and a few blacks. Everyone was partying, and the smell of pot was heavy and thick in the air. Anybody who didn't smoke weed would still wind up getting a contact high from the smoke in the room.

When the group, Santana, appeared on stage, the crowd went wild. When they started playing, people began to dance any- and everywhere. No one needed a dance floor; it was wherever the person stood. Dexter and Milvia began to party and dance; their chemistry was beginning to mix.

As they began to dance close, Dexter gave her a kiss. Milvia kissed him back and they embraced. When they came up for air, a white guy who looked like he was from Oxford bumped Dexter twice on his left arm. Dexter looked over, and the guy was handing him a joint. Dexter took the joint, took a hit then placed it in Milvia's mouth, where he held it for her to take a hit. After Milvia took the hit, Dexter took the joint and looked to his right, where a Latino brother was standing with his eyes glued to the stage. Dexter bumped him on the left arm, and he turned to see Dexter passing him the joint. The Latino brother took the joint, took a hit, and kept the joint moving.

Hit the joint and pass it on was the code of honor, and the joints were moving constantly. Everyone was stoned out of his or her mind. Hippies were dancing carefree, with no method to the movement. All they needed to do was move and they were dancing. Some were jumping in the air like Tinker Bell, and some white girls were doing ballet. Some people simply sat on the floor in a circle and held a powwow while passing water pipes filled with weed and hash as they grooved to the music.

Someone said that there were some bottles of wine being passed around that were laced with acid, so take care. When a bottle came around to them, they passed.

It was a carefree environment and nobody cared about who you were, what you looked like, or what you did. It was all about peace, love, and dope. It was exactly what Dexter needed. All the issues of home were gone and forgotten for the moment.

After the concert, they headed outside and Dexter grabbed a Berkeley Barb and a Black Panther Party newspaper. The four of them got into the Chevy, and Dexter drove up Market Street to the top of Twin Peaks. Dexter and Milvia lay down in the front seat, and her sister lay down with her boyfriend in the backseat. They all made love, and then Dexter took everyone home. He got up the next day and went to church.

The next few weeks were very difficult for Margaret. Hank was institutionalized, and he constantly called. The phone would ring, and Margaret could sense that it was her baby boy.

"Hello," she answered.

"Baba?" Hank said on the other end.

"Hello son, how are you?" she asked.

"Baba, I want to come home. I don't want to be here. I'll be good. I promise I will," Hank said, beginning to cry.

Margaret tried hard not to break down. She had to be strong. She told him, "Hank, the doctor says you're not ready to come home yet."

"But Baba," interrupted.

She continued, "Now Hank, listen to me, listen to me now. The doctor says you're making good progress. He told me that everyone there likes you, and that you're getting along with everyone and making friends."

"But Baba," he tried to interject. She cut him off, "Listen to me now. The doctor says that I can come and visit you in about a week. Nanny and I—"

Hank interrupted again. "When? When are you coming? I miss you, Baba."

Margaret then told Hank, "We'll be up to see you next weekend. Then afterward we'll see how well you do, so we can bring you back home."

There was silence. Then she heard Hank sobbing on the other end. Margaret's mouth became dry, and there was a lump in her throat. This was hurting her so much that she could barely contain herself.

"Hank? Are you there?" she asked.

"Yes Baba, I'm here. I just want to come home," he said.

"You will, baby. Let's just keep praying on it. Do you have your Bible? Are you reading your Bible?" she asked.

"Yes, Baba, every night I read it before I go to bed," he answered.

"That's good, son. God will see us through this. You know that, don't you, son? God can fix it. He can make everything all right. You just have to believe and have faith. I believe he can fix it. Do you?" she asked.

"Yes, Baba, I know God can fix it," answered Hank.

"I'm going to go now. You just keep on praying, and I'll see you in a week," said Margaret.

"All right. Bye, Baba," he said.

"Good-bye, son," said Margaret as she hung up.

After Margaret hung up the phone, she read a scripture, prayed, and then went to the piano to play and sing.

Dexter was in his room, reading the newspapers he'd picked up after the concert. The Black Panther paper had printed their version of the Oakland shootout. Eldridge Cleaver had gotten out on bail and fled the country. There was a column about how the Panthers had started a free breakfast program for children, and there was an update on Huey P. Newton.

The Berkeley Barb provided a different perspective on what was taking place with the war. It was the voice of social consciousness, with a radical point of view. Dexter read the articles from front to back. Angela Davis had joined the Communist Party and the Black Panther Party, and there was a complete schedule of protests and demonstrations that were going to take place in San Francisco and Oakland.

After reading the paper, Dexter decided to go to the Haight and pick up a few things. When he arrived in the Haight, it was the usual wild and crazy place—crowds everywhere, people doing something unusual or strange on just about every corner stump and stoop. Dexter was thinking, "Wow, it sure is different from when Hank and I went to school here. I wonder, does anybody here ever go home?"

Dexter's first stop was by the head shop to pick up some supplies. He also wanted to pick up a new poster or two. When he got to the counter, he noticed the variety of buttons on sale. They read, "Free Huey," "Black Power," "Power to the People," "Peace," and "Stop the War."

Dexter began to wonder what he was doing with regard to the power struggle and the war. Nothing! He wasn't doing anything at all!

He was very bitter and angry about all the things that had transpired. He thought about Dr. King, and about the Panthers, and about the brothers of his friends and church members who'd been shipped off to war. He began to think about Ali and Malcolm.

"Give me one of those, and one of those, and let me have that one and the one with the peace symbol," Dexter told the clerk. He walked down the street to a clothing store where he asked the clerk if they had any black leather jackets. She pointed him to where the jackets were and he walked over the area and began to browse.

There was a good collection. "Nah, I don't want no motorcycle jacket. Ahhh, this is a nice one," he said softly. It was a leather jacket, cut similar to a blazer. Dexter pulled the jacket off the hanger and walked to the mirror and put the jacket on. "Yeah, I like this. This is the one!" he said, talking to himself in the mirror.

"Do you have any berets?" Dexter asked the clerk.

"No, we don't have any here, but there's a place down the block and across the street that I think has some," answered the clerk.

"Right on. I'll take this jacket," Dexter told the clerk.

He had his buttons and his black leather jacket; now he needed a beret. He walked down to the shop the clerk had mentioned and found a black beret that would fit over his large Afro. He paid for the beret and left the store, and then he hopped on the bus and headed home.

18

The Nuthouse

The next Sunday, Charles arrived with Mary to pick up Margaret and Dexter to go and visit Hank in Napa. They piled into the hot rod and headed north, crossing the Golden Gate Bridge. The ride was bumpy and loud. Every time Charles took off after stopping at an intersection, everyone's head would jerk. It wasn't that Charles was trying to speed; it was just that the car was so powerful that he had a difficult time trying to start off slowly.

The family arrived at the hospital, which was an immense place and seemed more like a campus than a hospital. When they finally got to the ward where Hank was, he was beaming with joy. It was good seeing everyone, and they were all happy to see him. Hank looked good, and it seemed like it had been quite a while since Dexter had seen him without his makeup. The straightening was coming out of his hair and it was turning into a very large Afro. But Hank's eyebrows were still freshly plucked and he had a mole painted on his face.

Hank had stories to tell, and he wanted to introduce his family to his newly found friends. He started taking the family on a tour, and as they walked, they began to see that it was truly a nuthouse. It looked like a scene out of the movie One Flew over the Cuckoo's Nest. They walked into the ward and a middle-aged black man was talking to himself. Then there was a lady in a gown who was aggressively rubbing and scratching herself. The next person they saw was swatting flies that were not there, and someone else, in a corner, kept twitching.

Mary, Charles, and Dexter were amazed by what they saw, but they tried to act civil, as though they didn't notice. Hank said, "Boy, they got a lot of crazy people here. You think I'm crazy? I ain't nothing compared to these folks."

"I see," said Mary.

"This is where I'm staying," said Hank, as he showed them his bunk. "Let's go over to the recreation area. I want to introduce you to my friends," he continued.

As they passed through the ward, another man sat in a chair next to his bed, rocking aggressively back and forth. It reminded Dexter of Hank and the way he used to rock in the car and in bed, to go to sleep.

They entered the recreation area, and a large woman approached them, smiling. "This is Candi, everybody," Hank said.

"Candi, this is my mother, Margaret, and this is my uncle Charles. This is my grandmother, Mary, but we call her Nanny, and this is my brother, Dexter."

Slowly Candi greeted each person, taking his or her hand and shaking it. "Hello. Hi. How are you? Dexter, nice to meet you."

Everyone in the group responded with their hellos.

"Oh, we just love Hank, he is such a kick. We have a lot of fun with him," Candi said.

"Oh, that's nice," replied Margaret. "Good, Hank, you're making a lot of friends here."

Because Margaret couldn't see, she had no idea what the rest of the family was seeing.

A white man began to walk toward the family from across the room. Dexter was the first to notice him approaching. He was wearing a cowboy hat and boots, he had on a holster with a toy gun in it, and he wasn't wearing a shirt.

"Howdy," said the man, as he approached with his hand outstretched toward Dexter.

"Oh, everybody, this is Jessie, Jessie James," Hank said, as he introduced the man.

"Nice to meet you, Mr. James," said Dexter as he shook the man's hand.

"Hank's a good little buddy. We like him around these parts," said Jessie.

"That's great, Mr. James," said Margaret as she held out her hand.

Jessie shook Margaret's hand and said, "How do, ma'am! If ya'll need anything or have any trouble around here, just let old Jessie know."

"Sure, thanks. We'll be sure to let you know," answered Charles.

Hank and the family sat down at a table; Hank was laughing and giggling. "Candi, she's my best friend. She's here because she keeps taking off all her clothes and goes walking outside."

He continued to joke about her, "She did it last night in the middle of the night. They found her walking down the hallway butt naked."

Dexter looked across the room to where Candi was, and she smiled at him. Candi was about 6' 2" and was a brown-skinned black woman who weighed about four hundred pounds. He tried to picture her walking around naked and shook his head.

"Jessie thinks he's the real Jessie James," said Hank.

"Oh, I think we figured that out," said Charles.

"What?" responded Margaret, upon hearing what was actually taking place.

"Baba, there's nuts walking all around this place," explained Dexter.

"Lord Jesus, my God," Margaret said.

Margaret was beginning to question whether this was the best place for Hank. Was he really mentally unstable? Was being a homosexual a mental disorder? How was Hank going to improve around these people? Was he really going to be a better person when he left?

Hank told his family that he had participated in some group sessions. A group of them would sit around in a circle and talk about whatever was on their minds. He felt that the sessions were good for him because he was able to get some things off his chest. Hank went on to explain that he'd had a number of one-on-one sessions with a doctor and that the doctor was very understanding. It was good to see that Hank felt that the stay was helping him. It made things much easier for the family when it was time to leave. When they left, Hank didn't cry or ask to leave. He simply said good-bye, and everyone in the family hugged him and told him they loved him.

That summer, Mattock and Dexter applied for jobs at the Youth Opportunity Center. Dexter had had luck with them the prior summer, when he'd landed the gardening job, so he told Mattock there was a good chance they'd be able to get work there.

Because Dexter maintained good grades, had prior work experience, and had taken a couple of courses in mechanical drawing, he was able to get a summer job as a draftsman with the U.S. Army Corps of Engineers. Mattock also obtained a job at the Corps, working in the mailroom.

The drafting job proved to be a very good one for Dexter. Having worked the summer before had really prepared him for this job because he'd learned to respect authority and take instruction. Plus, he had tested very well, demonstrating his drawing and mathematical skills. After a couple of weeks of feeling Dexter out on the job, they put him on some bridge, dam, and highway projects.

Whenever Dexter and Mattock received their pay, the first thing they did was shop for clothes. They'd go to Howard Clothiers, The Brass Lantern, or Park Avenue clothing shops in downtown San Francisco and spend half of their checks. Before long, Dexter had assembled a large collection of suits, sport coats, sweaters, slacks, shirts, shoes, belts, and hats. It was at the National Shirt Shop where Dexter and Mattock purchased dress shirts in every color, complete with French cuffs.

Most of the people who worked at the Corps were mature middle-class white people. The majority of the men wore white shirts, striped or paisley ties, and wing-tipped shoes. Mattock and Dexter thought themselves to be the sharpest dressers in the building, but to the workers, they looked like a couple of hustlers, pimps, or entertainers.

Even though their choices were clothes of bright and loud colors, the clothing they purchased wasn't cheap. The majority of their clothing came from Italy and was of high-quality materials. They wore fine silks, wools, and blends. No longer were they wearing cheap shoes from Flagg's. Now they were wearing shoes made of fine leather and skins from Thom McCann's, Howard's, and Florsheim Shoes. Whenever Dexter purchased clothes for himself, he usually picked up something for Hank too, only he couldn't get too much because Hank's taste in clothes had changed.

Dexter struck up a good relationship with a Jew who owned a jewelry store on Market Street, not far from where he worked. Dexter often stopped by and purchased a watch, ring, or cuff links, all of which were costume jewelry. Soon Dexter convinced the owner that he could sell his merchandise for him. The Jew was smart and really sharp, and he had a way about him that seemed more Italian than Jew. He also wore fine Italian menswear, and he appeared to be street-smart. He knew that Dexter worked at a decent job for a sixteen-year-old and that he seemed well grounded. Plus Dexter dressed sharper than any sixteen-year-old he'd ever seen. The jeweler decided he could trust Dexter, so he fronted him a few watches, a couple of rings, a medallion or two, and some cufflinks.

Dexter had come to be quite an entrepreneur. He held a steady job, sold jewelry, and still sold marijuana. He was making money in several different ways and began to think about purchasing his first car.

Not long after starting to work at the Army Corps, Dexter picked up the book The Autobiography of Malcolm X. He read about Malcolm, and he related to what Malcolm was about and what he'd gone through. For one thing, Malcolm used to be a hustler, like Dexter, so he felt they had that in common. The other thing that he loved about Malcolm was that he'd risen up above his challenges to become a leader. As he read, he wished that he'd paid more attention to Malcolm when he was alive. But Dexter was just too young to be that aware at the time.

America was still in a daze from King's assassination, but many social groups were trying to come together to ease the tension between the races. Their efforts were quickly disrupted. Two months after the assassination of Dr. King, the brother of President John F. Kennedy, Senator Robert F. Kennedy, was also assassinated. Anger, hatred, frustration, sorrow, fear, and disgust were the feelings of many Americans.

Margaret read the scriptures and prayed diligently to deal with the signs of the times. She was concerned, like most parents were, about her two young men. She worried about how they were going to be affected by the events that were taking place in the world.

"Dexter, the devil is busy. We have to walk in faith and trust in the Lord," she preached.

Dexter was sixteen, about to turn seventeen, and like many young people, he was searching for the answers to many questions. He just didn't understand why there had to be so much hatred in the world.

Often, when he read the newspapers or watched the news and listened to the country's leaders, he'd ask himself, "Why are all these things happening? Why is there so much hatred? Why can't people get along? What is this war all about? I'm tired of all the riots and the killings."

It was a confusing time for teenagers. Things that didn't seem too important before were now becoming very important in their daily lives. For one thing, the draft was looming.

The Concepts had to get ready for a show. It was going to be their first official performance. The gig was performing for a local labor union that was having a political event. The group got together to practice, and they decided which songs they were going to sing. It was going to be a compilation of mostly Temptations songs, along with a couple of others. They did their usual warm-up of "Farewell, My Love" and "I Love You So."

After their warm-up, they practiced "Please Return Your Love to Me," with Raul taking the lead as sung by Eddie Kendrick. Then Mattock took the lead and they sang "Ain't Too Proud to Beg." Next it was Cary's turn, and the group went into a sultry "Oh Baby, Baby" by the Miracles. They then decided to mix it up with "Born Free." The final cut was the Temptations' hit "Don't Look Back," with Dexter taking the lead. The group practiced their steps then decided to call it a wrap.

"Let's go to St. Michael's and play some basketball," Raul suggested. Everyone was up for it, so they headed off to the schoolyard, smoking a joint along the way.

When they arrived at the schoolyard, there were a couple other kids on the court whom the group knew.

"What's happening?" Raul said to the two on the court. "Can we join you?"

"Yeah Raul, we can play some three-on-three," said one of the boys.

"I can dig it," answered Raul.

"Hey, we heard you guys singing down the street. You guys are right on," said the other boy.

"Yeah, we got a show coming up that we have to be ready for," said Mattock.

"You guys hear about the Temptations?" said the other boy.

"No, what?" asked Dexter.

"Otis kicked David out of the group," said the boy.

"What?" replied Raul.

"Yeah, Otis kicked David out of the group, and word has it that they have a new guy."

This was devastating news. They could not believe what they were hearing. Without David it was not conceivable that there could still be a group called the Temptations.

"Bullshit, this is fucked up! It's not the same group without David. David is Mr. Temptation. He makes the group!" Dexter complained. "I don't care who the new guy is, I won't accept him."

"It's over, the group is done. This is fucked up," added Mattock.

After hearing the news, the group decided they didn't feel like playing. To them, the news was worse than anything else going on in the world. Dexter went home and turned on the radio and listened for anything about the breakup. Nothing was said on the radio, so he walked up to the corner store and picked up a Jet magazine. He thumbed through the magazine and found an article about a new guy named Dennis Edwards joining the Temptations.

"This is bullshit," a customer overheard Dexter saying as he read. He put the magazine back on the rack and walked out of the store. He headed down the street, complaining as he went, "I won't accept him. I don't like it. This is bullshit!"

The following weekend, the group got ready to perform but the band never showed up. So they decided to sing a cappella, and the show went off like clockwork. The mostly-white crowd loved their singing, energy, and showmanship. The group ended the show with "Don't Look Back," and danced the "Temptation Walk" as they left the stage.

People from the audience approached them to congratulate them on a fine performance. It felt good to be admired; the performance was a bright moment, especially for Dexter, who was being torn by the situation in his family life and with the state of the country. To Dexter, it seemed like the world was closing in on him, and that everything was going wrong.

When Dexter arrived back home, Margaret and Leon were there and they were arguing, so Dexter left the house, walked to the store, and asked a man going inside to buy him a small bottle of Ripple. After getting his wine, he headed back to the house. When he arrived, Margaret and Leon were still arguing.

Instead of heading upstairs, he cut through the garage and out the back door into the backyard. He closed the back door behind him and copped a sit on the concrete stoop. Dexter then twisted the top off the bottle, tilted his head back, and took a long drink, gulping down half the bottle. He then pulled a joint out of his pocket, lit it up, and took a long drag.

Dexter sat there for a moment and looked at the grounds of the backyard. It didn't look like a perfectly manicured yard, but he was proud of the work he'd done on it. The grass was cut, and the plants and trees that he'd planted three years earlier had really taken off and grown. A palm tree that he'd planted in the middle of the yard, which he and Hank used to run and jump over, was now too tall to jump. This made him think of Hank being in the mental institution with a bunch of crazies. His mind wandered for a moment, and then he snapped to.

Dexter downed the rest of the wine in one long gulp. He took a long drag on the joint, exhaled, and then stood up to go back inside the house. Margaret and Leon were upstairs in the kitchen, still arguing. Dexter went upstairs, walked into his room, and closed the door behind him. He went to his record player and put on the Temptations album *Wish It Would Rain*. He walked over to his bed and lay back, looking at the empty bed next to his, where Hank would lie. Dexter continued to lie on his bed, staring at the ceiling. The Temptations were playing on the record player and David Ruffin was singing, "I could never love another … after loving you," and Dexter again began to think. Whenever he got loaded and was alone, his mind would churn. Soon he went to sleep.

When Dexter awoke, Margaret and Leon had stopped arguing. There was a knock at the door.

"Yeah," Dexter shouted.

Leon opened the door and walked in. He wanted to talk. Dexter didn't want to talk, but he didn't say no. Leon started complaining about how difficult Margaret was, and how she was the boss, and a man is supposed to be a man. And never marry a woman who will run your life, and I bet a man, and blah, blah, blah, blah, blah …

Dexter just sat in front of Leon, nodded his head in agreement, and said, "Yeah, yeah, yeah." After a while, he wouldn't even hear Leon or know what he was talking about. But he'd give him the courtesy of pretending to listen. Dexter knew that he was the only person in the house that Leon could go to because, if Hank were there, he wouldn't listen to it and might even jump into their argument. Dexter usually stayed out of it as long as it never got beyond yelling, and it never did.

Leon always said, "You know I'd never put a hand on your mother. I never will. Sometimes she goes to beating on me. But I bet a man I'll never raise a hand to her. She ought not treat a man like that."

After Leon left the room, Dexter was stressed and needed some kind of relief. "I know; I need a girl," he said to himself.

He picked up the phone and called Milvia. She answered the phone, "Hello?"

"Hey, whatcha doin'?" asked Dexter.

"Hey, sexy Dexy," she said on the other end.

"What are you doing this weekend?" he asked.

"It looks like I'm doing you," she answered.

Dexter laughed, "You got that right. Let's go see Sly Stone this weekend. He's going to be at Fillmore West."

"Far out! Okay, it's a date. I'll see you Saturday night," Milvia said with excitement.

"All right, later," Dexter hung up the phone.

Mary had given her second car to Charles, so Dexter had to borrow it from him. Charles said it was fine but that he had to have it back in the morning because Cynthia would need to use it.

That Saturday night, Dexter picked up Milvia, again waiting around the corner because her father didn't like blacks. She got into the car wearing a short skirt and a sexy blouse, showing a little cleavage. Dexter liked what she had on. She leaned over and, reaching around, put her hand on the back of his head and kissed him firmly on the lips.

Dexter responded with his tongue and squeezed her right breast with his left hand. She moaned and let her hand slide down his chest and onto his knee and then rubbed his crotch. It was just what he needed.

Dexter sat upright, turned the key in the ignition, and Milvia slid close to him. He opened the ashtray, pulled out a joint, and handed it to Milvia. They drove off and headed down to Market and Van Ness—destination, Fillmore West.

The Carousel Ballroom had become Fillmore West. Bill Graham had taken it over, and it was the premier venue for the new music of the day. It was psychedelic, far out, and right on!

Dexter and Milvia were stoned, and Sly, Freddie, Rose, Cynthia, Gregg, and Jerry were on stage, and the music was taking them higher. Black people were singing, "Don't call me nigger, whitey."

On cue, white people sang, "Don't call me whitey, nigger," and the crowd was going wild.

"You Can Make It if You Try" brought the crowd back into a mellow groove, with people rocking and swaying as the music intensified. Things got outrageous and electric when Freddie's guitar struck a chord and Larry's bass came in from the bottom with "Sex Machine."

Everyone fell into a groove that put each one into another dimension of his or her own world. They played "Sex Machine" to an orgasmic climax, with Gregg killing the drums.

Finally, Sly kicked off a song and took people to a level of consciousness about what was taking place in the world, while asking everyone to take some sort of position. He called for everyone to "Stand," and the place was in a frenzy. Dexter and Milvia were jumping up and down, and everyone threw their hands up and cheered.

When Dexter walked out of the Fillmore, all his cares and worries had disappeared. He was going to take Milvia out to Ocean Beach, but she wanted him to take her home. She told him she was going to sneak him into her house.

Dexter had to wait outside for her to get settled before she could slip him in. After about twenty minutes, Milvia came downstairs and opened the front door. "Shh, follow me," she said, as she led the way. Dexter followed her upstairs, made a left, and tiptoed down the hall to her bedroom.

Once inside her bedroom, she told Dexter to get undressed and climb under the covers. Milvia quickly undressed, put on her robe, walked to the door, then turned and said, "Stay put, I'll be right back."

Dexter stayed under the covers with only his underwear on, feeling nervous. Milvia lived at home with her sister and her father. He didn't know why, but there was no mother in the house.

A few moments later, the door opened. Dexter lay under the covers, holding them up over his head. He heard some shuffling around and took a peek. It was Deanna, Milvia's sister, and she was undressing and getting ready for bed.

Dexter hadn't noticed the extra bed in the room. When he moved slightly, he startled Deanna.

"Shhh," Dexter said, putting his finger in front of his lips.

"What are you doing here?" Deanna asked Dexter.

Just then, Milvia came back into the room. "You two be quiet; Dad's going to get suspicious."

Deanna just shook her head. "You hide your face."

Dexter was getting even more nervous. "Maybe I should go."

"No, just stay there," instructed Milvia.

Dexter turned over and pulled the covers up over his head. Milvia turned out the light and walked over to the bed where she disrobed and climbed in. She was naked, and her body felt great next to Dexter's.

Dexter turned toward Milvia. She put her arms around him and pulled herself close and kissed him passionately. Dexter kissed her too and began to get aroused. The softness of her skin felt good to his touch. Her long jet-black hair periodically got in the way. Milvia would pull her hair away, turn her head up, and shake it back. He loved it when she did that.

Milvia then pushed Dexter onto his back, climbed on top of him, and then slowly mounted his manhood. She was moist and wet, and he slid right in. She pushed the covers back and sat up on Dexter's midsection, taking him in deeper. She rubbed her hands on his chest and began to ride. Dexter looked up at her, with her long black hair hanging down and flowing over her full but perky breasts. She looked down at Dexter. "Happy birthday, my sexy Dexy," she said, looking him in his eyes with the sexiest look he'd ever received from a woman. Then she smiled.

After making love a couple of times, Dexter got out of bed and got dressed, then snuck out of the house. Instead of driving home, he headed for Charles's house. Dexter had a key to his uncle's house, so he let himself in and crashed on the couch. It was 5:30 in the morning. When he awakened, he and Charles drove up to visit Hank for his birthday. The following week, Hank was released from the hospital and returned home.

One day, while Dexter's supplier was dry, he and Mattock traveled to the 'more to visit Tree's Pool Hall to try and cop a matchbox to hold them over. The Black Panthers had one of their offices at the corner of Fillmore and Eddy. Dexter decided to pick up a BPP Newspaper. While he was at it, he picked up a copy of Chairman Mao Tse-tung's Red Book.

While walking, he read through the BPP Newspaper and saw a notice for a "Free Bobby" demonstration being held at San Francisco State University. The university was near his home, so this was his chance to get involved.

When the day of the rally came, Dexter donned his all-black outfit, complete with black leather jacket and beret. He pinned his buttons on his jacket lapels and left the house. As he walked up the street to catch the bus, he walked proudly through the neighborhood. Familiar faces looked at Dexter; they were not used to seeing him dressed this way. As they looked, he smiled and raised a clenched fist in salute, "Black power." He was on his way!

When Dexter reached the university, there was a sea of people. There were people of all colors from all walks of life. "I thought this was a Black Panther rally," Dexter thought to himself. But he soon learned that people of all colors were against the injustice to others, no matter what color they were.

The Panthers were out in full force. It was an impressive display of discipline and authority. They stood tall and proud in soldiers' formation while other members patrolled the scene to keep order. On stage, there were many leaders of the party. They talked about Bobby Seale being kidnapped and arrested by the racist pigs, claiming that he had incited a riot at the Democratic Convention. They called the action a farce and a setup and demanded the release of Bobby, with chants of "Free Bobby." The crowd chimed in.

The speakers took turns on the stage and spoke about their leader, Huey Newton, and about the injustice the party was experiencing because they, as American citizens, had a right to defend themselves. They then demanded the freedom of Huey with chants of "Free Huey," and the crowd chimed in. Shouts and chants of "Free Bobby" and "Free Huey" escalated in a sea of raised fists. Dexter was in the crowd with his fist raised, chanting along with the crowd. These chants were followed by chants of "Power to the people," and "Black power," then "Stop the war," and "When do we want to stop it?" "Now!"

There was a sense of unity and purpose that Dexter had never felt before. He looked at the police who were standing near, in the event that things got out of hand. The people stayed steadfast and made their demands heard. For once, Dexter felt he was doing something and that he was a participant in the movement.

After the rally, Dexter went home. Margaret had cooked dinner, and Hank was home. He wanted to know all about the rally, so Dexter told him all about the experience and about how he felt he was now doing something about the struggle. He went on to inform Hank that there were people of all colors participating in the rally, and that he'd even seen someone carrying a sign that read, "Gay Pride." Hank found that to be very interesting, and Dexter suggested to him that maybe he'd like to come the next time he went. Hank was very happy that his brother had invited him and accepted the invitation.

In 1970, Huey P. Newton announced the Black Panthers' support for the equality of gays and lesbians. It was the first pro-gay announcement to come from a black civil rights organization. The Black Panthers went on to form a relationship with the Gay Liberation Front. The gay rights movement was just getting under way. It was a good thing for those who were soon to be coming out of the closet. But Dexter felt it was just a little too late. Maybe if Hank had waited a little longer, it wouldn't have been so painful for everyone involved, especially Hank.

Margaret sat down and ate dinner with her sons. It was the first time in quite a while that the three of them had eaten together. It felt good for all of them to be sitting together at the same time, and the conversation was good. It was a time to bond and be a family again, with no discussions of negative things. Dexter mentioned to his mother that he wanted to go and visit Joy. Margaret said it would be fine, if he took Hank with him. Dexter had no objection and said it was fine if Hank came along.

Joy was still Dexter's heart. He cared for her deeply, but he was interested in having sex and Joy wasn't. Whenever Dexter came to visit her, they'd sit in front of the television and neck, but when it came down to having sex, she'd refuse. Dexter was feeling frustrated and tired of the rejection, and began to consider ending the relationship. There was only one problem: he really felt that he loved her, and if he broke if off, it would hurt him and her. After dinner, Dexter called Joy and told her he was on his way. It took about an hour to get to Joy's house on the bus.

Dexter decided to change clothes and get out of his revolutionary uniform. He went to the closet and opened the door. "Umm, let's see," he said, scanning his wardrobe. "Sweater, suit, or sport coat? Or maybe just a starched shirt and some slacks with my leather maxi-coat?" He looked at the long, heavy, grayish-lavender, leather coat. It reached down almost to his ankles, and when he wore a brim with it, he looked real slick, and he really liked to impress Joy with his dressing.

But it was too nice out for the maxi-coat. The fog hadn't rolled in and it was going to be a clear night. If the weather was nice in Lakeview, then the weather would be nice anywhere in the city. "I'll wear a sweater and some slacks with a lightweight leather blazer," he said, speaking to himself.

He pulled a crew-necked, double-knit pullover out of the closet. It was one of about a dozen sweaters he had. All of them were beautiful and Italian-made. This particular sweater was an olive-green color, with five panels across the front, separated by raised olive ribs. Each panel was the same width from top to bottom; the center panel was white, bordered by two gold panels, which were bordered by the two outer panels that were cocoa-brown.

The sweater looked good with either olive, brown, or gold slacks, all of which Dexter had. "Okay, which slacks?" said Dexter. He looked at his shoes; the cocoa-brown alligators stood out. He picked the gold wool slacks, which had a silk-like look; they matched the gold panels in the sweater exactly. Brown pimp socks, a brown alligator belt, and a cocoa-brown leather blazer topped the outfit off. "Let's see, should I wear my brown stingy brim?" Dexter asked Hank. Before Hank could even answer, Dexter said, "Nah."

Dexter took a shower and got dressed, and Hank followed. Hank put on some blue cotton pants and a light green alpaca sweater. He decided not to be in drag because he knew it bothered Dexter. However, he still had to tie a scarf around his neck. He also wore a tad of makeup.

They were ready to go. Dexter asked Hank, "How do I look?"

"That's my brother. There ain't nobody dressed sharper than my brother!" Hank said as he snapped his finger in the air and shook his head.

Dexter laughed at Hank and said, "Hank, you're crazy," then the two of them left for Joy's.

At that time, the Castro district had not yet become the Mecca for gays in the city of San Francisco. There were only one or two gay bars in the area at the time. While Hank and Dexter waited at the bus stop on the corner of Market and Castro, they noticed a few gay couples walking about. They were not being too obvious, but if you were observant, you could tell. All of them were grown white men.

When the boys arrived at Joy's house, she had a couple of visitors. Her girlfriend, Shirelle, was there. Dexter had introduced Mattock to Shirelle, and Mattock had starting having sex with her on a regular basis. She asked Dexter where Mattock was, and Dexter told her he hadn't talked with Mattock, even though he knew Mattock was having sex with Ellie that very moment.

The other friend at Joy's was Olive. A few months before Hank had come out of the closet, he and Dexter and Mattock had gone to Shirelle's house with Joy and Olive. Mattock and Shirelle had gone into one bedroom to have sex, and Dexter and Joy had gone into another bedroom and necked. Hank and Olive had remained in the front room, talked, and did some necking. It was one of the few times Hank engaged romantically with a girl. Olive was much older than the rest of the group and was about four years older than Hank. She really liked Hank, but he only liked her as a friend. He was no longer interested in girls!

After being at Joy's house for a while, Hank decided that he wanted to walk to the corner store. Olive offered to go with him, but Hank insisted that he wanted to walk alone. She seemed a little offended, but she understood.

Once Hank left the house, Olive began to talk about Hank.

"Girl, goddamn, he's fine. Um-uh, what a waste! He's too fine to be gay. I bet I can change him!" said Olive.

"You ain't gonna change shit," said Dexter.

"He's a sissy, and he ain't interested in no girls, and there ain't nothing you can do to change that. I know, I'm his brother," Dexter said sarcastically.

"Humph, shit. One hour with this pussy and I'll make him a man," Olive said confidently.

"He ain't having it," Dexter repeated. "You can try if you want to, but you're gonna get your feelings hurt."

Soon Hank returned, and the five of them sat around and watched television and chatted. Shirelle decided to leave and dismissed herself. Olive was contemplating making a move on Hank then decided not to approach him. But she did stay awhile longer until they were all ready to leave.

Once it came time to leave, Hank and Olive walked out of the room, and left Dexter and Joy alone to say their good-byes. Dexter and Joy kissed and hugged, and when they parted, it was time to go. Hank and Dexter then caught the bus and trolley back to Lakeview.

Upon summer's end, Dexter entered his senior year and Hank entered his junior year at Balboa High School. The summer seemed long and eventful. Dexter maintained his drafting job while attending school, participating in the four-four plan that allowed students to attend school for four hours a day and earn school credits while working for four hours.

On the first day of school, Dexter sported his black velvet, eight-button, three-quarter-length blazer with gold wool slacks and a gold turtleneck. On his feet, he wore some black alligator loafers with ribbed, sheer, black pimp socks. He didn't take a stash to sell that day. He just took a few joints to smoke. Once on campus, he located the crew. There was Mattock, Cary, Jonnie, and Worrell. Raul was attending a trade school.

Worrell was the oldest student in the school. He was stuck in the twelfth grade and was repeating his senior year for the third time.

Everyone liked Worrell. He was a good kid, but he was lazy and wanted to get high all the time. Dexter had tried on several occasions to get Worrell to keep his grades up and be more responsible. Worrell would listen respectfully, but he'd never act on Dexter's advice.

Sometimes Worrell hung with the crew and tried to sing with the group. He didn't have the best of voices, but he was okay to fill in when Raul wasn't around.

"Dex, you selling any joints?" asked Worrell.

"Nah, but I'll smoke one with you!" answered Dexter. Everyone was up for that.

They still had about twenty minutes before homeroom, so the group walked around the corner and stood in the driveway of someone's home.

"Here, fire this up," Dexter said, as he handed it to Worrell.

Worrell fired up the joint, took a hit and coughed, then passed it to Jonnie. Jonnie took the joint, put it to his lips and took a drag, then immediately bent over and coughed.

"Damn, what kind of shit is this?" asked Jonnie.

"Thai Stick," answered Dexter.

Just then one of Cary and Jonnie's younger brothers approached them. It was Morris, one of the twins, and he was carrying a ghetto blaster with James Brown screaming through the speakers, "Say it loud, I'm black and I'm proud." The song had just debuted on the airwaves.

Jonnie was probably the biggest James Brown fan there ever was. He knew every cut James Brown had ever made. He knew the drummer parts, the horn parts, the guitar, and every instrument. Jonnie would say, "Okay, check out the drums," and he'd mimic every beat with his lips and air play with imaginary drumsticks. "All right, listen to the horns," he'd say, mimicking the horns, and so on. He'd get everybody into it and have each of them mimicking one part until the whole group was playing the song, with their voices sounding out the instruments. On cue, Jonnie would scream, "Ayeee," just like James. "Say It Loud" was a monumental hit. For the black students on campus, it was a call of unity and black pride. For non-blacks, it was a notice that black people were no longer accepting a second-class status in anything.

Cary's twin brothers, Horace and Morris, had the same look as Cary. They were extremely handsome, with light golden skin, sandy-colored hair, and green eyes. They wore large, soft and fluffy Afros, and were short, with athletic builds. They were also professional thieves. The twins were just turning fifteen years of age and could get you almost anything you wanted. Audio or photography equipment were their specialties. They kept the latest music cassettes and sold all the hits for pennies on the dollar. You could put in an order, and they'd have it the next day. Morris wanted to hit the joint. The group standing around getting high was beginning to grow, so Dexter fired up another joint and gave it to them then left.

Hank and Dexter received their schedules for classes and they were off to a good start. Hank settled in with his crew and they paraded around campus in semi-drag, flirting with the males, and strutting their stuff.

It wasn't long before Hank began to cut classes. He and his friends got into taking pills and drinking alcohol. They sometimes left campus and went to someone's house whose parents were away at work. Soon it came to Margaret's attention that Hank was getting back into his old habits. He was becoming rebellious again and was capable of going off at the drop of a dime. Margaret was at her wit's end and didn't know what to do, so for the time being, she just prayed.

The Black Student Union at Balboa had become very active, politically and socially. The events of the time, as they related to civil liberties, had a direct impact on the planning of their activities. Soon there were calls for walkouts and demonstrations on campus, so the voices of black students could be heard. At the same time, there was a consensus from the general student body population that students needed to be more involved in the protest against the war. So there was a concerted effort of the socially conscious student bodies to have walkouts and demonstrations together.

It wasn't long before there was major unrest on the campus, with walkouts and demonstrations becoming commonplace. On the days when a protest was scheduled, Dexter would don his BPP uniform and participate. It was just a matter of time before things began to get out of hand.

One day, there was a walkout scheduled, and everyone walked out of their classes and gathered outside on the streets around the campus. A few fights broke out, and soon the police came out in full riot gear, and like clockwork, some of the thugs on campus began to throw rocks and bottles at the police.

Dexter was standing in a crowd that was chanting, "Stop the war! When do we want it stopped? Now!"

Next came shouts of "Hell no, we won't go!"

Dexter was chanting and raising his fist along with crowd, yelling at the police.

The police then lined up shoulder to shoulder. They had their helmets with face shields on, with billy clubs in their hands. A police commander lifted a bullhorn to his mouth and instructed everyone to disperse and go home. No one budged. Instead, the chants and raised fists got stronger.

Again, the commander shouted through his bullhorn, urging the students to disperse and go home, but his appeal was met with more protests, and someone threw a bottle and hit one of the officers. The police had had enough. The commander waved down the street, and a police van came around the corner and backed up behind the row of officers.

The commander gave notice that it was his last appeal for the crowd to disperse, and that if they didn't, the police would take it upon themselves to disperse the crowd and they'd begin to arrest people. This time his request was met with a shower of bottles, rocks, and cans. The police then scrambled out in all directions, chasing the students and tracking them down. The crowd then panicked, and people began to run in all directions.

Dexter began to run. When he looked back, he saw a friend of his being grabbed from behind and hit in the head with a billy club. He watched as his friend's body went limp. The policeman dragged him by the collar and lifted him into the paddy wagon. Dexter then noticed a policeman heading toward him, and from the look on the officer's face, he knew he was the target—probably because he was wearing the complete Black Panther Party outfit.

Dexter took off running, with the policeman in hot pursuit. He ran down the block, turned the corner, went a few yards, and then stopped to see if the officer was still following. The policeman hit the corner and charged toward Dexter. Dexter turned and ran as fast as he could down an alleyway between Balboa and Denman. They were now a good block and a half away from the center of the violence and the officer was still pursuing him.

Just past the alleyway was an opening that was bordered by the school stadium and Denman's schoolyard mesh fence. Children were playing in the Denman schoolyard. Dexter ran and jumped onto the fence, which separated the schoolyard from the walkway. He quickly climbed over the fence and ran into the schoolyard where the kids were at play. He looked back and saw that the policeman had stopped and decided not to follow him into the yard filled with children. Dexter turned and held up a finger and said, "Fuck you, pig," then turned and ran to the other side of the playground and through the gate at the other end of the yard. He then headed up to San Jose Avenue and on toward home. The next day school was back in, and everyone tried to bring things back to normal.

19

Take a Stroll Through Your Mind

When school let out for lunch, Dexter would leave the campus for work and catch the 14 Mission Street bus downtown and make his way to the Corps of Engineers' offices which were at the foot of McAllister Street. He'd get his assignments from different engineers then get to work drawing. One of the projects he was currently working on was the Warm Springs Dam project.

There was a white engineer named Ben, who was one of the lead engineers on the project. Dexter often interacted with Ben on many of the drawings he was working on.

Dexter found Ben to be an interesting person. He was from Canada and was in his late twenties. He'd been recruited to the United States to work at the Corps. There were no black people where Ben came from, and Dexter was one of the first blacks he'd come in contact with on a regular basis. He was very intrigued by Dexter.

At first Dexter thought Ben was a little weird, and he even thought that Ben might be gay. But Ben wasn't gay; he was just from a different country and culture. Plus, he was real square. He was very nerdy and also a borderline eccentric. He was an academic whose specialty was mathematics, and he was extremely intelligent, with a high IQ.

Ben was about 5' 11" tall, weighed about two hundred pounds, and had a beer belly. His clothes were real plain, and usually his dress consisted of a white or simple plaid shirt, some khaki pants, a funky tweed sport jacket, and a pair of penny loafers or wing-tipped shoes. He washed his shirts and pants himself and very seldom cleaned his three jackets, which all looked almost alike. Ben's hair was a dirty blond and kind of curly. The longer it got, the curlier it was, and he always waited until it got real sloppy before he'd cut it.

Whenever Dexter came around, Ben would smile because he knew Dexter was going to say something to make him laugh. For one thing, Dexter spoke two languages—street and educated, just like his mother did. Dexter spoke one way when he was at home or with his crew, but when he was around church folks, white people, or business people, he spoke good English. But for some reason, when he was around Ben, he spoke like he did with his crew.

Ben would watch the transformation in Dexter and be amused. He'd watch Dexter talk conservative around the office and then walk over to him and talk jive. Soon Dexter and Ben became good friends, and they were like the odd couple—different as night and day. Ben was Dexter's first white male friend as an adult, and Dexter was Ben's first black friend ever. Ben lived just a few blocks from the office. He lived in the Tenderloin in a rented studio apartment at 340 Eddy Street.

It wasn't long before Dexter found out that Ben liked to smoke weed, so naturally, he became a customer. Dexter thought Ben was funny because he'd buy some weed from him and then want to smoke it with him. Most people Dexter dealt with would buy some weed from him and then want Dexter to smoke his stash with them, so they could save what they purchased. Sometimes Dexter would accept the invitation to go over to the apartment after work and smoke a joint or two.

Ben drove an old Dodge when he and Dexter first met. But soon he purchased a brand new 1968 Pontiac Firebird, Formula 400. It had a 400 cubic-inch engine, with a Hurst linkage, and over three hundred horsepower. It was a powerful car.

Dexter had yet to purchase a car, so sometimes Ben taxied him around after work. Dexter began to show up with Ben around the crew, and they'd be curious about who the white cat was.

They'd ask Dexter, "Man, who's this white dude?"

Dexter would answer. "Ah man, don't trip; he's cool. He's all right. He's with me!"

Ben thought that hanging out with Dexter and his friends was exciting. They'd be singing, capping on each other, and jiving around. Ben really tripped out one day when one of them referred to the other as "nigger."

One evening, Ben was with Dexter and they were over Mattock's house in the basement where the group was practicing for a show. They were smoking weed and drinking beer, and Raul got the giggles and just busted out laughing while he was looking at Mattock.

"What? Whatcha laughin' at?" Dexter asked Raul.

Raul began pointing at Mattock. "Look at that muthafucka's nose," Raul said, as he started laughing uncontrollably.

"Fuck you, nigga," Mattock responded.

Dexter and Cary now started laughing and cracking up because Mattock did have a large nose.

"I'm from Panama and that nigger's nose is wider than the Panama Canal. I've seen the canal, and it ain't as wide as that muthafucka!" said Raul.

Everyone was bending over laughing and stomping and pointing at Mattock.

Mattock came back and said, "Ah, muthafucka, look at your nose. You can't talk. You got a nose like that buzzard that's always trying to catch Bugs Bunny, nigga."

Now Cary and Dexter were rolling over laughing.

At first Ben didn't understand what was going on. To him they were insulting one another. Soon Ben finally figured out that the boys were playing when they talked about each other like that, and soon, he too began to laugh.

The weed and beer had everyone loaded and then they started in on each other's mommas and it got even more hilarious. Ben was laughing so hard tears were coming out of his eyes, which were turning red. His cheeks, too, began to turn red as beets.

Mattock saw Ben laughing at him and turned to him and said, "Ah, muthafucka, what you laughing at? Look at them damn clothes you wearing, muthafucka."

Everyone busted out laughing, and they all began to focus on Ben.

"Damn, where you buy them shoes, muthafucka?" asked Dexter.

They couldn't stop laughing.

Ben looked down at his shoes and said, "What? I happened to pay a hundred dollars for these shoes."

"Well, you need to get your money back for them sons of bitches," said Raul. "And look at your hair, muthafucka. Why don't you get a damn haircut? And what the fuck is that smell?"

They couldn't stop laughing because it was so hilarious.

"Shit, muthafucka smell like white folks!" capped Mattock.

"Well, I am white," Ben said seriously.

Raul came back, "You sho' is, muthafucka!"

Soon everyone got their laughs out, and they calmed down and got back to practice.

Ben gave Dexter a ride home, and as they were driving, Ben asked Dexter why they referred to each other as "nigger." Dexter explained that it was not considered a derogatory name when used amongst buddies within a context of fun or friendship.

He went on to tell Ben that, anytime a white person used it to refer to a black person, it would be considered an insult. He told him, "Don't you ever call a black person a nigger. You understand?" Ben said he understood.

Once they arrived at the house, Dexter got out of the car and walked toward the house, shaking his head as he laughed about the fun they'd had, then he went into the house and went to bed.

Shortly thereafter, Tommy Smith and John Carlos raised their clenched fists during the awards ceremony at the Olympics, and their action was covered heavily over the televised news. Most of white America was outraged.

"Yes, yes!" said Dexter as he saw it replayed on TV. "Yeah, brothers, right on! Black power, muthafuckas, black power. Take that shit!"

Dexter said screaming at the television. "Oops," he said as he covered his mouth, thinking his mother might have heard him.

It was a controversial moment in black history, and black America seemed torn between the old and the young. Some felt it was a symbol of violence and made blacks look bad. But most young people felt it was a symbol of black pride. Many older Negroes even felt that it was too "in their face" to accept the word black as the description of themselves, while many young blacks embraced it with expressions like "Black is beautiful."

The civil rights movement was in full swing, and black Americans throughout the nation were standing up and taking pride in themselves and in their history. The older Negroes were leading the charge with organized demonstrations, but the young people were the true energy and the strength of the movement, and Tommy and John were a symbol of that strength. They were the best athletes in the world, and they were black!

Dexter loved it when the holidays rolled around. It was a time when the entire family got together. Everyone visited Mary's house for a big dinner. Mary, Annie, and Cynthia would cook just about every traditional dish for the feast. Margaret usually took a break from cooking.

The table would be set with roasted turkey, roast beef, and ham. Cynthia made the best dressing, and she'd serve string beans and turnip greens, along with boiled potatoes and rice and gravy. Potato salad, macaroni salad, green salad, cranberry sauce, and yams, and sometimes even gumbo, topped off the meal.

Cakes, pies, and cobbler adorned the table behind the dining table, which seated eight. The children ate in the kitchen, while the adults ate in the dining room. Before anyone ate, however, everyone gathered around the table and BD would say grace. Once grace was said Annie would say her usual, "Rise, Peter, slay and eat."

It was Thanksgiving, and everyone was present—Annie, Mary and BD, along with Charles and Cynthia, and their daughter, Lady. Annie's sister, Aunt B, came over from Berkeley with her daughter, Wilda, who favored Mary. Wilda's child, Sonja, was also there. Margaret, Hank, and Dexter arrived a little late. Leon wouldn't attend.

Annie's older sister, Aunt Mine, was missed, having passed on a few years earlier. It was funny how all three elder sisters each dipped snuff. They'd picked up the habit in Arkansas during the late 1800s. The children hated when Aunt Mine used to kiss them, because her kisses were always wet from the snuff in her mouth. The three sisters used to sit around in rockers, with their empty Folgers coffee cans sitting on the floor, and spit.

Everyone sat around the tables, eating, and having a good time. There was some gospel music playing on the Magnavox stereo console in the living room. It was a joyful occasion.

Mary was the leader of the family. She was the glue that kept the family together, and her house was the central meeting place for the entire family. The three elder sisters had long ago passed the torch on to her.

Since Charles was an adult now, with his own family, he began to take on more of a leadership role. He was a strong young man, and he seemed a natural for it. Although BD was the eldest male in the family, he was a more passive man, and he didn't have the dominant characteristics to take on the lead. Charles was the next-oldest male behind BD, so it was fitting that he took on the role as the most dominant male. The only other males were Hank and Dexter. Leon didn't seem to count.

Although Dexter looked up to Charles as an older brother, Charles tried to be more of a father figure. In many situations, when Margaret or Mary was having problems with the boys, Charles would step in and try to get a handle on them, usually with a belt. But Hank and Dexter had put a stop to that a couple of months earlier.

Margaret and Leon had taken a trip out of town to Texas and left Hank and Dexter to themselves. Like most teenagers when their parents are away, they were having a good time. They didn't have any wild parties, but they did have their friends visit, and they stayed up late.

Charles called one evening and wanted to know why they were up so late. He also heard talking in the background and asked who was there. Hank told him that it was Dexter's friends, Mattock and Raul. Charles told Hank that everyone had to leave. Dexter overheard Hank telling Charles he wasn't his daddy, and they knew how to take care of themselves.

Upon hearing the way the conversation was going, Dexter grabbed the phone from Hank. He put the receiver up to his ear and said, "Hello," and right away, Charles told him that he was coming over with his belt, and that everyone needed to be gone when he got there, then he hung up the phone.

Dexter was seventeen years old and Hank was sixteen. When Dexter hung up the phone, he looked at the fellas and said, "I'm tired of him thinking he's my daddy and always thinking he can whip me. My momma don't even whip me no more."

Hank chimed in, "Yeah, he's always thinking he's our daddy and shit. I'm tired of it too, and I'm not taking it anymore."

So they sat around and plotted how they were going to handle Charles when he arrived. Mattock and Raul agreed to be a part of the plan.

In about twenty minutes, the doorbell rang and Dexter went and opened the front door. Standing at the gate was Charles. He didn't have a shirt on, and there was a leather belt looped over one shoulder.

"Open the gate," commanded Charles.

Dexter stepped into the entryway, reached over, and hit the buzzer to let him in.

Charles stepped into the house; Mattock was sitting at the bottom of the stairs, looking straight at him, and at the midway point up the stairs, where they turned, Raul was sitting, looking straight at him as well. Charles stepped around Mattock, started climbing the stairs, and then stepped around Raul. When he hit the curve in the stairs, he saw Hank standing at the top. Charles continued to the top of the stairs and stood by Hank in the hallway where he announced, "Mattock, Raul, you two have to leave."

Dexter tapped Mattock on the shoulder and motioned for him to follow him up the stairs. Mattock got up and followed Dexter and was followed by Raul. They got to the top of the stairs and surrounded Charles.

Dexter informed Charles, "They don't have to go nowhere. We're tired of you beating on us, and we're not having it anymore. We're too big for you to be beating on us."

Charles took a look at the four boys who had him surrounded. Mattock was itching to fight. He was short, stocky, strong, and solid, and it had been a little while since he'd had a good rumble. Raul, Hank, and Dexter all had the height advantage over Charles. They really didn't want to fight, but were prepared to. Charles was twenty-four at the time.

Charles made the right decision and decided to leave. He turned and descended the stairs and left the house. Hank celebrated and yelled out, "Yeah, go home, monkey." They all chuckled about how Charles had made the right decision before he got hurt.

Charles got into his car and drove home. Little did they know, Charles was more hurt than afraid! He felt he could have taken them all on, but the hurt overrode his anger. His little nephews had taken a stand against him. He hadn't cried in many years, but he cried as he drove his car home.

After eating the Thanksgiving dinner, Dexter went into the living room. Hank was still in the kitchen, sitting in the breakfast nook, eating. Wilda, Lady, Sonja, and Aunt B were also in the living room. Margaret had taken a seat in the kitchen where Mary and Cynthia were washing dishes. BD had gone downstairs to his television and Annie had gone to her bedroom and sat in her rocker.

Margaret was feeling very troubled about Hank and the way he was behaving by cutting classes in school. She voiced her concern to Mary, who began to question Hank just as Charles walked into the kitchen. Eventually, voices began to rise in the kitchen. Dexter was in the living room and could tell that an argument was stirring. He was feeling disappointed that a good evening was turning sour. He looked at Wilda, who shook her head disapprovingly.

Soon the talking turned to shouting. Dexter couldn't tell exactly what was being said, but he heard Hank clearly say the word bitch.

The next sound coming from the kitchen was the sound of rumbling and tumbling and furniture moving about. Hank and Charles were fighting in the kitchen. Dexter's first thought was to get up and go into the kitchen, but he decided to let them have it out. The next thing he knew, he saw Hank dart out the front door and run downstairs to the street. Charles followed in hot pursuit. That was when Dexter finally jumped up.

Mary came running down the hall, shouting to Dexter, "Dexter, you go and bring Charles back here, because Hank carries a knife, you know."

She was right! After Hank had come out of the closet and confessed he was gay, he began to carry a knife for protection because people sometimes harassed him, and he wasn't going to take any shit from anyone.

Dexter ran out the front door, skipping steps as he climbed down. When he reached the bottom of the stairs, he stepped out onto the sidewalk and looked around for Charles and Hank. He eventually saw Charles across the street; he was lying down on the sidewalk. Dexter darted across the street to where Charles lay, and saw there was blood on the ground. Charles was curled up in a fetal position.

"Charles, Charles, what happened?" he yelled.

"Hank stabbed me. Get an ambulance!" Charles yelled, in pain. He was hurt; he was hurt bad!

Dexter looked back across the street; Mary and Margaret were standing in front of the house in the dark. Mary was looking in his direction, trying to make out what was happening. He yelled to his grandmother, "Nanny, call an ambulance. Charles has been cut. I'm going after Hank."

Margaret cried out, "Oh no, Lord Jesus," and Mary ran into the house to call the ambulance.

Cynthia came outside and ran across the street to see about her husband. Dexter looked up the street and saw Hank running toward Third Street, just over a block away.

Dexter ran off after Hank. It was starting to rain. His heart was racing, and his emotions were in a turmoil. He wanted to cry but couldn't do that. He was scared for Hank, and even a little fearful for himself. He was worried about Charles too.

Hank was crying when Dexter caught up with him. Tears were flowing down his face, and mixing with the rain. He was holding the bloody knife in his hand, while apologizing for stabbing Charles. "I'm sorry, Dexter. I'm sorry. I didn't mean to cut him. I told him to leave me alone, but he wouldn't. Dexter, I'm sorry."

Dexter stared at Hank in disbelief. His mouth was trembling as he tired to speak. He reached out for the knife and said, "Hank, give me the knife."

Hank did as his brother requested and slowly handed Dexter the knife.

With his voice trembling Dexter said, "Hank, you have to come back."

"No, no, I can't go back there. I can't," he said, shaking and crying. It was cold and dark and the rain continued.

Dexter held out his hand and said, "Come on, Hank. I'll be with you. You have to come back. I can't let you go. You got to come back."

Dexter took hold of Hank's shirtsleeve and began to tug.

Hank pulled back; Dexter pulled a little harder. He kept on talking, "Come on, Hank, let's go. Let's go."

Hank stopped resisting and began to follow. He was tired and weak. Dexter held on tight and pulled him along. Hank kept crying loudly and apologizing for what he had done. Dexter was wiping his tears, but the rain was coming down across his face, so it really didn't matter.

They got to within a short distance from where Charles was lying. He saw Hank and tried to get up as though he was going to go after him, but Cynthia made him lie down. Soon, the ambulance came, and then the police arrived. The paramedics put Charles on a gurney and lifted him into the ambulance. Dexter spoke with the police after they'd sat Hank in the backseat of the patrol car. They wanted to know what had happened, and Dexter explained as best he could. Then they questioned Mary.

Dexter stood by the patrol car as the police conducted their investigation. Hank wanted Dexter to ride with him, and he said he would, but when the police finished up, they refused to let Dexter ride with his brother. Fear began to take hold of Hank, and he started to beg. Dexter felt helpless to help his brother. They told Dexter where they were taking Hank and said that he could come down to the station.

It was a tragic end to what was supposed to have been a joyous occasion. Several family members went to the hospital, and others went home. Dexter went to the jail.

Hank didn't spend much time in jail. They ruled that Hank had acted in self-defense, saying that it was Charles that had initiated the fight.

Charles was seriously hurt, but the doctors said he'd recover. They said if the cut had been over another half an inch, it could have killed him. The doctors said he was lucky, but it was God that stepped in and saved him.

Margaret contacted Duane. She told him that she was at an end and didn't know what to do with Hank and that he was uncontrollable. Duane came to San Francisco; it was the first time they'd seen him in almost five years. Dexter was seventeen, and the last time he'd seen his father was when he was twelve years old.

Dexter was bitter toward his father, but he still loved him. All his memories of him were good ones. He'd missed him a lot when he was a kid, but now he felt like a man and he understood things much better.

When Duane learned that Hank had proclaimed his sexuality, he was a little surprised, but he wasn't shocked. Duane knew quite a bit about psychology and sexuality and said he thought he understood what Hank was going through. He offered to take Hank with him to live in San Jose where he'd care for him. Margaret agreed with Duane because she didn't know what else to do. Hank packed his clothes and moved down the peninsula with Duane.

The holidays came and went, and things were not the same. There was no longer a sense of family unity. Margaret was at a loss about Hank, so she did what she always did in a time of need—she stayed close to God. She prayed, read the Bible, and sang. Dexter began to visit the church where his mother performed, and he began to spend more time with her. He also began to pray.

Margaret's diabetes was beginning to act up again; she had another insulin reaction and had to be hospitalized. While she was in the hospital, Leon was gone most of the time, so if he wasn't visiting his mother, Dexter was at the house alone.

It was 1969; it was a difficult time in America, and it was a difficult time in the Evans residence. Many things had taken place, and many changes had come about. More changes were in store.

While at home, Dexter got bored and his focus began to change. Girls now occupied his mind. A girl named Sherice, who transferred to Balboa from a junior high school, replaced Joy. But Dexter wasn't used to having a girlfriend in the same school, and eventually the relationship ended.

One evening, Dexter went downtown to shop and catch girls. He dressed in a lime-green, three-piece, 100 percent silk suit. It had narrow lapels, with a single button on the jacket. The vest was double-breasted with four buttons, two on each side. The lining was green satin, and it fit Dexter's tall slender body like he was born in it. The dress shirt he wore was the same green color as the suit, and he wore a white tie and white slip-on loafers. His Afro was freshly cut and he knew he was clean.

Dexter was depressed, although he didn't know it. The many things that had taken place were heavy on his mind. Margaret and Leon were constantly arguing. His mother was ill. All the issues with Hank were burdening him, as well as the pressures of school, dealing weed, going to work, singing in the group, and singing in the choir.

Other burdens were the world issues he'd become conscious of—the war in Vietnam and the civil rights movement. It was a lot for a teenager to be taking on. Instead of turning to the Lord, which is what he was taught to do, he turned to marijuana, beer, shopping, and girls.

While downtown, Dexter went to his favorite clothing stores to shop. He visited Howard's Clothier, The Brass Lantern, and Park Avenue. While at Park Avenue, he pulled a suit off the rack. It was a high quality, Italian, three-piece silk suit. It was gold in color, actually more like a burnt orange, with money-green, narrow, iridescent pinstripes that changed from a light to a dark green sheen, depending on how the light shone on it.

The lapels on the jacket were narrow without any break in the outline. It had only one button, square in shape, with rounded edges, and made of polished wood, which looked to be burl or redwood. The vest was double-breasted and had two buttons on each side that buttoned about four inches from each hip. "Wow, this is a bad suit. I got to have this one," Dexter said to himself as he went to try it on. The suit fit almost perfectly. It just needed a little tailoring, so he had to leave it to be chopped.

Dexter left the store and walked across the street to the Brass Lantern and purchased a suit that was a little more conservative. It was something he could wear to church. As he left the Brass Lantern, he walked down Market Street to Walgreen's where he purchased some candy for his mother in the candy section, and then left the store.

Once outside of Walgreen's, he walked to the curb to cross Market Street and stood waiting for the light to change. When the light changed, he stepped off the curb and proceeded to cross the street. Halfway across the street, his eyes met with a girl's eyes, and he stopped dead in his tracks. "Damn," he said under his breath, as the girl walked by. His head turned to follow her as she passed; she smiled a bright smile in his direction.

The light was changing and Dexter had to make a quick decision, so he turned in her direction and darted across the street then jumped up on the curb to avoid the traffic.

He approached the girl and said, "Hi, how you doing?"

"Fine, how are you?" she answered.

"I'm cool. I was hoping I could slow your pace down to a stop," he flirted.

"That's cool," she replied, as she looked him up and down. She was trying to size him up.

Dexter was clean from head to toe. He had one ring on his left hand and two on his right. She saw the gold watch with a row of diamonds around the rim and on the other wrist, a gold, chain-link charm bracelet. He was also wearing diamond cuff links, which sparkled just below his jacket sleeves. She was impressed, and he was coming at her strong.

At the same time, Dexter was sizing her up. First, he noticed she wore lots of makeup, even though she had a naturally pretty round face. Her hair was ratted, and she was wearing a fall to make it appear longer than it was. She wore a nice two-piece suit with a ruffled blouse, open to show her cleavage. The skirt was short and tight and was about midway above her knees. She was also wearing high-heeled shoes with nice sheer stockings. Her nails were manicured and polished.

"What's your name; where you from; where you going; how old are you?" Dexter asked all at once.

"Damn, are you going to let me answer those one at a time?" she asked.

"I'm listening," replied Dexter, as he looked at the girl she was with.

"This is my girlfriend, Mattie. We're just doing some shopping," she said.

"Nice to meet you," smiled Dexter. "So can I give you a call?"

"You don't even know my name yet," she said.

"I don't need to know your name to know I want to call you. What's your name?" Dexter countered.

"DeeDee," she answered.

"I'm Dexter, but you can call me Dex," he said, extending his hand. "So can I call you?"

"I live in Alameda," she responded.

"That's cool, I can come over there," Dexter replied.

"All right, you can give me a call," she said.

Dexter handed her his Parker pen, along with a small leather note pad he always kept. "What are you doing this weekend? Can you get out?" asked Dexter.

She told him that she could but to give her a call.

"All right, I'll give you a call," Dexter said as she turned to join her friend.

"Bye," she said, and she smiled and waved.

Dexter gave her a nod and said, "Later."

He watched her as she walked off. She was short and petite, with pretty brown skin. Her teeth were white and straight, and she showed a little gum when she smiled. She had a wide grin. As she walked off, he noticed that she had sexy bowlegs and they were nice and slender, but not skinny.

"Damn, she's fine!" Dexter said to himself. He was thinking that she was a little flashy, and almost looked like a ho. But he knew he was flashy too, and he thought that she'd look good on his arm. He liked that! She reminded him of Mary Wilson of the Supremes; they had the same look, even down to the hair. She was a redbone.

The next day, Raul came by and Dexter told him about DeeDee. Raul wanted to know if she had any friends. Dexter said yes, but he really didn't remember that much about her, only that her girlfriend had huge titties and was dark-skinned. "Shoot, that sounds cool to me. Call her up, set it up," said Raul, sounding excited.

Dexter called DeeDee, and she answered the phone. They chatted a little, and then Dexter asked her if her friend would like to meet his friend, Raul. Once he described Raul to her, she said that her girlfriend probably would. He asked her if she wanted to go to the drive-in to see a movie that weekend and bring her friend along. She agreed.

That Saturday night, Raul drove his car; it was a 1959 Oldsmobile. They drove over to Alameda, which was across the bay on the other side of Oakland. DeeDee lived in a housing project that was used by air force personnel, because her father was in the air force.

When Dexter and Raul arrived at her home, they both walked in to meet DeeDee's family—her mother, father, and brother. Dexter was very polite and charming. Her mother thought Dexter was a nice kid, but her father was suspicious. He took one look at Dexter and thought, "This boy is fast." He knew his daughter was fast too, and Dexter looked just like what DeeDee might like. He knew she was impressionable. He gave Dexter a firm and strong handshake and said, "Don't you keep my daughter out all night."

"Don't you worry, sir, I won't," responded Dexter.

The four of them walked outside, and DeeDee and Dexter introduced Raul to Mattie.

"Whew, man, I thought your daddy was going to cut me with those eyes," Dexter said to DeeDee.

"Oh, he's just trying to be Dad, that's all. Don't worry about him," she answered.

They all hopped into the car; Dexter and DeeDee got into the backseat, while Mattie got into the front seat and slid right beside Raul. Raul started up the car and drove through the Alameda tunnel and headed for Oakland. There was a drive-in theater in Oakland, not too far from where they were, so they decided to go there. It didn't matter what was playing, they'd watch whatever it was.

When DeeDee sat next to Dexter, he placed his arm around her. He wasted no time; he began to kiss her on her cheek, and she loved it. He started to squeeze her gently and rub her up and down her arms. She smelled really nice, and he told her he liked her perfume.

"You look good, baby," he said, looking into her eyes. She looked up at Dexter, gazing into his eyes, and Dexter moved in for the kiss. She parted her lips to receive Dexter, and they embraced with passion. Dexter continued to kiss her until they reached the drive-in.

Raul pulled into the drive-in, and Dexter paid the entrance fee for all of them. Once inside, Raul drove to the opposite side of the lot and took a space in the last row, backing up to a fence. Once they were parked, Raul got out of the car, went around to the trunk, and came back with a brown paper bag. Inside the bag were a couple of four-packs of Ripple. He handed everybody a bottle, and Dexter fired up the joint. They sat in the car, getting high on the weed and Ripple while talking through the movie. The girls said they were hungry, so Dexter and Raul went to buy some food.

As they walked to the concession stand, Dexter asked Raul, "So what do you think?"

Raul said, "Damn, she's got some big titties. I can't wait to suck on them suckers."

Dexter started to laugh, "Yeah, she got some huge ones all right. I bet they're nice, too."

"Shit, I'm going to find out, that's for sure," answered Raul as he slapped five with Dexter.

Dexter and Raul pimp-walked on the way to the concession stand. They were buzzing and felt like boss players. They knew they had two fine young ladies back in the car, so they were on top of the world.

"Damn, I'm gonna do my best to get me some tonight. I've got to pull out all the stops on this one. She's fine as hell. I can't wait!" Dexter blurted.

Back in the car, the ladies' conversation was similar to the fellas'.

DeeDee asked Mattie what she thought about Raul.

Mattie answered her, saying, "Girl, you know, he's about 6' 3". I grabbed me a handful when we were busting slob and, ump, girl, there ain't nothing short about him."

"Ohhhh, I know that's right," replied DeeDee.

DeeDee began to talk about Dexter, "Well, Dexter is so fine, and he's so clean. It's just something about those San Francisco niggas that is so different from these squares around here."

Mattie responded, saying, "Girl, I know what you mean. But you better watch that man. He's dangerous. He looks like a heartbreaker to me. He's too sharp and he's too slick for the average girl. You can see how smooth he is. He's not like Raul, who's not quite so smooth."

DeeDee thought about what she was saying, "I know what you mean, girl. Did you check out the clothes that he wears? And he seems like he has money too."

Mattie heard her girlfriend and gave her another word of caution, "That's what I mean, girl, it's too good."

Raul and Dexter returned to the car with the concessions, and they all ate and then drank some more Ripple. They were all nice and buzzed, so the mood was set. Raul turned on the radio and the Dells were singing "Oh, What a Night." Raul started singing along with the radio, and then Dexter chimed in. The girls sat back, listening, and realized that the young men sounded pretty good. This added flame to the fire.

Dexter leaned over to DeeDee and kissed her, and she moved to lay back. Raul and Mattie did the same in the front seat. Dexter's hands began to explore DeeDee. Her breathing became deep and passionate, and she began to rub Dexter on his chest. Raul was in the front seat on top of Mattie, and she was moaning. The sounds of kisses and moans of excitement filled the cabin of the car, and soon the windows began to fog.

Dexter's skilled hand unbuttoned DeeDee's blouse and exposed her beautiful breasts. She was a petite girl with a full 34 C-cup. Once he had her blouse open and her breasts exposed, he paused and moved back to have a good look. He looked her in the eyes and gently caressed one breast in his hand. She moaned and responded to his touch.

As he caressed her, he said, "Ohhhh, you have the most beautiful breasts. Your body is nice and sexy."

She liked the way he was talking to her. It made her feel so feminine. Dexter began to give her breast the attention she wanted.

DeeDee moaned and called his name, "Oh, Dexter."

Hearing her speak his name made him excited, and he was so aroused he felt like he was about to explode with fire.

Dexter lifted up her skirt and rubbed her pussy through her hose. He reached around to pull down the hose, but she stopped him so she could do it herself. She didn't want to snag them and go home with a run. After taking off the stockings, she left the panties for him to remove. Dexter slid his hand into the front of her panties and began to rub. She was wet and ready. She breathed deep with excitement in anticipation of what was to come. She then reached down and began to rub Dexter on his crotch.

Dexter sat up and pulled off his slacks and underpants. He moved into position to mount her, then paused and opened his shirt to expose his chest. Dexter gently climbed on top of her and she opened her legs to receive him. She took her hand and guided him in. She was so wet that he slid in effortlessly.

Slowly he began to pump and grind. Raul and Mattie were in the front seat, also in full swing. DeeDee was wet and very warm to Dexter. He'd never been inside a woman who was so warm. He kept pumping and grinding, and she was taking all he had.

She pulled him close and kissed him feverishly. "Give it to me, Dexter. I want it. I want it all," she spoke softly.

Dexter responded by saying, "Oh, baby, you are so sexy. You are so fine. I love it, girl. I want it. Let me have it, baby, let me have it all. Oh, you so fine."

Dexter's words made her even hotter. She began to move more rapidly and cling to his manhood. Her muscles pulled on his member, trying to drain him of all he had. Suddenly, Dexter began to feel something he'd never felt before. The more he pumped, the more the feeling came. It felt like he needed to go to the bathroom, but he knew he didn't. He felt like he wanted to stop and pull out of her, but DeeDee felt his penis become strong and stiffen and begin to throb. She increased the rhythm and pulled him ever so tight. She was hot and on fire. Dexter sensed her desire and joined her in intensity. They went harder and stronger, and they felt as one. The feeling took over his body, and he lost control and began to shake. His penis exploded deep inside of DeeDee.

"Yes, baby, yes. Give it to me, sweetheart. I want it, I want it all, Dexter," she said as she gripped him tight and wiggled around to take all he had to give. They both went limp, and Dexter lay on top of her, catching his breath.

As Dexter lay on top of her, he kissed her and smiled and gently stroked her face with the back of a finger, admiring her beauty. He knew from that moment that she was going to be his girl. When he finally got up, his midsection was soaked. He moved to put on his shorts and pants, but DeeDee stopped him. She took some tissue out of her purse and handed him some, then cleaned herself up and got dressed.

Raul and Mattie were lying in the front seat, fast asleep. DeeDee lay back in Dexter's arms, and they kicked back and watched the movie. Once the movies ended, Dexter and Raul drove the ladies home and headed back across the bay. Although Dexter had had sex on several occasions prior to DeeDee, he'd never experienced an orgasm. It was the first time he experienced one; now he knew he was a man.

DeeDee replaced Sherice as his girlfriend. Actually, Sherice quit Dexter as a payback for some dirt he'd done with another girl. The breakup hurt his feelings, but he knew he deserved it, and he quickly got over it with the help of DeeDee.

Soon Dexter let Milvia go too; Joy was already out of the picture. All the remaining females he was close to were just friends he flirted or talked on the phone with. It was just he and DeeDee—at least for the moment!

One day, there was a shooting not far from the school. The young people involved were not from Balboa. It happened in the middle of the day, about a block from Bal at the Tick Tock hamburger drive-in on Ocean Avenue. News of the shooting shook up the school.

Apparently, a group of young black men had gotten into a confrontation with some young white men. An Italian teen from Excelsior had been shot and killed, and it set up a chain reaction. The Italian youth at Balboa wanted revenge, and they banded together to voice their outrage to the blacks in school.

Things were beginning to get out of hand, and soon other whites joined with the Italians and were ready to fight. The Mexicans were divided right down the middle, with half for the whites and half for the blacks. The Samoans joined sides with the blacks, and the Asians stayed out of it.

The two sides faced off across the street from each other, screaming and hollering back and forth. When the violence looked like it was about to erupt, several members of the faculty came outside and took control of the situation. The Italians vowed retaliation, and shouted that it wasn't over. To the blacks, it didn't matter; they had them outnumbered.

That Saturday night, there was a dance, and the show was taking place in the auditorium at Woodrow Wilson High School. Cary's brother, Jonnie, and his group, the Marcels, were going to perform along with the Whispers and several other groups. Dexter and Mattock decided they were going to go.

DeeDee heard about the show and asked if she could attend, so Dexter invited her along. Since Dexter wasn't able to get a car that weekend, DeeDee would have to catch the bus to the East Bay Terminal in downtown San Francisco, where Dexter would meet her, and they'd catch the bus together out to Woodrow.

Although Dexter was very fond of DeeDee, he'd grown frustrated by her tardiness. She was always late, and sometimes he'd have to wait for her in the terminal for over an hour. Part of the frustration was that her house was the last stop before the bus hit the bridge, and from her house, the next bus stop was the terminal. Also, the bus ran about every fifteen or twenty minutes, so there was no logical excuse for her to be so late when planning in advance.

DeeDee's problem was that it took forever to get herself ready, to look the way she did. Because she wore a fall, she needed time to get her hair together. She applied makeup like a model, which took a long time, and she wore the best clothes. DeeDee always waited until the last minute to get started. Dexter cared for her quite a bit, but this tardiness was draining their relationship, and his patience was wearing thin. He was too busy a man to be sitting around in the terminal waiting for an hour or more. She was cutting into his time and his money.

Mattock was hard on his women, and he felt Dexter was soft. They both were reading Iceberg Slim's book, Pimp, and Mattock's head was full of the game. He often beat his girlfriend, Ellie, as a form of keeping her in line; Dexter never understood why she stayed with him.

Sometimes Dexter questioned Mattock as to why he was always slapping his girlfriend around, and Mattock's response was, "To keep her ass in line. Plus, she really likes it. She knows that I love her, and she likes to be slapped around a little."

Dexter thought it was a strange relationship. He told Mattock, "You've been reading too much of The Story of O and Pimp."

Mattock and Dexter had both read The Story of O, a book about total male domination over a woman. They had read it as a homework assignment.

The last time Dexter had spoken to DeeDee, he'd made it a point to emphasize that it was important for her to be on time, especially this time! He even went so far as to tell her to never ever be late again, but just as she had been before, DeeDee was late!

Mattock and Dexter hung around the terminal, waiting for DeeDee and Mattie to arrive. Mattie was coming because she was hoping to see Raul, but he'd cut her off and moved on. She didn't catch him on this trip; he was nowhere to be found. No one was aware that she was expecting his baby; not even DeeDee was aware of this.

After a half an hour passed, Mattock started in on Dexter, saying, "Man, if she was my bitch, I'd beat her ass. She'd never be late again."

Dexter dismissed it.

One bus arrived, and then another, and still no DeeDee. Then an hour had passed; three more buses arrived, and still no DeeDee.

"Damn, the bus stops right in front of her house, and it's the last stop before getting on the bridge, and then it comes straight here. She should be here," Dexter complained.

Mattock started in again. He was in Dexter's ear. "Man, you ain't supposed to take this kind of shit from no bitch! If I was you, I'd slap the shit out of her."

Dexter was getting angrier by the minute, and Mattock wasn't helping the situation any.

After an hour and a half and about seven buses later, a bus pulled up, and Dexter could see DeeDee and Mattie on the bus. Mattock egged Dexter on. "You need to slap that bitch silly. She'll respect you for it. I'm telling you the truth."

Dexter was highly pissed. He'd been waiting an hour and a half, and they still had a long way to go to the show by bus. He was steaming. When DeeDee stepped off of the bus, she could see the anger on Dexter's face. She made the mistake of smiling as though it was funny.

"Come on," Dexter snapped at DeeDee as he turned and walked away.

Mattock was in front of Dexter as they walked down the ramp to a second ramp to get to the street level. Dexter made the turn to go down to the second level; he was steaming.

Mattock looked back at him and whispered, "Go on, man, do it."

Dexter turned around; DeeDee was walking about two steps behind. He raised his hand high, then slapped her across the cheek with a backhand. The blow knocked her back, and as she reached for the railing, she missed it and fell to the ground. The motion of her fall caused her legs to fly up into the air, exposing her undergarments. When she came to a stop, her fall had moved out of position and was crooked on the top of her head.

She grabbed her cheek and began to cry.

"Didn't I tell your ass not to be late again? Didn't I?" Dexter hollered at her.

Mattie stepped back and got out of the way.

DeeDee was still on the ground, crying.

"Get your ass up and go into the bathroom and fix yourself up. And stop that goddamn crying. I mean don't take all fucking day, either!" he yelled.

Mattock was standing behind Dexter, cheering. "Yeah, yeah. That's what I'm talking about. Don't take that shit from no bitch."

Dexter could hear Mattock in the background. "Shut up, Mattock," Dexter snapped.

"What? What did I do?" replied Mattock.

Mattie helped DeeDee up off the ground and they went into the ladies' bathroom to get her straightened up. Dexter felt bad about what he'd done. He didn't like it at all. But he was still mad nonetheless. Dexter also knew that he'd never have done that if it hadn't been for Mattock egging him on. It was out of his character; he was a lover, not a fighter.

When DeeDee came out, she had fixed her hair, freshened up her makeup, and stopped crying. She wasn't smiling either.

"You walk three steps behind me. Let's go!" Dexter instructed, and they left the terminal. Mattock and Dexter led the way, and DeeDee and Mattie walked three steps back.

When the bus pulled up, Dexter stood back and let DeeDee and Mattie get on first. When he got on the bus, he sternly told DeeDee, "Sit your ass down right there, and I don't want to hear shit."

Mattock loved every minute of it. Mattock and Dexter sat together and talked men's talk while Dexter had DeeDee and Mattie sit behind them in the next row. They were on the 14 Mission Street line and got off at Silver Avenue to transfer to the 51 line, which would take them to Woodrow Wilson High School.

When they transferred to the 51, Dexter sat next to DeeDee.

He then apologized for striking her. "Baby, I don't want to be slapping on you like that. You know I love you, but you've got to respect what I say and what I want. When I say don't be late, I mean don't be late. You understand what I mean?" asked Dexter.

"Yes, baby, I understand. I won't be late again, I promise," she answered.

Dexter said, "All right, baby, that's cool. Now give me a kiss."

She reached over and gave Dexter a kiss on the lips. He then scanned her face to see if she was all right. She was okay, and there was no sign of a slap.

"You have some money, baby?" Dexter asked.

This caught DeeDee by surprise. He had never asked her for money before, and he always had money.

"Yes, why?" she asked.

"How much you got?" asked Dexter, without answering her.

She opened her purse and found that she had fifty dollars.

"Give it to me," Dexter ordered.

"How much you want?" she asked.

"All of it; give it to me," Dexter said again.

DeeDee gave him all of her money. He took the money and put it in his pocket. At the end of the night he gave it back to her. Dexter was just testing her to see if she'd do it, and she had. When he gave her the money back, he again apologized for striking her. He had given things some thought and realized that it wasn't just her that had angered him. It was the accumulation of everything that was taking place in his life, and he'd taken it out on her. He promised her that he'd never strike her again, and he never did. He also never asked her for money again.

Soon they arrived at the show; they'd only missed the first act. There was a group on stage called the Performers, who were from the Sunnydale Projects. Dexter knew one member of the group. They had a hit recording currently being played on local radio, named "I Can't Stop You." The performance was good and the crowd enjoyed them.

The next act to come to the stage was Jonnie's group, the Marcels. They danced out onto the stage, and the girls in the audience went wild. They sang their medley of the Intruders' hits, with Ray out in front, wooing the crowd. Next they performed a James Brown hit, and this time Jonnie was out front, screaming like the Godfather of Soul.

The final act to perform was the Whispers, and they were two cuts above all the rest. They were professionals. They were dressed in tuxes, and their steps were smooth like silk. One of the twins, who was a lead singer for the group, was missing; he was serving his country in the war.

After the show, Dexter and Mattock went backstage, and DeeDee and Mattie tagged along. Dexter's reason for going backstage was to connect with Jonnie and the rest of the group, and congratulate them on their performance. Once they all got together backstage, Jonnie decided to take the bus along with them because he didn't have a car, either.

When they were about to leave, Robert, who was the bass and baritone of the group, decided to join them as well, as did one of the members of the Performers. Robert also had a lady friend with him, who came along too. But the main reason everyone really wanted to come along was they knew Dexter had the weed.

So they all left the auditorium and headed out. Altogether it was Jonnie, Dexter and DeeDee, Mattock and Mattie, one of the Performers, and Robert and his lady friend. There were seven in all.

While waiting for the 51 bus to arrive, the group milled about the bus stop, singing and smoking weed. After catching the 51, the bus soon arrived at Silver and Mission, where the group departed to transfer to a Mission Street bus. They still had to head downtown and drop off the ladies at the East Bay Terminal.

When they got off the bus, they walked across the street and stood at the bus stop on Mission, waiting for the next bus. While waiting there, something suddenly dawned on Dexter. He thought to himself, "Hey, we're in the Excelsior District, and we're a bunch of niggas in the

Italians' territory, and they're pissed because of the shooting yesterday." So he figured he'd better keep an eye out.

DeeDee stood next to Dexter, trying to stay warm. Dexter scanned the streets and watched every car as it passed by. The rest of the group was not paying much attention; they were singing, and they were stoned. A car rolled by slowly, and Dexter noticed there were about eight white boys piled into the car. It was being closely followed by another car with about six boys inside. He overheard someone in the car say, "There go some niggers!"

Dexter didn't panic, but he watched as the cars turned the corner on Silver Avenue. He then looked to see that the 14 Mission Street bus was fast approaching.

"Hey fellas, we got trouble," Dexter said, as he pointed down the street toward the corner.

The group looked to see a mob of about fourteen white boys, walking around the corner and heading toward them. Just then, the bus pulled up right in front of Dexter and stopped. The driver was a white man who opened the door, then looked up and saw the mob coming around the corner. Someone from the mob yelled, "You niggers get on that bus, we going to kill your asses!"

The door was about six feet away from where Dexter was standing at the curb. The driver reached over to pull the lever and close the door. Dexter leaped into the air as hard and as fast as he could, just making it between the doors while they were about six inches apart, and forced the doors back open. "Get on the bus, get on the bus!" he yelled, and everyone in his group piled onto the bus.

The light was red so the driver sat at the bus stop, leaving the doors open. The white boys were trying to climb on. They had clubs and chains and a couple had knives. Jonnie, Robert, and Mattock were fighting them off to keep the mob from boarding. The girls ran to the back of the bus, and sat on the opposite side holding onto each other tight.

Dexter pulled the other guy in his own group to stand close to him next to the driver. "Look, if you don't close those doors, we're going get you before they get us," Dexter warned the driver.

The guy standing with Dexter backed up the claim, "Yeah, we gonna fuck you up."

The driver then quickly reached over and pulled the handle to close the doors. As they closed, the fellas kicked the arms and legs of the mob back off of the bus. The mob began to surround the bus, yelling and cursing at the group inside. Dexter looked out the windows at the mob and saw some familiar faces. These were guys he always got along with in school. One of them was even a member of the Latino family he was a part of.

The kid who'd stood with him by the driver was walking through the bus, antagonizing the mob by pointing at them and saying, "Yeah, I know you. Yeah, I'll see your ass again at school."

Next, someone from the mob slapped a chain across the window and it cracked. Just then, they noticed two old white ladies, midway to the back of the bus, sitting on the opposite side; they started screaming.

The bus was still standing at the bus stop and the light had turned from red to green to red again. The bus driver was stalling; he wanted the mob to get them. Jonnie and Dexter went back to the driver and told him to move.

The driver said, "It's a red light."

"If you don't run that red light right now, we're gonna whip your ass!" Dexter threatened.

The driver took his foot off the brake, slammed on the gas, and ran the red light.

Dexter stepped away from the driver and took a seat. He mumbled, "Thank you, Lord," under his breath.

Everybody took a seat, and the driver continued with his route as if nothing had happened. After about three stops, Robert noticed that his girlfriend was not on the bus. "I got to go. I got to go back and get my girl. She didn't get on the bus," exclaimed Robert.

"Man if you get off this bus and go back there, you're a dead man. She ran the other way, man. I'm sure she's okay. They're not going to mess with a woman!" said Jonnie. It sounded convincing.

"I got to go back. I'm sorry, I'm getting off," said Robert.

He got off at the next stop, only to find that she was on the bus behind them. The bus driver continued his route, and they rode the bus all the way downtown.

Dexter saw DeeDee onto her bus, and then the group traveled back to Lakeview. The police never came, and as far as they knew, there was no report.

To Dexter, it had been a terrifying experience; they were outnumbered and had no weapons. It could have been a disaster. But by the time they were back in school, everyone had calmed down and went about their business as though nothing had happened.

20

Busted

Down on the peninsula, Hank was adjusting to a different way of life. Duane had started a new family, and he and his girlfriend had a son. They were also raising a daughter she'd had prior to knowing Duane. Hank was accepted warmly into their home, and he was doing well, away from the influences of the big city and his friends. For the first time in a long time, he wasn't gay and he wasn't straight; he was just Hank. He was happy and enjoying himself. Duane wasn't working, as usual, so he was always at home with Hank.

Hank did miss his mother and brother, but he realized that this was a much-needed break, so he welcomed it. Margaret still worried about her baby boy. Duane had never really represented stability to her, so it did raise some concern. But she knew that Duane was wise and very intelligent, levelheaded, and reasonable. He could communicate very well, which was what Hank needed. Hank needed someone to talk to who'd listen to his thoughts and feelings. So his real father was there for him, and it was refreshing.

Margaret was still under stress, even with Hank away for a while. She and Leon continued to have differences. Leon wanted to be sexual with her, and she didn't share the feeling. He also wanted to get back to fishing and hunting, which would take him away from the house for two to three days at a time. But Margaret wasn't going to allow Leon to go away for very long. Even though Dexter was home and was always there for his mother when she needed him, she preferred the luxury of riding in a car to wherever she needed to go. Dexter had to transport her on the bus, so they'd take much longer to go to-and-fro.

Leon constantly had to take Margaret shopping, to visit the doctor, pay bills, or run errands, and many times he also had to cook. These were all the things Dexter and Hank used to do. But Dexter still had the main responsibility of keeping the house clean and the yards groomed.

Dexter was feeling stressed from the tensions at home, and occasionally he skipped a class or two. Sometimes he called in sick to his job too. He'd have DeeDee cut school and he'd go over to her house while her parents were out, and they'd lie in bed, having sex. Other times he traveled to other high schools and visited girls that he knew on the other campuses. Sometimes he'd just hang out with Cary, Mattock, and Morrell. Many times they just rode the bus around the city or traveled downtown or visited Fisherman's Wharf.

Dexter called DeeDee one evening and asked her to play sick and stay home from school the next day; she agreed. The next morning Dexter rode the trolley downtown and then took the bus to Alameda. When he arrived at DeeDee's house, she was in her pajamas and she greeted him with a kiss.

Although Dexter flirted around and played the field, he really did care for DeeDee. She was his main squeeze. DeeDee was infatuated with Dexter and would do just about anything he asked of her.

At DeeDee's request, Dexter had begun to use condoms. He didn't like them, but he used them anyway, to satisfy her. Once the two of them became comfortable, they made love. It was a long and passionate session, and afterward they needed to rest, so they napped.

While lying in bed, DeeDee heard a noise, which startled them. Someone was trying to open the front door. DeeDee jumped up, to see who it was; Dexter jumped up and reached for his underwear and pants.

Just as Dexter was pulling his pants up, DeeDee's younger brother walked into the bedroom and saw him.

"Uh huh, I knew something was up when you weren't at school today. I'm telling Momma," he said.

"Ah man, you ain't got to be telling nobody. Why you want to tell on your sister like that?" asked Dexter.

DeeDee's brother answered, "'Cause she should be in school instead of running around after you. She's way too young to be sleeping with anybody, anyway."

"Ah, you just a little punk. A sorry-ass little punk," said Dexter. "Just because you ain't got no girlfriend, you gotta be a little tattletale on your big sister," Dexter continued as he got dressed. Once dressed, Dexter kissed DeeDee good-bye and then left.

On his way home, Dexter thought about what happened and wished that he would have bribed DeeDee's brother with some money, but it was too late.

That evening, after dinner, Dexter was in the bathtub taking a bubble bath, when he heard the phone ring.

Margaret answered the phone, "Hello? Oh yes, hi, this is Dexter's mother."

Dexter sat in the tub and listened to his mother's side of the phone call.

"What?" Margaret said, sounding as though she were shocked.

"Damn!" Dexter said in a low voice from the tub. He knew what the call was about.

DeeDee's mother was on the phone, informing Margaret of her son's activity with her daughter.

"Well, I want to thank you for calling. I'm going to have a serious talk with Dexter. I didn't raise him to be like that, and he knows better. I appreciate your calling. And thank you again," Margaret finished up the conversation and hung up the receiver.

"Dexter, you hurry up in that tub and come in to see me," Margaret yelled out from her bedroom.

"Yes, Baba," he answered. Dexter got out of the tub and put on some pajama bottoms, then walked into his mother's bedroom, "Yes, Baba?"

Margaret let him have it. She talked about how it was a sin to have sex before being married. She talked about how girls and boys should act. She also said that good girls don't allow boys to do those kinds of things to them, and she questioned his choice in girlfriends.

It was a conversation that was a little too late. But Dexter was always respectful and courteous when his mother chastised him. He didn't talk back; he was patient and listened. She had him sit in the chair next to her bed and open his Bible. "Turn to Exodus 20:14 and read it for me."

Dexter began to read, "'Thou shalt not commit adultery.'" Margaret had Dexter assure her that he knew exactly what that meant.

She continued with another passage for him. "Now turn to Revelations 2:22 and read it to me."

Dexter fidgeted around in his seat and began to read, "'Behold, I will cast her into a bed. And them that commit adultery with her into great tribulation, except they repent of their deeds.'"

"Now, first you need to acknowledge that this is a sin. Next, you must acknowledge that you have sinned. Finally, you need to ask for forgiveness. Can you do that?" Margaret was trying to get him to recognize what his behavior meant.

"Yes, ma'am," Dexter answered, itching to leave the room.

"All right, you can go to your room and do what you need to do. You're on punishment for a week."

Dexter left her room and walked down the hallway to his bedroom and said a quick, "Sorry, Lord," then turned on the TV. It didn't take long for him to get back to his sins.

Eventually the Army Corps of Engineers released Dexter. He called in sick one time too many. He was really disappointed in himself; he knew it was a good job and that he'd blown it. They'd been grooming him for a possible career, but now it was almost certain his career would be going in a different direction. He didn't know which direction he was going to go, but he wasn't going to ponder over it for long. He still had his hustles.

One day when he should have been in class, he was walking off campus with Cary and Morrell. A car with three white men inside pulled up to the curb next to them. It was the assistant dean, Mr. Murphy. He got out of the car and stepped in front of the three boys and held out one hand, "Hold up, boys." Dexter became nervous because the two white men in the car looked like undercover police officers, and the car they were riding in looked like an unmarked police car. He had a baggie full of joints and a couple of lids in his pocket.

Mr. Murphy approached Dexter, "Dexter, you go directly to my office and wait for me. I'll be there shortly."

With a sigh of relief, he replied, "Yes sir."

Mr. Murphy approached Cary and Morrell, "You two either get to your classes or leave the vicinity." He then turned away, got back into the car, and they drove off.

The boys stood and watched the car as it pulled off. They were all relieved that it wasn't any more serious than it was. Dexter looked at his friends and wiped his forehead. "Damn, that scared the shit out of me. "I'll check ya later," he said as he ran off to the dean's office.

Dexter was surprised that Mr. Murphy knew his name. They'd never had an encounter before, or even a conversation. Even though Dexter was a pretty flamboyant individual, he kept a low profile and usually avoided trouble and the troublemakers. Plus, he was always polite. He never had a bad attitude with the teachers, students, or staff.

"How did he know my name?" Dexter thought. "I got to put my stash somewhere. I have to hide it where no one will find it." He looked for a place then stowed it in some bushes near the school.

Dexter hurried to the dean's office, where the secretary told him to have a seat in the hall and wait. As Dexter sat outside the dean's office in the hallway, students walked by and stared. They knew, seeing him sitting in that seat, he must have gotten into some sort of trouble. Dexter was feeling very uncomfortable because he'd never been in that seat before, and it took until his senior year for it to happen.

When Mr. Murphy arrived, he called Dexter into his office and told him to have a seat in front of his large desk. Dexter took a seat and glanced around the room at the pictures and plaques on the desk and walls.

Murphy opened a bottom drawer in his desk and pulled out a folder; it was Dexter's file. He put the file in front of him and opened it up. He grabbed a few documents, glanced over them, then looked at Dexter, "Dexter, you have a good file, with good grades. Your teachers like you, and you've even held down a good job. You're supposed to graduate in four months, but now you decide to start cutting school."

Dexter was sitting erect in his chair; he dropped his head. He couldn't look the man in his eye, and he was feeling humiliated.

Mr. Murphy continued, "If you don't get your act together, you will not graduate, and I'll make sure you don't! How would you like that?"

Dexter raised his head and looked Mr. Murphy in the eye, "I wouldn't like that, sir."

"I don't think that you would. Do you feel that you can keep from cutting school?"

It was sounding like maybe he was going to get another chance, so he perked up, "Yes sir."

Mr. Murphy wanted another confirmation "Are you sure?"

"Yes sir, I'm sure," Dexter answered confidently.

The dean looked over Dexter's file again, and then looked up at Dexter. "Okay, I'm going to give you a chance. You leave my office, and I don't want to see you back here again." He motioned for Dexter to leave.

"Thank you, sir; I appreciate this, sir," Dexter was glowing.

Dexter left Murphy's office and breathed a sigh of relief. He was glad it had turned out the way it did, and he was ready to get back on track. He looked up toward the ceiling and said, "Thank you, Lord. Thank you, Jesus." He knew again that God and his guardian angel were watching over him, trying to keep him on the right path.

He straightened up his act and got back into class. One of his favorite classes was English because the teacher, Mr. Brasso, was so cool. Occasionally, he had given Dexter passes when he'd cut a class.

Mr. Brasso was an intelligent teacher who knew how to relate to kids. In order to get them to read, he let them read books that would be of interest to them, no matter what the subject matter. He could sum up a kid, determining what they might like, and then make a book recommendation.

The first book he recommended to Mattock and Dexter that they completed reading was Pimp, written by Iceberg Slim. He'd made the recommendation based on how the boys dressed, talked, and carried themselves. They both got deep into reading the book and would call each other to discuss it. They completed the book in about two weeks and prepared a book report together. Both of them received a grade of A+.

Mr. Brasso's class was the only class where the teacher allowed them to swear. He had only one requirement, and that was not to call each other names. All the students in his class had to respect each other.

Their new assignment was to read The Autobiography of Malcolm X by Alex Haley and to prepare a book report. Dexter became enthralled with the book. The struggle of the black man in modern-day America was at an all-time high, and the words of a man as powerful as Malcolm X were all-inspiring to many young black men. Dexter was no exception. He buried himself in the book and identified with the experience of the life that Malcolm had lived. Mattock identified more with Iceberg Slim.

The news reported that Eldridge Cleaver had fled the States some months back, and the Black Panthers were under constant attack across the nation. J. Edgar Hoover had named the group as the most dangerous threat to society, and it seemed as though Black Panther members were being killed or incarcerated on a daily basis.

Current events were discussed regularly in Mr. Brasso's class, and Dexter always had input in the discussions. He had developed a habit of reading the newspapers almost daily when he'd had his paper route, and continued the habit after he discontinued the job.

Dexter also developed a habit of watching the news on television. These things, as well as reading The BPP Newspaper, The Berkeley Barb, Ebony, and Jet magazines, are what kept him informed and satisfied his desire to know and understand what was taking place with regard to blacks in the American society. Mr. Brasso recognized this awareness in Dexter and he tried to take an interest in his need to know, and his need for answers. He was good at getting young teenage black male students to read.

Dexter's next assignment was to read Manchild in the Promised Land. It was another book about a young black man who had to hustle and struggled to survive in the inner city. He was able to rise above the life of crime and the temptations of the life of a hustler and become a productive member of society.

Dexter read his books and sometimes lay back in his bed, thinking about his future. He wanted to be an architect, but he'd lost his drafting job. He wanted to go to college, but didn't know the first thing about how to go about it. His mother was educated and had graduated from college. She had mentioned on more than one occasion that she wanted him to go. But what was the plan? There wasn't one, and no one was giving him any direction—no relatives, no counselors, no friends, no one. This was a problem that plagued many young black males with potential in the inner city. So how would he rise above the streets that were calling him?

One day, Margaret awoke from a deep sleep and wasn't feeling well. Dexter was away at school, and Leon hadn't yet come in from work. She was feeling groggy and felt that she was having an insulin reaction, so she got up to get some orange juice and sugar. After Margaret drank her orange juice and sugar, she decided she wanted to read her Bibles and proceeded to go downstairs to get a few books. When she turned the corner in the hallway to make her way to the stairs, she misjudged her first step. Her foot slipped out from under her, and she hadn't yet found the banister.

Margaret began to fall. She reached out, but to no avail; there was nothing to hold onto. The steps were steep, and they turned in the middle of the flight halfway down. As she tumbled, her left arm, just below the elbow, hit the corner of the wall. The pain sent shockwaves up her arm.

When she stopped tumbling, she moaned, trying to gather herself together. "Lord, help me, Lord Jesus," she said as she tried to get up. She was unable to use her left arm, but since she was right handed, she was able to maneuver her way back up the stairs to her bedroom, where she got into bed. Soon after Margaret's fall, Leon came home and found her in bed complaining about the pain in her arm. She explained what had happened, and Leon took her to the hospital.

Margaret had fractured her left arm below the elbow. The doctor applied a small cast that covered her entire forearm and informed her that she'd have to wear the cast for approximately six weeks. This meant that she wouldn't be able to play the piano, which also meant she wouldn't be able to work or perform.

On the way home from the hospital, Margaret noticed that Leon smelled of alcohol and voiced her displeasure.

Leon was tired and didn't want to hear it, "You always got something to say."

Margaret dismissed his comment, "Well, it certainly is too early in the day to be drinking. Lord knows you don't need to be drinking this early."

Leon became angry. He had worked late into the morning and was ready to get some rest, "Look, woman, leave me alone. I'm a grown man, and I don't be trying to tell you how to handle your business."

Margaret was also tired and didn't want to argue, so she let things be. Plus, she was still not feeling 100 percent because of the insulin reaction she'd had earlier in the day.

A couple of weeks later, Dexter awoke early, so he got up, took a shower, and then dressed for school. It was going to be a sunny but brisk day, so he decided to wear a V-neck sweater, a button-down-collar dress shirt, and some slacks. After checking on his mother, he fixed the two of them some breakfast and cleaned up the kitchen. He then got his books together and stood at the kitchen window, watching for the 26 Valencia bus to cross Brotherhood Way down the road.

When Dexter saw the bus cross the overpass, he quickly kissed his mother good-bye and dashed down the stairs and out of the house. He made a quick run and jaywalked, crossing the dangerous five-way intersection. He got to the bus stop just in time to board the bus that would take him to within two blocks of Bal. Dexter got off at Ocean Avenue and proceeded to walk to school.

The morning started off well, with the usual routine of hooking up with his buddies and peddling a little weed. He got rid of a couple of lids, two matchboxes, and several joints. Since he'd lost his job, he'd begun to sell joints again. He made forty-five dollars, which wasn't bad to start out the day.

It was still a little early, so he walked to the courtyard and joined in a card game of Tonk, at twenty-five cents a hand. He lost about a dollar before the bell rang. He headed off for class.

Leon came in from work at about 9:00 that morning. He unloaded all his belongings in the garage and laid his jacket over the side of his fishing boat. He headed upstairs and took a peek into his bedroom to see that Margaret was asleep. Leon then went into the kitchen and fried some oysters for breakfast, along with some rice and eggs. After eating, he went downstairs and grabbed a bottle of bourbon and took a swig. He waited a moment and took another swig. Leon had been up all night and the liquor took hold pretty quick. It was not long before he began to mumble and talk to himself.

Leon was feeling angry and depressed about his life. He felt he wasn't able to do the things he wanted to do, which were to hunt and fish. He was feeling as though he'd become more of a servant and a chauffer for Margaret than a husband. The sex issue was really taking a toll on him, and he realized that he wasn't happy.

Leon then went to the downstairs closet and took out one of his rifles. It was a shotgun. He was thinking that he wanted to go hunting. He hadn't been hunting for quite some time. He thought about going out in the field with his buddies and their greyhounds, hunting for rabbits. They'd spread out and walk across a field in a row of about four or five men. Sometimes he took Hank and Dexter along.

A couple of the guys would hold the dogs, and when a rabbit jumped out and began to run, they'd take turns on who would have the next shot. Other times, when a rabbit appeared, they'd let the greyhounds loose and the dogs would take off after the rabbit, eventually tracking it down.

Leon began to imagine being in the field. He raised his shotgun, took aim, then shouted out, "Boom, boom."

From upstairs, he heard a call, "Leon, is that you?"

"Woman, what you want?" Leon hollered from downstairs.

Margaret didn't like his reply, so she snapped back, "Man, come here, I need you to go to the store."

"Hold your horses, woman. I'll be right there," answered Leon.

Leon then started to put his shotgun back in the closet, but he got an idea. "I'm going to go upstairs and shout, 'Boom' with this rifle and put a scare on Margaret." Leon then proceeded to walk up the stairs. When he reached the top of the stairs, he held his shotgun up and aimed it toward the bedroom door down the hall. Slowly, he walked down the hall, then he stopped just outside the open bedroom door, where Margaret lay in bed with her broken arm.

Leon then jumped into the doorway, aimed the shotgun at Margaret, and yelled, "Boom."

Dexter was in his mechanical drawing class when a school counselor walked into the classroom and approached the teacher. She whispered something to the teacher, then turned and walked out. The teacher called for Dexter to come to the front of the room, "Dexter, there's been an emergency at your home; you need to go there right away." He quickly grabbed his belongings, stopped by his locker on his way out, and then left the campus.

As Dexter headed home off the campus, he wondered what the emergency was. Most likely his mother was slipping into a coma and needed to go to the hospital emergency room, like on so many occasions before. He'd get her to the hospital where she'd receive a shot, along with some care, and be back to normal within hours.

As he passed through the courtyard, he ran into a student who lived near his home. She saw him walking in her direction and yelled, "Dexter, you need to get home right away. I heard you momma's been shot." A jolt shot through his heart, and then panic immediately set in. He took off running.

He ran the two blocks to the bus stop, but there wasn't a bus in sight, so he decided to keep running. He headed up San Jose Avenue; it was mostly an uphill climb. He was about a half mile from school and was getting tired. "How could this happen? Was the girl right about what she said? Who would shoot his mother? Is she alive? Is anybody there?" All these questions and more began to race through his mind.

As he approached Lakeview Avenue, he looked back and saw the 26 bus line coming. He jumped out into the street, flagged the bus down, and the driver stopped. Exhausted and out of breath, he jumped on the bus, paid the fare, and took a seat in the first row next to the driver, watching the street as the driver drove him toward home. It was just a couple of more stops to Sagamore and Orizaba. When the driver stopped, he jumped from the bus and ran down the street and around the corner.

When he arrived at the entrance to the house; the gate and front door were wide open. He stopped and paused and tried to check out the scene. He was afraid. What would he find inside? He was afraid that his mother was dead. He didn't know what to think. The house was quiet, and it seemed as though no one was there.

Dexter walked through the gate and entered through the front door. He called out, "Anybody home?" There was no answer. He then ran up the stairs, skipping a step with each leap. He looked down the hall toward his mother's bedroom; the door was wide open. "Baba?"

he called to his mother. His heart was beating fast, and he was out of breath. He reached the doorway and looked in the direction of his mother's bed. It was covered in blood.

It was a ghastly scene, but Margaret wasn't there. Blood was splattered across the walls, and there were small bullet holes from buckshot in the headboard and in the wall. The pillow where his mother laid her head was blown apart and covered with blood. There were pieces of flesh on the bed, lying in a pool of blood, and there was blood all around the floor. Dexter covered his mouth as fear set in. Tears immediately formed in his eyes, and he began to cry, "Baba, Baba."

Suddenly, the phone rang, and Dexter ran to the phone in the kitchen, "Hello?"

It was Annie. "Dexter, where have you been, boy? Leon's done shot your momma."

He was shocked at what he was hearing, "What happened? Why?" He was numb and thought he was dreaming.

Annie continued to speak, "Look, Dexter, she's at the hospital, and she's alive. You better get over there right away."

The news was promising. He knew he needed to get to his mother's side as soon as possible. He had to be with her. "Momma, where's she at, what hospital?"

Annie replied, "She's at San Francisco General Hospital."

Dexter locked up the house and left. He had to take the bus to San Francisco General Hospital. "What was the quickest route?" he began to think. The 26 line wasn't very regular that time of day. The M trolley would take him way out of the way, so he decided to run over to Mission Street and catch any bus that went in the direction of the hospital. It was the longest ride of his life.

He got off at Twenty-fourth and Mission and ran the six long blocks to Potrero. When he got to the emergency ward, Mary, BD, and Charles were there. Mary was crying, and Dexter approached her, "Dexter, Leon shot your mother. That nigger shot my baby. How could he do this? How could he do this?"

Dexter hugged and tried to console his grandmother, trying to fight back his tears. But he needed answers. "How is she?"

"She's in the operating room, and they said they think she'll make it. She's lost a lot of blood, but they believe they can save her. They won't let us in to see her. How could he do this, Dexter? She can't even see! She was lying in bed, and she had a broken arm. What harm could she do to anybody? She didn't deserve this." Mary was crying, angry, and confused.

Dexter became angry, tears filling his eyes as he held onto his grandmother. His heart was racing, then he looked at Charles. "Where's Leon?"

"They don't know where he is." Charles was looking at Dexter, and he was reading his mind. He knew what Dexter wanted to do, and they were both on the same page. They wanted to find Leon and kill him.

"I'll be back," Dexter said, and then he walked outside and headed around the corner, where he leaned up against a metal-barred fence and began to sob. A couple of people walked by and tried to not stare. He thought about doing what he was taught to do when things seemed hopeless, when there was no one else to turn to. He turned to his God, and he prayed, "Dear Lord, please, God. Help my mother get through this, dear Father. You know how she lives to serve you, Lord. You are her life and her everything. Dear God, I beg of you. Reach down and touch her soul, dear Lord. Give her the breath of life, as only you can do, dear Father. All of these blessings I ask in your Holy Son, Jesus's, name. Amen!"

Dexter gathered his composure and headed back into the hospital. He was angry, and Leon was constantly on his mind. When he got back, he went to Mary, "Has anyone called Hank?"

Mary replied, "Yes, Duane is bringing him back home. They should be on their way."

The family waited around the hospital for several hours. Finally, a policeman came in and told the family that Leon had turned himself in and that he was out on bail. Dexter was angry at the news; he didn't understand how they could have let him go.

The policeman said that Leon had told them it was an accident, and that he had been playing with the gun and only meant to scare her, when the gun went off.

"How can he scare her with a gun when she can't even see it? How can he do that? He knows she can't see the gun, so how can he scare her with it?" Dexter kept repeating himself as he questioned the policeman.

The officer didn't have an answer and only shrugged his shoulders. He understood how Dexter felt, but he couldn't offer an acceptable explanation.

A doctor came out soon after the policeman left and announced that Margaret was going to be fine, but it was going to take some time for her to recover. He explained that Margaret had been shot in the left side of her neck and that she must have raised her hand when the shot went off because she'd also lost a finger. He also said that she was probably lucky that she'd raised her hand, because the shot could probably have caused more damage to her neck and maybe even killed her.

He also said that there was some buckshot they'd had to leave in her neck because it was too close to some of her vital organs, so it would be better to leave it alone. He continued to say that, over time, the buckshot might cause her some discomfort, but otherwise, she should be fine.

However, the doctor said he had some more troubling news. He said that he understood she was a singer and played the piano. Because of the gunshot wounds, her face would be disfigured, and she probably wouldn't be able to sing again. He also said the loss of her finger meant she probably wouldn't be able to play the piano either.

Upon hearing this news, Mary became distraught with grief. Now her baby, who hadn't been able to see from birth and had been given a gift from God to sing with the voice of an angel, had had it all taken away. She didn't want to hear any more bad news. Next to death, it was the worst thing that could have happened to her daughter.

Duane and Hank soon arrived and were filled in on the news. Hank too became distraught and cried uncontrollably. Dexter and Duane tried to comfort him, and Charles decided to let the bad blood between them go. He hugged Hank, and Hank hugged him; it was one moment of happiness in a sad situation.

Soon they allowed the family in to see Margaret. They walked into her room to see her heavily bandaged about the neck, head, and left arm, which was already broken. Her hand was redressed, with her fingers sticking out from the cast. She was missing one: it was the index finger.

Margaret was weak, tired, and sedated. She'd been in surgery for several hours and needed to rest. She wasn't able to speak because of the injury, so the family decided to leave and let her rest. Duane left and headed back to San Jose. Mary took Hank and Dexter back to the house. They all walked into the house, and Mary went upstairs and closed Margaret's bedroom door. Hank noticed that someone had been to the house and taken some of Leon's things.

Mary walked through the house and approached the boys, "Hank, Dexter, you two leave Baba's door shut. I'll be back tomorrow to clean up her room. Are you two going to be okay here by yourselves?"

They both paused and wondered if they really wanted to be home alone. Looking at each other, they were glad to be together again and answered, "Yes Nanny, we'll be all right."

Mary turned and motioned for BD to return to the car.

Charles lagged behind and assured Dexter, "I'll be back in about an hour."

Dexter nodded in agreement.

Dexter didn't have a gun, but he knew where to get one. He told Hank to stay at the house and that he'd be back soon. There was a barbershop in the neighborhood where a few of the local thugs hung out. He knew he could buy a gun from somebody there.

He was able to buy a .25 caliber revolver and some bullets. He then returned home and waited for his uncle. When Charles arrived, Hank got into the backseat and Dexter took the passenger's seat at the front of Charles's car. Charles had an angry look on his face. "Okay, where do we go?"

Dexter glanced at his uncle, who was staring straight ahead as he drove off. "I know a few places where he might be. His kids are probably hiding him, and I know where most of them live."

As Charles drove off, he showed Dexter his gun and told him that he was going to do the shooting, but that they were all together. Dexter didn't reveal to Charles that he had a gun too because he'd made up his mind he was going to take the first shot, and he didn't want Charles to know.

As they rode around the city, Dexter began to think about the scriptures, "Thou shalt not kill." Annie had told him that if you ever killed someone, it was the one sin that God would not forgive, and if you killed someone, you'd be doomed to burn in hell for all eternity. He decided that he didn't care. He was going to kill Leon if it was the last thing he did, and Leon's kids better not get in the way.

When they arrived in the Fillmore, they visited one residence at a time, then planted themselves outside and lay in wait. They spent most of the night hunting for Leon, but there was no sign of him or his kids, anywhere. Leon had to know they were out to get him, and Leon's sons were sure to be aware of it as well.

After an exhausting search, they decided to give it up and go home. It was just about an hour before daybreak, and they were exhausted. Once home, Dexter rolled up a joint and fired it up. He took a drag and sat on the couch in the living room.

Hank went into the kitchen, paused, and walked to his mother's bedroom door. "You don't want to look in there," Dexter hollered from the living room.

Hank thought about what his brother said, but decided, "I have to see." When he opened the door and saw the horror, he began to cry. Hank walked down the hall to his bedroom, went inside, and lay across his bed, sobbing.

Dexter turned on his transistor radio. Jerry Butler was singing, "Only the Strong Survive." Dexter took another hit then put the joint out and lay back on the couch and fell asleep.

It was just about noon when the doorbell rang and woke the boys up. It was Mary; she'd come by to clean up the room. Hank let her in, and she said she'd already been to the hospital and would drop them off there when she was done cleaning. She also told the boys they had to get back to school, and that she felt they were old enough to take care of themselves until Margaret came back home. Hank and Dexter agreed.

The boys took care of themselves and maintained the house pretty well. They took turns cooking and cleaning, and there was plenty of food in the house. The freezer in the garage contained half a side of beef with every kind of cut you could possibly want. There was also close to a quarter of a pig.

Every day, Dexter and Hank visited the hospital to check on their mother. If they didn't both go, they took turns. One day, after several weeks, Dexter went to the hospital alone. Margaret was recovering pretty well and was able to talk. The left corner of her mouth was stretched downward where it had been pulled tight from the neck surgery. The operation had left her mouth twisted and her face disfigured.

While visiting, a nurse came by to check on Margaret and motioned for Dexter to follow her into the hallway outside the doors to the ward. Dexter followed her. Once outside the ward, she turned to Dexter and said, "I'm not sure if you're aware of this, but your father has been coming in here late at night, after hours, visiting your mother."

Dexter was shocked. He didn't know what to say, "No, I can't believe this. Are you sure?"

The nurse knew he'd be alarmed, "Yes, I'm sure."

He asked her to describe him and she described him right down to his crooked hand.

Dexter scratched his head and, with a puzzled expression, answered, "Thank you, Miss. I really appreciate this."

The nurse had taken a personal interest in Margaret, and she was appalled at what had happened to her. She often thought about how this man had shot a blind woman, and the question of how any man could shoot a woman did not sit well with her. So when he showed up to try to make up with her, the nurse couldn't sit back and watch what was taking place without the family knowing.

Dexter returned to his mother's bedside and called to her, "Baba?"

"Yes Dexter?" she answered, sensing some concern.

Dexter informed her, "Baba, I have to ask you something."

She replied, "What is it, baby?"

Dexter took a deep breath, "Baba, I hear you've been seeing Leon after hours!"

"That ain't none of your business," she snapped quickly.

"But it is my business. You're my mother, and I'm concerned about what you're doing, and I have a right to know." Dexter was trying hard to control his emotions. He was feeling anger, disappointment, frustration, and confusion. He tried to remain respectful.

Margaret was feeling cornered. Leon had been coming in late at night and begging her forgiveness. He explained that it had been an accident, and that he'd been playing and was only trying to scare her. But he was also aware there would be a hearing, and he'd have to face a judge. If there was going to be a trial, Margaret would have to testify. He needed to have her say it was an accident.

Leon knew Margaret was a devout believer in the Word, and the Bible teaches to forgive and forget. By his being sincere and asking for forgiveness, Leon believed she'd forgive him. During his visits, he begged for mercy. He promised to take care of her and told her he'd never leave her side. He confessed his love for her and confessed his love for the Lord. He put his hand on the Bible and swore the things he said.

Margaret thought about her situation. She realized that her sons would soon be grown men and would eventually need to leave home. Without Leon in her life, who would care for her? She thought about Hank; she knew that he'd probably be the one who'd want to stay, but she didn't think it would be fair. He needed to go off and be a man on his own.

After quite a bit of praying and consideration, Margaret decided to forgive Leon and accept his explanation that it had been an accident. Margaret realized that it was just a matter of time before she'd have to deal with her family regarding her position. The time came sooner than she expected, but she was ready for it.

When Dexter pressed her on the issue, she firmly said, "It was an accident."

"An accident? How can you say it was an accident? He shot you! You just don't go around shooting people by accident." Dexter couldn't believe what he was hearing. It was appalling to him. He couldn't even imagine what his mother was thinking.

Margaret stood her ground, "Well, I said it was an accident, so it was an accident."

Dexter was beginning to feel hopeless. He thought of how he could reason with her but he knew, by the tone of her voice, she'd made up her mind.

Dexter decided to move on to the issue he felt was next—the possibility of Leon coming back home. "Baba, I hope you don't plan on having him back at home."

"If I do, that ain't none of your business," she responded sharply.

It was coming down to either Leon or him. "If he moves back into that house, then I'm going to move out," Dexter said, asserting his position and forcing her hand.

Margaret snapped back, "Then I guess you'll be moving."

Dexter was shocked and saddened. After he had always been there for her, his mother had taken the position against him and with Leon. "I'm sorry, I have to go now," Dexter said and walked away. His body felt limp and a lump began to form in his throat.

He walked out of the hospital ward, disbelieving what had just taken place. He went home and called his grandmother and gave her the news. Mary couldn't believe it either. She told Dexter that she'd go to the hospital and get things straightened out. Dexter then informed Charles and Hank of his conversation with his mother. He let them know what his position was, and how he was feeling betrayed.

Mary went to her daughter's bedside, where Margaret tried to explain how it had been an accident. Mary sat next to Margaret's bed and looked at her daughter's face, disfigured and covered with bandages. She couldn't believe how Margaret could say the things that she was saying. Finally, she couldn't bear any more hurt, so she left the hospital room, saddened and disappointed.

The district attorney's office held a hearing and accepted Leon's story that it had been an accident; they didn't care when black people shot each other, anyway. Leon moved back into the house, and Dexter moved out. Hank stayed because he wanted to protect his mother. He was going to make sure that nothing would happen again as long as he was around. It would take some time for the family to even be in the presence of Leon again.

After the shooting, Dexter purchased his first car. It was a 1962 Chevrolet Impala two-door convertible. It was black, with a red interior and a red stripe running along the side panels from front to back.

Dexter's friend, Bill, let him move into his Tenderloin studio, and Bill moved into a larger place on Russian Hill. Dexter was seventeen years old and still in high school. He was now living in his own apartment and had his own car. He was determined to finish school, and he attended his classes every day. To support himself, he continued to hustle.

Leon brought Margaret home from the hospital, and the two of them began a healing process that was not easy for everyone to accept. Hank remained in the house, keeping clear of Leon, and Leon stayed clear of him. Leon had to wait on Margaret hand and foot. For the time being, she was totally dependent upon him. Hank kept a watchful eye.

Margaret was constantly in a great deal of pain, and she developed high blood pressure. This, along with the diabetes, caused her a lot of stress. Leon gave her the daily shots she required and monitored her blood sugar. He kept track of the different medications she needed for her pain and her blood pressure.

Dexter wasn't able to stay away from his mother for too long. Mary was putting pressure on him to go to visit his mother. Margaret had been asking about him; she missed her oldest child. After a few months, he finally went home to visit. During the first couple of visits, Leon was away, but eventually Dexter would run into him.

21

Manchild

Over the last few weeks of school, Dexter traveled back and forth between the Tenderloin and school. He knew the importance of finishing school and was happy that he'd soon be graduating. He continued to hustle to pay his bills.

The senior prom was approaching. He asked Sherice if she'd accompany him, and she agreed. Even though they were no longer a couple, they were still good friends. He didn't trust DeeDee to be on time.

They attended the prom, then afterward went to a performance at Basin Street West on Broadway to see the Watts 103rd Street Rhythm Band." The warm-up act was Richard Pryor, and his show was hilarious.

In June of 1969, Dexter graduated from high school. Margaret wasn't able to attend, but his grandmother, Mary, and his Aunt Cynthia did. Charles was working as a guard at San Quentin and wasn't able to attend; soon he'd leave to work for the IBM Corporation. The ceremony was nice, and Dexter was proud of his achievement. He was glad that Mary had come to his ceremony. She really felt more like a mother to him than his mother did.

Margaret was always so dependent on Dexter that he felt they'd never had a mother-and-son type of relationship, the way most mothers and sons did. Even though Margaret was a very independent woman by nature, she depended heavily on her children. She seldom went anywhere without them.

Sometimes Dexter would recall the few times that his mother had ventured out without him or anyone else, and how he'd always worried about her during those moments. He felt that Mary was always there for him. When he was young, she'd cuddle him and kiss him, like a mother does her son. She treated him like he was her own son and showered him with lots of love and affection. As a baby, Hank was partial to his mother, but Dexter was partial to Mary.

As teenagers, Mary kept her doors open to the boys, and although she loved Hank very much, the scars and the pain from the incident with Charles took time to heal. She often called upon Dexter for assistance with chores and various needs, and he always tried to fulfill her requests.

After graduation, Dexter knew that he had to do something to earn a living. Having finished school and left Lakeview, most of his clientele was gone. He needed to get a job. College would have to wait; he was really disappointed that he wouldn't be able to attend full-time like some of the others in school. Unfortunately, he had to survive!

In a way, living in the Tenderloin was a wake-up call for Dexter. It was full of pimps, prostitutes, pushers, junkies, and hustlers. As a regular in the Tenderloin, he began to know and recognize who all the real players were. He lived at 340 Eddy Street, which was in the heart of the Tenderloin, where the prostitutes were in full force, with many having turfs on the same block where he lived.

On many occasions, when he returned home late, the hos were posted up in the stairway. He'd walk by and say, "Hello, ladies," and they'd flirt and smile and respond with, "Hi, Dexter." They thought he was so young and cute. The prostitutes developed into some of his best customers, and, sometimes, when the heat was on because of a police crackdown, they'd visit his place and hang out until the heat was off. He never approached them for any favors, and they never asked him for anything. He was about business, and if they wanted any smoke, they had to buy it.

Dexter didn't hang around or linger in the Tenderloin. He never visited the bars, cafes, or pool joints. He understood that it was a one-track road to nowhere if he got entrenched there. The only things he did there were eat and sleep. He'd come in and get some rest and get up and go. He just kept to himself. Sometimes Cary came and visited, but he didn't have too many other visitors.

Dexter obtained a fake ID and began to frequent a few nightclubs in the city. This was where he could continue his hustle until the job market developed for him. He began to frequent many clubs in San Francisco—places like the Rickshaw, Charlie's Half Note, the Sportsman's Inn, and the Moroccan Club.

Since he had a car now, he began to venture more into Oakland and frequent the many nightclubs across the bay. He visited Uppy's on the Square, the Black Knight, and the Square Apple.

Since he was a good dancer, he also entered dance contests as another way to make money. He'd find out where a contest was being held and arrive early so he could survey the women to find which attractive single lady was the best dancer. Once he identified the best dancer, he'd approach her and ask for a dance. On the dance floor, he'd determine if the chemistry was right and then coax her into entering the contest with him. Many times he'd win, and often he would at least place. It was a good hustle and it was legal, but it still was not enough. He also began to tire of hustling the jewelry.

Dexter had experience in finding work, so it didn't take very long for him to land a job. He was able to find employment with a graphics firm by the name of Chad Litho. It was a black-owned business and was doing some good things. The company landed a nice contract with Bank of America, printing forms, booklets, and brochures for the bank and for other firms.

Two black men spearheaded the company—Chad, who was the CEO, and Phil, who was the president. Chad focused on marketing, and Phil focused on operations. Besides Dexter, there were five other employees: two pressmen to operate the large printing presses, a stripper, who worked the darkroom, a salesman, and a secretary, who also was in charge of administration.

It was a tight-knit family, and they took Dexter under their wing and began to teach him about every aspect of the trade. He enjoyed the work and absorbed information like a sponge. He worked on the printing presses and also went out on sales calls. Sometimes he spent time in the darkroom, and other times he helped with the billing. One thing that was funny to him was that most of the staff smoked marijuana during breaks. Instead of taking coffee breaks, they took pot breaks.

Everything seemed to be falling into place for Dexter. One weekend, the Veterans Day Parade was taking place downtown, not far from the Tenderloin, so Dexter decided to walk down to the parade.

He was enjoying his new life without the steady stream of friends coming around; he enjoyed the sanctity of being alone. He was off to the parade, and he was going alone, with no friends, no brother, and no girl.

As he walked the route of the parade, he was struck by something he saw. It was a girl. He happened to look up across the street, and there was this beautiful exotic girl looking straight at him. He paused and returned her stare; she smiled and waved at him. That was all that he needed. He stepped off the curb and walked right through the parade, heading in her direction. The girl looked shocked and seemed like she was about to panic.

When Dexter approached her, she immediately grabbed a girl that was standing next to her and said, "Hi, I'm Sally, and this is my girlfriend, Zoe." She then grabbed the arm of a young man standing to her left, and introduced him as her boyfriend.

Dexter looked at him, and the young man returned a look that said, "What the hell are you doing here?" He looked like a square and Dexter dismissed his glance, but they acknowledged each other. The young man could tell that something wasn't right, but Sally had played it off real well. Dexter had come over for Sally, and she had passed him on to her girlfriend so quickly that everyone had to go along. Dexter remained cordial and talked with the girlfriend. They exchanged phone numbers, and then he went on his way. He knew he'd get back to Sally eventually. However, during this time, he had several other girlfriends.

Not long thereafter, the Concepts landed a gig they felt was going to be their big break. The Marcels' manager was producing a showcase at Mr. D's on Broadway, and the booked headliner was the Whispers.

The Concepts were booked as the first act and would be followed by the Marcels. Next would be the Windjammers, who'd changed their name from the Emotions because of a conflict in names with another recording group of the same name. The TCBs were booked as the band to provide entertainment and backup.

The group got together and began to practice. Dexter had some new steps for the group, being fresh from going to the dance clubs and knowing the latest dances. They practiced their songs, got the timing down perfect, and were ready to perform.

The group needed to have some 'fits, so they went to Selix Formal Wear and rented four royal blue dinner jackets with black satin collars, tuxedo slacks, and black patent leather shoes. They picked out some white ruffled shirts with black piping along the ridges of the ruffles, as well as some black bow ties. Next, the fellas went to the barbershop together and had their Afros cut real tight. They were now ready for the show.

It was showtime! And Mr. D's was popping. The place was packed and jumping. Dexter had invited all of his girlfriends; they were all in the audience at the same time, only they didn't know it, but he didn't care. A true player, for real!

Backstage was frantic and exciting. The group was checking out the scene when one of the coordinators approached them and told the group it was time to go on. Mattock, Raul, Cary, and Dexter had been waiting for this moment for a long time, and they were ready for it.

The lights were dimmed and the fellas walked out onto the dark stage and took up their positions. A dim blue light appeared as a backdrop and cast an outline of four silhouettes. They were standing side by side with their legs slightly apart, and each member had his hands clasped together just in front of his crotch. Their heads were bowed.

A voice came over the mic, "Ladies and Gentlemen, it gives us great pleasure here at Mr. D's to bring to you a group that's been making a name for themselves right here in the heart of San Francisco. Ladies and gentleman, we bring you the Concepts."

The lights remained dim while the band began to play the intro. On cue, the spotlights came on as they raised their heads, brought their feet together, and then raised their hands up in front of their faces, in a praying position.

They did a short bounce, then sang, "Please, return your love to me, girl. Forgive me for the wrong I've done. Oh, baby."

Cary took his mic and started on the lead, "I cry myself to sleep at night for fear of another holding you tight," and "Oh, Baby."

On cue with their steps, the remaining three came from behind Cary, and stepped up to their mics and sang out, "Oh, Baby," with their hands flowing away from their mouths and down to their sides.

The girls in the audience went wild. Dexter looked out into the crowd and saw the reaction, and he smiled. This resulted in girls screaming. It was the moment the fellas lived for. They sang three other tunes, including the one Dexter led, "Don't Look Back." The set ended with a dance routine, choreographed by Cary, to the Isley Brother's hit, "It's Your Thing." They danced their way off the stage and waved to the crowd as they exited. Once backstage, the group celebrated and bonded, enjoying the moment.

After the Mr. D's performance, the group never booked another gig. Raul was drafted into the army, and Mattock took up a life of crime. He tried to get Dexter to do a burglary job, but Dexter declined and told him he wasn't going down that route.

It was a pivotal moment in his life. It was a moment when he could choose the left or the right. Annie's preaching always came back to him in those moments. It was at times like those when he heard her voice saying, "Train up a child in the way he should go. And when he is old, he shall not depart from it."

So he and Mattock parted ways, and from then on, they got together only occasionally. Mattock had also started snorting heroin, and Dexter wanted no part of that either. He had a lot more sense than that.

Many of the young black males from his neighborhood became victims of the war, drugs, or crime. Many ended up as junkies, dead, homeless, or in prison. Being young, gifted, and black wasn't enough to get ahead in America.

Cary and Dexter remained close friends after graduation. So, when Dexter finally got in touch with the girl from the parade, he invited Cary along.

When they arrived at Zoe's house, Dexter introduced Cary to Sally, and he proceeded to court Zoe because that had been where Sally had directed him. Soon it became evident that it was Dexter and Sally who were interested in each other.

Sally stood about 5' 6" and weighed about one hundred pounds. She was really slim and wore a D-cup bra, which Dexter loved. Her light-skinned complexion was soft like a baby's. Her hair was jet-black, fine, and curly, and she wore it cut in a cute, short hairstyle. She was exotic-looking, with cute, narrow, pouty lips, and her eyes had an Asian look to them.

She was from Bermuda, by way of the East Coast, and she spoke with the cutest Bermudan accent. It was an accent Dexter hadn't heard before, and she expressed herself with words he'd never heard. Sometimes he couldn't even understand what she was saying. Sally's background was part Bermudan and part Chinese. She was striking and beautiful. After Dexter started dating her, he began to see less of DeeDee, who became suspicious. She could tell that something was up, but she couldn't really catch him in anything.

Sally's mother had sent her to the West Coast to stay with her aunt because she'd delivered a baby girl. Her mother kept the baby on the East Coast, so that Sally could get her education and get herself stabilized. There was one problem with this idea: Sally was a stubborn teenage girl who was strong-willed. She had her own ideas as to what she wanted to do. School was not a priority with her, and her aunt was having a difficult time keeping her from cutting school.

Sally's aunt became really fond of Dexter, once she got to know him. Soon she appealed to him for help with her niece. Dexter said he'd do the best that he could in encouraging her to finish school, and went so far as to pick up Sally in the mornings, and drop her off at Mission High School on his way to work. But she just continued to cut classes once Dexter had dropped her off.

Cary was always partial to Latino women, and his girlfriend was no exception. Angel was his main squeeze, and she and Sally hit it off right away and became the best of friends. The four of them would get together often and double date. But at that time, Dexter had still made no commitment to Sally, nor had Cary made a commitment to Angel.

There was a white girl that Cary was dating, who had a black girlfriend whom she wanted to introduce to Dexter. At first, Dexter was apprehensive about the arrangement, but he finally agreed, so Cary arranged for the girls to come to Dexter's crib.

Cary arrived at the pad early, so he and Dexter drank some Champales and smoked some Acapulco Gold. When the girls showed up, Dexter looked at the sister, and she was out of sight. She was gorgeous! Her almond complexion was smooth as velvet, and her smile was hypnotic. She had bright brown eyes with long eyelashes that batted in a way that had the effect of flashing lights. Her petite slender frame was like a Barbie doll's, and her Afro was full, soft, and puffy. She was dressed real mod in a leather vest, and she wore a leather headband around her forehead that penetrated her Afro. A long tail of leather, beads, and feathers hung from the right side of her headband and flowed down over her shoulder. The yellow, see-through chiffon pullover blouse she was wearing had puffy sleeves with a large Hi-Boy collar and a V-neck that displayed her cleavage. Her crisp bell-bottomed blue jeans fit like a glove, and her brown leather, high-heeled boots gave her a stance that would make any man humble.

Her name was Alma, and the more she and Dexter looked at each other, the more they began to look familiar to each other. As it turned out, they had known each other when they were children. Their families had been good friends. Her family belonged to Macedonia Baptist Church, the same church that Mary used to belong to when the family first moved to San Francisco from Richmond. Charles had dated Alma's sister, Vanetta, who'd become a famous black actress in Hollywood.

When Dexter realized who she was, he remembered the pretty little girl he'd been smitten with who'd worn two long, thick, braids of hair, one on each side of her head. She was about a year younger than Dexter, and they'd played together sometimes when they were younger.

This made the attraction between them even stronger. The four of them sat around and got their buzz on, and Alma and Dexter began to catch up. She asked about Hank and the family, and Dexter asked about Vanetta and the rest of her family.

Suddenly there was a knock at the door, and Cary said, "I'll get it." He got up from the couch, walked to the front door and opened it. He quickly slammed it shut. Whoever was on the other side of the door had just had it slammed in their face.

Cary was standing at the front door, leaning with his back against it. He had a look of shock and surprise on his face.

Dexter was puzzled. "What's going on?"

Cary whispered across the room, "It's Angel and Sally."

Dexter jumped up from the couch and walked over to the door and opened it. They were gone!

He turned to the ladies. "Excuse me, I'm sorry, but you have to leave."

The girls were real polite and said they'd go, but Dexter didn't wait for an answer. He took off running, leaving Cary in the apartment with the girls.

When he reached the street, he didn't see the girls anywhere. They could have gone in any direction, so he had to make a choice. He asked a stranger on the street if he'd seen the two girls; the man pointed up the street. Dexter ran up the block and saw Sally and Angel walking down Leavenworth Street toward Market, about two blocks away. He ran the two blocks and eventually caught up with Sally. He proceeded to beg for her to return. Sally was very upset and started cussing him out. She called him every name in the book.

When he kept insisting that she return, she blurted out, "Hell no, muthafucka, what do you take me for, a fool?"

At this point, he was about to give up but decided to give it his all. He reached for her hand, and, looking into her eyes, he said, "Sally, I'm sorry, but there was nothing going on. We were just sitting around chatting, and she was an old friend of mine. We didn't do anything. You know you're the girl for me, and it's only you that I care about. Please, please, forgive me and come back to the crib."

Sally finally agreed to return. Angel decided to continue on, so she left.

Dexter took Sally by the hand and led her down the street. He looked at her, and she was looking good. She was wearing a new, shiny, crumpled, black patent leather maxi-coat with black patent leather, knee-high, high-heeled boots. With the boots on, she stood almost five foot ten. The coat flowed softly in the slow breeze, which blew gently through her soft, fine hair.

As they walked back to the pad, they approached a bar that had a couple of pool tables inside. It was known to be a hangout for pimps in the area. As they passed the bar, Dexter noticed a high-yellow pimp who was a familiar face in the Tenderloin; he was standing by the pool table with a cue stick in his hand, waiting to take his next shot. Dexter had seen him on many occasions, but they'd never spoken. Dexter knew he didn't like this cat from the first time he saw him.

Dexter took Sally's hand and placed it around his arm to display that she was his. As they passed by the open door, the pimp, who was about to take his shot, looked out and saw Sally walking by holding onto Dexter's arm. He stopped his play and stood erect with the pool stick in both hands.

He shouted out, "Maxi-coat Slim!"

Sally's eyes stayed fixed straight ahead, and Dexter glanced over at the pimp with a raised eyebrow and a look of disapproval. The pimp then acknowledged Dexter by giving him a nod; Dexter turned his head away and kept walking. After that encounter, the pimp never again interfered with Sally and Dexter whenever their paths crossed.

Not long after the Alma incident, DeeDee found out about Sally. She was hurt, frustrated, and felt betrayed. She wanted revenge and felt the need to get back at Dexter. So she decided to sleep with one of his friends.

Jonnie was a good friend of Dexter's, and he'd gotten married at the early age of sixteen. Jonnie, along with his wife and daughter, lived in an apartment in the Valencia Gardens housing projects in the Mission District. Dexter and DeeDee had often visited their apartment and used one of their bedrooms to have sex. It was Jonnie that DeeDee decided to sleep with. Somehow, DeeDee was able to get the message to Jonnie that she wanted to sleep with him. He was more than willing to oblige.

After their encounter, Jonnie didn't hesitate to contact Dexter and inform him of the affair. Although Jonnie was a dog and would never turn down pussy, he wasn't a backstabber. He had to tell his boy and be straight up about it. It was a code between the brothers. Jonnie told him that DeeDee was upset about his relationship with Sally and used it as an excuse to get back at him. He said he hoped there would be no hard feelings between them and that he was just being the dog that he was. Dexter told him it was cool, and it was the excuse he needed anyway.

Dexter couldn't get upset anyway because of the code. The code was that you always respected your homeboy's woman and never made a pass at her. But if she made a pass at you, you could take her, and if she could be taken, then you never had her in the first place.

Jonnie went on to explain that DeeDee had felt guilty after they did it. He said she really felt bad and started to cry. She also felt bad because he was married, and she knew his wife. He said she was confused and didn't know what to do. He told Dexter that she didn't want to lose him and had asked Jonnie to talk with him to help her keep him.

But Jonnie's way of explaining things was not the best way to get a point across. He simply said, "Dexter, you should keep her. She got some good pussy."

Dexter looked at Jonnie and snickered, "Right, yeah, I should keep her. She got some good pussy. Right!"

He thought about the time Jonnie had told him about Brenda. He laughed at Jonnie and told him he was a dog muthafucka, and Jonnie acknowledged and said, "I know."

After DeeDee's encounter with Jonnie, Dexter cut her loose. It was something that he'd wanted to do anyway because he was becoming attached to Sally. DeeDee tried to make a comeback by apologizing for the incident, but it was too late. She even offered to trick for him, but he didn't have the heart to pimp.

Over the course of the next two months, Sally had to move out of Zoe's house and move back with her aunt, but when she wouldn't abide by her aunt's rules, she moved to live with her cousin. That didn't last either, so Dexter finally invited Sally to live with him.

When Sally moved in with Dexter, Mary and Margaret both became very concerned. For Mary, Sally was pretty and yellow like she liked, but she knew that Dexter was too young for any kind of commitment. She told him he hadn't yet sown his oats and hadn't been on his own long enough. For Margaret, they were living in sin. They were shacking up! And that was against the Word of God. She said they wouldn't be blessed because of it.

Margaret kept the pressure on about living in sin. Although Dexter had come into worldly ways, he was still well grounded in his religious beliefs, so his mother's constant preaching about living in sin and about infidelity was working on him. He began to feel guilty, so he asked Sally to marry him, and Sally accepted. Charles tried his best to talk Dexter out of getting married, but he wouldn't listen. Soon they were married at First Union Baptist Church, and Charles was the best man. Dexter was eighteen years old, and Sally was seventeen.

The week after they were married, Dexter lost his job. Chad Litho went bankrupt and had to close their doors. But not long after he lost his graphics job, Dexter applied for a job at the IBM Corporation and landed it through an affirmative action program.

IBM put Dexter through a rigorous six-month training program, complete with a two-week crash course in typing. The next thing he knew, he was in charge of the mail room and had the responsibility of purchasing supplies for the branch office, and he was also responsible for typing the entire branch office's Teletype messages. Within three months on the job, Dexter was able to type more than one hundred words per minute.

Not long after they were married, Sally became pregnant, and they had their first baby. It was a baby girl. They named her after Margaret and gave her the nickname Mimi. Margaret was proud to have a granddaughter named after her. But as Mimi began to grow into a toddler, Margaret became jealous of Mary. Mary was crazy about Mimi, and she showered her with love. Mimi was equally fond of Mary.

Mimi never wanted to be held by Margaret. Being a small child, her senses could determine that something was wrong. Margaret, disfigured from the accident, was intimidating to Mimi, so she was afraid of her. Margaret tried to overcome her granddaughter's fear and coaxed her to come to her. She'd reach out and hold Mimi when she came near, but she was a little too aggressive.

Margaret tried to joke and laugh, "Ah, come here, girl. Stop that crying and come to your Baba."

Mimi would holler from fright and reach out for her mother or father or Mary. It was a tough situation for the family. Everyone wanted so badly for Margaret to be able to enjoy her grandchild, but they couldn't force it. Only time might be able to mend the process.

Margaret wasn't in a position to be able to do any babysitting. She was ill and couldn't get around as well as she used to. She continued to try and cook, but she often burned the food. On more than one occasion, she set the kitchen on fire. She had to be watched with a careful eye, which she resisted. Her diabetes was getting worse, and the pains from the wounds of the accident were constant. Soon she began to drink a little wine for relief.

A few years had passed since the accident, and although the doctors had told Margaret that she'd never play or sing again, she refused to accept their comments. The last thing anyone could tell her was that there was something she couldn't do if she wanted to do it. Margaret even thought she could drive if she wanted to. She and Dexter had gotten into arguments before because she'd said on more than one occasion that she wanted to buy a car and learn how to drive. Dexter kept telling her that there was no way she could drive because she couldn't see, but she never wanted to accept it. She just could never understand why she couldn't drive.

So when she was told that she'd never sing or play the piano again, she began to practice. She'd sit at the piano and play for hours. Having the missing finger was difficult for her, and she'd keep hitting the wrong keys. Nonetheless, it wasn't going to stop her; she was determined.

Eventually, she attempted to sing too. Her voice was not the same. It was still her voice, but the notes didn't come easily anymore. Her voice would strain and crack, and when she'd try to hit the high notes she'd been used to hitting, her voice would fade.

For the family members, hearing her attempt to sing was depressing. Dexter had a hard time being around his mother's house when she was practicing and often left. When the boys were around, Leon would leave the house if she began to sing, because he knew it only made them think of him and that it was his fault.

Leon knew it was his fault, and he had to live with that. Margaret's attempts to play and sing served as a constant reminder of the damage he'd caused, and it tormented him. Whenever Leon came in contact with Dexter, he'd constantly apologize for the accident. Dexter no longer called him Dad but referred to him as Leon. He learned to tolerate Leon; he knew that Leon's life was now that of a servant. Margaret fussed and snapped at Leon constantly, and there was nothing he could do about it.

Leon would corner Dexter and say, "Dexter, you know, you're the sharpest of the bunch. I mean, even between my own, I love you, boy."

Dexter would just stand there and nod his head, trying to give him some respect, but he wouldn't say much.

Leon would continue, "You know I love your momma. Lord knows I hate what happened. If I could change things, I would. I bet a man I'd trade places with her any day if I could."

Margaret, who still had sharp ears, would hear Leon and shout out, "Leon, leave Dexter alone. Get out of his ear! Leave him alone, man, now."

Leon would just walk off. "Okay son, you take care. You keep doing a fine job now. I'm proud of ya."

Margaret kept practicing her playing and singing. One evening, she had played for hours and gone to bed exhausted; she was so tired. The little wine she drank to help ease her pains hadn't helped much.

As she lay in bed sleeping, something began to rouse her. Something had come about her body and was engulfing her. She started to open her eyes and there was a glimmer of light. She could see a light; it was a light she'd seen only once before in her life, when she was a little girl. It was becoming brighter and was shining white. She looked directly into it as it engulfed her. Margaret sat up in her bed, and the light disappeared.

"Glory be to the Father; it's a miracle." She climbed out of her bed and got on her knees and prayed. "Dear Lord, heavenly Father. Once again, your light has touched me from heaven above. I don't know what it all means, Father, but you have your way with me, O Lord. Touch me, O Lord, and give me strength that I may serve you in the way in which you would have me do.

"Thank you, Lord, for you have brought me from a mighty long way," Margaret prayed as her voice began to rise. "Dear God, you know that I only live to serve you. They tried to take me from this planet, Lord, but you weren't ready for me to leave," her voice was now cracking, and she was beginning to cry. "My God, you are a mighty God. Holy would be thy name, dear Lord."

Margaret got up on her feet and raised her arms toward the heavens, and she began to shout, "Have your way with me, dear Father! Show me which way to go. Guide me with your guiding light, O Lord.

422

Hallelujah, Hallelujah, great God almighty." She threw her arms down, embraced herself hard, and shook back and forth. She was full of the Holy Spirit, and she hadn't had that feeling in a long time. She soon calmed down and returned to bed.

The next morning Margaret got out of bed and Leon came in and fixed her something to eat. She didn't say anything to Leon about what she'd experienced. In fact, she wasn't going to tell anyone. It was between her and the Lord.

After breakfast, Margaret got dressed, which was something that she usually didn't do unless she was going somewhere. But this morning she got dressed even though she was staying home. As she began to button her dress, she noticed that her hand didn't hurt anymore. Margaret's pain was gone, and she didn't have any problem with the buttons; it was easy for her.

After she got dressed, she wanted to listen to some gospel music. So she went into the living room and put a record on the hi-fi phonograph. She couldn't tell which album it was, so she just settled for whichever one she grabbed. The album was the Clara Ward Singers; they were one of her favorite gospel groups. The song "In the Upper Room" was playing, and she stood by the hi-fi and hummed along.

Margaret then turned the volume up and walked into the kitchen. Leon hadn't washed the dishes, so she decided to clean up the kitchen. She stood at the sink, washing dishes and listening to the music. She was bouncing and tapping her feet to the music when she noticed that she wasn't having any problem with the dishes and there was no pain.

She continued to hum along with the music. Her feet kept tapping, and the music was sounding good. She was shaking her hips and bouncing up and down and just having a joyous good time, cleaning and listening to the music. Soon, one of her favorite songs came on. It was "Jesus Will Fix It," and again she began to hum along. The music was sounding so good to her that she began to sing.

> Jesus will fix it.
> Jesus will fix it.
> Jesus will fix it,
> By and by.

At first she didn't notice it, but her voice was sounding clear. There was no cracking, and there was no strain. Once the dishes were washed, she began to dry them, wiping them and storing them on the cabinet shelves.

She kept drying and singing, and the music was sounding good. Slowly, she began to realize something. It was dawning on her that her voice was sounding normal. She was singing! Margaret sang louder and louder then stronger and stronger.

She put down the dish she was holding and navigated her way into the living room and walked over to the phonograph. She stood by the hi-fi and sang along with the music. She was singing perfectly with the record, and a joy came over her and uplifted her spirits. When the song ended, she walked to the piano and sat down on her bench.

After she positioned herself on the bench, she raised her hands to the keys. Her hands glided back and forth over the keys as if caressing a fine jewel. Once she found her position, she began to play, and she began to sing.

> Our Father
> Which art in heaven
> Hallowed be thy name
> Thy kingdom come
> Thy will be done
> On earth as it is in heaven.

As Margaret sang "The Lord's Prayer," she was feeling happy in a way she hadn't felt in a long time. Her voice sang loud and clear, and she was feeling very thankful. Tears began to fill her eyes, and joy filled her heart. She completed "The Lord's Prayer" and began to cry. She pushed the bench back away from her and closed the piano. She then kneeled down and began to pray.

"Dear Lord, my Father. Never have I forsaken you. In my darkest hour, I never gave up on you, Lord, and you have rewarded me for my faith. Thank you, Jesus; thank you, Father. When there is no way, you make a way. When the Jews were blocked by the Red Sea and Pharaoh's army was behind them, and they had nowhere to turn, they turned to you, Lord, and you delivered them.

"You have delivered me, O Lord, and I'm thankful. I've dedicated my life and my voice to you so that I may serve you all of my days. It's a miracle, dear God, and I thank you. Thank you, Jesus! Thank you, Lord!"

Margaret rose from the floor and sat at the piano and continued to play and sing. She practiced for hours. Over the next few weeks, she played constantly until she felt she was ready to go back to work.

Margaret dreamed of the day she could get back to work. She made some phone calls, but none of the churches she had relationships with had openings. Either they already had enough choir directors or they'd heard of her accident and were told that Margaret could no longer sing or play. But she didn't give up hope.

Margaret continued to practice and pray. Leon came in and out of the house and heard her practicing and continued on about his business. But it didn't matter to Margaret because she was going about the Lord's work.

Hank would often hear her and sit with his mother and encourage her. He'd sometimes join in and sing while she played. It was like old times, and the two of them enjoyed it.

Finally, one day the phone rang, and it was the pastor of a small start-up church that needed a pianist. The congregation had recently grown large enough to have a choir. The pastor was aware of Margaret's situation and figured he'd be able to get her pretty cheap. He was right; he offered her pennies on the dollar, and she accepted the position. The money didn't matter to her. What the pastor didn't know was that she'd have played for nothing. She just wanted to sing and play and evangelize for the Lord.

Dexter had gotten away from the church since becoming a grown man with a family. His daughter was going on two, and he and his wife lived in a small house in East Oakland. Between his work at IBM and his family, it wasn't often that he got over to San Francisco to visit his mother.

One Saturday evening, after Sally and Mimi had gone to bed, Dexter went into the living room to kick back and listen to some music. He'd purchased his first stereo-component system and had hung the speakers on the wall, one at each end of the room.

FM radio was now broadcasting in stereo, and Dexter wanted to listen to something new and different because soul music was still being broadcast on AM in mono. He grabbed his new headphones and turned on his brand new Sony stereo system. He switched the dial on the receiver to FM, and began to scan the airwaves. He came across a radio station that had a female deejay. It was unusual to hear a female's voice on the radio, especially as a deejay. Her name was Dusty Street, and she was a white girl with a whole lot of soul. Her voice was smooth as silk and, to Dexter, she sounded so cool, almost as if she were black. The radio station was KSAN.

He kicked back on the couch and listened as Dusty played some Aretha, Tower of Power, and then some Sly Stone. Dusty came back on the air and said she was going to play a real treat; she was about to play some Jimi Hendrix after the break. Dexter had only heard of Jimi and seen his name on posters for concerts at the Fillmore. The hippies were deep into his music, but the black community had failed to embrace him. His music was not played on the soul radio stations like KDIA and KSOL. So when Dusty said she was going to play some Hendrix, Dexter lay there, ready to take notice and listen.

The break was over, and Dusty began to talk about Hendrix, giving a little background. She called him the best guitarist on the planet, placed the record on her turntable, and the guitar began to play. The music began to bounce through the headphones in a way he'd never heard a stereo sound before. He sat up and tilted his head to catch every sound, "Wow, this brother is bad. Damn, how come I never really heard him before?"

"All along the Watchtower" was playing on the radio, and Jimi's guitar was turning Dexter on. "I got to pick up some of his stuff," Dexter thought as he lay back on the couch.

He relaxed back on the couch and listened to the stereo. Suddenly he noticed his German Shepherd sit up with her ears on alert. She was looking at the front door. Dexter looked at the front door, and saw that someone was trying to open it by picking at the lock from outside.

Dexter got up slowly and quietly grabbed his gun. He walked to the door, placed his hand on the knob, and looked down at his dog. "Okay, get ready, girl." The dog was in position and ready to go. Just as he put his hand on the doorknob, he heard someone run down the stairs just outside the door. Dexter opened the door and the dog took off around the side of the house toward the backyard.

Dexter followed his dog in hot pursuit. When he got to the backyard, his dog had caught the prowler by the pant leg as he was trying to climb over the back fence. Dexter placed his gun to the back of the prowler's head. The burglar felt the cold steel of the gun barrel on his neck and froze. Dexter grabbed the burglar by the shirt collar, pulled him off the fence, and threw him to the ground.

He called his dog off and told her to sit and stay. He was holding his gun on the prowler when he noticed that he was a kid about eighteen years old.

Dexter lived on 105th Avenue, near the freeway in Sobrante Park, and he recognized the kid from around the neighborhood. "Muthafucka, you gonna try and rip me off?"

The kid lay on the ground, looking up at the gun barrel pointed at him. "I'm sorry, I'm sorry, I didn't know you live there."

"Man, I ought to turn your ass in." Dexter held his outstretched arm with his gun aimed straight at the boy.

"No, please, man; don't turn me in." He looked at Dexter, begging and pleading.

"Stand your ass up!" commanded Dexter, with his dog sitting near. The boy stood in front of Dexter, who moved the gun and held it pointing skyward. "You lucky I didn't pop a cap in your ass. I should just go on and drop a dime on you." Dexter looked at the young man, who really wasn't that much younger than he was. He was thinking about what he wanted to do with the boy.

"I ain't going to turn you in because I don't want to see you get a rap. But I'm gon' beat your ass, and you're gonna take it, too! And don't you ever let me catch your ass near my house again." Dexter held his gun in one hand and made a fist in the other. He pulled his lean arm down and reached way back. "Don't you move, muthafucka." He came up with his fist and landed it squarely across the boy's left jaw.

The teenager fell back against the fence.

"Stand up, muthafucka," Dexter commanded, and the boy grabbed hold of his face.

He stood up, and Dexter changed positions, still holding the gun. He stepped to the left and turned sideways, then he pulled back and let a right cross go to the boy's stomach. The boy bent over, gasping for air, and, as he did so, Dexter caught him with his knee to the forehead. That's when the boy fell back and hit the ground. Dexter then kicked him once in his ribs.

Dexter scolded the kid, "Get your ass up and get the fuck out of here. You need to get you a job, muthafucka, and stop breaking in people's houses."

The boy slowly got up and began to walk off. He watched the boy walk toward the driveway and yelled, "I didn't hear you say thank you."

"Thank you," answered the boy.

"Thank you for what?" Dexter demanded.

The boy stopped and turned back to face him, and with a grimace on his face, he said, "Thank you for not calling the pigs."

"All right," answered Dexter as he let the boy go. He never saw or heard from the boy again.

Dexter went back into the house, opened the refrigerator, and pulled out a Colt 45 malt liquor. When he went to open the top, he noticed that his hand was throbbing and swollen. He'd hurt it when he hit the boy, probably on his jaw.

He then turned off the radio and took out an album to listen to. "Ah, let me see—Temptations, Psychedelic Shack. Yeah, that's cool." He put the record on and lit some incense. Sally and Mimi were sound asleep in the bedroom. He grabbed his shoebox, rolled a fat joint, and lit it with a match.

Dexter inhaled and then exhaled a cloud of smoke. He noticed that the fireplace, in which a fire was burning, was in need of some more wood, so he took a few small logs and threw them onto the fire. He then walked to the couch, lay back, and began to think. "This is all right. I have a nice family, a beautiful wife, and a lovely daughter. I've got a nice home and a car and a good gig. This is what's it's all about. God's been good."

He then took a swig of the Colt, another long drag on the joint, and kicked back, listening to the music. The only light on in the house was the flames burning in the fireplace. The Temptations were singing on the stereo. He could hear Eddie Kendrick sing.

One drag, that's all it took
Oh, oh, I'm hooked.
Take a stroll through your mind
    sometime,
You'd be surprised at what you might
    find.

"Yeah, Eddie, sing the song," Dexter said, as he began to fly. Suddenly, the phone rang.

He reached for the receiver, "Hello?"

"Dexter?" It was his mother.

"Baba?" he said, surprised.

"Hi, son." It was good to hear her voice.

"Hi, Baba, what's up? How are you?" It was late, and he wondered why she was calling.

"I'm calling to ask you a favor," she explained.

"Sure, what do you need? Do you need me to take you somewhere?" asked Dexter.

"No, honey," Margaret said. "I just got a new job. I'm playing for a small church on Sutter Street, and I'm having a musical with Hank on Sunday evening. We'd like you and the family to come."

This was something that Dexter did not want to do. He'd been out of the church for over three years and didn't really care for going. He'd attended church so much in his life that when he turned eighteen, he didn't want to go anymore. Although he did believe and know that there was a God, his faith had been diminished by the circumstances of his life.

He thought about his mother's request and said, "Ah, Baba, do I have to? I really don't feel up to it."

"Now, come on. I know you haven't been going, but I want you to do this for me. I've been working real hard to get back to playing, and this is something really special for me and your brother. I'd love it if you were there, and you should bring your family too!" She said, not taking no for an answer.

Dexter really didn't want to go. He also had a problem listening to his mother sing. He wasn't used to hearing her sound the way she did. He asked, "How about the next one, Baba? Maybe I'll go to the next one."

Margaret held her ground. "No, now, I want you to come to this one. I don't ask you for much, so the least you could do for me is do this."

Her voice was stern and direct. He knew that when she sounded like that, she meant it, so there was nothing he could do but obey.

Reluctantly, he answered, "All right. Where is it at and what time?"

"The church is on the 2600 block of Sutter Street. The program starts at 6:00, so don't be late."

"Okay, I'll see you then." Dexter said and hung up the phone.

He lay back down and noticed the fire was getting low. The record had come to an end on the stereo, and the incense had burned out. It was getting late; he knew Mimi would be up early in the morning, and she wouldn't let him sleep. He got up from the couch, took another swig of the beer, made a pit stop in the bathroom and hit the sack. He was out like a light.

The next day, Dexter called his grandmother to see if she was going. She told Dexter that she wasn't ready to see Margaret perform in the condition she was in. She said she just couldn't take it, so she wasn't going. Dexter thought he would try and reach Hank. His efforts failed, and he was unable to track him down.

Dexter then tried to persuade Sally to go, and she said she didn't want to, but he could take Mimi. He knew he couldn't force Sally to go, so he left it alone. As he began to get ready for the evening, Sally got the baby ready. She dressed Mimi up in a pretty, red, frilly dress with some pretty panties that had little ruffles around the booty. Mimi also had on some nice little, black, patent leather shoes and white socks with lace trim. Her hair was combed nice and neat, with little braids and red and white barrettes.

Dexter put on a double-breasted, Edwardian-cut, beige, double-knit suit with bell-bottomed pants, along with a white shirt. He wore a wide beige and red tie and some platform shoes. He picked out his Afro and was ready to go.

He and Mimi rode the Chevy over the bridge, took the Franklin Street exit, and then made a left turn onto Sutter Street. When he arrived near the church, he found a parking space exactly in front of the house he remembered living in when he was two or three years old. It didn't dawn on him until he got out of the car and picked up Mimi.

He remembered the fire, and then he thought of his godfather Wilber, "I wonder where Godfather is?"

Dexter held Mimi in his arms, looking up at the apartment building, and then said to her, "Daddy used to live there when he was just like you." He pointed to the building.

Mimi looked at where her father was pointing, and she raised her little hand and pointed. "Dare, Dada, dare?"

Dexter smiled and laughed. "Yeah, there!"

He hugged and kissed her; she was so precious to him. Mimi was almost three years old.

Dexter crossed the street and headed up the block. He began to think it was ironic that his mother was beginning her comeback right up the street from where she'd begun her gospel-singing career in San Francisco. They were right back where they'd started. First Union was just around the corner, two blocks away. He thought about how he and Hank used to hold hands with their mother and guide her up the street to the church.

When Dexter arrived at the church, the service had already started. It was a small church, but it wasn't exactly a hole-in-the-wall. The choir consisted of about twenty members, and there were at least eighty people seated in the pews. There wasn't much room toward the front of the church, so he and Mimi took seats in the rear.

Margaret was sitting in the front row of the church with Hank beside her. There was another woman at the piano. The pastor got up and said a prayer; the ushers passed around the plate for tithes and offerings. Dexter put five dollars in the plate.

It was getting close to Mimi's bedtime, and she was getting restless. She began to play with some children who were sitting in front of them, so Dexter turned her around to face him, and she began to play with a woman sitting behind them. No matter what Dexter tried to do, Mimi wouldn't sit still. She wasn't used to being in church, so she didn't know how to act. With Sally not there, Mimi was really becoming a handful.

Dexter was trying to get control of Mimi when the pastor announced that he wasn't going to preach a sermon, but instead he wanted to read a scripture and say a few words before starting the musical portion of the program. That was Dexter's cue; he picked Mimi up, and then walked outside with her.

When Dexter got outside, Mimi was holding on; she thought they were getting ready to leave. Dexter walked to a tree and tore off a little switch. He then held Mimi in front of him and looked her in the eyes, "You see this switch?"

"Swish?" Mimi asked, pointing at the switch.

"Yes, switch! If you don't sit down and be quiet and stop playing, you're going to get this switch. Do you understand?" Mimi started to cry.

Her father rarely raised his voice to her, and he seldom punished her. Usually it was her mother who put her in check. But the look in her father's eyes, staring into hers, was enough.

"Are you going to behave?" Mimi nodded her head.

"Okay, stop crying." Dexter wiped her eyes and headed back into the church.

Once inside, he noticed a program sitting on a table near the entrance. He picked up a copy and stared at the picture on the cover. It was a portrait of his mother and Hank. He hadn't seen the picture before, and it was a surprise to him. He glanced at the portrait and couldn't get over the fact that Hank looked like a woman. His hair was styled in a woman's fashion, and his eyebrows were heavily arched. Margaret's smile was crooked because of the surgery from the accident. Dexter decided that he didn't care for the picture; it served as a reminder of the drama his family had been through.

This time Mimi sat in her father's lap and didn't say a word. A couple of the members looked at them and chuckled because they knew Mimi was acting a whole lot different when she came back inside. Dexter smiled at the members, acknowledging their thoughts.

The pastor stood in the pulpit and announced, "And now we'll turn this portion of our program over to one of our new choir directors, Margaret Evans." Hank then stood and reached for his mother to assist her to the piano. She was wearing a two-piece, off-white cashmere suit with a beige scarf around her neck to cover the scars. Her wig was freshly styled, and she was wearing makeup. Dexter knew Hank had taken great care in preparing his mother. The vision of Hank fussing over her brought a smile to Dexter's face. Hank had made a fuss over how she looked from the time they were very young.

After Margaret was seated at the piano, Hank then moved to the side, standing near the piano. Margaret positioned herself on the bench, then raised her hands to the piano keys and found her position on the keyboard. She then raised her head and announced that the choir would first sing a selection, led by her son, Henry Vizinau. Hank stood near, holding his hands together in front of him. He looked out into the crowd and smiled. He glanced around the church and discovered where Dexter was sitting and nodded. Dexter nodded in return. Margaret then announced that the choir selection would be followed by a solo of her own.

Margaret was ready to begin. It was the moment she'd been praying for—her debut, recognizing her comeback. She sat at the piano and turned her head in the direction of the choir. She lifted her hand to about shoulder height, paused, and then raised it higher. The choir reacted to her gestures by standing. Margaret then placed her hand on the piano keys and began to play the introduction.

On cue, the choir began to sing.

Oh, happy day
Oh, happy day
When Jesus washed
When Jesus washed
He washed my sins away.

Hank's voice filled the church. His voice was strong and clear and sounded beautiful. He had taken after his mother and could sing a song in a way that would move people. Margaret's hands were playing on the piano keys and her feet were tapping on the pedals. She felt like she was in heaven. Her baby boy was leading the choir, and she was playing again, and it felt good. Hank got the choir to begin clapping their hands, and the congregation joined in. Margaret was smiling and moving on her seat, rocking back and forth, banging on the keys. She was doing what she was born to do—singing, and praising God. Margaret was rejoicing the name of Jesus by lifting up his Word. She was serving the Lord.

Once the choir finished their first selection, Margaret scooted the bench back away from the piano and stood. Dexter sat with Mimi in the back of the church with his eyes fixed on his mother.

Margaret began to speak to the audience. "The next song I'm about to sing is a song that has a special meaning to me. It has a special meaning to me because it's a song that people have come to associate with me. But even more important is the fact that this is a song that was given to me by God. Years ago when I was a young girl in Arkansas, at the age of twelve, the Lord came to me, and he showed me the way. That was when I came to know the Lord and Jesus Christ as my savior. Now, I may not be able to see," her voice now began to crack as she continued, "but my God has shown me the light. I know it because I saw it for myself. I don't know about you, but I know that his light shines on me. I've seen it for myself."

Margaret was visibly choked up by her testimony, and she was on the brink of tears. But she held on and reached down to feel the piano stool and scooted it back into place. Several members of the choir and congregation were touched by the words spoken by the blind woman.

Dexter sat in his seat; a lump had developed in his throat, and his heart was racing. He knew what his mother was speaking of, and he knew more than anyone else in the room that what she said was true. He bit down onto his lip to compose himself. Mimi was wondering what was wrong with her daddy.

Now it was time for Margaret to sing and play. She sat at the piano, and her hands flowed over the keys, and the notes rang out with joy. It was the moment she had prayed for and worked so hard for. God had done a miracle and healed her hands so that they could again play his music.

The choir then sang out loud and clear, "Shine on me." Then again, "Shine on me." They continued, "Let the light from the lighthouse shine on me." The choir sounded beautiful, and it lifted Margaret even higher. She was now ready for her part, the lead.

Margaret held her head back and opened her mouth to sing. She heard the words flow through her vocal cords, "I heard the voice of Jesus say, 'Come unto me and rest.'" She was feeling so proud of herself. She could hear her voice sounding like it had three years ago, before the accident. She was thinking, "Thank you, Lord, thank you, Jesus, for touching me and healing me and making me whole."

Dexter sat in his seat, trying his best to be attentive. There were two boys, around ten or eleven, sitting in the row ahead of him, and they were laughing at every missed note Margaret made on the piano. When his mother sang and her voice cracked, the boys would lean forward and cover their mouths, laughing.

Dexter was hurt. He looked around; some people were grimacing, while others were trying to contain their laughter. Other church members were getting angry with those who were not being respectful. The tears began to form in Dexter's eyes, and his heart became heavy. He hung his head and wanted to weep. But he needed to be strong for his mother. He tried not to allow his pain to be obvious. He again looked in the direction of the boys in front of him. "Kids can be so cruel sometimes," he thought to himself. He tried not to get upset with the two boys and almost found humor in their humor.

He tried to compose himself and to watch and listen as his mother tried to sing and play. But even though the choir stood firm and sounded great, his mother's singing and playing sounded less than satisfactory. He couldn't help but remember how she used to sound and how she could tear a church up and have them jumping and shouting in the aisles. "Those boys don't know whom they're laughing at. If they only knew that she was a great singer," he thought to himself.

Finally Dexter couldn't take if any longer, and he got up and excused himself then stepped outside. Once outside, he held onto Mimi and put her head on his shoulder, and cried. "O God, how could you let this happen? How could you take away everything that my mother lived for? Why? Why? I don't understand, God. I just can't understand it."

As he walked away from the church toward his car, he could hear the echo of his mother's voice as he made his way down the street. He held onto Mimi, wiping his eyes as he placed her in the car. The two of them remained in the car until the service was finished.

Margaret finished her song, and then she and Hank sang a duet, with the choir singing in the background. It was one of the happiest moments in her life. God had touched her and healed her. She was singing beautifully and playing eloquently. She knew that soon people would be shouting and singing and stomping in the aisles while praising, "Hallelujah" by and by.

Epilogue

I'd like to take this opportunity to talk about miracles. By definition, miracles are events that can't be explained by human nature. Mankind can theorize, rationalize, or use science to begin to define the circumstances of these events in an attempt to find an answer. But in the end, there is no rational explanation.

In most cases, when we think of miracles, they are acts associated with God. The Bible shows us that a person, place, or thing can be used as an instrument for the events of miracles. For example, in Joshua 10:12–14, the Bible tells us that Joshua (a person) demonstrated the power of God by commanding that the sun and the moon stand still. In Numbers 22:28, God opened the mouth of a mule (an animal) to speak to Balaam. In Daniel 5:5, at a temple of God (a place) in Jerusalem, a finger appeared before King Belshazzar and drew handwriting on a wall, which could only be interpreted by Daniel.

Many miracles associated with people are personal. When a person experiences a miracle, who is it to say that it's not so? Simply because one person can't see or understand another person's miracle doesn't mean that it's not real.

Let's take, for example, situations that most of us are familiar with. While scanning the different stations on my cable television, I came across a program featuring an evangelist who was in the process of healing people in his congregation. I was a little surprised when I saw this because it's not seen very much these days on national television.

I watched as the preacher laid his hands on the many people who had lined up to be healed of whatever affliction ailed them. My first thought was that this was a scam. I must add that the majority of these people were black and that the evangelist was a white man.

A woman stood before the healer and said that her hip was going out, and that the doctors had told her she needed to have an operation to have her hip replaced. The preacher asked if she believed in the power of God. Next, he asked her if she believed that the power of God could heal her. To both questions, she answered, "Yes!"

At this point, the healer placed his hand on the woman's forehead, applied some pressure, and began to call on the power of the Lord to touch and heal this person. When he lifted his hand off the woman, she began to praise the Lord and announced that she was healed.

"What did you say?" asked the healer.

The woman looked into the camera, with tears in her eyes, "I've been healed."

"Let me hear you say that again," the healer asked her.

"God has healed me. My hip, it's all right. I don't feel any pain. I can walk; I can walk!" the woman proclaimed.

"Praise God almighty, let everybody shout, 'Hallelujah,'" the preacher shouted out to the congregation, who responded by rejoicing.

The woman began to jump up and down, and the camera focused on her.

"Run, run," instructed the preacher, and she took off, running up and down the aisles.

One by one, the Evangelist began to heal people with every known affliction and ailment, from cancer to high blood pressure to back problems. I sat there watching him, thinking the whole thing was staged and it was all a fake, even though I do believe in miracles.

In retrospect, I now believe that it was a miracle that my mother was healed, and was again able to sing and play the piano. For all I know, God could have touched her and caused her ears to hear her voice and playing as it once was. Or maybe he placed it in her mind to think this. For whatever reason, she believed that she was healed and was able to sing. So therefore, because I, like everyone else, heard her voice and playing as it really was, does that mean that it wasn't so? What's important is that, for her, it was! And this is what makes a miracle personal.

The woman with a bad hip may have had enough faith that, for her, the bad hip was no longer a problem because she didn't feel the pain. Perhaps, if she visited a doctor, she'd find that the problem still existed, or perhaps, as in some cases, the problem would be gone, much to a doctor's dismay.

It all boils down to faith! What do you believe? If you believe in the power of God, all things are possible. My mother was a woman of great faith. It was a faith so strong that it could never be measured. She believed in the power of Jesus Christ and, for her, that power was real, and that is what healed her, and it was a miracle. If it was a miracle for her, it was a miracle for me. I thank God with all my heart for restoring the gift that he gave her and for causing her to be happy in the end.

Over the next ten years, Baba continued to sing and play the piano. She worked and performed from one hole-in-the-wall or start-up church to another. Sometimes she'd be paid for her services, and other times she wouldn't. It didn't matter to her; she was doing the work of the Lord.

In 1982, on Thanksgiving Day, my mother passed away in her sleep. She died of heart failure just before her fifty-fourth birthday. She was a very happy woman, and she was at peace. By then, I had moved back into the house on Orizaba with my two children and begun to care for her.

At the time, Mimi was eleven years old, and my son, Duane, was eight. Baba loved having her grandchildren around, and they were old enough to have outgrown their fear of her. By then, I was a single parent, and living with her also provided me with a built-in babysitter. She was so happy to be able to help me take care of the children.

Sally and I had separated in 1980, and we eventually divorced. When we split up, the children stayed with me. Duane was five years of age and Mimi was eight. Mimi stayed with me until she turned sixteen, when she returned to live with her mother. Duane stayed with me until he turned eighteen.

I eventually gave up drugs and continued working for the IBM Corporation for twenty-two years. Eventually, I made my way into management and retired with thirty years of service from an early-retirement buy-out program.

While at IBM, I obtained numerous outstanding recognitions and was awarded the highest honor obtainable for "suggestions." One of my ideas saved the IBM Corporation over four million dollars in revenues in the first year of its inception and saved many more millions for several years thereafter. IBM compensated me for my suggestion to the fullest amount allowable.

I eventually went back to the church, and today I'm married to a fine Christian woman. We have two sons, and I have one daughter from a prior relationship. I have five children altogether.

Upon leaving the IBM Corporation, I started my own consulting business firm in Oakland, California, and have been in business for over ten years.

Hank moved to Oregon in the mid-eighties and then to Denver during the late nineties. He recently moved back to California.

Hank has devoted his life's work to providing shelter for the homeless and continues to do so today. My brother loved and always will love the Lord; he is a person of great faith. Homosexuality is now more accepted in our society than it was when we were teenagers in the sixties. However, it's still a very controversial issue. I feel that his sexuality has caused him to endure a tremendous struggle, and I'm glad that he's at peace with himself. I love my brother dearly and will stick by him always.

My great-grandmother Annie passed away in 1977; she was eighty-five years old. It seemed as though Momma was old as long as I can remember. Just like she had taken care of her father until he passed on, my grandmother, Nanny, took care of her until her last days. Momma's teachings of "Honor thy mother and thy father that thy days may be long," still echo throughout our family today. I tell my children the same stories she told to me.

Annie's constant preaching, "Train up a child in the way he should go, and when he is old, he shall not depart from it," have held true for me. I believe if you instill these beliefs in an individual from the beginning, it will have such a profound effect that even the most hardened sinner will one day realize the mistakes that have been made and seek repentance.

These teachings are something that have been lacking in the last few generations of my people and the effect of it shows in our society today. There's a difference between those who do wrong and know they've done wrong and those who don't know the difference between right and wrong. This is what the church has given to me. I understand the difference between right and wrong. I know when I have sinned, and I know how to ask for forgiveness.

Charles is retired and still lives in the home of my grandmother in San Francisco. He and I had grown apart, but in recent years, have again become close. He lives with his lovely wife, Cynthia, and their daughter, Lady, lives with her husband and two children in southern California. Charles and Cynthia are both Christians and are active members in their church congregation.

In 1981, Leon was attacked in a robbery attempt while visiting relatives in Texas. The incident caused him to lapse into a coma, and when he awakened, he had suffered brain damage.

Margaret arranged for him to be transported back to California, and he was admitted into Laguna Honda Convalescent Hospital, where he spent the rest of his days.

In 1990, although still somewhat bitter as a result of the shooting accident, Nanny wanted to pay a visit to Leon in the hospital. When she and I arrived at the hospital, he looked surprisingly well and young for his age. His skin was bright and soft like cotton. Leon was sitting upright and could eat well and look about.

We were glad we had decided to see him, and were happy that he looked so well. He briefly recognized me, and when I mentioned Margaret's name, he looked at me with tears forming in his eyes as he tried to mumble her name.

While walking out of the hospital ward, holding Nanny by the arm, I glanced over and noticed a man lying in a bed near the ward entrance. The man looked familiar to me, and I knew I'd seen this man before, years before.

He was a tall, brown-skinned black man, and he had the type of eyes you see on some people who are blind, eyes that are sunken deep into the skull. He had a large protruding forehead, as if he had an enormous brain. His eyeballs twitched back and forth and went up and down as if he were trying to scan. It was John, the man who had lived next door to my family on Sutter Street when I was three years old.

I looked at the name posted above his bed and said, "Nanny, look. Look at his name."

Mary stared at the nameplate above the bed. It read, "John Vizinau." She was puzzled. She turned to me and said, "Vizinau? His name is Vizinau?"

We approached the bed where John was lying and I said, "Excuse me, sir."

John responded, "Yes?"

I continued, "I couldn't help but notice your last name."

Quickly John asked curtly, "What of it?"

I remained polite while Nanny looked on and said, "Well, it says your name is Vizinau."

"So?" he answered.

I explained, "Well, my name is Vizinau too, and I was wondering where you got it from?"

"I took it," John said smartly.

"You took it?" I asked.

"Yeah, I took it!" he said, challenging me.

Anger quickly overcame me; he was being a jerk, but I remained calm, "Did you know Duane and Margaret?"

He answered, "Yes."

After he answered yes, I took my grandmother by the arm and led her away. When we got down the hall, Nanny turned to me and said, "Can you believe that? He took it, just like that. He took it!" I didn't comment, and we just walked on.

The next year, on April 17, 1991, at the age of eighty-three, Leon passed away. Nanny and I attended the funeral. There were many friends and family in attendance, and he passed on as an ordained minister.

Later that year, on November 9, 1991, Nanny, my grandmother, Mary Dillard, passed away after a fierce battle with lung cancer. She was about to turn eighty-one. It was a great loss to our family because she had been the glue that held us together. Our family gatherings passed away with her; she was the leader of the family! A few years later, BD passed on. Charles and Cynthia had cared for him until the day he died.

My father, Duane, and I lost touch with each other in the late seventies. I was disappointed in him for some things that had taken place during that time period. In 1989, while in Santa Cruz on an outing with my girlfriend, I decided to try and pay him a visit. I hadn't seen or heard from him in several years and wondered if he still lived in the same house.

At first, I was apprehensive about going to the house, but my girlfriend convinced me. We parked in front of the house and I sat there, hesitating. My girlfriend coaxed me out of the car.

When I knocked on the door, a white man whom I didn't recognize answered the door. I asked if Duane was in, and he suspiciously answered, "No." I then asked the gentleman to tell Duane that his son, Dexter, had come by. This caught the gentleman completely by surprise. I don't know if it was because I was black, or because he didn't know Duane had a son, or what.

Once I informed him that I was Duane's son, the gentleman asked me to wait for a moment and closed the door, leaving me standing there. After a few moments, the gentleman opened the door and told me that my father was there in the back room, and I could go in and visit. It was a very peculiar situation!

I then waved for my girlfriend to leave the car and come inside with me. When we entered the house, it was his typical residence. There were so many books in the house that they were stacked up, forming aisles, and we had to navigate around them to get to the back room. The place looked like an old library.

When we reached the back room, my father had just gotten out of his bed and put his trousers on, and he was zipping up his pants, with no shirt on. He looked like an aging hippie. The top of his head was bald, and his hair was long and flowed down past his shoulders. He also wore a long beard and mustache.

Just past him, in the bed, was a young lady who could not have been more than twenty-five years of age. She was naked and was holding a sheet over her breast, trying to keep herself covered.

Duane was excited to see me, but he was stoned out of his mind. He was fidgeting around, trying to figure out what to do. I looked around, and on top of the dresser, I noticed some cocaine on a mirror and a crack pipe nearby.

I introduced him to my girlfriend, and he introduced me to the young lady. As she reached out to shake my hand, she dropped the sheet, exposing her breasts. My girlfriend was standing right next to me, and I was never so embarrassed in my life. The young lady then grabbed the sheet and pulled it up over her breasts while shaking my hand and my girlfriend's hand.

Duane then told me how happy he was to see me and asked me if I wanted a hit on the pipe. And, boy, did that hurt! I hung my head and shook it back and forth and said, "No, Daddy, that's all right, I'll pass. I don't do drugs."

I'd seen enough; it was time to leave. I gave him a hug and a kiss and told him that it was good to see him. He walked me to the door and we said our good-byes. When I got in the car with my girlfriend, I felt like crying. I thought I'd prepared her for my father prior to going into the house, but I hadn't prepared her for that. She felt my pain, and told me to not try and explain things, that it was all right.

During the eighties, while working at IBM, I got into producing nighttime entertainment venues as a side business. As always, I had to have a hustle. I began to promote dances, fashion shows, comedy shows, nightclubs, and so on. I made quite a name for myself in the Bay Area, and became very popular.

In October of 1998, I had a nightclub venue in Oakland that I was promoting on the weekends. A partner of mine, Douglas Sanders, approached me and said, "I'm sorry to hear about your father."

This really came as a surprise, because I hadn't seen or heard from my father in almost ten years. Also, almost no one who has known me since I was five years old knew my dad.

I looked at Doug and said, "What, how do you know about my father?"

"Oh, I'm sorry, but my wife Mona said she read about him passing away, in the newspaper."

I was puzzled. "My dad?" I asked.

Doug continued, "Well, I thought it was your dad. Maybe not, but it gave his name. I think she said it was Duane Vizinau, and it talked about your mother and your brother, and it named you."

"What paper?" I asked.

"I think she said it was the Oakland Tribune," answered Doug.

As it turned out, Duane had passed on, and his sister had put a notice in the Oakland Tribune obituaries, hoping that I, or someone who knew me, would see it. She also left a phone number at the newspaper's office so I could contact her. Well, it worked; I contacted my aunt, and it was good to speak with her and catch up. I hadn't seen or spoken with her or her children since I was a child. I was glad to know the final outcome of my dad. I'm not happy about how things ended between us, but I did love him and I know that he loved me.

For the most part, it's the good times when we were together that I remember the most and cherish. He taught me quite a bit, and most of what he shared with me still remains with me today. There is a lot about him that is also in me.

Printed in the United States
139277LV00002B/1/P